PSYCHOLOGICAL HEALING THROUGH CREATIVE SELF-UNDERSTANDING AND SELF-TRANSFORMATION

By
Dr. Max Hammer

With Dr. Barry J. Hammer and Dr. Alan C. Butler

Strategic Book Publishing and Rights Co.

Strategic Book Publishing and Rights Co.
12620 FM 1960, Suite A4-507
Houston TX 77065
www.sbpra.com

ISBN: 978-1-62857-075-5

Design: Dedicated Book Services (www.netdbs.com)

Dr. Barry
Hammer

Dr. Max
Hammer

Dr. Max Hammer

AUTHORS' VITAE

The late **Max Hammer, PhD**, 1930-2011, is the primary author of this book. He had a distinguished career for almost three decades (1961-1990) as a professor of clinical psychology at the University of Maine. As a beloved, dedicated, insightful, and talented teacher, supervisor, researcher, and writer, he profoundly influenced students and colleagues alike in his understanding of the psychological and spiritual growth process. He also had extensive experience as a practicing psychotherapist. Dr. Hammer was years ahead of his time in his initial writings on psychological and spiritual growth, or developmental transformation, as well as in his understanding of the actual and potential impact of humanistic and transpersonal psychology on contemporary western and global society. As a practicing psychotherapist, he published almost thirty articles in the field of psychological health and psychotherapy, as well as two previous books in the area. He served on the educational board of the *Journal of Psychotherapy: Theory, Research, and Practice*, and the *International Journal of Symbology*. Furthermore, Dr. Hammer was a member of the American Academy of Psychotherapists (AAP), the American Psychological Association (APA)—Division of Clinical Psychology, Psychologists Interested in the Advancement of Psychotherapy (PIAP), and the International Society for the Study of Symbols. This book, and those to follow, is primarily comprised of Dr. Hammer's original writings, thoughts, and lectures to students; they contain invaluable insights into psychological and spiritual development, interpersonal relationships, society, and the future of humanity.

Alan C. Butler, PhD, helped Max Hammer write the original *Psychology of Self-Growth* manuscript on which much of the present book is based. Dr. Butler is a clinical psychologist, recently retired from his full-time position as staff psychologist and pre-doctoral psychology internship director

v

at the University of Maine Counseling Center, a program that he developed in 1978. As a cooperating associate professor of psychology, Dr. Butler also taught undergraduate and graduate students for over thirty years. Both he and Dr. Max Hammer remained close colleagues, and utilized the initial material from the *Psychology of Self-Growth* manuscript in their personal growth classes, seminars, and supervision of students. Dr. Butler continues to work part-time in private practice as a clinical psychology consultant and psychotherapist.

Barry J. Hammer, PhD, has extensively edited and expanded the *Psychology of Self-Growth* manuscript on which this book is based. He is the eldest son and lifelong confidant of the primary author, Dr. Max Hammer. Barry Hammer has a doctorate in the history of world religions from the Graduate Theological Union in Berkeley, California, as well as a Masters degree of theological studies (MTS) degree from Harvard Divinity School. He has taught university courses in the history of world religions and has a longstanding interest in the relationship between psychological, spiritual, religious, and societal transformational development and counseling.

TABLE OF CONTENTS

INTRODUCTION

By Dr. Barry J. Hammer

This book presents an understanding of psychological factors that can enhance or impede genuine, uncensored, or creative self-understanding of the actual experiential truth of oneself, as well as self-transformation into greater levels of emotional well-being, constructive functioning, and maturity of character. We authors are using the terms "creative self-understanding" and "genuine understanding of others" to refer to insights that come from direct experience and from openness to the deepest core integrity level of one's own being, unrestricted and undistorted by any preconceived interpretive presumptions and self-censoring. In this book, "creative self-understanding" refers to a dynamic process of self-exploration of personal feelings and other experiential states, not a static self-definition or unchanging self-concept.

The authors of the original manuscript of this book, my father, the late Dr. Max Hammer, and his colleague, Dr. Alan C. Butler, were both formerly professional psychotherapists and professors of psychology at the University of Maine, who together wrote an incomplete manuscript for a book, originally titled, *The Psychology of Self-Growth*, that included a chapter discussing the process of developing psychological self-understanding and healing of emotional pain, which is chapter 1 of this book, as well as three other chapters focusing on the psychological dynamics of human relationships, which are not contained in this book, but, instead, will be included in another book focusing specifically on the topic of developing deeply caring human relationships and meaningful interpersonal communication processes. This book focuses specifically on the development of psychological self-understanding and self-transformation. In addition to chapter 1, other materials included in this book come from Max Hammer's articles published during his lifetime, and are reprinted here with written permission from the particular journals in which they were originally published, as well as some unpublished articles, verbal discussions, and extensive written notes dictated by Max Hammer to me, his eldest son, Barry Hammer, over a period of many years, until he passed away on June 14, 2011.

Prior to his death, Max Hammer asked me to publish his writings posthumously. He gave me permission to organize and edit his writings in whatever manner I deemed most appropriate, as long as I tried to remain true to his intended message, as best I understand it, which is what I am conscientiously attempting to do. My father also consented for me to update his older writings to incorporate some of his newer ideas and insights, as well as to add some related insights and ideas of my own that he found to be consistent with his viewpoint and with the basic message that he wished to communicate through this book and his other writings. Dr. Alan Butler has also graciously given me his consent to publish the *Psychology of Self-Growth* manuscript as two separate books, including this book, focusing on the process of "Creative Self-Understanding" or the development of psychological self-understanding that is truly authentic, directly observed (not mediated by preconceived presumptive interpretations), unrestricted (uncontrolled), and that facilitates meaningful self-transformation or genuine psychological growth. The other book, not yet published as of this date (Summer 2013) and focusing on enhancing the development of fulfilling interpersonal human relationships, is tentatively titled *Deepening Your Personal Relationships: Developing Emotional Intimacy and Good Communication*. (To be published by Strategic Book Publishing and Rights Co.)

For many years, I worked closely with and resided with my father, serving as his writing collaborator, confidant, personal secretary, and housekeeper, which enabled me to develop an in-depth as well as broad understanding of the development and essential existential significance of his ideas. He communicated those ideas to me through daily written notes and verbal conversations, as well as through the above-mentioned manuscript. Many of the dictated notes and verbal insights focused on the topic of healing psychological pain by deeply understanding the illusory nature of the conceptually-derived ego-personality, which is the basic source of unnecessary psychological pain, as well as related forms of inner conflict and distorted, inauthentic self-perception. He often distinguished between the ego-personality as a presumptive, conceptually defined, basically illusory sense of identity, continuously engaged in narcissistically self-preoccupied inner monologue, or what he often referred to as the "personal life story daydream fantasy" or "mind chatter," in contrast to the real self, consisting of intrinsic talents, interests, predispositions, and other natural inclinations, as well as authentic feelings and other experiential states, spontaneously arising within the individual from moment to moment, or aroused through responsive relationships with other individuals. The ego is basically a separate, psychologically disconnected sense of self-awareness and identity, while the experiential real self inherently is being a relational self, naturally inclined to psychologically connect to others in a caring way, especially through a process of non-dualistic empathic communion. This book emphasizes Max Hammer's view that the ego's mostly subconscious commitment to validate, defend, and aggrandize its positive, and sometimes even negative, self-definitions and self-evaluations or value judgments produces distorted self-perception, because it "blinds" or desensitizes us to intrinsic natural inclinations and momentary authentic experiential states that are not consistent with, and that threaten to invalidate, those desired self-concepts.

Although this book may be relevant and useful for various readers, it is particularly dedicated and directed to open-minded, open-hearted readers who feel inclined to explore the actual experiential truth of themselves, no matter where it may lead, without defending any kind of biased preconceptions, and not seeking comforting presumptions or idealized conceptual abstractions, divorced from the authenticity of their actual experiential states, and the life energy that they contain, and not mediated by any kind of preconceptions or selective self-censorship. This book is particularly directed to readers who are willing to courageously open themselves to the risk of possibly experiencing emotional pain as a basis of achieving transformational developmental growth of enhanced self-understanding and creative functioning by exploring deeply into uncomfortable feelings, inner conflicts, and creative potentials, even at the risk of moving beyond their current "comfort zone," which may involve no longer defending and holding on to their old, familiar but basically false sense of identity, psychological security, self-esteem, and habitual, overly-programmed, rather superficial ways of functioning.

Whatever is written in this book should have personal, existential truth and value to you, the reader. It should intuitively ring true in your own experience. If not, then you should reject it or at least seriously question it; continue exploring the experiential truth of yourself and accept only what fits with your own understanding and experience.

This book explains how emotional pain can be meaningfully resolved, and thereby overcome by inquiring deeply into its origin. This liberates energy from uncomfortable feelings to use for enhanced vitality, sensitive alertness, and creative, insightful, productive functioning. The alternative is distracting yourself from emotional pain at the cost of numbing or desensitizing your energies. Then you become like a hardened empty shell, lacking a real heart, with an absence of authentic "juices of life." Instead, you become overly dependent on addictive, unhealthy substances and sensations for an artificial sense of inner vitality, euphoria, comfort, and psychological security. We will discuss the basic process of liberating yourself from psychological pain, as well as from various kinds of unhealthy addictions that are used to avoid the experience of psychological pain. This involves outgrowing identification with what is unreal in yourself, as well as growing in conscious understanding and creative development of what is experientially real in yourself. Through this inquiry, you can understand and undo psychological factors, or impediments to psychological growth, that block and distort your own energy force, producing psychological, dyadic, and societal pain and pathology.

A related topic discussed in this book is how deeply exploring, understanding, and letting go of false psychological and social masks, coverings, or presumptive ideas about yourself can enable you to uncover, or discover, what is experientially real and genuinely alive in yourself. Later in this book, we explain how you can develop greater awareness coming from deeper levels of your psyche that contribute to the development of greater self-understanding and enhanced creative functioning, such as integrity, intuition, empathic insight, and inspiration. We invite you to enjoy the ongoing process of exploration into the actual experiential truth of yourself in particular and of the human psyche in general, rather than seeking premature closure by demanding a definitive sense of direction and certainty beforehand in terms of where the journey of self-discovery and self-transformation may lead.

The book also discusses the following topics: What does enhanced psychological maturity involve? How is it achieved, and why is it important to grow or be transformed toward enhanced maturity? This book takes the position that enhanced psychological maturity involves developing strength of character, as well as letting go of illusory psychological and social masks, involving presumptive ideas of ourselves that cover over, or distort, awareness of our intrinsic predispositions and current authentic experiential states or momentary feelings. Another related issue addressed in this book is what psychologically damaging effects occur if we are psychologically immature, and how the ego undermines the process of growth toward greater psychological maturity. This book takes the position that achieving greater psychological maturity involves growing in the conscious awareness and actualization of the individual natural potentials that are inherent to our real life energy force, and growing more conscious of what is experientially real for ourselves, from moment to moment, as the basis of developing an optimal sense of authenticity, integrity, and sincerity. This book will also discuss how psychological growth is related to the growth of our ability to relate to other people maturely and constructively, which enables us to actualize potentials that are related to other individuals. Obviously, if we are not psychologically mature, we will relate to other people in a psychologically immature, non-constructive manner, so our relationships will be psychologically immature and unhealthy. Those who are psychologically immature tend to have unrealistic, inappropriate expectations and demands that they place upon others, like young children who feel very needy and expect many things from their parents and others in their lives. We will explore what prevents us from maturing psychologically and what keeps us fixated or stuck in psychological immaturity.

This book will discuss how to develop full, fulfilling, or optimal psychological health, beyond what other psychologists and non-specialists describe as reasonable health, relative health, or normality. We postulate that full psychological health is something qualitatively different from normality, and may not necessarily even be on the same continuum. We view psychopathology as the result of extreme rejection of inner and outer experiential realities; psychological normality as reflecting greater but not full unification of the conscious psyche with painful experiential realities; and optimal psychological health involving an unconditional sense of psychological security, fulfillment, well-being, and integrated wholeness, as intrinsic qualities of the transpersonal self or relational core of being, beyond the ego's separate sense of selfhood and dualistic self-awareness with which individuals evidencing psychopathological and normal levels of functioning tend to be primarily identified. The divided conceptual self, as an ego in conflict with itself, is the basic cause of psychopathology; the experiential self, as the ego unified with and accepting of most of its own experiential states, is the basis of psychological normalcy; while the individual consciousness no longer exclusively identified with the separate ego and attuned to the relational nature of reality or of "love-life energy" is what we call the transpersonal self or the real self.

Although we have questioned whether full psychological health and fulfillment is on the same continuum as relative psychological normalcy and psychopathology, it can be helpful to view them on a continuum in the context of recognizing that virtually all human beings experience negative emotions or feelings of deficiency, such as fearful anxiety, anger, depression, and inner emptiness at some time in their lives. However, individuals differ in the extent to which they are dominated or even debilitated by these kinds of turbulent feelings. In some individuals, they can develop into a serious psychopathological disorder if they feel extremely insecure and deficient, perhaps instigated by environmental stress or innate predispositions. Our view is that even psychologically unhealthy innate predispositions or longstanding learned patterns can be overcome with enough therapeutic insight and the development of greater levels of psychological security. As individuals develop a greater sense of wholeness by consciously unifying with their own painful experiential states, developing genuinely caring personal relationships with others, and becoming less identified with divisive egoistic self-definitions, they increasingly experience a sense of fulfillment that is intrinsic to the natural undivided wholeness of relational love-life energy. In this book, we will discuss in greater depth and detail how and why fulfillment realization is the inherent nature of the real self, as an undivided wholeness of energy that comprises one's own distinctly individual being but which is also naturally relational to others.

Most essentially, the basic purpose of this book is to clarify the process by which our partly conscious and partly non-conscious psyche can grow in developing greater consciousness of its actual momentary experience and intrinsic permanent real being. This developmental growth of consciousness enables our formerly unconscious life energy force, or our being, to liberate itself from self-imposed illusions, along with related psychological pain and pathology, and regain the full stature or full grandeur of our inherent being, as a dynamic process of attunement to the core integrity level of ourselves, other individuals, and the transpersonal relational whole of being, from moment to moment. Metaphorically represented by the Statue of Liberty holding high the sacred torch of liberty, this book discusses the process of consciousness liberating itself from all illusions, blockages, addictive cravings, inhibitions, and self-constraints that prevent our conscious and non-conscious life energy spirit from being fully free, unrestricted, and triumphant in its development or ascension into greater levels of self-understanding, self-transformation, self-empowerment, and fulfillment. In this book, we will discuss how the life force within us and as us, individually, and as a collective whole society, is naturally urging us to develop greater consciousness of the experiential truth of ourselves, as a way of overcoming impediments, fixations, blockages, or distortions in the natural, spontaneous, healthy, regenerative, flow of our energy, experience, ideation, and functioning, as the fulfillment of the basic meaning or purpose of life. We will discuss how we can live a responsible life by taking greater active responsibility to understand and develop what is experientially real in others and ourselves as the basis of developing greater psychological self-understanding, self-transformation, self-liberation, and self-healing. That is how we live a life of responsible liberty, without irresponsible, reckless license.

CHAPTER 1

THE PROCESS OF PSYCHOLOGICAL SELF-HEALING AND SELF-TRANSFORMATION THROUGH CREATIVE SELF-UNDERSTANDING

"And ye shall know the Truth, and the
Truth shall make you free."
—St. John 8:32

Unraveling Today's Human Dilemma

Most people living in today's society find themselves confronted with a psychological dilemma. This dilemma arises out of society's pressure to achieve a sense of identity, adequacy, self-worth, and approval from others. The value and overemphasis that society places upon the success of these strivings encourages us to erect and identify with various self-concepts, idealized images, or other psychological masks or stereotyped social roles which remove us from our more genuine and spontaneous self, including our enduring conscious energy presence and its momentary experiential states. The overemphasis upon these societal values also inevitably leads to our immersion in the "competitive arena." This leads not only to being constantly evaluated by others, but even more importantly, it leads to our own constant evaluation of ourselves. These self-evaluations, and the tendency to constantly "put ourselves on trial" in the attempt to prove such things as our adequacy, worth, and identity, inevitably result in self-induced anxiety and psychological pain.

1

Therefore, these self-evaluations are at the core of most if not all psychological disturbances because they inevitably produce a process of painful self-conflict or dissonance between our actual experiential states and what we presume we "should be" or "should not be" experiencing, and how we "should" or "should not" define and evaluate ourselves in a given moment. Thus, for each of us, the dilemma can be essentially stated: *How can I wear the various self-concept psychosocial masks necessary to be financially successful and socially approved without losing contact with what is most psychologically genuine, spontaneous, and creatively alive in myself?*

Since we live in a society where self-worth and approval are not viewed as intrinsic and therefore unconditional at birth, we learn that the gratification of those needs must be conditionally earned by our successes achieved through competition with others throughout our life. In order to achieve these successes, we learn that we must play various prescribed social roles, and acquire and display various social masks and possessions valued by others in our society. To the extent that we are successful in fitting into these valued psychosocial masks and prescribed roles, society praises and rewards us. But even with extensive praise and rewards, at a deeper level, we may continue to feel relatively empty, bored, and unfulfilled. We are aware that something is still missing in our lives. There is still some inability to deeply contact and understand ourselves, to feel fully vital, creative, and spontaneous, which no self-concept, possession, praise, or reward seems to replace.

The problem which has emerged is not that humankind's valuing of competition and success is necessarily incorrect or harmful per se, but that we often become preoccupied with it. This excessive preoccupation tends to make us overly identify with the various concepts, labels, or images of self that we have created, which may result in the loss of contact with what is most creative and real in ourselves. For example, because society puts a high value upon the person who is always strong, independent, and self-sufficient, we tend to overly identify with these traits, which often results in our inability to let ourselves cry, be open to our tender feelings, or recognize our natural longings for and reliance upon others. Thus, the over-identification with various self-concepts greatly restricts our functioning and our awareness of ourselves, and makes us feel like prisoners confined behind the psychological walls of our self-created psychosocial masks, predetermined self-images, and self-definitions. The idealized self-concept also functions as our inner judge, which produces the pain that comes with our self-evaluation, blaming, punishing, and conflicting with ourselves for not always living up to an idealized image of what we presume we "should be" or "ought to be." In addition, the over-preoccupation with competition and success also tends to lead to the over-valuation of the end product of whatever we are doing. We have become too concerned with how our efforts will be evaluated and not concerned enough with just enjoying and appreciating the activity for its own sake.

The over-identification with the personal self-concept as well as the over-emphasis upon its validation and enhancement produces an excessive devotion to achieving an absolute sense of self-protection, self-affirmation, self-integration (self-consistency), and self-enhancement. Without the gratification of these basic egoistic psychological needs, the self-concept cannot feel itself to be a real, consistent, permanent, psychological entity. However, these needs can never be fully or realistically gratified because all psychological traits are only relative in nature, and can never become absolute, or exclusively and conclusively validated. We can never be or validate a particular trait all the time. We also cannot be more of a trait than others all the time. For example, we cannot always be kind, intelligent, attractive, strong, etc., and we cannot always be more of this trait than anyone else. Therefore, we cannot realistically be and validate any trait absolutely or exclusively. These traits are intrinsically relative rather than absolute because they involve comparisons with others. For example, we may hold ourselves to be relatively intelligent if we compare ourselves to an intellectually challenged person (a person of very low IQ), but we may hold ourselves to be relatively unintelligent if we compare ourselves to a great philosopher or scientist like Albert Einstein. In view of the fact that we can never realistically achieve a sense of absoluteness in regard to any personality trait, our efforts in this regard are in vain, and so feelings of frustration, inner conflict, emotional pain, and fearful anxiety are inevitable and relatively frequent in many of us.

In addition, the overemphasis on the validation and aggrandized enhancement of the egoistic self-concepts also results in the diminished capacity for expressing what is truly real, creative, or spontaneous in us. That ability is related to true self-transformation, psychological growth, or greater psychological maturity, and achieving a real sense of inner substance and vitality. As a result, we frantically search for new exciting sensations to recapture our lost sense of what is substantial, intensely alive, and experientially real in ourselves (e.g., our constantly changing feelings, emotions, impulses, desires, and needs, in contrast to the unchanging self-concept or basic idea and image of ourselves, as our self-defined presumptive sense of psychological identity). To make up for the threatening sense of dullness and inner emptiness that comes from the loss of our natural real sense of vitality, we turn to a variety of escapes, and diversions to generate an artificial sensation of vitality, which we take to be real. Examples of some of the many escapes and sensationalist diversions that may pervade our lives include the habitual use of recreational drugs, alcohol, sex, TV, stereo, movies, and computer-based "virtual reality" as well as the compulsive drive to accumulate possessions that we do not really need. In addition, because of our superficiality, created by the identification with the personality roles, psychosocial masks, and self-concepts, as well as through the pursuit of shallow sensationalist thrills, our capacity for relating and loving more intimately, deeply, and honestly becomes severely impaired. We continually seek different relationships once the excitement and sense of vitality of each new relationship wears off, and the basic superficiality and dullness of the relationship is recognized.

In short, we become so preoccupied with the gratification of the egoistic desires arising from our yearning to become, achieve, validate, enhance, or aggrandize our idealized self-concepts that we often fail to recognize our true moment-to-moment yearnings, feelings, inclinations, and natural potentials stirring in us to be actualized. Without clear awareness of these actual feelings, we lack the means of knowing who we really are or what we really want in life. This lack of clarity about our own real feelings, needs, desires, and other actual experiential states at any given moment intensifies our feelings of confusion, emptiness, and alienation from others and ourselves. This, in turn, sets up a vicious cycle or downward spiral increasing in momentum of psychological negativity, by encouraging an even greater, potentially addictive dependency upon artificial and distracting sensations as a means of covering over and blocking out the conscious experience of that sense of emptiness, deficiency, dissatisfaction, and unhappiness. Only the *self-discovery* of that which is experientially real and truthful about ourselves liberates us from the grasp of constant feelings of deficiency, inner conflict, tension, and boredom created by identification with self-concepts and excessive dependency upon sensations of excitation.

Eventually, self-discovery of our actual experiential realities leads to that non-evaluative, non-judgmental, or totally self-accepting and unified state of consciousness which is the essential basis of psychological health, peace of mind, and the means by which we come to feel fully and creatively alive and fulfilled.

Many of us consciously or subconsciously recognize this recurring human dilemma. In quiet moments, we are sometimes able to put our egoistic efforts toward achieving a greater or absolute sense of identity, security, self-worth, and approval into its proper perspective, so that it does not overwhelm us and dominate our lives. But all too often, we seek to acquire these goals at the cost of overlooking our deeper needs, motives, and feelings, thereby creating a great sense of confusion, inner conflict, and emotional pain for ourselves.

If we wish to discover the way out of this dilemma and eliminate our ever-increasing sense of alienation, loneliness, worthlessness, boredom, and lack of vitality, we must neither escape from the moment-to-moment experiential truths of ourselves nor reject our natural human needs to feel successful, recognized, and worthwhile. Instead, we must listen sensitively and non-judgmentally to what is actually experientially real in ourselves, from moment to moment, so that we may once again discover what it is really like to feel fully alive and genuine, and thereby gain the self-understanding and self-integration that leads to real psychological growth, involving greater transformational development of what is experientially real in ourselves, and outgrowth of what is not experientially real in ourselves, such as presumptive self-interpretations and related psychological pain, pathology, and inner conflict. That compassionate, empathic, nonjudgmental caring for and nonselective openness to all that is actually experientially arising in yourself is what it means to be a caring good friend to yourself. Learning to be a caring good friend to yourself in this way also enhances your ability to be a caring good friend to others in various kinds of interpersonal relationships as well, because the more open you are to the experiential truth of yourself, the more awareness, insight, energy, empathy, and compassion you will be able to bring to your encounters with others, whereas self-estrangement often causes estrangement from others.

The Process of Creative Self-Understanding and Self-Growth or Transformational Self-Development

The basic premise of this book, which you can verify through your own personal experience, is that the way toward real self-growth or healing psychologically painful inner conflict, enhanced fulfillment, and constructive personal transformation, can be achieved only through a process of nonjudgmental, nonselective (uncontrolled), experiential self-understanding. Growth of greater self-understanding by being open to the experiential truth of oneself enables us to outgrow what is unreal and psychologically unhealthy in ourselves, and grow in what is real and truly fulfilling in ourselves. Any other process is basically a form of self-deceit, in which you attempt to escape from what is emotionally painful or deemed to be objectionable in yourself. This self-distracting escape can provide, at best, only the illusion of transformational psychological growth, through the fact that you are no longer fully consciously experiencing the painful feeling, but it can never lead to real self-growth in terms of enhanced understanding and self-actualized transformational development of what is experientially real in yourself. Real self-growth involves increased experiential self-understanding, self-acceptance, and self-integration, as well as increased tolerance of psychological pain. This results in greater freedom of expression, greater inner peace, and greater openness to both internal and external reality. Only by facing the actual experiential truth of yourself, from moment to moment, can real transformational growth occur, involving an ongoing process of outgrowing what is unreal in ourselves and growing more consciously aware of and developed in what is real in ourselves. We outgrow, transform, or further develop what we see the whole of, or understand completely in ourselves, for we must be completely beyond a particular aspect of ourselves in order to have the perspective necessary to view the whole of it. It is only the process of creative self-understanding, achieved by facing the actual experiential truth of yourself that enables such a growth-producing perspective to take place.

In essence, you are either facing the truth about yourself or avoiding it in some form or another. Because creative self-understanding essentially involves facing and understanding the experiential truth of yourself, it is the only process of psychological healing and transformational self-growth that does not involve self-rejection, distracting escape from yourself, or distortion of reality. Self-rejection and escape do not eliminate the existence of psychologically painful feelings and experiences. It only functions to preserve what is being rejected and used as an escape at a more subconscious level of awareness. The more that you reject and escape from yourself, by rejecting and repressing awareness of your actual experiential states, or the more that you condition an insensitivity to psychological pain in yourself, the more this eventually generalizes to become an insensitivity to experiencing all intense feelings in yourself. This kind of habitual insensitivity to the experiential truth of yourself is a kind of psychological numbing, inner deadening, or dehumanization of yourself. Not only does it severely alienate you from yourself, but it also alienates and makes you insensitive to others. Thus, the attempt to escape from the actual experiential realities of yourself can never lead to psychological healing, pain removal, or real growth of liberating transformation, but only to greater pain and pathology. Only facing the moment-to-moment actual experiential truth of yourself can yield the alert sensitivity necessary to achieve the creative self-understanding and self-integration which results in real self-transformation and the elimination of painful feelings.

To maximize creative self-understanding and holistic self-integration, we first need to fully and consciously contact and unconditionally accept as part of our indivisible experiential wholeness those painful experiential realities which we have previously rejected and from which we were previously trying to escape. These experiential feelings need to be directly and fully contacted so that the underlying unexpressed message within each feeling can be easily and fully understood. In order to fully contact a painful feeling, it is necessary that you stand ready in consciousness to experientially unify with your changing feelings that arise spontaneously (i.e., not deliberately initiated, anticipated, or controlled) to conscious awareness from moment to moment, rather than identifying with some fixed, static, or permanent self-concept, as a pre-conceived sense of identity and a selective filtering of your experience. To develop genuine self-understanding, liberating insight into the underlying source of psychological pain, and a capacity for authentic self-transformation, you must be in a condition of non-duality, unity, identity, or oneness with your own spontaneously arising experiential realities, instead of identifying with some self-concept which stands outside of, or dualistically apart from, these feelings as their judging and censoring observer.

You must speak *as* the feeling, and never *for* the feeling. You must speak as though you were being only the painful feeling, *speaking for itself*, and not speak for the feeling by making interpretive assumptions and conjectures in regard to what the feeling has to say. More specifically, you must *take your stand as being the message within the feeling*, speaking for itself, and not stand as any other self in consciousness, dualistically detached from the feeling, as the reactive interpreter of it. When you take your stand in consciousness as being no self other than the spontaneously arising and creatively speaking message within the feeling, then there exists the full experiential contact with the feeling necessary to lead to its complete understanding, drainage, and dissolution. This condition of non-duality or oneness with the feeling, including fully contacting, unifying with, and welcoming the energy and message abiding within the feeling, is achieved when we relate to the feeling that spontaneously arises within us without labeling it or making any judgments of good or bad with regard to it, and when there is no attempt to escape from it, oppose it, control it, overpower it, suppress it, repress it, interpret it, distort its reality, or change it in any way. All of these are forms of rejection of our actual feelings and experiential states, and means of separating ourselves from the actual feeling, as the reactive, judgmental, selective, interpreter of it. This distancing of ourselves from the feeling makes the hearing and understanding of the message within the feeling impossible, which is necessary if the feeling is to be fully and permanently dissolved.

Essentially, creative self-understanding involves learning to *let be what is*. The letting be what is, which is to say, the letting be of whatever experiential reality arises spontaneously to our conscious awareness, from moment to moment, ends the influence of the observer as the self-concept which selectively judges and censors all experiential realities that are unacceptable to itself. When the process of labeling and judging ourselves ends, all the self-rejection, self-opposition, self-conflict, and self-escape will also end. When all such mind movement away from what actually is ends, the mind becomes quiet on the surface of consciousness. When the voice of the judging and censoring self-concept on the surface of consciousness is quiet, then this allows us to clearly hear and understand the softer, quieter, inner voice of the rejected and repressed painful feelings that are submerged at the deeper levels of consciousness. This leads to their full drainage and most immediate elimination.

Consequently, if you do not interpretively speak for, label, judge, or react in a partisan way for or against or try to control the painful feeling in any way, but just let it be and quietly listen for its underlying message, then all that inevitably remains is for that message to spontaneously arise and creatively (unrestrictedly) speak for itself or play itself out to conclusion. It will then be fully understood, and the repressed psychological energy contained within it will be totally drained, thereby releasing, healing, or transcending the inner conflict and psychological pain that the feeling originally involved. Through this process, the unexpressed message and its accompanying repressed energy, which is the thread that holds the fabric of the feeling together, will be completely released, and thereby the painful feeling will totally and permanently dissolve. There can be no more immediate or effective means than this for the eradication of painful feelings, and the achieving of real transformational self-growth or greater psychological well-being and constructive functioning. It is only through creative self-understanding that real change and growth (i.e., liberating transformation and enhanced constructive functioning) takes place in us, and that creative self-understanding arises only out of a consciousness in non-duality or full unification with spontaneously arising feelings and experiential states.

The state of consciousness in non-duality with one's actual feelings and experiential states is the only truly therapeutic and transformational growth-producing state of mind because it is the only conflict-free state of consciousness. This is in contrast to the intrinsically conflicted state of duality, which is our more typical state of mind. In the state of duality, we are identified with two selves at the same time. One self is comprised of the observed moment-to-moment actual feeling, and the other self is functioning as the dualistic, reactive observer, interpreter, judge, censor, or controller of those feelings. The observer and the observed selves both exist simultaneously in consciousness, as two distinct entities. They may assume forms such as the thinker and the thought, the judge and the judged, the censor and the censored, the "I" and the "me," the self as subject and the self as object, the self as conceptually presumed ideal and the self as actual experienced feelings. The psychological entity that operates as the judging, interpreting, and censoring observer is essentially nothing other than an idealized, presumptive self-concept. It has no actual reality but is merely fabricated out of one's ideas of what one ideally or absolutely wants to be, in contrast to what our feelings and experiential states actually are. The idealized self-concept judges our spontaneously arising feelings in terms of whether those feelings are in accord or discord with its goal of achieving an absolute sense of psychological protection, security, affirmation (validation), integration (self-consistency), and aggrandizement. It is constantly "putting itself on trial," or judging itself, in order to affirm or validate its sense of security, identity, consistency, and worth or esteem. As a result, the idealized self-concept is constantly confronted with the threat of being invalidated, and endures related feelings of frustration because of the impossibility of ever realistically, conclusively, definitively, permanently, exclusively validating idealized, absolutist, perfectionist self-definitions. Thus, the judging self-concept is at the root of all psychological pain, fearful anxiety, tension, and the various other negative or objectionable experiential states.

Since the idealized conceptual self that operates as the observer-judge-censor is not real, we should take the position in consciousness that we are only the experiential selves that change from moment to moment. Some moments may be elation, but other moments could be sadness, tenderness, destructiveness, fear, loneliness, etc. Therefore, for example, we should not say that this moment, "I *have* hostility," but, rather, "I *am* hostility." The first statement implies an additional self to whom the experiential reality of hostility belongs. In reality, there is no other self to whom the particular feeling belongs. There is only the feeling itself. All other selves are only conceptual and illusory ideals of what you presume you ought to be. You then realize that nothing can be done about what is experientially arising at this moment. Having no choice in the matter, you can only adopt an attitude of unconditional acceptance in regard to what is, which leaves nothing else to do but to let the feeling speak for itself and express its message completely. You must not try to control or interpret that process in any way because that only keeps the feeling stuck and therefore unresolved, by interposing a controller and interpreter between the feeling, itself, and your pure conscious awareness, as the knower or observer of that feeling.

You must understand clearly that *you* cannot get rid of any painful psychological condition. The "you" that tries to get rid of the painful feeling is actually the prime contributor to the creation of that painful feeling. That self that tries through effort to get rid of painful feelings is not your real self, but only a presumptive self-concept fabricated out of your values and what you believe you ought to be. *No painful or pathological psychological condition can be eliminated through deliberate effort.* A painful feeling can only get rid of itself by permitting it to spontaneously arise into your consciousness, in full experiential unification with it, so that it can speak for itself and play out its message to conclusion, which enables the energy within the feeling to be fully, cathartically released, drained, liberated, and thereby fully healed. This occurs only when you assume the position in consciousness of being no self other than the painful experiential self that is actually arising, this moment. In this way, a condition of inevitability or necessity exists in which you can do nothing but let this painful feeling be, and permit it to creatively or spontaneously speak for itself to conclusion, without any form of interference or judgmental interpretation. When your consciousness is just listening to and not interpreting or reacting to the particular painful experiential reality that has spontaneously arisen in this moment (so that there are no connotative labels, evaluative judgments of good or bad, and you are totally without desire or goal in regard to that painful feeling), then the consciousness will be in what is called the *state of being* or the condition of non-duality. In this non-dualistic state of consciousness, where the judging self-concept is quiet and inoperative, so that all egoistic efforts are absent, the message contained within that painful feeling is free to creatively, spontaneously, and unrestrictedly speak for itself to conclusion, bringing full understanding of the feeling, and total drainage or full liberation of the pent-up psychic energy encapsulated within the unexpressed feeling. That is how the painful feeling comes to eliminate itself, because *that which is fully drained out and understood leaves no trace of itself in consciousness.* The unexpressed message that held the feeling together unravels itself when consciousness is in a state of non-duality with it. Therefore, no deliberate effort is ever necessary or effective for the purpose of fully dissolving painful psychological feelings or symptoms. As the prominent psychologist Frances Vaughan suggests, "At the emotional level, healing awareness implies recognizing both positive and negative feelings . . . A cathartic release of suppressed emotion can relieve depression, reduce anxiety, and contribute to feelings of inner peace . . . The willingness to allow awareness of emotions is a key to release . . . Emotional healing lies in the identification, acceptance, and communication of true feelings."[1]

It is important to point out that this process of non-duality or communion with painful feelings or experiences does not mean identifying with or personalizing those feelings, and inappropriately acting out upon them in our actual behavior, by holding them to be intrinsic to our permanent being, sense of self-definition, identity, or essential nature, as if to say, "I am always or exclusively being or agreeing with the anger, fear, or tension that I currently feel" as an illusory, partisan, sense of holding ourselves to be the feeling by reacting as the feeling, approving of it, justifying it, siding with it, letting it define our sense of self, and automatically, impulsively influence our values, attitudes, and behaviors, even if it urges us to respond inappropriately to a particular situation or individual that has aroused the negative feeling in us. *That is, identification involves reacting as, agreeing with the feeling, internally and/or externally, rather than being in non-dualistic communion with the feeling as the non-reactive, undisturbed, impartial observer of it.* Identification involves letting the negative feeling define you as itself, as a reactive, partisan, often enduring and exclusive sense of automatically agreeing with the message, volitional intention, or viewpoint of the feeling, and impulsively acting upon negative feelings, even when it is inappropriate, irresponsible, and even dangerous to do so. Identification with negative feelings diminishes your ability to consider other appropriate options by obligating you to adhere to the feeling's viewpoint. This can lock you into rigidly predetermined, involuntary, inflexible ways of perceiving and functioning. Therefore, you must non-dualistically unify your nonreactive conscious awareness and relaxed, undisturbed, pure feeling energy with negative feelings without identifying with them, siding with or against them, or inappropriately acting upon them. This enables you to liberate your pure conscious life energy force from the superimposed negative feelings and from their incessant, intensely demanding, potentially addictive and enslaving reactivity, by enabling the intensely energized reactive negativity to subside, like a wave of water, back down into your nonreactive pure conscious awareness, where it dissolves into pure, calm, conscious-energy, and loses its negative, disturbing, quality.

The negative feeling may urge you, in an intensely demanding tone of voice, to react in identification with, approve of, side with, or agree with its perceptions and volitional intentions, as an internal assent or consent and/or by expressing it or acting it out, because you have let the feeling influence, control, possess, dominate, and define you by identifying with it, rather than just communing with it in a non-reactive, undisturbed, impartial manner. Negative or disturbed feelings are only temporary, whereas your being is permanent, just as a pure glass mirror is not affected by images that are temporarily reflected on the surface of the mirror. Similarly, you can be in a state of non-dualistic communion with painful, angry, fearful, disturbed, or other negative feelings, so that you are willing to "be" them in a given moment, as an uncontrolled process of not distancing yourself from full, direct, and immediate experiential contact with the feeling, without personally identifying with those feelings, and thereby becoming attached to them, by letting the feelings exclusively control your attention, energy investment, volitional intentions, and perception of yourself, other individuals, and particular situations. Thus, you let the feelings exclusively define your sense of self, values, attitudes, and behaviors, by reacting as or in favor of the feeling with which you have personally identified.

That kind of inappropriate identification and partisan siding with negative feelings can involve feeling compelled to impulsively act on or inappropriately express negative feelings with which you have identified, as an illusory forgetting that you have an intrinsic, permanent, calm, relaxed, unconditionally loving, cheerful nature, beyond the temporarily experienced feeling of disturbance with which you have become falsely identified. *Thus, it is important to distinguish between being unified with a particular negative feeling as a process of being in non-dualistic, nonreactive, nonpartisan, experiential communion with the feeling, versus being the feeling by identifying with the feeling, which involves reacting as the feeling, by siding with, justifying, agreeing with, and possibly acting out the feeling in a partisan, exclusive manner.* It is also important to distinguish between our temporary, disturbed, negative feelings and our permanent being, which is an unconditionally relaxed peace and intrinsic well-being that is not capable of becoming conditionally disturbed and is not naturally inclined to identify with negative feelings that have an oppositional volitional intention, reacting against someone or something in an antagonistic manner.

The state of consciousness in being or nonreactive, nonjudgmental non-duality must be distinguished from consciousness in a condition of duality or what we call the *state of conceptually reactive, judgmental becoming.* In this state, the "me" as a self-concept is constantly preoccupied with striving to *become* absolutely aggrandized, affirmed (validated), integrated (self-consistent), and protected. Consciousness is then in an intrinsic state of self-rejection and self-conflict because that self-concept is judging and rejecting what consciousness actually is being, experientially, at this moment, in order to pursue what it believes that it ideally ought to become. Consciousness in a state of becoming or judgmental duality from our actual experiential states is in an intrinsic state of self-rejection and self-conflict, and therefore it is the basic cause of all psychological illness, fear, and pain, as well as preventing psychological healing and growth into greater levels of genuine self-understanding and self-transformation. Thus, it is important to let be feelings of deficiency, dissatisfaction, or disturbance by being in non-dualistic communion with them, so that they can thereby drain out, be released and dissolved in your nonreactive conscious awareness, without identifying with those feelings, by reacting as them in a partisan, judgmental manner, and trying to achieve or become a compensatory, conditional, acquired sense of greater proficiency, wholeness, and well-being. Instead, the state of being that is the basis of psychological healing, health, fulfillment, and growth, or maturational development, involves recognizing that your permanent being is already an intrinsic, unconditional, total proficiency, wholeness, and well-being, regardless of the temporary negative feelings that bring a contrary sense of deficiency or disturbance.

Although this self-healing process of creative self-understanding may seem quite new, unfamiliar, and unnatural to you, or perhaps contrary to what you have always heard of or done in dealing with psychological pain or fear, you must understand clearly that negative, painful feelings or objectionable symptoms of psychological turmoil are eliminated only by diving deeply into their midst (i.e., being in non-duality with them). To alleviate psychological pain or fear, you must yield to it—let it be, lose yourself entirely in it, make fully conscious experiential contact with it, rather than try to avoid it. Through being in non-duality with the pain, you will learn that this does not cause you to experience greater pain. Instead, you will come to see that the pain will be diminished and transcended, gradually if not immediately.

Psychological pain involves the mind recoiling away from itself, in the form of inner resistance to some experiential state currently arising in consciousness. *If there is no self-judgment and no reactive inner resistance, control, or selective censorship of our feelings and other actual experiential states, there is no enduring psychological pain. Enduring psychological pain is not inherent in any particular feeling, per se, but arises only after the intent to reject the feeling arises. The feeling of psychological pain is created essentially by the attempt to fragment or separate consciousness from itself, by rejecting fully conscious experiential contact with painful feelings.* This involves the splitting of the natural inherent unity of consciousness into the duality of a reactive conceptual judging observer who tries to run away from, distort, control, or overpower the rejected observed feeling. *If consciousness in duality is the cause of the pain, then only consciousness in unity or non-duality can bring the elimination of the pain.*

Prior to having been acquainted with the process of creative self-understanding, you may have operated under the assumption that to eliminate painful psychological states, you must either escape from the pain, or the awareness of it, oppose it and overpower it, or distort its reality in some way. We have been suggesting that these are all forms of self-rejection of your actual feelings and of your own energies invested in those actual feelings. All forms of self-rejection are intrinsically pathological and painful at some level. Therefore, they will never eliminate the pain, but will actually function to preserve the painful feeling likely beyond your immediate conscious awareness. In this condition, it is less available to you; therefore, its influence is more insidious and damaging. These various forms of self-rejection of your actual experiential states are potentially very harmful, and inevitably lead to the creation of greater pain and psychological illness, as the products of unresolved self-conflict and emotional self-numbing, like a kind of psychological Novocain. That is a process of desensitization to your uncomfortable feelings, which also desensitizes you to the experience of love, joy, and beauty by divorcing your consciousness from its own experiential energy flow as you attempt to control it and thereby block that energy flow to prevent uncomfortable feelings from arising to your conscious awareness. *However, the process of creative self-understanding, because it does not involve self-judgment and self-rejection, is entirely conflict-free, and therefore relatively pain-free. It represents the essence of what is meant by nonjudgmental unconditional self-acceptance. It is the most expeditious and completely effective process by which you can liberate yourself from various painful psychological states and achieve self-growth or greater understanding and transformational development of what is experientially real and genuinely alive in yourself.* If this process is continued, it will ultimately lead to optimal psychological health and fulfillment.

Many readers, when they first learn about the process of creative self-understanding and the necessity of surrendering the dualistically separate observer-judger-controller-interpreter of feelings, in order to be in non-duality with their feelings, resist it consciously or subconsciously. They fear that it will lead to the acting out of their objectionable feelings, such as hostility. Such a fear is truly unfounded. Nothing could be further from the truth. Actually, the continued conflict, resulting from the rejected or repressed feeling pushing for discharge and the accumulated tension this creates, is much more likely to lead to acting out of the objectionable feeling than is yielding to it in non-duality. Merging or unifying in non-duality with your rejected feelings actually removes the cause or need for acting out, rather than facilitating it, as long as you do not identify with, side with, or react as those aggressive or disturbing feelings.

The rejected and repressed feelings constantly push for drainage and entry into conscious awareness, not behavioral expression, because they are obeying the basic principle of consciousness, which is to try to restore itself to its natural condition of being a unitary wholeness by bringing full conscious awareness and acceptance of all that has previously been rejected in oneself. Therefore, those repressed feelings are not necessarily pushing for acting out or discharge through expression into behavior; instead they may be pushing only for reintegration into the whole of conscious awareness, so that they can thereby achieve complete drainage and release of their repressed and encapsulated psychic energy. This occurs once each feeling is fully acknowledged into conscious awareness as the momentary experiential truth of oneself, rather than being rejected, distanced, and treated as a not-self, and also without identifying with the feeling as one's exclusive, partisan, reactive, sense of self. Once the message speaks for itself, and its repressed psychic energy and tension is thereby fully drained out into conscious awareness, then all impetus or need for acting-out is eliminated, as long as one does not react as or side for or against the feeling, as an exclusive, partisan identification with the feeling, but instead is non-dualistically unified with the underlying message and energy of the feeling as the nonreactive, nonpartisan, nonjudgmental, naturally calm observer of it. This liberation from painful, fearful, disturbed, or aggressive feelings occurs because the energy charge of the rejected or repressed feeling has been completely defused. In short, creative self-understanding does not necessarily lead to acting out of objectionable feelings, but rather, can be the best assurance against such acting out.

However, sometimes it is prudent to be alone with particularly intense negative feelings rather than in the presence of others at times when those feelings may be pushing for some kind of aggressive or explosive discharge, and then resume dialogue with others later when the explosive intensity of negative feelings such as anger or aggressiveness has begun to subside, and when one is beginning to experience a greater sense of calmness, clarity (liberating insight), and compassion. Intensely aggressive or disturbed feelings can be like inner wild animals or inner demons that first need to be tamed in solitude through the gentle power of nonjudgmental loving compassion for oneself and others, and the liberating insight that that process of unbiased, nonreactive exploration of the experiential truth of oneself brings, before we can safely return to the presence of others and communicate our negative feelings constructively and not abusively or even violently. If one is not able to calm down explosively intense aggressive, angry, fearful, painful, and/or other negative feelings on one's own, sometimes (not necessarily always) it can be helpful to discuss those feelings with a professionally trained, licensed, well-reputed psychotherapist or others who are not the target, object, or source of arousal of one's negative feelings, especially someone who one deeply trusts and respects, and who can be relied upon to help one explore those feelings in a truly compassionate, warmly caring, empathic, calm, nonjudgmental, unbiased manner. With these and/or other appropriate safeguards, permitting yourself to fully consciously experience negative feelings in a nonjudgmental, nonreactive manner is usually the best way to defuse and transform those feelings and the energy within them, whereas rejecting awareness of them and thereby repressing them into the unconscious actually increases the dangers of discharging those feelings in inappropriate or even violent behavior. This is described by Ken Wilber:

> We can tame evil only by befriending it, and we simply inflame it by alienating it. Integrated, evil becomes mellow; projected, it becomes quite vicious, and thus those who would seek to eliminate evil have added substantially to its victory . . . As a matter of fact, violent anti-social aggressive acts are a result not of integrated aggression but of suppressed and alienated aggression, for by "holding it in" the force of aggression greatly increases, just as the tighter you clamp on the lid of a pressure cooker the greater the force of steam becomes, until it finally results in violent explosion. Again, it appears a moral imperative to integrate and make conscious our aggressive tendencies.[2]

The process of creative self-understanding is the mind's natural means for healing and fulfilling itself by restoring itself to its natural condition of being an indivisible unitary whole. The mind naturally seeks the resolution of all of its inner states of conflict and tension, which is relaxed peace, its natural state of being. The mind wants to heal itself of all of the ego's self-created divisions, contradictions, and self-rejections in order to restore itself to its natural condition. The mind will heal and fulfill itself if we permit the mind to do what it naturally wants to do. The mind will naturally bring all of our rejected and repressed experiential realities to conscious awareness for integration if we will just not interfere with it by setting up a dualistic self, in the form of a self-concept, which functions as a judge, censor, and replacement of our actual experiential realities. If there is no sense of opposition to this natural therapeutic process and to what is actually arising as experience within consciousness in a given moment and if we can just let be what is, then self-integration, self-understanding, self-healing, and self-growth will take place most naturally, immediately, effectively, and least painfully as possible.

Creative self-understanding, arising out of a consciousness in the state of being or non-duality with our actual experiential states, is not only the most expeditious and effective means for ridding consciousness of painful and objectionable experiential states, but it also is the only means by which consciousness can achieve a real sense of peace, love, joy, beauty, spontaneity, creativity, health, and fulfillment. Each of these ego-free positive states requires a consciousness that is whole and free of self-conflict. It is only consciousness abiding in the non-dualistic state of being, not fragmented by identification with any self-concept, or rejection of any uncomfortable feelings, and therefore, free of all egoistic desire to become anything other than what it experientially is actually being this moment that is true psychological wholeness and health, completely conflict-free. With rare exceptions (e.g., those whose contact with reality is severely impaired, as in some kinds of psychosis), the process of creative self-understanding can help anyone achieve the liberation, health, and fulfillment we all crave.

The Process of Creative Self-Understanding: Illustrative Examples

The typical tendency is to try to escape from a painful feeling by trying to superimpose upon it a more tolerable feeling. For example, let us assume that what actually is arising, experientially at this moment, is your painful feeling of depression. Underlying that painful feeling of depression may be a message related to feelings of worthlessness. This message, were it recognized, would be a great threat to the ego's sense of existence because the ego, usually subconsciously, equates a feeling of being totally worthless with being a psychological nullity, or no psychological self. Thus, the labeled and negatively judged feeling of depression is itself an attempt to disguise and escape the full awareness of the ego-threatening message contained within it. As long as you are experiencing the feeling of depression, without exploring why you feel that way, you continue to remain unaware of its more threatening underlying message.

In addition to the painfulness of the message, the painful feeling of depression may be judged as being too threatening for you to endure. The experience of it may be too painful and might overwhelm your ego, or it may not be congruent with your self-concept as a cheerful, carefree, or happy-go-lucky person. As a result, you reject the actually arising experiential "what is" and try to escape into what presumptively "ought to be." You reject your negative and painful feeling of depression, and seek to superimpose upon it some compensatory, distracting, good, or pleasant feeling. You seek to indulge yourself in some kind of pleasurable activity or sensation that will provide you with a feeling of gaiety or vitality. Among these activities may be attending a fun party, taking a drug or alcohol, eating your favorite food, engaging in sexual relations, talking with a friend, or going on a buying spree. But have you really grown or changed yourself, psychologically? Have you really transformed the feeling of depression through this distracting effort?

It should be clear that you have actually not eliminated the depression through the above-mentioned activities; you have merely engaged in a process of self-deceit by hiding or concealing the feeling of depression from yourself. This has distracted you from the actual experiential truth of yourself at this moment, which is the ego-threatening message of worthlessness lying beneath the depression. This attempt to escape from the painful experiential truth of yourself does not eliminate the depression but only functions to make it unavailable to your conscious awareness for hearing and understanding its underlying message. The avoidance of fully consciously experiencing your depression ensures the continued preservation of its existence at the subconscious or subliminal level of your psyche. It is now submerged within the subconscious depths of your consciousness, instead of existing at the surface level of conscious awareness, where it was originally abiding. It now lies dormant and hidden, but not dead, and not resolved. Consequently, your escape from the depression is not a real transformation of the feeling, but only the illusion of transformation. The pent-up psychic energy contained within the message of the unexpressed feeling continues to remain encapsulated and not really discharged or resolved. Only when that energy is totally drained, by letting the message in the feeling spontaneously flow into one's full conscious awareness and speak for itself to conclusion, without any kind of censorship, control, distracting escape, or preconceived interpretation as a way of speaking for the feeling rather than letting it spontaneously speak for itself to its natural conclusion is the feeling totally transformed, released, resolved, and thereby, truly eliminated. Even if you were to gain the intellectual awareness that you feel depressed because you feel worthless, this conceptual understanding by itself alone would not be sufficient to bring liberation from its associated emotional pain. You must actually let the message speak for itself and bring its own accompanying emotional arousal and experiential energy discharge before liberation can be complete.

We reiterate for emphasis, you should not identify with the feeling when being in non-duality with it; for example, you can let yourself fully, nonjudgmentally experience feelings of worthlessness or insecurity without holding yourself to inherently *be* a worthless, insecure nature.

A feeling is totally resolved and transcended only by fully draining its underlying message and the pent-up energy associated with it. This can occur only if the feeling is not rejected or disguised with preconceived, presumptive interpretations. Only then can you clearly listen to the message and thereby provide an opening for its release, by letting it speak for itself to conclusion, so that it can fully drain out in your conscious awareness. *Being in non-duality or experiential communion with the feeling and its message, rather than observing or interpreting it from outside of the feeling, permits the door of repression to open and the message with its related energy to be totally drained.* Therefore, instead of rejecting the feeling, or moving away from it in any way as a detached observer or dualistic conscious knower, you must *let it be* by letting your conscious awareness be in full experiential contact or non-dualistic communion with the feeling, not attempting to control, eliminate, interpret, or speak for the feeling in any way. This permits the message within the feeling to speak for itself to conclusion. You must never speak for the message within the feeling, by superimposing an intellectual interpretation upon it. All you need to do is just listen and let the message speak for itself. This yields true self-understanding, which results in real self-growth. Mere theoretical interpretation or analysis alone cannot yield real transformational growth or liberation from psychological pain.

Thus, for example, do not *tell* yourself or provide explanations to yourself of why you feel depressed. Instead, let the feeling of depression speak for itself without any kind of controlling interference or superimposed, preconceived interpretation, so that the feeling of depression can spontaneously reveal its own answer and understanding of why this painful feeling exists in consciousness this moment. An explanation is not a genuine answer. The only real answer or liberating insight to the question of why the depression exists and how it is to be resolved abides only within the feeling of depression itself that is alive within you this moment. Only that alive, creative, spontaneously arising, actual experiential truth speaking for itself can bring about the true self-understanding, which yields a healing therapeutic effect or produces transformational self-growth (growth of what is experientially real and constructive in oneself, and outgrowth of experientially false, non-constructive psychological masks and habitual reactive patterns). This psychologically therapeutic, growth-oriented outcome of following the actual experiential truth of oneself, from moment to moment, involves developing enhanced levels of liberating self-understanding, constructive functioning, relaxed inner peace, and psychological well-being. Analytical or intellectual explanations applied to the feeling from the outside are non-creative (not open to spontaneously arising new experiential insight), non-transformational, non-healing, non-liberating, and dead, merely conjectures or presumptions rather than experiential insights. Such speculative interpretations are incapable, by themselves alone, of bringing a full cathartic release of the feeling's pent-up energy, and therefore are incapable of contributing to its being dissolved and resolved, as long as our actual feelings remain buried under superimposed conjectural interpretations, controlling defenses, and distracting escapes. It is only when the message contained within the feeling is permitted to spontaneously arise and creatively or directly speak for itself, without control, censorship, or interference of any kind, that the full release or drainage of the energy contained within the feeling can occur.

When you initiate this self-healing process, you may discover that your feeling of depression contained not only feelings of worthlessness, but also unexpressed feelings of hostility. You may discover that this hostility is covering over even deeper feelings, such as frustration, impotence, vulnerability, fearful insecurity, inner emptiness, or inner nothingness. If you permit this process of creative self-understanding to run its course, the entire complex of this feeling of depression will be spontaneously revealed to your conscious awareness and thereby dissolved. Therefore, it should be clear that no deliberate effort is ever necessary or effective in bringing about a true change of growth within consciousness. *Consciousness in the state of non-duality, which leads to creative self-understanding, is the mind's essential, natural, self-healing, integrative process.*

A more specific example will now be offered to illustrate some of the typical difficulties and psychological defenses that you are likely to encounter when you first learn the process of creative self-understanding and attempt to listen to and understand the messages underlying your feelings. The following example is taken from the actual experience of one of the authors (Max Hammer) in his early experimentation in developing this process of creative self-understanding. This experience was instrumental for him to eventually understand and formulate some of the basic principles of self-growth and psychological health discussed in this book.

I observe myself experiencing, verbally expressing, and on the verge of acting out very destructive feelings toward another person to whom I usually feel loving. That is the experiential truth of "what is" this moment. I observe that my immediate reaction to this experiential truth of myself is to rationalize my destructive feeling by trying to justify it in some way. I tell myself, for example, that this is just a bad day for me and that my anger must be an expression of the tension related to a multitude of frustrating situations that I encountered that day; or I just didn't get enough sleep the night before; or it's her fault and she deserves my anger because of the unacceptable way that she has just behaved toward me. Some of these reasons may, in fact, be related to my anger, but at this moment, they reflect only my attempt to justify my anger. It is an attempt to excuse it, so that I will not have to face the real truth underlying its current presence in my consciousness. All of these justifications reflect my attempt to convince myself that this destructive feeling and urge to be violent that is currently dominating my consciousness is not truly me. I do not want to take responsibility for its creation or its continued residence in my consciousness. I prefer to place the responsibility outside of myself.

As I observe what I am doing, I recognize that I have been trying to deceive myself into believing that some other person or some unusual circumstance outside of my own volition is responsible for putting the anger into my consciousness. Recognizing the self-deceit in trying to justify my anger, I now am prepared to face it and listen to it again, so as to learn what it is really all about. However, my previous attempts at justification have separated my awareness from my angry emotion. I try to review in my mind the events that led to the arousal of my anger, hoping that this will arouse it again, so that I will be able to readily hear and understand it. I observe myself asking the other person, with whom I have been angry, to do something for me. But she refuses and suggests that I do it myself. The more I try to convince and persuade her to do what I want, the more resistant, defiant, and adamant she becomes in asserting that I should do it myself. I now observe clearly that my anger is rising, and I see that the more resistant and adamant she becomes, the more my anger intensifies.

The issue is no longer: *who shall do what needs to be done?* We are now locked in a battle of wills, and I am determined to win. The more that I feel myself losing the battle, the more intense my anger grows. As my anger grows in intensity, I label myself as violent, and I become filled with self-hate and fear that I might lose control of this urge to be violent. As I observe this intensification of my anger, I come to realize that the labeling of a feeling and its associated connotation actually adds to the intensity of the feeling. I see that it also contributes to the negative judgment and rejection of the feeling, which I have labeled as violence. I can clearly see how the process of labeling my feeling actually makes it more difficult for me to establish contact with and understand the message contained within the feeling.

I can now also see much more clearly that it is I, and not the other person, who is directly responsible for the arousal and intensification of my angry feeling. I do this through the negative interpretations, labels, and judgments that I place upon her behavior and my own feelings. Now I realize that I cannot justify my anger, and that I am responsible for my own painful feeling. I judge myself as a bad person for having been so intensely angry with her. This makes me feel very guilty, and I proceed to heap a great deal of abuse upon myself. As I observe this, I realize that I cannot accept the truth of my rage because I cannot tolerate judging and seeing myself as a bad person. As a result, I vow to make stronger efforts in the future to control my anger and to work hard to become its opposite. In this way, I will not have to judge myself as a bad person, and feel so terribly guilty and worthless.

Now, as I look at what my mind is doing, I recognize that I am trying to escape from the actual truth of what is by trying to become what I ought to be. Right now, I am being my impulse to be violent. That is what is, but I am telling myself that I ought to be its opposite. I ought to be nonviolent, peaceful, kind, loving, gentle, accepting, and the like. This is not to suggest that I never am actually encompassing these traits. There certainly are experiential moments when I truly am these qualities, to some degree, but not right now. Right now, these traits only represent what I ought to be because right now, the experiential reality is my urge to be violent. I have also been telling myself that I ought to practice more self-control and willpower in regard to inhibiting the expression of my anger. However, when I cease to tell myself about what I should be with regard to my willpower, and just non-judgmentally observe what willpower is and listen to it speak for itself, I recognize that willpower is an attempt to reject "what is" for "what ought to be." It involves a pitting of one part of myself against another part of myself and thereby creates a condition of intrinsic conflict within myself, which produces tension and pain.

As I continue to observe what happens to my angry feeling when I attempt to control it, I become aware of the fact that no matter how much I try to suppress and control my anger, or try to avoid the expression of my angry feeling by striving to become or act like its opposite, the angry feeling will still be there, shadowing me and pushing for expression and drainage. I will either be forever in conflict with myself, trying to resist and deny these feelings, or else I will end up expressing them in some distorted or muted form. I can see the conflict and pain inherent in this process of trying to deny and escape from what is experientially real in myself, and I can see that conflict and pain can never really free me from my anger, but will only intensify it. As I observe what is involved in the attempt to act as if I were being the opposite of my destructive feeling I realize that *acting as if* will never be the same as actually *being*. Acting as if I were not violent, through such typical means as softening my voice, constantly smiling, compulsively trying to please other people, or continuously making declarations to myself that I am love and not hate, is not the same as truly being nonviolent. In doing these things, I would just be a violent person acting nonviolently rather than truly being free of my violent feelings. I clearly see that as long as I continue to act as if I were nonviolent, my feelings will continue to prevent me from ever really being nonviolent. As long as the violent feeling remains unexpressed and not drained, it will continue to endure in my consciousness at some level, and sooner or later, it will inevitably express itself in some way.

To really be nonviolent, I need to completely transform the violent feeling and not just pretend that I am its opposite by acting the role of its opposite. I recognize now that my urge to be violent must really end, rather than ignoring it and pretending that it does not exist within me. To accomplish this, I see that I must first *let be* this actual experiential truth of myself, which is my urge to be violent, in order to have it available to me, so that I can listen to it and come to understand it. But I immediately recognize that if my *goal* is to be free of my urge to be violent, then again I am rejecting "what is" and pursuing "what ought to be." This yearning to understand my destructive feeling in order to be free of it is a subtle form of rejection of that feeling, which distracts me from being able to make contact with it; therefore, I will not be able to hear and understand it. I see that I must be able to let this feeling be. It must be all right for me to be it. In fact, I must care about it for, in a sense, it must be there for a good reason, or else I would not have created it. However, I find that the truth of myself in this moment is that my mind is still resisting being one with my anger. Rather than tell myself that I should not be resisting, I let it be and listen to it speak for itself.

The creative awareness or experiential insight suddenly arises in me that if I accept the fact that I am a violent person, then this image of myself will be inconsistent with and totally destroy the image of myself that I am trying so hard to validate, which is a person who is nice, kind, gentle, good-natured, loving, and helpful. How can I be both violent and loving? My conviction is that if I am the one, I cannot also be the other. This apparent contradiction of my being both violent and also loving would make me question if I am any psychological self at all. If I am not what I always believed myself to be, then my entire sense of identity is threatened. I begin to catch a hint of how tenuous my sense of conceptual identity is, and how deeply I fear being a psychological nullity, an inner void, and a nobody. Now I understand better why I work so hard to affirm my identity as a gentle, kind, and loving person, and why my mind has been so resistant to accepting this momentary experiential self of my impulse to be violent. I have also learned that, if I am resistant to accepting some momentary experiential self, it is better to be, or let be, that feeling of resistance, and to look at it and let it speak for itself, rather than try to be what ought to be, which is nonresistant. Only understanding resistance, rather than avoiding or resisting the resistance, ends it.

Recognizing now that I am not really my self-concept of what I presume I ought to be, but only my changing moment-to-moment actual experiential reality, which at this moment is my anger, I no longer try to judge, control, or filter my thoughts or feelings, and my attention returns to the feeling of anger. I see more clearly now that it is not a case of my being angry, but more correctly, that I am anger at this moment. Anger is not just an attribute or feeling apart from me, as some detached conceptual self, but rather, I am anger totally in this moment, and no other personal psychological self. Therefore, I have no choice but to just yield to it, let it be, and listen to its message speak or play itself out to completion. Being one with my anger, rather than just the observer standing outside of it, and just passively and receptively listening to it speak for itself, I come to see even more clearly how my anger is related to my inability to control and influence the other person. I recognize now that I was trying to control and influence the other person, but I was meeting with resistance, which was producing feelings of failure, helplessness, and impotence within me. I was also feeling that she was trying to control and influence me into doing what she wanted, which was making me feel even more weak and impotent, especially as I became aware that I was losing this battle. I observe my anger intensifying at the thought of being controlled and influenced by another person, especially one that I label as being weaker or less potent than I am, and I recognize my inability or impotence to impose my will upon and influence the other person. I see this so clearly, as I just permit myself to be my anger and listen to what it is trying to do and say.

As I continue to listen to the message within the anger, I now gain the creative realization that my anger, as a form and expression of potency or power, is really an attempt to cover over, compensate for, and help myself deny my more underlying feelings of being weak, helpless, impotent, or powerless, and thereby, vulnerable to emotional hurt or psychological destruction, as an experiential negation of my sense of self. The greater my frustration or inability to control, influence, or impose my will upon the other person, the greater are my feelings of weakness, helplessness, impotence, and vulnerability to being psychologically destroyed. The more intense these feelings become, the more intense my anger grows. My anger intensifies because I need to deny these feelings of impotence. I attempt to deny them by expressing their compensatory opposite feeling of potency, which my anger represents. My anger is my attempt to demonstrate that I am really powerful, and not helpless and impotent of will, as I really feel. I see that my anger is essentially just an intensification of the need to impose my will and prove its capacity to influence the other person.

As my attention returns to my feelings of helplessness, weakness, impotence, and vulnerability, I try to explain away these feelings by being reminded of something that I had read at one time. This reading had suggested that these feelings are related to, or reflect doubts about feelings of masculine potency or castration anxiety. Although any of these explanations may, in fact, be part of my psychological make-up, I quickly recognize that, once again, I have detached myself from the creative free-flow of my thoughts, and have proceeded to stand outside of my own experiential self. I have intellectually interpreted, or analyzed myself. I have treated myself as though I am something to be understood theoretically, instead of permitting any of these theoretical explanations to arise creatively to me as a directly experienced truth, if indeed they were true. I have deliberately interjected them and imposed them upon my awareness, in an attempt to satisfy myself that I had really achieved self-understanding, thereby putting to an end the creative and free-flowing stream of my consciousness. Fearing where my thoughts were freely going, I intentionally provided myself with a set of theoretical explanations of what I was feeling in order to put an end to the creative uncovering of my experiential self-understanding. I see clearly now how all explanations and interpretations that come from outside the feeling itself, and outside of my own experiential self-discovery of its message, create a sense of duality or divisiveness within me. This only prevents really hearing and understanding the truth of my momentary experiential self. With this understanding, my attention spontaneously returns to my feelings of frustration, weakness, helplessness, impotence, and vulnerability. Now I see that each of these feelings are not essentially different but are really basically the same. They are just different labels for the same underlying experiential reality, reflecting the impotence or non-efficacy of my will to influence what I have put myself on the line to influence.

At first, a feeling of great fear arises, as I attempt to escape from acknowledging these feelings as being my self. As soon as I let be and accept the reality of the existence of these feelings as being me, both my anger and fear completely fade. But this time, content to just stay with these feelings of impotence of will, and letting them say whatever they have to say, there comes the understanding, in a flash of sudden insight, that my inability to influence and control the other person made me feel extremely impotent and fearful. I tried to cover this over with a feeling of power through my anger because the feeling of impotence of my will made me doubt my own psychological existence. Now I can really see clearly that I have been trying to affirm my own sense of self through the power of my will to influence the other person. I was equating my sense of self with my will, and I was equating the existence of my will with the freedom to express itself and its capacity to influence the other person in the way that I wanted. I was trying to affirm the potency of my will, and thereby affirm the existence of my will and affirm the existence of the sense of self with which it is identified. I was attempting to do this through my ability to produce the desired influencing effect of gaining some sign of surrender from the other person. This would be achieved if I could persuade her to do what I wanted her to do, even though I knew that she didn't want to do it. Failing that, if my anger could produce a reaction of fear or crying in her, then I could also construe this as a surrender to my potent will. I could then conclude that I am something substantial and real. However, if I fail to produce the desired effect that I have put myself on the line to achieve, then I must conclude that my will is without potency or efficacy. If I cannot produce the intended influencing effect, then I must conclude that I am no cause, my will is impotent, and therefore I am nothing. If my will is not able to feel itself to be the cause of any effect, then I feel as though I do not exist. This would be true for anyone. To be a non-influencing will is to be no will at all. To be no will is to be no agent or self.

Now I understand the full implications of why I was so angry with the other person. I can also now see clearly that what I reject in others is directly related to what I reject in myself. I see that my inability to accept what she was being and expressing in this moment, which I was interpreting as being psychologically more powerful than I was, was directly related to my inability to accept the resulting feelings of impotence, vulnerability, and psychological nothingness. Were I able to accept all such experiential realities in myself, then I could surely let her be whatever experiential self she had to be, in a given moment, because whatever her experiential self triggered in me would be acceptable to me. There would be no need for me to change her or try to control her. There would then be only the desire to understand her, and her momentary experiential self, but not the desire or need to change her or reject what she honestly had to be in the here and now.

Seeing the truth of all this, letting be my feelings of impotence of will, and realizing that I still continue to exist, rather than feeling like a nullity as I fear I would if I let myself recognize my feeling of impotence, I now recognize that all traces of anger, fear, and impotence are gone. I can clearly see that once I can let be and feel that it is really all right to be my negative feelings, such as impotence, vulnerability, insecurity, or nothingness, then these feelings vanish. There is now a deep feeling of acceptance and compassion toward myself that immediately leads to acceptance of and feelings of compassion toward the person to whom I have felt violent. The self-discovered truth has liberated me. I now see very clearly what true self-acceptance really is and its relation to real self-love. I see that when there is no labeling or conceptualizing of myself by myself, no judgment of good or bad applied to myself, and no demands placed upon myself to be anything more or different than what I am actually being this experiential moment, in essence, when I can just let be what is, then I am in a state of nonjudgmental or unconditional self-acceptance, which is the essence of true self-love. I also realize, at the same time, that when I am self-love, I am also naturally loving toward the other person. When I am not labeling the other person, and therefore am not fragmenting her wholeness by making a concept out of her, and when I am not judging her as good or bad, not making any demands that she be anything other than what she is this experiential moment, then feelings of love, tenderness, and compassion spontaneously pour forth from me. This occurs without my purposeful intention and without being the result of the other person soliciting my love and compassion in any way. I not only feel very loving, but I also feel a great sense of peace and joy. There is now the profound realization that love-joy-peace are not three different realities, but are really one and the same reality, which may be referred to as Bliss. Even more importantly, there is the realization that my and every other person's consciousness is intrinsically that triune reality of bliss. Now I have the first hints of the nature of true fulfillment. I realize now that true fulfillment does not abide outside of me, outside of my own intrinsic consciousness. It is not something that I must make an effort to become or something into which I must convert myself. I am always and intrinsically being that state of wholeness and fulfillment, but have previously failed to realize that, ironically because I have been so busy striving to attain it.

When I am free of all attempts to label or conceptualize myself, free of all attempts to judge myself as being either good or bad, and free of all egoistic strivings, expectations, and demands upon myself, and do the same for all that confronts me, then I realize my true inherent wholeness, which is one with love-peace-joy and real psychological fulfillment. I feel privy to a very great secret that this creative awareness and realization has bestowed upon me, like a gift from a deeper part of my own consciousness. It is as though a veil of ignorance had been removed from me by a source that seems to be outside of me, and yet I know that it is truly not outside of my whole being. I have been permitted a peek into my true nature, my essential substance, and my real being. I realize now that if anyone lets be and follows the spontaneous stream of consciousness of their moment-to-moment experiential truth, then eventually, this current will carry their conscious awareness to union with the sea of their ultimate Truth, Being, or Source, their Real Self, which is the realization of intrinsic true fulfillment. Several distinctions can be offered to help further clarify the process of creative self-understanding.

Creative Self-Understanding vs. Contrived Self-Understanding

Creative self-understanding or uncontrived, unrestricted, genuine, self-understanding often comes in a spontaneous flash of sudden insight. It is free to come only when the self-concept operating as the psychological self, which is the observer-thinker-judger-censor of thought, is surrendered. It is called creative self-understanding in contrast to contrived self-understanding, which is under the influence, control, and bias of the self-concept. Contrived self-understanding is meant to validate the self-concept's idealized view of itself. The self-concept blocks the intrusion of creative insight, as direct, immediate, non-conceptually mediated contact with and realization of the actual experiential truth of us in a given moment. Because of the self-concept's devotion to protecting its sense of internal consistency of its self-definitions or sense of inner cohesiveness, it must first filter every thought and feeling that arises to conscious awareness in order to make sure that no thought or feeling will be recognized that might contradict the traits with which the self-concept is defined and identified, and thereby jeopardize its sense of being real.

Creative self-understanding, on the other hand, arises from our indivisible holistic self, which is open to all experiential aspects of itself, and not from our egoistic self-concept, which is inherently divisive, comprised of a duality between the actual feelings and the conceptual interpreter, controller, and judger of them, as well as comprised of various opposite, contradictory self-concepts, such as good and bad, strong and weak, secure and insecure, etc. The conceptual self is our more contrived, fabricated, presumptive, or counterfeit self, derived from conjectural self-definitions and reactive self-evaluations, whereas the holistic self is our more essentially real, authentic, inherent, or unconditioned self, as our enduring whole energy field or being, and its momentary experiential states. The holistic self is naturally devoted to bringing conscious awareness to the realization that your real self is already intrinsically an indivisible unitary whole, and therefore, is already naturally healthy and fulfilled. It is this natural urge or basic drive of consciousness to restore our natural wholeness by undoing unnatural self-division, arising from rejecting and distancing ourselves from our painful feelings and experiential states, that causes the previously rejected, repressed, and nonintegrated experiential realities, along with their creative self-understanding, to be spontaneously propelled into our conscious awareness. This occurs once the inhibiting self-concept (as dualistic observer and reactive, partisan, divisive interpreter of the contents of consciousness) is surrendered. It is only our identification with our intrinsically divisive, selective, partisan self-concepts that prevents the realization of our intrinsic wholeness, and makes us feel fragmented and deficient. The egoistic self-concept from which contrived or presumptive self-understanding emerges must first be surrendered and made inoperative by not labeling, judging as good or bad, or having any kind of desire, goal, censorship, control, or conjectural interpretation with regard to the experiential reality that exists or arises within ourselves in a given moment. At that point, creative self-understanding and the psychological integration that it brings can enter our awareness and produce the elimination of the painful feeling, which creates a healing effect, as transformational self-growth.

Creative Self-Understanding vs.
Intellectual Self-Understanding

Creative self-understanding is more than just intellectual understanding or conjectural self-interpretation. Intellectual understanding is knowing about yourself via theory, explanation, analysis, or presumption, in contrast to knowing yourself directly, by letting your moment-to-moment feeling spontaneously arise and creatively, unrestrictedly, directly, immediately, authentically speak the experiential truth of itself, without any distortion or superimposed, preconceived, interpretive bias. In intellectual understanding, a state of duality exists because you stand outside of your own experiential self, acting as its observer, analyzer, or interpreter. For example, you might feel depressed, and try to understand the reasons for your depression, believing that this would be sufficient to relieve you of your depression. If your consciousness is in a state of duality from direct contact with the actual experiential truth of yourself, as it is during the process of intellectual understanding, the observer or judge of your feeling might offer any one of a number of possible interpretations or explanations to help explain away your painful feeling. For example, you might attribute your depression to the loss of someone you love, to an un-gratifying job, or to a growing sense of frustration or boredom. Even though some of these intellectual explanations may, in fact, be related to your depression, they all represent a form of guesswork. They are, at best, sophisticated forms of opinion or conjecture, which are superimposed upon the real message contained within the feeling, thereby obscuring that message, and preventing it from being truly heard and understood. The guesswork, as nearly everyone can attest to through their own personal experience, is not the total and direct experiential self-understanding sufficient to liberate you from the depression, but letting the real experiential message creatively speak for itself to completion is the necessary self-understanding that will provide that liberation.

Creative Self-Understanding vs. Emotional Self-Understanding

Creative self-understanding is more than just emotional understanding. Emotional understanding is the identification with a particular labeled emotion that you are feeling in a given moment. For example, you might recognize that you are feeling angry or sad when you have not been aware of that before, and consider that recognition a reflection of real self-understanding. This recognition of that emotion you are actually feeling may, at times, be helpful in leading you to real self-understanding, but unless you are also sensitive to the underlying message contained within your anger or sadness, which is the reason *why* you feel sad, you are only partially in touch with yourself, and therefore have only partial and usually rather superficial self-understanding.

Emotional understanding, by itself alone, is not sufficient to bring the full understanding of the message hidden within the emotion. It is therefore not sufficient to bring about true, full, and enduring, liberation from that emotion. In fact, experience of the emotion often inhibits real self-understanding because it covers over the awareness of that which really needs to be directly experienced and thereby understood. *That which really needs to be experienced and understood usually relates to what is threatening the ego in this moment. It is the full understanding of the ego-threatening message contained within the painful emotion, and not just the awareness that you are experiencing a particular emotion, per se, that is the true creative self-understanding capable of producing a liberating and therapeutic effect.* It is the authors' experience that once the message within an emotion is fully experienced, and thereby understood so that its accompanying psychic energy is fully drained or released, you will then feel not only relieved of the painful emotion, but will also experience a real and deep sense of peacefulness and well-being.

Creative Self-Understanding vs. Self-Awareness

Many people may confuse creative self-understanding with terms currently in vogue, such as "self-awareness." However, the self being referred to here is usually just the physical body. The self-awareness movement has emphasized the importance of being more clearly in touch with the sensations, energies, and experiences of the physical body as an essential means of achieving a sense of integration and identity. Through various individual and group exercises and techniques, individuals are encouraged to become aware of the movements of their bodies and their physical sensations. Those people who use self-awareness to mean just bodily awareness are involved in a fragmentary approach to self-understanding. It may be that being more aware of your physical self is extremely stimulating, relaxing, and grounding, but that kind of self-understanding by itself alone is incomplete and lacks sufficient depth for the purposes of true psychological liberation, which requires keen, direct observation and undistracted insight into the momentary experiential truth of yourself.

For example, if you were to become sensitive to the physical sensations in your body, you might identify a part of your body that feels all tied up in knots and under tension. This tension might then correctly be translated or converted to its underlying feeling of hostility, which you could easily express in a number of ways, such as pounding your fist into a pillow. If, in this way, you drain the physical energy associated with your hostility, it is true that you might eventually feel greatly relieved. However, unless the message contained within your hostility is also fully experienced, fully understood, and completely drained, the relief will be neither deep nor enduring. The acting out of your hostility may still keep you ignorant as to the origin or underlying cause of the hostility, and so it will soon build up again. Being aware that you feel hostile without directly experiencing the underlying reason why you feel hostile is still only a form of duality or distancing by making only superficial experiential contact with the feeling. Through creative self-understanding, as opposed to exclusively physical self-awareness (but which may or may not include physical self-awareness along with direct observation of deeper, nonphysical feelings and experiential states), you might not only recognize your urge to express hostility, but through being in non-duality with this feeling, it would give way to its more underlying causal real message, involving an attempt to alleviate the ego's sense of inner deficiency and help it to feel better about itself, such as the need to express hostility as a display of power and providing the means by which you are trying to deny a more pervasive underlying feeling of impotence, weakness, helplessness, or vulnerability. It is not when the physical energy associated with a feeling is drained out, per se, but only when the psychic energy associated with the message within a particular feeling is fully understood, and thereby fully drained out that a true integration and enduring liberation of the whole psyche can be obtained. That is to say, full liberation from painful feelings requires not only being aware of the actual feeling, per se, but also directly experiencing the underlying message of the feeling, which provides liberating insight into *why* the feeling has arisen in the first place and why it has persisted until now.

Thus, if we thoroughly understand the process of creative self-understanding, we will not confuse it with terms that sound similar or with other processes that claim to achieve the same ends. By the same token, if we thoroughly understand the process of creative self-understanding, we will recognize that the same essential process can also be referred to in different ways by terms such as the way of being, the way of non-resistance, the natural way to self-growth, awareness without choices, nonjudgmental awareness, non-duality therapy, transpersonal therapy, quiet mind therapy, experiential therapy, holistic therapy, or creative self-understanding therapy. Whatever the name may be, if the process involves a consciousness in non-duality with our actual feelings and other experiential states, then it is essentially the same as what we call the process of creative self-understanding.

In order to gain at least a thorough intellectual understanding of the essence of the creative self-understanding process, the discussion of this process contained in this chapter may need to be reread several times with considerable reflection and thoughtfulness. There is much here that will likely be new and unfamiliar to the reader and much that is not easily comprehendible at first glance. The degree to which the reader will be able to enter into non-duality or experiential communion with what is written in this chapter, and let it creatively or spontaneously speak for itself, and thereby provide its own understanding of itself, the deeper and more authentic that understanding will be. However, even if a thorough intellectual understanding were achieved, it would still not be sufficient for liberating psychological self-healing to occur. To understand the process of creative self-understanding thoroughly, so that it can be most effectively utilized, requires more than just the process of reading about it and the intellectual understanding of it. In addition, you must actually *practice* it consistently and diligently. If you do so, your psychological growth, and increased sense of well-being and fulfillment can be enormous.

THE PROCESS OF PSYCHOLOGICAL SELF-

HEALING AND SELF-TRANSFORMATION

THROUGH CREATIVE SELF-UNDERSTANDING

Ceasing to identify with psychosocial masks such as predetermined self-definitions, idealized self-images, positive and
negative value judgments (or approved and disapproved self-
evaluations), and predetermined social roles enables us to
liberate our energies from psychological self-confinement,
and also enables us to gain liberating transformational insight into the actual experiential truth of ourselves as well as
resolve painful psychological inner conflicts rooted in rejecting our actual experiential states in favor of a presumption
of what we "should be." Self-discovery of our actual experiential realities and nonjudgmental unconditional acceptance
of them eventually leads to inner peace, arising from resolution of psychological inner conflict, as well as enabling
us to feel more joyfully alive and fulfilled by liberating our
energy from confinement in preconceived self-interpretations. The only effective way to resolve psychological pain
is to let yourself experience it fully consciously, whereas
escaping from psychological pain, such as by superimposing more positive self-definitions and pleasant experiential
states, actually preserves the psychological pain, often in
subconscious levels of the psyche. We must let our painful
feelings spontaneously speak for themselves to conclusion,
rather than controlling, censoring, and speaking for them
with preconceived conceptual interpretations. The state of
consciousness in non-duality with our actual feelings and

experiential states is the only true therapeutic and transformational growth-producing state of awareness, because it is the only conflict-free state of consciousness. However, unifying with our painful feelings does not necessarily mean identifying with them, agreeing with them, siding with them, justifying them, or acting upon them. Consciousness in non-duality with and nonjudgmental unconditional acceptance of our actual feelings and experiential states is in a state of being or natural indivisible wholeness; however, when consciousness seeks to validate, defend, enhance, or aggrandize, its egoistic self-definitions, then it is in a state of becoming or presumed deficiency and compensatory desire, seeking to become more than what we believe that we already are. The attempt to deny and reject awareness of our actual experience by trying to become or validate some kind of ideal self-image or presumptive self-definition that we presume to be "better" or more acceptable to ourselves puts us into a process of self-division and inner conflict, which perpetuates and exacerbates psychological pain.

CHAPTER 2

REFLECTIONS FOR ENHANCING EXPERIENTIAL SELF-UNDERSTANDING

> No man can reveal to you aught but that which already lies half asleep in the dawning of your knowledge. The teacher who walks in the shadow of the temple, among his followers, gives not of his wisdom, but rather, of his faith and his lovingness. If he is indeed wise he does not bid you enter the house of *his* (italics mine) wisdom, but rather leads you to the threshold of *your own mind.*[1]

Author Khalil Gibran's statement suggests that the kind of self-knowledge and self-understanding that is necessary to produce transformational growth and psychological health comes only through your own *self-discovery*. No teacher, counselor, analyst, or guru (i.e., spiritual advisor and guide of whatever religion or philosophy) can ever know your truth as well as you can know it. The truth has no prescribed route to it. It is spontaneously arising within you from moment to moment, and no one's mind other than your own is able to alertly be with that momentary experiential truth of you. To discover the real truth of yourself, you must be without guidance from others and without being taught because any preconceived ideas or goals will distract you from alertly observing whatever experience is actually arising in yourself in a given moment. Looking at the truth of yourself is what it means to be your own guru or teacher of truth. The liberating insight that leads to appropriate and transformational action is not something that can be coaxed out of you as you sit across from some kind of counselor, whose only claim to wisdom hangs framed as a degree on his office wall. Likewise, it does not come out of sensitivity training sessions in which everyone plays the now popular game of exchanging hang-ups. It comes only when the mind is totally alone with itself and quiet, not striving to reach any kind of predetermined goal or knowledge, but simply content to alertly observe whatever experience is spontaneously arising in a given moment. That kind of relaxed quiet and open receptivity of mind enables you to alertly observe whatever experience spontaneously arises in yourself in a given moment, and that non-reactive process of observation effortlessly brings insight or understanding of the truth of yourself.

This, in essence, is what the process of reflection or self-exploration is all about. It is an attempt to help you get to know yourself and understand yourself better, to be in better contact with the reality of the actual experiential truth of yourself. Being open to alertly observing whatever experience is actually arising in you so that you can be real or truthful with yourself and others is the basis of psychological health. Being psychologically healthy with the ability to appreciate life most creatively and to its fullest involves the capacity to be sensitive to the reality of yourself, as well as the reality of the outside world.

Probably the most difficult sensitivity for us to develop is toward ourselves in terms of developing authentic self-understanding. We tend to run from the actual experiential truth of ourselves, spontaneously arising in a given moment because it is so often in conflict with our idealized image of what we think we should be. We tend to feel that growth is the progression toward the goal of becoming, achieving, or validating that idealized image. However, growth toward some ideal is not real growth at all, in terms of developing greater genuine self-understanding, self-transformation, and self-healing of inner conflict and psychological pain by developing greater self-acceptance. Instead, trying to become, achieve, or validate some kind of idealized image of yourself is really only the solidification, elaboration, and expanding dead weight of an artificially contrived psychological and social mask, which conceals and distorts what you really are. It is all imaginary presumption because you never stop being what you are by turning your back on what you actually are being or experiencing in a given moment and pursuing an idealized image or positive concept of what you assume you ought to be as a desired trait or experience. When you escape from the actual experiential truth of yourself by pursuing some kind of idealized concept of what you presume you ought to be, then what you are actually being or experiencing continues to cling to you as a heavy burden, like a monkey on your back, incessantly harassing you in the attempt to capture your conscious attention so that it can be reintegrated back into the natural wholeness of your being, rather than being divorced from your conscious attention, as an unnatural, psychologically unhealthy, process of self-escape, self-division, or self-splitting. As you reject more and more of the actual experiential truth of yourself, in your attempt to fulfill your idealized image of seeking to become something else that you presume you ought to be, the psychological burden of internal self-rejection and self-conflict becomes heavier and weighs you down more and more, until you break down and collapse under the strain, at which time, painful, pathological symptoms of emotional disturbance manifest.

Like a dog frantically chasing its own tail, the mind becomes weary and disturbed, repetitively going around in circles, trying to escape from the actual experiential truth of itself, but not really being able to outrace or sever some rejected aspect of our own indivisible whole being. Like the dog that is unable to bite off part of its own tail, we cannot really detach ourselves from any of our actual experiential states, no matter how long and intensely we try to deny and escape them. We pursue some kind of presumptive self-enhancement that our pure conscious awareness can never really attach to itself, like the tail of the dog that the dog is not able to grasp in its mouth because its body cannot naturally twist itself to that extent. Similarly, our conscious awareness feels unnaturally "bent out of shape" as the painful experience of tension, frustration, and inner conflict when it tries to grasp its intrinsically unknowable inner being, or indefinable objectless pure subjectivity, as an object of knowledge of itself. The most subjective knower cannot naturally "turn around" or recoil inward upon itself to dualistically know itself as an objectified conceptual self-definition, just as a dog cannot naturally turn around its front side far enough to grasp its own tail or hindquarters, as the eye is unable to naturally turn inward to see itself, as pure clear light cannot naturally turn inward upon itself to illuminate its own essential nature, or as the ear cannot hear itself, but can naturally hear only sounds coming from outside of itself.

What draws you away from the truth of yourself is your unconscious commitment to yourself to run away from psychological, mental, or emotional pain. This commitment stems from your deep inner conviction that the pain is *absolutely* intolerable to bear, and if you do not run away from it, it will overwhelm you. The origin of this fear and conviction goes back to the time of early infancy when you felt extreme pain from the experience of hunger, and because your thinking apparatus was not very much developed, you reacted physiologically to this pain and felt that this pain was going to annihilate you. You were helpless in your own efforts to reduce the pain, and you had no means of understanding that the reduction of this pain was dependent upon someone else coming with milk. Thus, if your mother did not come promptly when you screamed, you reacted physiologically as though you were helpless to eliminate the pain you were under, that it would likely never cease, and therefore it threatened you with annihilation. That's why, even today, when you are more mature, it still frightens you to feel helpless and vulnerable, and it explains why, at the first sign of tension and pain—physical, mental, or emotional—you immediately try to reduce it. That is also why most people are more frightened of being abandoned and helpless in the face of unalterable pain than they are even of death.

The psychological, mental, or emotional pain from which you run away is often in the form of an uncomfortable thought, feeling, or impulse, such as some kind of fear, anger, guilt, sexual impulse, or loss. The loss may either be in the form of a loved person, either through death, abandonment, or rejection, or the loss may be the result of diminishing of self-esteem. Loss of self-esteem usually takes the form of a failure to fulfill a valued goal or an esteemed image of yourself. For example, you may have an image of yourself as a very intelligent person, which becomes severely threatened when you receive a low grade on an examination. You may have an image of yourself as a very unselfish person, and then someone tells you that you behaved very selfishly in a particular situation. You may have an image of yourself as a good parent, but your child lowers that image by doing poorly in school or getting into some kind of trouble in the community.

Many people have also learned to run from uncomfortable thoughts, feelings, impulses, problems, and conflicts because the tension and psychological pain that such confrontation produces tends to undermine the ego's basic sense of security, willpower, identity, worth, inner substantiality, inner animation, psychological vitality, or self-awareness. As a result, we tend to avoid and escape into diversionary distractions, which drown out the emotional pain that we are trying to avoid consciously experiencing, by superimposing intense comforting sensations coming from potentially addictive substances or sensationalist entertainment media that may be unwholesome, toxic, and/or excessively consumed. These kinds of substances and entertainment media often serve to produce an artificially contrived sense of euphoria and relaxation, as well as inner psychological numbing, deadening, or desensitization of our consciousness to the emotional pain that we are trying to avoid. But that process of desensitization also decreases our ability to experience true love, joy, relaxed inner peace, beauty, creative insight, inspiration, and various other reality-oriented aspects of true goodness, fulfillment, and well-being. In that sense, the desensitizing effects of misusing various kinds of substances, entertainment media, and insincere psychological games (involving self-deception, as well as deception of other individuals) as a means of escaping from actual or anticipated psychological pain are psychologically comparable to using Novocain.

Psychological health, maturity, and strength of character necessarily involve being willing and able to tolerate painful feelings and experiences; otherwise, we increasingly withdraw from various aspects of life and deaden ourselves psychologically by continuously, addictively using some kind of controlled experience to block the possibility of psychological pain. These methods include addictive substance abuse, obsessive thinking, or frequently losing ourselves in fantasy. Unless we are willing to face possible psychological and physical pain, we retreat into a self-imprisoning kind of psychologically escapist "womb" or "tomb" as a means of guarding against any uncontrolled experiences that might possibly bring pain or discomfort. Escaping from the full conscious awareness of painful or uncomfortable experiential states through various distracting means can readily become addictive and dull our conscious alertness, impair our contact with reality, diminish our capacity for effective, adaptive, functioning, and adversely affect our psychological and physical health and well-being. Excessively using narcotics, compulsive fantasy, and intensely exciting sensations are often used as a means of distracting ourselves from uncomfortable inner or outer realities. Such escapist tactics only temporarily and superficially cover the uncomfortable experiential states at a less than fully conscious level of our psyche, where they continue to fester and become increasingly more pathological, like a wound that becomes infected when ignored or covered over and not properly medicated.

It is important that you clearly recognize that the issue is not one of "Shall I endure pain now or try to avoid it?"

That pain cannot be avoided indefinitely because it is abiding within you, and it has not been eliminated just because you are trying to ignore it or escape from it in some way. You can never really escape from yourself, and you are being your own painful experiential states occurring within your own psyche. Therefore, you can only escape for a time from your *awareness* of that painful experiential self. That process of escape, in which the conscious knower stands dualistically distant and separated from the pain, only preserves and intensifies the pain. Thus, the real issue is, "Shall I endure psychological or emotional pain now by surrendering to it, unifying my conscious awareness with it, so that it can thereby gradually drain out into my conscious awareness, and eventually be fully gone? Or shall I try to avoid it now, and therefore have to endure it for a longer time and with greater intensity later, when it inevitably eventually pushes past the resistance and forces its way into my conscious awareness?" Make no mistake about it, at some time in the future, when you grow tired of escaping from your painful experiential states, and the incessant internal struggle or divisive self-conflict that necessarily involves, or when your ego can no longer tolerate the constant pressure and tension of having to escape from your own thoughts and feelings, that pain will register in your conscious awareness with enormous intensity.

If you ever expect to be able to regain the energy trapped in rejected painful feelings so that energy can become available for productive, adaptive, enjoyable, living and for investing in developing and maintaining genuinely caring or loving relationships with other people, and if you wish to grow psychologically from your painful experiences, so that they are not a total waste, then you must learn to confront your pain head-on and let it do its worst. If you do that, your pain will dissolve relatively quickly, and you will heal the emotional pain and the self-conflict that it produces. But if you do not directly confront your pain, by permitting yourself to fully consciously experience it, contact it, embrace it, and welcome it to play itself out to completion in your conscious awareness without any kind of censorship, control, inhibition, or blockage, and without any sense of distancing or duality that process of self-escape from your painful experiential states necessarily involves, then whether consciously or subliminally/subconsciously, your pain will continue and your capacity for undertaking productive, adaptive, deeply enjoyable, fulfilling, functioning and real love relationships as well as your psychological stability will be severely impaired because the energy trapped in those rejected, blocked, painful experiential states will not be available to you. Metaphorically speaking, the energy trapped in painful experiential states that are rejected and therefore not free to flow spontaneously into your conscious awareness and play out to completion is like water that becomes frozen into ice, so that it can no longer flow and support life-sustaining activities, such as drinking, agriculture, hygiene, generation of hydroelectric power, and swimming, as well as providing a habitat for fish and other aquatic creatures, metaphorically representing the enhanced levels of psychologically constructive and productive functioning that become available when you liberate energy previously trapped in suppressed uncomfortable feelings and experiential states.

Unless we develop emotional pain tolerance, we lack the inner strength of character needed to function productively, effectively, and constructively, especially in the face of uncomfortably difficult circumstances, adaptive challenges, and responsibilities. The more that we avoid facing uncomfortable truths about ourselves, uncomfortable challenges and circumstances when it is truly appropriate to do so, or reject taking constructive, life-and-developmental growth-affirming risks that might possibly produce discomfort, the more we weaken and disable ourselves, psychologically speaking, by reinforcing the conviction that we are too inwardly weak and fragile to face pain even when continued avoidance can produce serious harmful consequences or even endanger our physical survival. However, development of greater pain

...ance enables us to develop greater strength of character, which brings greater psychological health, self-confidence, and self-understanding as we face uncomfortable truths about ourselves. Productive self-discipline, adaptive coping abilities, and the ability to risk pain or discomfort in order to contact and enjoy a wider and deeper range of life experience and activity also result. By taking such courageous, growth-oriented, psychological risks, we thereby grow more developed as a person, developing greater psychological health and maturity, as well as developing significant, rewarding, new skills and insights. As some apt old adages suggest, "no pain, no gain" and "without the hurts, the heart is hollow." Avoiding contact with uncomfortable or painful aspects of life experience makes us more superficial, inauthentic, and insincere as well as more divorced from our real life energy invested in rejected painful feelings and uncomfortable aspects of life experience that we avoid.

Sue Paton Thoele aptly describes rejected aspects of our being and experience as "inner orphans" or "sub-personalities" that need to be consciously accepted and thereby reintegrated back into our indivisible psyche in order to retrieve our natural wholeness, life energy vitality, well-being, and authenticity:

> Our society has taught us that we are tainted by innumerable unacceptable flaws and circumstances. From that judgmental concept, we have become adept at denying aspects of ourselves which appear unworthy or shameful. Unfortunately, denying parts of ourselves creates ambivalence and internal fragmentation. With each part of ourselves that is chastised and exiled, there is less life force available to us. In order to regain the gift of our entire life force, we need to find the inner orphans that we have cast out, and adopt them back into the fold. Underdeveloped, undernourished, and wounded, inner orphans carry our fears and our penchant for self-devaluation. Remembering

Rilke's statement, "All in us that is terrible needs to be loved," we can be reassured that, through love and acceptance, our seemingly terrible inner orphans can be healed, empowered, and set free to augment our life force and become compassionate lovers, beautiful expressions of our soul's luminosity.[2]

Ken Wilber is another prominent transformational thinker who views conscious embracing of sub-personalities as a way to integrate them into the whole psyche, so that they no longer function in a psychologically unhealthy manner by being buried in the unconscious, dissociated from the "conscious self."[3]

Similarly, John Powell points out that rejecting and denying uncomfortable feelings produces intense inner conflict, which can produce various physical, psychological, and social disorders, as well as impairing our ability to function effectively and be open to transformational growth possibilities in many aspects of our life:

Non-expression is not good, but the repression of emotions into the subconscious is even more self-destructive because, while we know that we are hurting when we have repressed our true feelings, we do not know why. We have hidden the source of pain in the "dungeon" of the subconscious. Repressed emotions unfortunately do not die. They refuse to be silenced. They pervasively influence the whole personality and behavior of the repressor. For example, a person who represses guilt feelings is forever, though subconsciously, trying to punish himself. He will never allow himself success or enjoyment without qualification. Repressed fears and angers may be "acted out" physically as insomnia, headaches, or ulcers. If such fears and angers had been consciously accepted and reported in detail to another, there would have been no necessity for the sleeplessness, the tension, headaches, or ulcers . . . Buried emotions are like rejected people; they make us pay a high price for having rejected them. Hell hath no fury like that of a scorned emotion. Lost or repressed emotions are not really lost. They continue, in one way or another, to remind us that we really didn't get away with the attempted rejection. Aside from this built-in system of painful sanctions, the essential tragedy of repression is that the whole process of human growth is shut down, at least temporarily. Psychologists call this state "fixation," an arrest of growth and development.[4]

As we have previously discussed, rejecting uncomfortable feelings and aspects of life experience can also produce unhealthy excessive dependence upon escapist substances, sensations, and activities. Some of the potentially addictive, often unwholesome, artificial, and toxic escapist substances and entertainment media that provide intense comforting sensations or illusion-oriented fantasies include various kinds of drugs, alcohol, cigarettes, excessive consumption of artificially sweetened foods and drinks, loud vulgar music, excessive computer-based virtual reality entertainment, video games, television, radio, movies, reading, hobbies, daydreaming, as well as various kinds of escapist, exploitative, interpersonal and sexual relationships. Some of those activities can actually be worthwhile and psychologically healthy when engaged in for their own sakes rather than utilized as a distracting escape from psychological pain. However, interpersonal relationships that are utilized for the purpose of generating distracting escapes from psychological pain, such as alleviating feelings of deficiency, inner emptiness, or lack of self-esteem, may involve functioning like a psychologically predatory or parasitic energy "vampire," so to speak, draining the energies of other individuals in overly demanding, unethically exploitative ways, so that we can thereby feel enhanced in some way. Some kinds of sensationalist entertainment media content that especially provide distracting escapes from psychologically painful inner conflicts and an artificial sense of excitement, inner vitality, or euphoria include pornography, horror shows, violent media entertainment programming, and frenetic, combative, and dangerous sports activities. Other escapist psychological defense mechanisms may involve avoiding confronting uncomfortable or painful feelings and experiential states through pleasurable fantasy, distracting obsessive thoughts, or exaggeratedly intense emotional feelings, such as manic-depressive mood swings, which deaden our conscious awareness and desensitize it to deeper threatening or disturbing feelings. Other mechanisms involve constructing a preconceived system of thought, such as a philosophy, psychology, or theology which offers a doctrine or a controlled, predictable method for giving you comfort and peace, such as "Never give up hope," "The power of positive thinking," the value of chanting sounds or mantras, concentration on a symbol of joy or peace, or some form of self-hypnosis.

Careful study of these "panaceas" will reveal that they are all, in one form or another, a subtle escape from what is, and the encouragement of the pursuit of what presumably ought to be. Psychological health and fulfillment can never come as a consequence of the rejection of the reality of what actually is, and the pursuit of the imaginary, presumptive what ought to be. For this is the essence of the pathological process. Emotional and mental disturbances (and perhaps some related physical bodily illnesses) are invariably the result of some form of withdrawal from reality. The only real and profound sense of peace and happiness that exists comes only when the mind quiets through self-understanding, which results when you confront, honestly, the moment-to-moment actual experiential reality and truth of yourself.

The process of constant distracting escape from self-disclosure prevents the self-discovery of the experiential truth actually existing within yourself, and it is the *self*-discovery of that which is real and truthful about yourself, from moment to moment, which liberates you from the grasp of constant inner conflict and tension, and is, therefore, the basis of having peace of mind and feeling fully and creatively alive. In essence, you have learned to condition yourself to run away at the first sign of anything negative or painful, and now you do it almost automatically, without being aware of it, which has resulted in an extensive dulling of your sensibilities. As soon as your mind catches the first glimpse of an actual or anticipated painful thought or feeling, it "turns its back" on it, so to speak, and pretends that it does not exist, focusing the attention on something else. The more psychological pain you run away from, the more insensitive to reality and emotionally disturbed you become, which often involves feeling inwardly weaker, more fearfully insecure, fragile, unable to endure psychological pain, discomfort, frustration, or disappointment. This is because avoidance of pain necessitates a distortion and escape from reality, not only internally but also outwardly, in order to guarantee that you will not become exposed to anything that could possibly threaten you or give you pain. Thus, for example, if you cannot face the pain of your own angry feelings, then you will avoid those people and circumstances that could possibly make you angry, and you will distort anything that is said to you that could possibly make you angry. Later on in the day, you may permit yourself to recognize what the other person was really saying to you, and you may then become angry because you are no longer in the other person's presence; therefore, you feel it is safer and less painful to now let the truth come to awareness. In some cases, individuals who have a very low threshold of emotional pain and discomfort tolerance become very controlling of self, other individuals, and situations, in order to prevent any kind of emotional pain or discomfort from arising. In extreme cases, this controlling avoidance of emotional discomfort can, consciously or subconsciously, take on a great intensity of chronic anxiety, panic, or frantic desperation.

It is important that you recognize that the more you run from psychological pain, the less pain you will be able to tolerate, and the more you will have to run, as an ever-accelerating escapist momentum because escaping from pain automatically increases feelings of fearful insecurity by reinforcing the conviction that you are too inwardly weak and fragile to be able to endure or tolerate pain without disintegrating, collapsing into nothingness, or falling apart psychologically. This kind of constant escape from uncomfortable experience prevents the self-discovery of the underlying significance of the experiential truth within yourself, and it is the self-discovery of that which is real and truthful about yourself which liberates you from the grasp of constant inner conflict and tension, and is, therefore, the essence of having peace of mind and feeling fully and creatively alive.

Do not expect books or any other person to give you the truth of yourself because the truth you learn by these means is basically just secondhand intellectual speculation on your part, and still keeps you away from direct contact with the actual experiential truth of yourself. This prevents the real holistic integration of the psyche necessary to yield the kind of self-understanding which liberates you from psychologically painful inner conflict, and produces related emotional growth of enhanced strength of character, as well as enhanced self-understanding and creative self-transformational development.

Thus, it is essential that you understand that your commitment to escape from psychological pain must be undone. You must come to see that pain is not intolerable or bad in an absolute sense. You must learn to acknowledge and be open to consciously experiencing your pain in whatever degrees you can handle it, and learn to see what is really causing you to interpret the event as painful. Come to recognize for yourself that just pinning the label of "painful" on an event contributes greatly to your experiencing it as such and trying to escape from it. See if you can learn not to put such a label on a particular experience. This will help you to stay in contact with the experience longer, and thereby come to understand what it is really all about. If you run away from painful feelings and experiential states, you can never come to understand anything about yourself or the thing from which you want to escape. For example, see how often you label an experience as being unbearable even though you have never really tried to bear it. See how it becomes much more bearable when you do not label it as unbearable but just passively observe it to see what it really is.

As previously mentioned, the self-alienation which results from your running away from the actual experiential truth of yourself produces a dulling or numbing insensitivity to yourself, which makes you feel inwardly dead instead of feeling a heightened awareness and sense of genuine vitality. Thus, in order to feel "turned on," such as experiencing a pulsating sense of inner vitality, you tend to turn to artificial euphoria-producing agents and stimulants like drugs, as well as other kinds of excessive, external thrill-seeking activities. In essence, you have not really changed or undone your estrangement from what is experientially real, genuinely alive, truly creative, and constructively transformational in yourself. Instead of being a psychological and social mask with a down-turned frowning mouth, you are now a mask with an up-turned-mouth, locked into a frozen pseudo-smile. Your gaiety is superficial and forced; it is without real substance and happiness, as if you were a "juiced up" mechanical robot. Pursuing artificially induced, mechanically contrived, controlled sources of euphoria keeps you only temporarily distanced from the actual experiential truth of your own inner sense of despair and emptiness, for eventually that truth must catch up with you, perhaps in an unguarded moment, or after a personal trauma, and then the price that you must pay in terms of psychological disability is substantially greater than had you confronted the painful truth originally. Psychological pain buried in the subconscious or subliminal levels of our being must inevitably arise to the surface of our conscious awareness eventually because it abides within us as part of our whole indivisible energy force from which it cannot be severed.

Because you make yourself insensitive to what is really going on within yourself, you come to feel alienated from yourself, and begin to wonder who you actually are, and then the self becomes basically nothing more than a series of artificially contrived roles which you play, like a cosmetic façade or masquerade. You become only a psychological and social mask that you show to yourself and to the world, and you forget that there is a real "face" that lies beneath or behind that mask, consisting of your current actual experiential states, as well as more enduring proclivities that are intrinsic to your being or life energy presence.

Excessive intense stimulation only distracts the mind from what is experientially real in itself, in terms of our actual feelings and natural inclinations, as well as the "still small voice" of intuition and core integrity, arising at a deeper, more substantial level of our being than the bombardment of vacuous "noise" filling the surface level of our conscious awareness. That intense sensory stimulation, along with related kinds of pointlessly irrelevant, mental-emotional chatter, forcefully captures the attention of the mind and keeps it in bondage with a continuous bombardment of inner noise that can distract us from contacting what is experientially real in ourselves and other individuals, as well as diminishing our contact with the reality of adaptive challenges in our social or physical environment, thereby undermining our ability to cope effectively and appropriately with the challenges of the moment. The repetitive reverberation of excessive stimulation and inner chatter taking place in your own mind can also make your responses to other individuals and circumstances overly routine, programmed, inappropriate, and inauthentic, as if you were functioning like a machine or robot. Thus, for example, after you watch TV, stay on the Internet, listen to the radio, or play video games for a long time, you find that your mind is still chattering with the things that have been imprinted upon it even without your consent and approval. You find yourself humming inane commercials or jingles that you may not even like, but they persistently keep intruding into your consciousness. It is necessary to stop constantly feeding stimulation to the mind and give it a chance to quiet; otherwise the level of adaptation to stimulation will become so high that you will become addicted to the need for stimulation, and you will one day likely find yourself in a state of constant frenzy continuously trying to find more and more forms of intense stimulation. The more addicted you become to the need for excessive stimulation as your "next fix," the more you feel as if you were inwardly dying when the stimulation begins to wear off, when you begin to adapt to it, or when you find yourself in moments of monotony and boredom. Addictive dependency on particular sensations and related substances increases the more intolerant we become of experiencing whatever uncomfortable feelings and experiential states inevitably arise when those sensations or substances are absent.

The craving for artificial sensations as a distracting escape from psychological pain is insatiable, leading to inevitable addiction, frustration, and misery because it is a false hunger for a false sense of security, vitality, and euphoria, which can never really be filled. It can never provide a genuine experience of any of the qualities of true goodness that are intrinsic to our real being or life energy presence, no matter how much we intensify those sensations. The more intensely, frequently, and enduringly we try to gratify the craving for addictive sensations, the less satisfying it gradually becomes. The initial surge of excitement and elation is increasingly followed by a subsequent process of deflation or depression of our energies, as the false enlivening sensations begin to reveal their truly deadening effects. Then our own real life energy becomes more and more covered over, pressed down, depressed, or blocked from naturally flowing into our conscious awareness because of the intervening superimposed false coverings of those artificial sensations.

Thus, it is really an exercise in futility to attempt to use artificial sensations and substances as a substitute to replace the genuine experience of inner vitality, joyfulness, inner peace, beauty, and grandeur, which are intrinsic to your real being. That intrinsic grandeur of being can be experienced only by going through it rather than attempting to circumvent or avoid your painful feelings and uncomfortable experiential states because only the process of being open to the actual experiential truth of yourself from moment to moment can liberate your energies from psychological pain. Following the trail of your actual experience and intuitively arising sense of core integrity from moment to moment can ultimately lead you through temporary painful truths that are currently rising to the intrinsic grandeur of your essential permanent being that abides above, beneath, behind, or beyond them at a deeper level of yourself. The inherent wholeness of being that is experienced when you stop all forms of self-divisive, self-conflicting, self-escape is an intrinsic inner relaxed peace, security, joyfulness, vitality, and all other sublime qualities of inner grandeur, beyond the power of thought to provide or adequately describe, as epitomized by the Biblical phrase "the peace that passes all understanding" (Philippians 4:7). Metaphorically speaking, the moment-to-moment process of following the experiential truth of yourself regardless of wherever it may lead is like following the "yellow brick road" in the children's story *The Wizard of Oz*. Reaching the wizard represents coming home to our own real being, our core integrity, sincerity, and authenticity, which is the source of all qualities of true goodness and sublime grandeur, including being the source of all of the temporary experiential truths eventually leading to the awakening of that essential core level of your own permanent being.[5]

The more that your mind and senses are dulled by the bombardment of intense stimulation, the more you become insensitive and unaware of the actual experiential reality of yourself, others, and the world. Ironically, the more alive and euphoric you try to make yourself feel, through the ingestion of artificial stimulants and substances, the more you are deadening yourself to real life energy experience because a genuine feeling of vitality comes only with clear and full contact with and awareness of that which is most deeply real and alive in yourself and in others you encounter. In order to achieve this, a quiet, non-distracted, non-chattering mind is necessary. Drugs and artificial stimulants only produce a pseudo "high" through the varied and intense sensations that they bring to the mind, but the mind is still as petty, superficial, inwardly empty, deadened, numbed, and divorced from its real being or life energy presence as it ever was. Only a mind that comes to be profoundly alert, quiet, and unified through progressively deeper and deeper levels of self-understanding can produce the real "high" that comes with the liberation from internal conflicts and from your identification with the false in yourself. Thus, real psychological growth involves the outgrowth of unreal or inauthentic patterns in yourself, as well as growth in the conscious discovery of ever-deeper experiential realities, including your temporary actual experiential states and permanent being or enduring life energy presence. This liberation from previously rejected and blocked painful feelings brings the release of formerly trapped and blocked psychic energy abiding within those feelings or uncomfortable experiential states, which then can flow into your conscious awareness, making available the experience of deeper underlying feelings of beauty, peace, joy, and love.[6]

To achieve the realization of that which is deepest and most real in yourself, it is necessary that you discover, by yourself, moment-to-moment experiential truths about yourself *without making any judgments* with regard to what you see, and *without trying to change them* in any way. Where there is a non-judgmental observation of what *is*, then your mind achieves a state in which the thinker and the thought, or your conscious attention and the experiential contents of the psyche, merge into one as a natural integrated wholeness of the mind. This state of mind is referred to as the state of *creative understanding* because it enhances your receptivity to unrestricted, nonselective transformational insights and productive capabilities coming from subliminal or not fully conscious levels of the psyche, beyond what is currently consciously known. This is in contrast to the ego's analytical thinking and imaginative fantasy, which are basically restricted to rearranging or reinterpreting what is already known, or wandering away from and distorting reality, rather than providing deeper, truly useful insights into reality.

When you are totally attentive to what is experientially real within yourself, without making judgments about it, analyzing it, interpreting it, or trying to change it in any way, then there is no longer a sense of separation between the thinker and the thought, the analyzer and the analyzed, or the conscious attention and your real feelings; when these two merge into one, then your sense of self or separate self-consciousness is lost. When you become self-forgetful, then the barrier between the known and unknown aspects of a problem, feeling, thought, etc., is removed, and the whole or entire truth of the underlying issue is immediately revealed with vivid clarity in a moment of sudden insight. With total absorption into the problem, you *become* the problem. By no longer being the outside observer of the problem and becoming non-dualistically totally integrated with whatever problem or experiential content is actually abiding or arising within our consciousness, the totality of itself becomes revealed.

As Krishnamurti says, "Awareness or sensitivity is the silent, choiceless, observation of *what is*. In this awareness, the problem unrolls itself, and thus it is fully and completely understood."[7] When you no longer identify with the ego as the dualistically self-conscious interpreter, controller, censor, judger, rejecter, and escaper of your real feelings and experiential states, that is to say, when you let go of the reactive mechanism that keeps your conscious attention divorced or distanced from those actual contents of the psyche, no longer standing apart from those experiential contents as the dualistic knower and reactive, partisan evaluator of them, then the energy tied up in keeping the truth from being discovered becomes liberated, and the mind effortlessly becomes quiet. Then you feel unburdened, peaceful, and happy, and you have enhanced energies available for greater levels of vitality and creative, productive functioning.

These moments of vivid clarity and creative self-understanding eventually enable you to see how many of your egoistic or narcissistic psychological motivations generate particular conditioned or learned habitual patterns of behavior, which may not necessarily reflect your current true needs and natural preferences, but may be rooted in "enslaving," compulsively driven, fear-based, psychological anxieties, addictive dependencies, and other presumptive deficiency-based needs. The clear recognition of your habitual ways of perceiving and functioning has an immediate liberating and transformational effect, for you now come to realize that no habitual way of functioning is really necessary, or absolutely independent, i.e., has a self-existing, unchangeable reality of its own, but that it is merely a reaction to a previous conditioning or a presumptive interpretation of particular kinds of experiences, situations, or individuals, which you are then free to relinquish if it is not really useful, beneficial, or preferable to you in the present moment. In this way, repressed or intensely demanding inappropriate desires and uncomfortable feelings float to the surface of consciousness, where in the strong clear light of a silent and non-judgmental mind, they are recognized for what they are, whereupon they spontaneously dissolve, never to come back. When preconceived habitual reactions fall away by being deeply understood, then we are free to function in a much more realistic, flexible, fulfilling, psychologically healthy manner. This falling away of predetermined habitual ways of functioning occurs if they are based mostly on fearful anxiety or distorted, rigid modes of perception rather than being an expression of your natural preferences and inclinations, which cannot and should not be eliminated, because they are intrinsic to your indivisible wholeness of being. As the Bible suggests, "You shall know the truth (or see the truth for yourself), and the truth will set you free" (John 8:32 KJV).

In truth, there is no such thing as a personal entity self, or a self-defined permanent identity, which we experience as "me." The ego as the "me" or the personal entity self functions as a sense of identity that defines itself in terms of particular conceptual traits, and divisively reacts for approved traits and against disapproved traits, as well as holding a dualistic sense of separate self-awareness and conceptual self-knowledge apart from other individuals, and also apart from the actual experiential contents of your own psyche. The entity self has just an apparent, presumptive, or imaginary semblance of reality, and consists basically of a collection of memories, interpreted experiences, desires, and motives, all held together with the tangled, fragile, breakable thread of some apparently consistent self-concept. All that we really are is what we are being from moment to moment, as what we are currently experiencing and expressing, indivisibly united to our indefinable, enduring, conscious energy force or our being, which includes our enduring natural inclinations and distinctive innate qualities, constituting our natural real experiential particularity, but there is no enduring self-defined entity or permanent identity that we can ever really be, because our real being already exists prior to, during, subsequent to, and beyond, all changing, presumptive, self-definitions, as our changeless, objectless, indefinable pure conscious awareness. Just be aware of what you are experientially being from moment to moment, and that will bring true self-understanding and liberating self-transformation. But identifying and siding with the ego's presumptive self-interpretations will produce only more dead self-concepts, dualistically divorcing your conscious attention from your real being as a spontaneously free flowing, indefinable, unpredictable, life energy presence.

Most if not all of the reactive ego's states of elation are due basically to the conscious or unconscious perception that some kind of accretion, enhancement, or aggrandizement of self has taken place, whereas the uncomfortable states or emotional feelings, such as depression, are basically the result of the perception that the personal entity self (the "me" feeling) has been diminished or lessened in some way. This is usually accompanied by the unconscious perception or fear that this lessening of self will ultimately lead to total non-being of self, or the inner void of utter psychological nothingness. Because we are so terrified of the seeming inner void and its symbolic manifestations in feelings of deficiency or lack, such as loneliness, emptiness, boredom, etc., we construct some kind of presumptive personal entity self in the form of a self-concept which we devote our lives trying to protect, defend, enhance, aggrandize, and in some way affirm and make permanent. Every egocentric, agitated, fear-based desire and motive has this as the basic aim: the inflation or enhancement of self, as the attempt to move further and further away from the nullity point. All of our strivings are directed toward making the "me" more. Observe your own strivings and see for yourself if this is not true.

As you sit in inner silence of non-reactive, non-interpretive, pure conscious awareness, not committing to or siding for or against any particular kind of experience, all kinds of thoughts, feelings, impulses, etc., may spontaneously arise in awareness. Let each of these experiences just rise and fall without labeling it in any way, without interacting with it in any way, or giving it any particular recognition, preconceived interpretation, or judgmental reaction. Do not judge what comes, or try to change it or interfere with it in any way. Just let be whatever experience arises in you. Let it rise and fall, and do not react to it in any way, for if you did react to it, you would then be reviving the dualistic state of thinker and thought, and the state of creative understanding would be lost, as spontaneous, uncontrolled, unrestricted insight coming from direct, non-preconceived, experiential contact with those arising contents of your awareness. Continue to sit in non-reactive, relaxed inner peace, without any desire, motive, or effort to become, achieve, or hold onto anything.

Sitting silently in peace, you are in being instead of the state of becoming, or striving to become something presumed to be more enhanced or better than what you are already being. Relaxed peace is what we are already intrinsically being prior to all controlled effort, rather than being the product or result of some kind of controlled effort. As long as there is some kind of preconceived image of ourselves or goal that we want to fulfill, then we are in the state of becoming or striving to become enhanced in some way, which must involve a state of conflict and tension with what we are actually being or experiencing in a given moment, which is rejected in the attempt to become or achieve something presumed to be "better." All such attempts at becoming are a rejection of what actually *is* arising in our conscious awareness, as a striving toward becoming what we presume *ought* to be our sense of identity and experience. There must always be tension and struggle as well as a distortion of reality in rejecting what is and striving toward what presumptively ought to be.

Psychological health and peace of mind essentially involve being sensitively aware of and totally present to what is without trying to change what is or avoid it in any way, whereas psychopathology is basically the result of the rejection of what actually is with an attempt to become or achieve what we presume ought to be. As you observe your own mind, are you not in a constant state of desiring and striving to become or achieve something? This constant state of turmoil, striving, and pursuing you call "living." Just sit in peace and silence, and see if you don't learn what living really is. Perhaps you are concerned about how you will solve a problem if you don't think about it. The solution to a problem lies in the problem itself, never outside or away from it. If you are lonely and depressed, you want to escape from those feelings, and you feel that you have solved this problem by running toward various kinds of activities, relationships, pills, or other addictive substances. But this is not a resolution of the problem; it is only an escape, which temporarily distracts you from the problem, but does not really eliminate it. The depression and the loneliness are still there, only you have temporarily successfully distracted yourself and turned your back, so to speak, to the reality of what is, but you have not resolved it, or eliminated it. In a quiet moment, it will catch up to you, and you will have to run away again from that constantly menacing specter of what you have rejected in yourself and presumed to be intolerably painful. That process of continuous distracting escape from painful, feared, despised, denied, or rejected feelings and experiential states makes you in effect an exile or *fugitive from your own being* or experiential energy force, producing self-division, self-conflict, tension, frustration, and chronic anxiety, like fleeing or hiding from your own shadow, or amputating part of your own body.

Thus, the solution to the psychological pain or problem lies *within* the problem. For example, it is important that you really and deeply understand why you are actually feeling depressed and lonely, instead of trying to distract yourself away from that immediate experience by superimposing some presumptively better, contrived, experiential state, or more favorable conceptual self-definition, such as telling yourself that you are not really feeling depressed and lonely, but you are a naturally joyful, popular person. Only this creative understanding, or uncontrolled, unrestricted, unmediated, experiential "insight," coming from direct contact with whatever problem or uncomfortable feeling you are actually experiencing, can liberate you from the problem, by enabling you to directly experience or immediately observe the underlying dynamics or causal source of the problem from the inside, rather than reactively interpreting it from the outside, which provides only a presumptive, often distorted understanding of the problem. Do not run away from the problem, and do not try to speak for the problem or interpret it from the outside, but just let yourself get inside of the problem and become one with it, experientially. Let yourself feel the loneliness and depression, but pin no such label on it; just stay with the energy or actual experience of the feeling, without superimposing any preconceived interpretation upon it from the outside. Then you will find that if you just stay with it without judging it, superimposing any kind of preconceived interpretation upon it, or trying to alter or remove it in any way (be satisfied for the moment just to be or feel lonely and depressed), then you will find that in a momentary flash of insight, the essential understanding of why you are lonely and depressed will reveal itself to you with vivid clarity, as well as a deep understanding of the nature of what all loneliness and depression really is. It will unravel itself and tell its own story, and your deep understanding will free you from continuing to be burdened by the problem or painful feeling because the energy in it drains out or is released and liberated when it is deeply understood through non-dualistic communion with the feeling, including the experiential energy-tone that underlies the feeling.

It is not difficult to solve a problem once you can see things from the calm, nonreactive, unbiased point of view of an onlooker who is fully aware of the real motives underlying every action or experience of psychological pain, pathology, and inner conflict. No concealing or distorting of facts is possible when your mind and heart are totally open, without any predetermined interpretive biases or judgmental expectations. Your most secret and hidden thoughts are brought to light, and your actions stand before you in all their nakedness or immediacy. Then you know what is right and what is wrong, the reasons for having done this or the other thing, and what has brought about someone else's reactions toward you. You will then feel marvelously cleansed and lighter of load. You must clear your mental storeroom lest it become overcrowded with fears, unresolved problems, worrisome thoughts, suppressed emotions, and thwarted hopes. Usually you keep all this bottled up until finally something explodes in the form of nervous symptoms, a serious ailment, or a violent reaction of one kind or another. The mind is like a sponge, or like an overflowing pot of boiling water; when agitated and overly confined, it can hold only so many mental impressions and can contain only so much blocked energy and related tension before it must make its own outlet as a way of trying to discharge the pent-up tension of the blocked energy, which can sometimes be very disruptive and damaging to you, as well as to others to whom you relate.

Just observe what is arising within you as a fact. If you observe something that you do not like to see in yourself, such as selfishness or angry feelings, do not react judgmentally with, "I ought not to be angry or selfish," and do not deny the actual occurrence of that tendency, but be open to observing, "I see that in that particular situation, I really was angry or selfish." You do not need to do anything about getting rid of these negative feelings and inclinations, for all such attempts are escapes from what is. Just stay with it, as a keenly attentive, unbiased, nonreactive observer, and then the deep understanding you achieve by observing or communing with the immediacy of your actual negative feelings or inclinations will be a sufficient basis to bring about a transformational change for the better. For example, if you deeply and truly see that you have really hurt another person because you have been selfish and insensitive to her or him, then compassion and sensitivity have already begun to set in. You don't become less violent, for example, by trying to behave nonviolently, but only by understanding why you feel an inclination to be violent. When you deeply understand the nature of your fears and tensions, then your violence will dissolve by itself.

Remember, just observe what is actually arising as experience in yourself, from moment to moment, but make no judgments about yourself, or else the spontaneous process that brings creative understanding will be halted. Also be careful not to try to prove something about yourself or interpret yourself with explanations of why you are thinking or feeling as you do, instead of letting your thoughts and feelings speak for themselves. This is just the mind's attempt to escape from the real truth, and prevents the truth from unfolding its own story. *Remember, do not guide or direct your thoughts in any direction or in any way. Just let it be. Let come whatever will.*

You must also be careful not to fall into the trap of accepting your problem in order to get rid of it, for that is also a form of trying to escape from your problem. Neither rejection nor acceptance of a problem is an appropriate solution. You should make no effort at all to change or get rid of your problem, but only be interested in being one with the problem. If your goal is to understand the problem in order to get rid of it, then you are back in the same trap. The effort to escape from the problem only puts you in the conflict of trying to make what is, what ought to be, and this conflict only functions as a distraction which prevents the full understanding of the problem. That nonjudgmental experiential understanding naturally produces and is actually being its own appropriate action or transformational energy, and is sufficient to bring a transcendence of the problem.

Another major error that many people make is to try to exert willpower over themselves in their attempt to coercively bring an end and resolution to their inner conflict. It is the attempt to reject the actual "what is" for a presumptive "what ought to be." It is pitting one part of the self against another part. An internal conflict can never be resolved through a means that involves more conflict with particular experiential aspects of yourself. The arousal of further conflict only intensifies the conflict and tension that you are already experiencing. Therefore, willpower can never be effective in resolving an inner conflict because it is, by its own nature, conflicting. At best, willpower can only temporarily suppress a problem but never resolve one. Willpower only submerges or suppresses one side of the conflict, but because it is still there within you, it is bound to ultimately bounce back and rear its ugly head again, sooner or later. Those who have tried to handle a problem such as dieting with willpower will, likely, understand this well. People usually eat too much, or consume unhealthy foods, in an attempt to reduce a high level of tension within themselves. When they exert willpower over themselves, they put themselves in further self-conflict, which only intensifies their already high level of tension, and then they end up wanting to eat or consume excessive amounts of other substances more than ever before. Willpower only sets up an internal war within yourself, and whichever side loses, you lose too for, indeed you are both sides of the issue. You really are *both* of the conflicting desires. Therefore, instead of dividing yourself in internal self-conflict, let yourself be only what you actually are experiencing, and not the ideal image of what you want to be or become, and then you will be in a state of integration and unity rather than self-contradiction. With a united mind, rather than a conflicting effort, there will be nothing competing or distracting to divide your attention and move it away from following the flow of your actual inner experiential dynamics to the essential underlying source of the problem. In that state, you will be able to clearly follow, for example, your intense drive to devour sweets, and ultimately come to understand and transcend this problem rather than just suppress it.

Try to remember that no problem can be finally overpowered or conquered; it can only be understood, which naturally leads to its elimination, or resolution, but it cannot be permanently conquered through willpower and struggle. They are two different processes, and the conquering process leads to further confusion and further fear, by merely suppressing and covering over the problem, rather than truly resolving and thereby eliminating it. To resist, to dominate, to do battle with a problem, or to build a defense against it is only to create further inner conflict, whereas the only way to understand the illusory nature of psychological anxiety or unrealistic fear is go into it fully, step by step. Explore the whole content and source of it, and then fear or any other kind of inner conflict will never return again in any form, once it has been fully understood and thereby resolved.

Now, what are we really afraid of or rejecting in ourselves as a source of inner conflict? Are we afraid of an actual fact or of an idea about the fact? Are we afraid of the thing as it actually is, or are we afraid of what we *think or presume* that it is? Take death, for example. Are we afraid of the physical fact of death or of the idea of death? The fact is one thing, and the idea about the fact is another. Am I afraid of the word "death" or of the fact itself? Because I am afraid of the word and of the idea, I never explore and try to understand the fact; I never look at the actual fact, so I am never in direct relation or communion with the fact. *It is only when I am in complete communion with the fact that there is no fear.* If I am not in communion with the fact, then there is fear, and there is no communion with the fact as long as I have an idea, an opinion, a theory, *about* the fact. If I am face to face with the fact, there is no need to interpret the fact or speak for it; the fact is there, to speak for itself, and thereby be understood on its own terms, and then I can deal with it because I am no longer resisting the actual fact by superimposing a frightening interpretation upon it. If I am afraid of the word, then I must understand the word, go into the whole process of what the word implies.

For example, as mentioned earlier, we are afraid of loneliness, afraid of the ache and the pain of loneliness. Surely, that fear exists because we have never really looked at loneliness face to face, never been in complete communion or direct contact with it. The moment we are completely open to the actual experiential fact of loneliness, we can understand what it is; but if we have an idea, an opinion about it, based on previous knowledge, it is this idea or opinion, this previous presumptive knowledge *about* the fact that creates fear. *Fear is obviously the outcome of naming, labeling, terming, of projecting a symbol or a preconceived interpretation to represent the fact; i.e., the experience of fear is not independent of the frightening word "fear."* There is freedom from psychological fear or anxiety only when there is self-knowledge or insightful self-understanding arising from direct contact with the actual experiential truth of ourselves. Self-knowledge, or direct insight into the actual experiential truth of ourselves, is the beginning of the true wisdom and liberating understanding that resolve psychological pain, which is the ending of psychological fear. This results in the undoing of fearful escape from the experiential truth of ourselves, because accepting direct and full conscious contact with the actual experience removes the frightening presumptive connotation of it being intolerable or unbearable.

Some people insist that they cannot permit themselves to be with the experiential truth of themselves because the truth is too ugly. We authors would like to point out that the truth could neither ever be ugly nor can it validly be called beautiful either, for essentially the truth is just a fact—it is what it is. If there is anything ugly at all, it is in your fearful attempt to reject and escape from the truth of yourself. As Gibran puts it, "Call nothing ugly, my friend, save the fear of a soul in the presence of its own memories."[8]

You deem the actual experiential truth in you to be ugly only because you live in the state of comparison in which you feel that you are not measuring up to the ideals and standards set by you or imposed upon you by others. In being honest and real with yourself, there is great courage, inner beauty, and true nobility of character. However, to defend yourself against the awareness of truth, in that there *is* something ugly because it involves a distortion of reality, which is a kind of destruction of life within yourself. To pursue the unreal fantasies and ideal images and reject what is honest and real in yourself is ugly because you presume to set yourself up higher than nature and reality; you have become a self-styled independent God, in your own right, by arbitrarily trying to replace what actually is with what you deem a better "ought to be" or presumptively interpreting what actually is arising in yourself as a worse "ought not to be." That process of removing yourself from the flow of real life experience by becoming lost in a reactive contrary flow or recoiled counter-flow of judgmental and interpretive thought taking place in your own mind is metaphorically depicted in the Bible (Genesis) as losing access to the Tree of Everlasting Life and the

Garden of Eden in which it abides, by eating of the forbidden fruit of the "Tree of Knowledge of Good and Evil." You have attempted to create or imagine yourself in the unreal, nonliving image of what you want to be instead of what you actually are. Only by being with the actual experiential truth of yourself is there ever any chance to grow beyond what you now are, and to grow into more psychologically mature, constructive, and fulfilling levels of your being, which are most deeply imbedded within you, but you cannot pursue it like another idealized image. Distorted, unconstructive ways of perceiving and functioning can be outgrown or transcended only by being deeply understood through communion with their underlying dynamics, whereas resisting and rejecting those patterns energizes and preserves them in duality from your reactive conscious awareness.

Only by being in that state of truth and clarity which Krishnamurti calls "choiceless awareness"[9] does growth and creativity occur. To be in choiceless awareness is to see the truth of what is, without uncertainty, ambiguity, or alternative. There is no room for "maybe," "perhaps," "it could be," "I think," "I believe." There is no room for opinion, theory, assumption, or conjecture if you are to ever understand the true nature of what is actually arising within you, from moment to moment. The truth or what is actual is really the easiest thing in the world to see, and, as a child, you were probably very much better at it than you are now as an adult. The truth is very precise, exact, simple, and the most obviously clear reality, if you do not obscure it by holding to a preconceived interpretation of it. The problem is that you are taught and also teach yourself to avoid seeing the truth. As you grow up, you learn to use psychological defenses and escapes, which make insensitivity and avoidance your automatic response to what is. In addition, your mind becomes conditioned with all kinds of biases, opinions, beliefs, and idealized images and standards, so that the actual experiential truth of what is becomes hidden behind a superimposed covering, maze, and barrier of psychological and conceptual irrelevancies, which makes the truth very distant and extremely difficult to apprehend. So that now, seeing a fact as a fact has become the most difficult thing in the world for you to do. Thus, to be open and sensitively aware of the temporary experiential truth and permanent reality of your being, you must first learn to identify your own particular defenses, escapes, biased conditionings, and false images. This may not be easy to accomplish, but its rewards are unlimited.

My best wishes for a glorious uncharted journey. May you find the peace you deserve, and return home where you belong.

Recommended Meditative Exercise for Enhancing Psychological Self-Understanding and Self-Healing

Before I [Max Hammer] discuss what meditation is, I will first try to eliminate some false notions with regard to some popular beliefs about meditation. There is nothing to fear in meditation. It is not a trance state in which you lose consciousness. On the contrary, in meditation, you will find that conscious awareness is more heightened than ever before. Meditation is not just daydreaming, but, instead, is basically a process of experiential self-observation. In daydreaming, the egoistic self determines and controls the specific content of thought, whereas in meditation, the egoistic self or controlling thinker is not active, and thoughts are permitted to come and go as they will. True meditation does not involve the following of any prescribed system, preconceived method, or effortful striving toward some kind of predetermined goal or outcome. It does not involve the repetition of words or sounds and does not involve any kind of chanting. In no way does it involve anything imitative or any kind of willpower. It is a totally spontaneous process, so that you are receptively open to new, unforeseen, creative insights of any kind that may arise. True meditation does not involve concentration, such as fixing the mind on one thought to the exclusion of all other thoughts. Concentration involves a rejection of whatever experience is actually spontaneously arising in yourself for some kind of preconceived goal, experience, or knowledge that you are seeking, as a presumed "what ought to be," which only produces effort, strain, and inner conflict, whereas true meditation involves a spontaneously free-flowing, non-directed, and non-controlled conscious awareness. Meditation is in no way any form of self-hypnosis or self-analysis. It is entirely without effort or purpose.

Essentially, meditation (the process of self-observation) involves facing whatever is spontaneously arising in you in the mirror of your own non-reactive, nonjudgmental, nondirective, unbiased mind or unfocused, non-predetermined, pure conscious awareness. Meditation involves being aware of every thought, every feeling, every motive, and every desire, no matter how trivial or transient. Never judge it as right or wrong, good or bad; just watch it as a fact and move with it. In that watching, you will begin to understand the whole movement of thought and feeling and out of this awareness comes a quiet and peaceful mind. Meditation is nonreactive pure consciousness aware of *its own* activities in creating thought, but not the separated thinker or observer being aware of his or her thought. Meditation is basically the unmediated, direct experiential understanding of the ego or personal entity self, and thereby the transcendence of that limited and false conceptual self, which brings your awakening to that most deep and real, limitless, non-conceptual, true self.

In order to obtain the best results in meditation, put aside at least one half hour a day, preferably just after awakening in the morning, but if this time is not suitable, then do it just before falling asleep at night. At these times, you tend to be in a rather drowsy or groggy state, which may be called the "twilight zone," in which the egoistic sense of self is least intact and influential, making possible the creative or uncontrolled intrusion into consciousness of those truths within you which have previously been rejected and repressed. Never sit in meditation when you feel pushed to go somewhere or do something; your time will only be wasted. Try to find a suitable time to meditate when you have no immediate appointments or tasks waiting for you. Make sure that you are in a room that is without noise or distractions of any kind, or at least kept to a minimum. The temperature in the room should be constant and comfortable. Sit up in bed cross-legged or on a chair with feet flat on the floor. Make sure that your back is erect. Lying down should be avoided for that will bring excessive rambling of thought or sleep. Then softly close your eyes (or keep them open if that makes you feel more comfortable and alert), and relax all bodily and mental tensions. Just let go and permit whatever wants to come into your awareness to come. Be in that state of mind in which there is no deliberate thinking. You need only permit the contents of consciousness to rise and fall spontaneously without making any effort of any kind to interfere with it, control it, or focus it in any way. There should be no labeling, condemning, justifying, resisting, controlling, directing, or initiating the contents of consciousness. These only interfere with the free flow of consciousness and function as a distraction, preventing you from being able to closely follow the movement of your spontaneously free-flowing thought. Be totally without desire, totally without motive, making no effort of any kind in any direction to do, become, or know anything. In essence, be in that state of mind in which there is no reaching out, pursuing, or volitional intention of any kind. Let go, and just be. Sit in effortless relaxed peace, the inherent, timeless "peace that passes understanding," prior to the arising of conceptual interpretation and volitional effort. The acquisitive, accumulating, striving drive of becoming a something or a somebody, of making the "me" more, must be put aside during this rest period. One day it will put itself aside when its true meaning is deeply understood.

You may find it very difficult at first to do so. Usually when you first begin to meditate in this way, the thoughts race about like monkeys swinging from tree to tree. Do not be discouraged. If you continue to persist, you will find that the mind will eventually begin to quiet, effortlessly, and you will be able to follow where it is going and why much more readily. The mind has been so overexposed to excitement and stimulation that when there is no input of stimulation, then the mind tends to race about in an attempt to provide itself with stimulation at the same level to which it has become accustomed; otherwise, you tend to react to the reduction in internal stimulation as a kind of psychological dying or loss of exciting energy experience. But if you continue to persist in this exercise, and you give the mind full permission to present to your awareness whatever it will, then eventually your mind will become drained of all that it has repressed and contained, and will become very peaceful and quiet. In one of those very peaceful and quiet moments, you may come to experientially know that glorious true self that is deepest within you. It will come uninvited, spontaneously, effortlessly. It will come only when you are content just to sit in the peacefulness of a quiet mind. If you pursue it, it can never come. If it comes, then you will directly know the meaning of the scriptural declaration that "The Kingdom of Heaven is within you" (Luke 17:21).

At the end of each meditation, perhaps it may be helpful to write a short journal related to your experiences or the essential things that you have learned about yourself or others. If you have forgotten most of what occurred during the meditation, do not be concerned. Write about whatever you do remember, and if you remember nothing at all, that is also all right. What is most important is not to purposefully keep a thought or experience in your mind in order to recall it later, for that will put a halt to the spontaneously unfolding process of creative insight and the mind's natural healing process. *Do not hold on to anything. Just let whatever comes to your awareness rise and fall as it will.* If something comes which is extremely significant or moving, then likely you will have some impression of it afterward, but if you do not, then do not be concerned. You need not write a journal entry for every sitting, but there should be at least one a week.

Do not force yourself to sit if you find yourself becoming overwhelmingly uncomfortable, but before you abandon the sitting for the evening, see if you cannot ask yourself what it is that is really making you feel so uncomfortable. Is it some kind of physical discomfort or fear of facing an uncomfortable feeling or problem?

Psychological Workbook

*(**Editorial Note by Barry Hammer:** Readers who are not interested in the contemplative exercises and questionnaires in this Psychological Workbook may wish to skip down to the Self-Disclosure Exercise on page 109, the Chapter Summary on page 118, or the beginning of Chapter 3 on page 120. Another possibility is for readers to quickly skim through the exercises in this Psychological Workbook to see if any of them may be of particular interest)*

One of the most useful instruments for long-term self-development is a workbook, diary, or journal. We use the term "psychological workbook" because many people tend to associate the word "diary" with recording often trivial and burdensome accounts of daily activities.

The type of workbook suggested here is for recording your inner life and its developments. Outer events may be recorded inasmuch as they are related to inner events (feelings, thoughts, observations), but the focus should be on the unfolding awareness of yourself and the world, and on the new meanings, values, and interrelationships that you are able to discover.

There are many purposes for keeping a journal or workbook of this sort. One of the most important is to help ourselves formulate our thoughts, feelings, and observations with greater clarity. And in the act of putting something on paper, we tend to commit ourselves to a greater extent or invest more of our energies and concentration. We are taking a step beyond simply thinking or saying something when we make the effort to write it down. Also, in the process of clarification of our thoughts and inner experiences through writing, we are obliged to choose between alternative points of view, so we are less likely to deceive ourselves by holding contradictory views without being aware of it. If there is a problem to be solved, or an area of real confusion, we are better able to gain clear, penetrating insight by organizing and developing our ideas and self-observations through the process of writing.

Thus, the act of writing is a great stimulus to the creative process. When we are trying to grapple with a problem or issue, it is a common experience that in writing down a few thoughts on the question, other related thoughts begin to stream in, through a process of association, and these ideas in turn open up new avenues of thought, new possibilities we may not have considered before. If we can learn to let our minds range freely in this manner, we will be truly amazed to discover the depth of the insights already within us, just waiting to be liberated.

Keeping a workbook or journal as a technique of self-development also functions in other ways. It gives us an opportunity to express in a harmless way any powerful and disruptive emotions we may have bottled up inside us. If we can learn to "let off steam" through writing, we will have a useful means of discharging tensions, and of becoming aware of what underlies them. Writing is also a useful exercise for developing the faculties of concentration and attention. It may help a person who is somewhat shy and reluctant to express herself in a face-to-face setting to explore certain aspects of herself more freely.

For all these reasons, keeping a workbook can be an important aspect of the psychological self-exploration process in that it is a method that you can employ on your own, as you take the process of your growth and self-realization increasingly into your own hands.

In addition to written materials, you can also make drawings and other visual aids a part of the workbook or journal. These may be of various kinds. In one category are images, which may come to you in the form of dreams, fantasies, or visualizations. In another category are diagrams, more abstract symbols or visual aids, which we can use to express our ideas in graphic form. This is useful in developing clear concepts and in communicating these concepts to others. A final category is what we call "spontaneous drawing." This should be done when we are in a relaxed state of mind, and when our attention is fixed on something else—as when we are doodling. Such drawings reflect the activity of the unconscious mind and may be of value in self-understanding. Thus, drawing as well as writing can be part of a complete workbook.

Here are possible headings for inclusion in your workbook. It is suggested that you choose among them the ones that, according to your own needs and experiences, are likely to be of greater value. But, of course, your choice can be revised at any time. It is important to date each entry to provide yourself with a developmental perspective.

Dialogue with ideas: Include a heading for any area of vital intellectual or existential/experiential interest in which you are trying to advance your own understanding—e.g., education, religion, sex, love, beauty, peace, freedom, etc.

Dialogue with people: Insight into or questions about your relationships and ability to communicate with others.

Dialogue with events: Your response to meaningful events in your life; note occasions on which you are aware of "synchronicity" or significant connections or relationships between various events and experiences of your life.

Inner dialogues: Miscellaneous thoughts, musings, fantasies, intuitions, questions, or speculations which do not fit under other headings.

Dreams: Description, context, associations, and amplifications of your night dreams (which are most easily recorded immediately upon waking).

Meditation: Notes on meditation with results obtained. Note any insights or intuitions that come through.

Creativity: Attempts and progress you are making to live more creatively and spontaneously.

Labeling: Awareness of your tendency to label people and things, as well as projecting your past conditioning and biases, instead of seeing the person or thing as they really are.

Self: Notes on your sense of personal identity or self-concept, responses to self-disclosure items, or answers to questions related to the inquiry, "Who am I?" Also include experiences with other meditative techniques related to the question of the essential nature of your being and of reality.

Techniques for transformational/developmental/psychological growth: Your experience with the various approaches that do not fall under other headings. Please note as fully as possible the circumstances under which the various approaches were helpful or not and your opinion of the reasons underlying success or failure with a particular method.

Peak experiences: Any high or deep experiences of peace, joy, love, expansion, awakening, etc., and their circumstances and effects.

Personal shortcomings: Personal weaknesses of which you are aware, and on which you would like to work. Particular emphasis can be placed on the techniques you can use to overcome them. Record also any negative reactions you have to other people, as they may clarify your own unrecognized and projected problems.

Contemplative Exercise to Enhance Self-Understanding as Experiential Insight into the Truth of Yourself and the Reality of Life

For those who are finding it extremely difficult to engage in the process of self-exploration discussed in earlier sections of this book, it is recommended that you lead into that process of self-exploration or self-inquiry by first spending some time in contemplation of other topics, which will help the mind become more disciplined and one-pointed. Choose one of the topics listed below, and explore the topic to the greatest depths that you can. You can engage in this kind of contemplative exercise with eyes open or with eyes closed, as in some kind of meditation practice, depending on which approach makes you feel most comfortable, relaxed, and open to new creative insights, which may come from deeper, subliminal, subconscious, or not fully conscious levels of your psyche, beyond your conventional everyday level of conscious awareness. Try not to think deductively or analytically about the topic; instead pose the topic to yourself, and see what thoughts come spontaneously, of their own accord, relative to this topic, and continue to explore the topic as deeply and as thoroughly as you can, until you find that nothing new is arising with regard to this topic. While in contemplation, do not make an effort to remember what you are learning about the topic, but after you are done, it might be helpful to write a short report or journal on whatever you do happen to remember or whatever lingers with you that was new for you. Each time that you sit down to contemplate a topic, you may choose the same topic to contemplate, or you may start with a different topic, but do not switch topics until you feel that you have exhausted your exploration of the one that you started with. If your mind wanders from the topic, keep bringing it back to the topic, even if it is not where you left off on the topic before your mind started to wander. Just bring your mind back to the topic, and see what thoughts then come about the topic. Don't inject what you may have previously read or learned about the topic. Instead, let it evoke only what you now discover about the topic, from your own self-observation and experience.

Recommended Topics for Contemplation

1. What is love?
2. What is harmony?
3. What is truth?
4. What is joy or happiness?
5. What is it to be perfect and/or imperfect?
6. What is it to be whole?
7. What is beauty?

8. What is freedom or liberation?
9. What is life?
10. What is death, and what dies?
11. What is reality?
12. What is it to be psychologically healthy or unhealthy?
13. What is desire, and how and why does it arise?
14. How and why does thought arise?
15. Who is it that observes your thinking?
16. Of what is the I-feeling and its sense of identity composed?
17. What is peace?
18. What is trust?
19. What is a feeling of worth, in essence? How does it come about? Does it necessarily depend on how others view us? Why or why not?
20. What is it that I want most of all, and why is that so important to me? What will I want next when I get it, and why is that particularly important to me?
21. What is fulfillment?
22. What is creativity?

If explored deeply, these topics when contemplated regularly have the capacity not only to bring you to a greater understanding of your own personal nature and experience, but should also enhance your experiential understanding and sense of existential connection to life as a whole as well as the world in which you live, both psychologically and physically.

Those who are interested in expanding their creative potential may find it helpful to contemplate the metaphorical or symbolic nature of various aspects of life. This will help them to become more sensitive to the intrinsically creative, precious, beautiful nature of all of life, and will also provide them with a renewed feeling of awe and wonder concerning the whole of life, as well as deepening their understanding of the whole of life, and how they fit into that whole. For example, one student contemplated a mountain somewhat as follows: "The mountain gives me a feeling of tremendous power. The snow on top reminds me of my father's gray hair and his power, also thought of power from the point of view of its pointed shape as a penis. It could also be a breast and symbolize mother. Mountains also give a feeling of protection and security. It also seems like a very egotistical person who is trying to stand taller than everyone else. It reminds me of ambition because people are always trying to climb to the top. Maybe a mountain represents man's supremacy over nature, man's ability to overcome all the obstacles of nature, and, therefore, one is more powerful than nature. Climbing to the heights also made me think of a spiritual journey to God. At the top of the mountain, I am as high, elevated, and as close to God, as I will ever get. I think that at the top of the mountain, I would be very tempted to jump off and merge with the infinite sky. I feel like I have become the mountain and I feel very powerful, very grand. I feel that it would be easy to feel myself to be one with all of nature and life."

Possible topics to contemplate, as a means of developing greater self-understanding and creative self-transformation: (Feel free to add some of your own.)

1. The sun and its emanated rays of sunlight, sunrise, noon, sunset
2. Springtime
3. Summer
4. Fall-autumn
5. Winter
6. Sky
7. Clouds
8. Ocean, river, lake, stream
9. Darkness of night
10. Snow
11. Rain
12. Wind
13. Tree
14. Flower

15. Grass
16. Earth
17. Seed
18. Birth
19. Death
20. Wind
21. Fire
22. Air
23. Water, ice
24. Breath
25. The moon
26. Stars
27. The ground that supports us; the "roots" of our being
28. The sexual act
29. House/Home
30. Car
31. The physical body
32. Marriage
33. Children
34. God
35. Spirit
36. Mind
37. Power
38. Illness
39. Work
40. Play
41. Color
42. Clothes
43. What is it to be good or bad?
44. TV
45. Father
46. Mother
47. Brotherhood/sisterhood
48. What essentially produces emotional pain and fear?
49. Art
50. Science
51. A garden

52. Pollution
53. Books
54. The physical senses
55. Bird
56. The solar system
57. Absoluteness
58. Infinity
59. Eternality
60. What is to be human?
61. Inner and Outer Beauty
62. Inner and Outer Sweetness
63. Love
64. Freedom and Responsibility
65. Life as a meaningful journey, story, process, or energy

Relaxation Exercise

Learn to take relaxation breaks like you take other kinds of breaks, such as for coffee, cigarettes, beer, candy, etc. These indulgences cannot bring real relaxation, but only an artificial illusion of relaxation. Unless the mind is fully relaxed by totally losing self-awareness, tension in the mind and related tension in the body prevents significant new transformational insights from coming. Take periodic relaxation breaks during the day by closing your eyes, taking a deep breath, and exhaling it as deeply as you can. With that deep exhalation, feel all of the tensions in your mind and body leaving your being, along with the exhaled breath. Stay in a kind of psychologically exhaled, "limp," non-resistive, relaxed mood until all thought and feeling has been exhaled from your mind, so that now your mind is very quiet and peaceful. Now concentrate fully on your breathing, feeling no purpose in mind with regard to it. Focus your complete attention on your breathing as it takes place naturally and spontaneously. Just watch your breathing, but do not try to influence it in any way, like trying to make it go faster, slower, or more smoothly. Just watch it, and place your entire attention upon your spontaneous breathing for about ten to fifteen minutes. Watch your breathing so intensely that there is no place for any thought, feeling, or awareness to enter your mind. The key is to watch your breathing with such total attention that you become totally absorbed into that breathing and lose all sense of self-awareness. The complete loss of that sense of self-awareness is the key to true mental and physical relaxation. Just let go fully, and with a "let be" attitude of complete absence of desire, just go along with the spontaneous movement of the breathing, as though you were a leaf limply floating atop a lake wave to nowhere in particular. Just go along with the natural and spontaneous rhythm of your own breathing, and let be all spontaneously arising thoughts and feelings as the non-reactive, nonjudgmental observer of them. If you practice this exercise regularly, then after some period of time, you will become one with the natural and spontaneous rhythm of your breathing, and your mind will feel very peaceful and relaxed. If you continue further with this exercise, the depth of your peaceful mind will continue to grow, and you will ultimately be carried to an experience of oneness with the natural and spontaneous rhythm of the cosmos, which will bring you "the peace that passes understanding."

Self-Concept Identification Inventory

The self-concept inventory is another means of helping you to get to know and understand yourself better and to help you to understand why you have adopted and identified yourself with the particular personality traits that you have. This will help you to transcend your identification with those relative traits, if you wish to do so, so that your experiential self-understanding and functioning is not exclusively restricted or limited to those particular traits. Instead, you can expand them to include other aspects of your being that are not part of any predetermined sense of identity.

If you are to derive any benefit out of this exercise, it is essential that you be as honest and candid in your responses as you can possibly be. The items designated as "male friend" and "female friend" are to be filled out by a close male and female friend who know you relatively well. Encourage each one to fill out the self-concept sheets as honestly as possible in terms of how each one really sees you, and not how they believe that you would like to be seen. Be sure not to let your friend know how you have rated yourself, and be sure that your male and female friend are not aware of each other's ratings.

Complete the following information:
(Do not write on these sheets.)

Male _____   Female _____   Birthdate _____

Highest educational level completed _____

If still in school, state your major field of study and career anticipated. _____

_____

If you are no longer in school, state your current occupation _____

Religion you were raised as _____

Religion you are now (if none, then state none, atheist, agnostic, spiritual but not religious, etc.)

_____

Relationship status:
   married _____
   engaged _____
   dating one person regularly _____

dating regularly, but not always the same person _____ dating infrequently _____

never had a date _____
bisexual _____
homosexual _____

Do not write on this page

Positive aspects of self-concept

Rate how often each trait is true for you: sometimes 1; often 2; very often 3; always 4.

1. adequate
2. casual
3. cute
4. famous
5. good son/daughter
6. idealistic
7. mature
8. proud
9. sensitive
10 successful
11. very feminine/masculine
12. admired
13. cautious
14. dependable
15. feared
16. good leader
17. independent
18. mentally healthy
19. relate easily to others
20. sexually attractive
21. swinger
22. wise
23. affectionate
24. cheerful
25. desirable
26. forceful
27. good listener
28. influential
29. modest
30. relaxed
31. shrewd
32. sympathetic

33. agreeable
34. clever
35. easygoing
36. forgiving
37. good mother/father
38. intelligent
39. morally correct
40. religious
41. sincere
42. talented
43. aggressive
44. comforting
45. uninhibited
46. friendly
47. good-natured
48. interesting person
49. non-conformist
50. respected
51. skeptical
52. tender
53. ambitious
54. committed
55. empathic
56. generous
57. good provider
58. involved
59. opportunistic
60. respectful
61. socially skilled
62. tough
63. a rebel
64. considerate
65. envied
66. gentle
67. good sexual lover
68. kind
69. nature or outdoor lover

70. responsible
71. special
72. trusting
73. athletic
74. communicates easily
75. aesthetic
76. good
77. liberated
78. physically healthy
79. rich
80. spiritual
81. understanding
82. good husband/wife
83. courageous
84. ethical
85. beautiful/handsome
86. good companion
87. helpful
88. loving
89. powerful
90. self-confident
91. spontaneous
92. unique
93. carefree
94. creative
95. fair and just
96. good conversationalist
97. honest
98. masterful
99. productive
100. good sense of humor
101. physically strong
102. psychologically strong
103. unselfish or self-sacrificing
104. hard-working
105. sensible
106. optimistic

107. sophisticated
108. patriotic
109. devoted
110. outgoing
111. very worthy
112. practical
113. immodest
114. open
115. secure
116. good self-discipline or willpower
117. good common sense
118. happy
119. neat
120. superior
121. conservative
122. real
123. happy-go-lucky
124. flexible
125. tolerant
126. warm
127. I know where I'm going
128. cannot be hurt
129. assertive
130. lovable
131. easy to please or get along with
132. not very needy
133. life of the party
134. prudent
135. down-to-earth
136. fun to be with
137. serious-minded
138. liberal
139. a comic
140. intellectual
141. orderly
142. conscientious
143. inspired

144. homosexual
145. popular
146. stable
147. hard to fool
148. imaginative
149. enthusiastic
150. fulfilled
151. wholesome
152. thrifty
153. artistic
154. daring
155. mannerly
156. frank
157. logical
158. outspoken
159. loyal
160. poised
161. sentimental
162. reliable
163. good-looking
164. well-organized
165. rational
166. dignified
167. contented
168. civilized
169. sexy
170. soft-hearted
171. unconventional
172. calm
173. realistic
174. romantic
175. determined
176. tactful
177. efficient
178. cultured
179. reasonable
180. limitless potential

If you feel that there are still some trait(s) not listed here that are part of your *positive* self-concept, list them at the end of all your selections under the heading "additional positive traits." To develop greater self-understanding, it might be helpful to reflect about why you have developed the particular personal qualities that you have selected as part of your self-description, and why you value or do not value them.

Rate how often each trait is true for you: sometimes 1; often 2; very often 3; always 4.

Do not write on this page

Negative aspects of self-concept

Rate how often each of the following traits is true for you: sometimes 1; often 2; very often 3; always 4.

1. inadequate
2. unpopular
3. emotionally cold
4. sexually cold
5. socially cold
6. unaffectionate
7. passive
8. conformist
9. ugly
10. lazy
11. a worrier
12. tense
13. not athletic
14. impulsive
15. unhappy
16. agitating
17. fearful
18. uncreative
19. plain
20. undependable
21. can't communicate
22. excitable
23. inhibited
24. immoral
25. a nobody
26. unforgiving
27. unfriendly
28. stingy
29. self-centered
30. rough
31. bad son/daughter
32. bad father/mother

33. bad wife/husband
34. bad sexual lover
35. bad provider
36. dishonest
37. dependent
38. authoritarian
39. unintelligent
40. a bore
42. inferior
44. indifferent
45. unkind
46. easily led
47. mentally ill
48. sloppy
49. slow
50. dirty
51. a prude
52. ill-at-ease
53. conceited
54. physically weak
55. psychologically weak
56. nervous
57. unrespectable
58. extremely talkative
59. extremely quiet
60. superficial
61. insecure
62. poor sense of humor
63. insensitive
64. sexually unattractive
65. insincere
66. confused
67. un-masculine/ unfeminine
68. under-sexed
69. over-sexed
70. shy
71. average

72. moody
73. proud
74. unemotional
75. overemotional
76. old-fashioned
77. mistrustful
78. too serious
79. wishy-washy
80. worthless
81. ungrateful
82. hostile
83. unlovable
84. controlling
85. stubborn
86. vulnerable
87. eccentric
88. jealous
89. demanding
90. defensive
91. an avoider
92. easily hurt
93. gullible
94. needy
95. pessimistic
96. uncompromising
97. submissive
98. abusive
99. compulsive
100. overly ambitious
101. overly introverted
102. overly extroverted
103. manipulator
104. defiant
105. impatient
106. overly pleasing of others
107. self-alienated
108. daydreamer

109. rigid
110. perfectionist
111. hard to please
112. self-rejecting
113. inner emptiness
114. guilt-ridden
115. self-punishing
116. very critical
117. evil
118. snobbish
119. reserved
120. perverted
121. a phony
122. a jinx
123. naïve
124. prejudiced
125. a gossip
126. cowardly
137. freeloader
128. greedy
129. poor self-discipline or willpower
130. handicapped
131. directionless
132. silly
133. self-indulgent
134. ruthless
135. bad personal hygiene
136. sickly
137. materialistic
138. a clown
139. aggressive
140. awkward
141. frustrated
142. too short
143. too tall
144. too fat
145. too thin

146. disagreeable
147. homosexual
148. a loner
149. competitive
150. unstable
151. disorganized
152. withdrawn
153. superstitious
154. rude
155. fickle
158. show-off
157. spendthrift
158. tactless
159. unambitious
160. idealistic
161. shiftless
162. temperamental
163. self-pitying
164. sarcastic
165. whiny
166. careless
167. conventional
168. nagger
169. cautious
170. cynical
171. cruel
172. unrealistic
173. addicted
174. reckless
175. immature
176. lacking conscience
177. formal
178. a punching bag
179. rationalizer
180. lost

If you feel that there are still some trait(s) not listed here that are part of your *negative* self-concept, list them at the end of all your selections under the heading "additional negative traits." To develop greater self-understanding, perhaps it may be helpful to reflect about why you have developed some of the negative traits that you have selected as part of your self-description.

Rate how often each trait is true for you: sometimes 1; often 2; very often 3; always 4.

Self-concept Exercise

1. For the positive aspects of self-concept listed on previous pages of this Self-Concept Identification Inventory, on a separate sheet of paper, write down the numbers of all of the positive self-concept traits with which you are identified, and next to the number of each trait, write down how frequently you see yourself as being this trait. If you see yourself as being this trait *sometimes*, *rarely*, or *never*, then record a number one (1); if you see yourself as being this trait *often*, then record a number two (2); if you see yourself as being this trait *very often*, then record a number three (3); and if you see yourself as *always* being this trait, then record a number four (4) next to the number of the trait. Thus, if you perceive yourself as *often* dependable, then on your sheet of paper, you would write "14-2." The number 14 represents the number of the positive self-concept item "dependable," and the number 2 represents your rating of *often* in regard to the frequency with which you see yourself as being this trait. If the next trait you see yourself as being is "sexually attractive," and you perceive yourself as being this trait *very often*, then you would next record "33-4." If, for example, the next trait that you identify with is number 55, "empathic," but you see yourself as being that only *sometimes*, then you would record this item as "55-1," and so on, until you have gone through the entire list of all the listed positive self-concept traits, indicating which of these

traits are part of your positive self-concept, and the frequency score that you perceive yourself as being each. After you have done that, if it occurs to you that there are still some positive self-concept traits with which you are identified, but are not contained in the lists on the relevant pages, then add these at the end of your list on your sheet of paper under the heading "additional positive traits."

2. Do the same for the negative aspects of your self-concept as you have done for the positive aspects of your self-concept.

3. Of all of the positive traits which you have listed as being identified with, now select out the ten which you value the most, and rank them from one to ten in order of being the most valued by you.

4. Now do the same for those ten negative aspects of your self-concept, and rank them from one to ten in terms of those that you most dislike.

5. Now go through the list of positive traits again, but this time, rank the ten traits that you do not have, but wish you did have, or those traits which you may have, but wish that you had more of.

6. Now rank those ten traits that you *most like* to see in members of your same sex.

7. Now rank those ten traits that you *least like* to see in members of your same sex.

8. Now rank those ten traits that you would *most like* your marriage partner to possess.

9. Now rank those ten traits that you would *least like* your marriage partner to possess.

10. Now ask your closest available male friend and female friend to rank the ten positive and ten negative traits that each feels most accurately describes or characterizes you. Encourage them to be as honest and candid as they can possibly be so that you can derive the most possible benefit from this exercise.

11. For each of the ten most positive and ten most negative traits which you feel that you possess as part of your

self-concept, as you have listed them on items three and four of this exercise, write a report discussing what you believe to be the origins of why you have come to identify with these particular positive and negative traits.

12. Compare your positive and negative self-concept with those traits that you like most and least in others, and see if you can identify any significant correspondence between them.

13. Compare your positive self-concept (item three) with your idealized image (item five) and write about why you feel the particular discrepancies between the two exist.

14. Compare the perception of you by your male and female friend with your perception of yourself, and write about the discrepancies or differences that you find.

15. On the next page, you will find a list of thirteen categories into which most positive self-concept traits will fall. See if you can determine which of these thirteen categories your ten most positive self-concept traits fall into most often, and write about the various influences and conditionings that have led you to most identify with this particular self-concept category. Also ask yourself how you would see yourself or feel about yourself if you were not this kind of person. In addition, observe if and how many of your negative traits also fit into these thirteen categories.

16. As a continuing exercise, each time you feel the threat of anxiety, see if you can identify which of your self-concepts is being put on the line and threatened with being disaffirmed, if it is a positive self-concept, and affirmed, if it is a negative self-concept; see if you can understand what it is about your current situation that is arousing that threat.

Self-Concept Categories

Below are a number of self-concept categories into which most of your positive self-concept traits will fall. See if you can come to understand how and why you have come to invest pride in those particular self-concept categories with which you have become most identified. Also try to recognize broader categories into which your negative self-concept traits fall, and explore why you have become identified with those particular self-concept categories, and see if they have any particular relationship to your positive self-concepts. Try to understand what particular psychological needs your negative and positive self-concept categories serve to gratify, and whether that sense of identity and need-gratification is truly an authentic, intrinsic aspect of your natural "real self," or does it seem like a kind of artificial covering that is not consistent with the "real you," and therefore can and should be outgrown at some point in your continued development. It might also be illuminating to explore whether your positive self-concepts may have a more negative or undesirable "down side," and whether your negative self-concepts may have a more positive or desirable "up side."

Often your basic self-concepts and values will predominantly fall into one or more of the following basic personality types.

A. *Machiavellian*: This person is primarily identified as a person of power, influence, prestige, and achievement. His sense of pride lies in feeling that he is someone of importance, and at the top of the ladder of success with mastery over others.

B. *Self-mastery*: This person invests pride in his ability to master all aspects of himself. It is important that he appears to be someone without any sense of tension or fear, and someone who is uninhibited and spontaneous with his feelings, emotions, and impulses.

C. *Unselfish Giver*: This person takes pride in his ability to be more unselfish and giving to others than anyone else. He may also often place himself in the role of the "martyr."

D. *Passivity or Peacemaker*: This person takes pride in his ability to be better than others with regard to avoiding conflict. He is proud of his ability to avoid contesting and opposing others, and of his ability to be non-aggressive, yielding, or submissive. He is chronically the "good child."

E. *Rationality*: This person invests pride in his intellect and in rational processes. Mental well-being and esteem of the mind is his greatest value and his basic identification is with his ideas.

F. *The Body:* This rank person invests pride in some aspect of the body, especially in terms of health or strength, or in the attractiveness of face and figure.

G. *The Idealist*: This person invests pride in values that are ethical, moral, or religious. He tends to gain a sense of superiority over others by concerning himself with non-materialistic values. He also tends to be a person of strong conscience development.

H. *Unique*: This person takes pride in being different from others. He loves to stand out in some way, and prides himself on being easily recognized, noticed, or especially unique.

I. *Sex-Role*: This person is identified with and takes pride in his ability to fit the culturally defined gender role of what a male or female should be better than others of the same gender.

J. *The Artist*: This person takes pride in being esthetic, sensitive, and concerned about beauty and creative or artistic productions and/or with regard to nature.

K. *Social*: This person takes pride in his social and interpersonal skills. The sense of relatedness is what he values most, and a sense of isolation or loneliness is what threatens him the most.

L. *Autonomy*: This person takes pride in his ability to be independent and self-sufficient, and un-needful of others. He constantly needs to demonstrate his internal strength, self-reliance, and/or independence of will to others, and is very sensitive and defensive about others trying to influence him.

M. *The Parent*: This person takes pride in being aggressive, dominant, and controlling of others. He is basically taking the role of the parent and treats others as weaker children.

Other basic personality types may also exist, and various combinations of the basic types listed above may exist.

The object of this exercise is basically to help you identify the various self-determined labels or concepts with which you are identified, and then help you to dis-identify from all of those labels of self-definition, by demonstrating to you the relativity and dynamically changing or fluid nature rather than the absoluteness or rigid quality of all of these various traits. You can now recognize that these labels are not what are most truly real for you, most essentially, naturally, intrinsically. You can see that, at times, you are also the opposite trait, and that you are not these same traits with all people at all times. Thus, it basically helps you recognize who you are *not*. Other exercises will help you get closer to who you most really *are*.

Self-Disclosure Exercise

Sometimes exploring our own inner struggles, unresolved feelings, and other aspects of the experiential truth of ourselves with other individuals, and helping others explore theirs, in dyadic relationships or group settings can enhance our self-understanding, beyond what we could discover about ourselves alone, through some kind of solitary, introspective, process of self-inquiry. Self-disclosure to other people of our own feelings, as well as other, related, inner struggles and experiential states can enhance self-understanding because our real self is a relational, responsive nature, and does not exist apart from others. As Jiddu Krishnamurti explains:

> In enquiring into ourselves, we are not isolating ourselves from the rest of the world. It is not an unhealthy process. Man throughout the world is caught up in the same daily problems as ourselves, so in enquiring into ourselves, we are not being in the least neurotic because there is no difference between the individual and the collective . . . I must become aware of the total field of my own self, which is the consciousness of

the individual and of society . . . I can observe myself only in relationship, because all life is relationship. It is no use sitting in a corner meditating about myself. I cannot exist by myself. I exist only in relationship to people, things, and ideas, and in studying my relationship to outward things and people, as well as to inward things, I begin to understand myself. Every other form of understanding is merely an abstraction, and I cannot study myself in abstraction; I am not an abstract entity; therefore, I have to study myself in actuality—as I am, not as I wish to be.[10]

People can disclose aspects of themselves to others in a group setting with varying degrees of comfort depending upon how personally threatening the particular area of self-disclosure is to them and depending on whether they have confidence that the other people in the group will respond to their candid self-disclosures in a nonjudgmental, unconditionally accepting, emotionally supportive, genuinely caring manner. Psychologists, such as Sidney Jourard, have long recognized the contribution of mental health to our ability to freely and openly disclose and reveal ourselves to others in a group setting.[11]

Self-disclosure contributes toward becoming more integrated and whole as a person because it puts to an end the self-divisive process of avoiding, escaping, and denying to ourselves and others certain unacceptable truths and aspects of ourselves. The accepting of these formerly rejected truths about ourselves is the first step toward greater holistic self-integration, inner peace, and enhanced contact with reality. It helps us to be more experientially real, genuine, or authentic, rather than to live by the dictates of certain social and idealized images and standards which have been imposed by influences outside of us, and with which we have become identified, as a presumptive sense of self, instead of the real self, grounded in our actual experience, and in our basic sense of authenticity and integrity. It also helps us to build trusting and meaningful relationships with others, for we cannot possibly be honest with others as long as we practice dishonesty and self-distortion with ourselves. If we cannot face the truth in ourselves, then that truth is not available to share with others, and, conversely, if we do not disclose the truth of ourselves to others, we may be unable to discover that experiential truth through some kind of solitary process of self-inquiry or self-exploration because many of our own psychological dynamics and individual creative potentials remain dormant and unrecognized until they are aroused through our responsive interaction with other individuals. Therefore, open, sincere, authentic self-disclosure contributes to the enhancement of our own self-understanding, and also contributes to the enhancement of our capacity for intimate, honest, intensely vibrant, and deeply satisfying, personal relationships with others, by enhancing our capacity to communicate well with others. It is when our relationships are deep, sincere, intensely passionate, and intimate that our experience of joy is greatest, which is what makes us feel most fully alive, and makes us feel that we are living to the fullest.

Many individuals, because it seems easier and less threatening, have the tendency to keep themselves in reserve, to hold back and not reveal their deepest selves to others, and after many years of behaving in such a pattern, this tendency becomes a habitual lifestyle, which makes real intimacy, honesty, openness, and sharing very difficult to accomplish later in life, when successful marriage and parenting necessitates it. Being open and sharing ourselves easily with others makes it possible for others to make full contact with that which is most real and alive in us, which is what enables close and gratifying relationships to develop and endure. This capacity for openness, honesty, and sharing cannot come by itself overnight. It is a skill that you must learn and continuously practice; otherwise, it is easily lost. This exercise is designed to help you enhance that skill.

In this exercise, we would like you to first disclose the experiential truth of yourself to yourself, which is usually the easiest way to begin, by writing a detailed report or journal containing your reactions and answers to any of the self-disclosure items listed later in this section. Now that you have disclosed yourself to yourself, you are now in a better position to more easily and comfortably disclose yourself to the group. Don't panic. It has been my (Max Hammer's) experience that although some students expect candid self-disclosure of their inner struggles and uncomfortable feelings to be a painful experience, after they have actually done it, they usually feel more relieved, liberated, "cleaner," and more experientially real, genuine, or authentic. They find that they like themselves better than they ever have before. I would like you to disclose yourself to the group at first only on those items that you feel would produce no more than a little discomfort in you. The goal is for you to then disclose to the group more and more items about yourself that you have previously been unable to share with the group. I would also like you to do this outside of the group setting and take the opportunity whenever it presents itself for you to disclose yourself to *others* around you, to whom you would feel it to be appropriate during your daily activities. Try to be as sensitive as you can about what is really true about yourself, and try to share that truth with others as honestly as you can.

After each time that you have had a particularly significant experience in which you have disclosed yourself, either in the group setting, or to others outside the group, it might be helpful to write a short journal describing all your feelings about it, and why you think it went well or poorly. Also include what you believe the feelings were of those to whom you directed your self-disclosure, and why you perceive that they felt as they did. Feel free to add to this report anything that in your judgment is relevant to your experience.

A Sample of Recommended Self-Disclosure Items:

Please feel free to add to this list any items that you feel are essential aspects of your personality, or of significant concern to you, and which you feel you need to disclose to other individuals, in a group setting or in dyadic relationships:

1. The pastimes I most enjoy doing or being involved with.
2. The kind of habits about other people or myself that I most like.
3. The traits of personality that I dislike most in other people.
4. The traits of personality that I like most in other people.
5. My feelings about God, religion, and the basic meaning or purpose of life.
6. My feelings about my marriage, or about the possibility of becoming married, or about the institution of marriage.
7. My feelings about my children or about the possibility of having children.
8. My feelings about my father.
9. My feelings about my mother.
10. My feelings about my brother(s) and/or sister(s).
11. The things that frighten me the most and/or give me the most anxiety.
12. The things that make me the most angry.
13. The times I have felt most lonely.
14. The times I have felt most guilty.
15. The times I have felt most happy.
16. The times I have felt most loving.
17. My feelings about today's political situation.
18. How I feel about my body image.

19. Those qualities in members of the opposite gender that make them most sexually attractive to me or that turn me off.
20. The past relationships that I have most regretted losing.
21. The things I often dream about.
22. The things I often fantasize or daydream about.
23. What I like(d) or dislike(d) most about school or about my job.
24. My general attitudes and values about sex.
25. My sexual needs and habits.
26. What I believe most members of the opposite gender think about me.
27. What I believe most members of my own gender think about me.
28. My evaluation of my own intellectual capacities and/or problems.
29. My evaluation of my own emotional capacities and/or problems.
30. My evaluation of my own sexual capacities and/or problems.
31. My evaluation of my own social skills and/or problems.
32. The kind of work I like to do most.
33. The kind of work I like to do least.
34. My attitudes and values in regard to money.
35. What holds my interest the most
36. What I value the most in life and why.
37. My more immediate personal goals.
38. My more future personal goals.
39. How I define love and what it means to me.
40. My earliest memory.
41. What people must do in order to convince me that they can be trusted.
42. My feelings about the changes going on in society today.
43. The unhappiest moment of my life.
44. How most people view me and how that compares to my view of myself.

45. My feelings about making a total commitment to others.
46. My feelings about being physically close to others.
47. My feelings about being emotionally close to others.
48. The time I lost my temper the most.
49. My feelings about the socio-economic status of my family.
50. My negative feelings toward myself and/or what I like least about myself.
51. My positive feelings about myself and/or what I like most about myself.
52. What I want and expect most from my friends.
53. The times that others have hurt me emotionally the most.
54. The things I most regret having said and done.
55. My beliefs about an afterlife after death.
56. My most secret wishes.
57. The things I remember most about my childhood.
58. My feelings about members of the opposite gender.
59. My feelings about members of my own gender.
60. My feelings about taking drugs, alcohol, or cigarettes for pleasure and relaxation.
61. What the term "respect" means to me.
62. My feelings about masturbation.
63. My feelings about having sexual affairs.
64. What I want most out of life.
65. The areas in which I need to be able to take more risks.
66. What I would do on my last day if I knew that I had only one day to live.
67. The greatest mistakes I ever made.
68. What embarrasses and/or humiliates me the most.
69. My greatest faults.
70. My greatest strengths and/or virtues.
71. My realistic self-concept of myself.
72. The self that I try to show to others or want others to see me as being.
73. My idealized self-image, i.e., the kind of person I would like most to be.

74. The things that I am most curious about.
75. My feelings about sports.
76. What I would do first if I were president of the United States.
77. My feelings about expressing myself in a large group.
78. The things that are most apt to make me cry.
79. The areas in which I tend to compete with others the most.
80. The things I am most envious about.
81. My feelings about growing old.
82. The times I have cheated.
83. The most serious lie I have ever told.
84. The possession that I have that is most valuable to me.
85. The times I have felt depressed.
86. The times I considered committing suicide.
87. The places I which I would most like to live.
88. My definition of success and what it means to me.
89. A discussion of my greatest failures and defects.
90. My definition of sin.
91. My greatest frustrations.
92. My ideal marriage partner.
93. The things that tend to make me laugh.
94. My definition of psychological maturity and where I am relative to that definition.
95. What is your view of true love, peace, happiness, beauty, freedom, virtue, wisdom, and creative inspiration? Why do you hold that view?
96. What kinds of people do you most admire and respect and why?
97. What kinds of people do you least admire and respect and why?
98. What is the best way to cope with pressure, stress, worry, or anxiety?
99. What is the best way to deal with grief related to losing loved ones through death, separation, or breakups?
100. What is the best way to develop authenticity, sincerity, courage, patience, perseverance, inner strength, and nobility of character?

Insights derived from this process of self-exploration and self-disclosure should be applied as a means of further developing or growing in what is most authentically real in yourself, as well as outgrowing inauthentic ideas, beliefs, and presumptions about yourself that are not grounded in what is natural or intrinsic to your being, and that produce unnecessary self-conflict, emotional burdens, and self-defeating habits, rather than producing a liberating discovery or uncovering of what is vibrantly alive and naturally joyful in you. Preconceived presumptions, value judgments (value judged "should-be's"), and self-images often block our awareness of various aspects of our actual experience, and prevent us from being open to useful insights and options that do not conform to those restrictive definitions of others, and ourselves whereas letting go of those restrictive self-interpretations can enable us to become open to liberating new possibilities.[12]

CONCLUDING SUMMARY OF

CHAPTER 2

REFLECTIONS FOR ENHANCING

EXPERIENTIAL SELF-UNDERSTANDING

Experiential self-understanding arises when the mind is open, receptive, relaxed, quiet, without preconceived ideas, and not following the views of others. Various kinds of intensely exciting sensations and soothing substances are used to escape from the actual experiential truth of oneself, and can readily become addictive and psychologically unhealthy. Psychological health, maturity, and strength of character involve being willing and able to tolerate painful feelings and experiences; otherwise, you withdraw from various aspects of life and psychologically deaden yourself. The process of escape, in which the conscious knower stands dualistically distant and separated from the psychological pain, only preserves and intensifies the pain. Courageously contacting our psychological pain head-on, and letting it do its worst, enables us to regain energy trapped in hitherto rejected painful feelings, so that more of our energies can become available for productive, adaptive, enjoyable living. Facing our psychological pain heals and dissolves it. Escaping from painful feelings and experiential states produces a kind of psychological numbing or desensitizing and alienation from what is experientially real and alive in you. Experiential self-understanding can liberate you from psychologically burdensome, restrictive, often learned, fear-based, self-defeating, habitual patterns and behavior. The personal entity self or conceptually defined sense of identity is merely a presumptive illusion, whereas our real self includes our moment-to-moment responsive experiential states, as well as our indefinable

118

timeless permanent being or transpersonal self, as objectless pure conscious awareness indivisibly united to our vibratory life energy, and its natural inclinations and innate qualities, which comprise our experiential particularity or distinctiveness, which need not be conceptually defined. The ego fears presumed inner emptiness and nothingness, but when we cease to escape from the indefinable pure simplicity of our being, we experience its intrinsic qualities of inner peace and joyful life energy. All of the ego's basic motivations are designed to escape from the inner nullity point, as an attempt to make the "me" more. We authors have recommended various reflective exercises to enhance authentic self-understanding, grounded in direct self-observation rather than any kind of preconceived, presumptive self-definition.

CHAPTER 3

PUBLISHED ARTICLES
BY MAX HAMMER:

HOW PSYCHOTHERAPISTS
CAN BEST FACILITATE THE
PSYCHOLOGICAL HEALING
PROCESS IN THEIR CLIENTS

Introductory Editorial Note
By Barry Hammer

The articles included in this chapter are reprinted here and edited by me with permission from the relevant journals where those articles were originally published. The editorial asides and commentary that I have added are based on typed notes dictated to me by my late father, Dr. Max Hammer, over many years. These articles and some additional typed notes that I have included in part B of chapter three discuss the essential process of psychological self-understanding and therapeutic healing of emotional pain, serving to elaborate on the introductory discussion of that process presented in chapter one and chapter two of this book. After some of the articles, I present interpretive commentary of my own, discussing how some of Max Hammer's later views diverged from certain ideas presented earlier in those articles. Occasionally, I, Barry Hammer, have inserted my own interpretive commentary in square brackets [ ] within the text of particular articles in order to clarify and expand particular ideas, whereas Max Hammer's own asides are contained in parentheses ( ), which were included in the original journal articles.

The published articles that I am including in this chapter are:

1. "The Essence of Personal and Transpersonal Psychotherapy." *Psychotherapy, Theory, Research, and Practice* 11, no. 3 (Fall 1974): 202-210. This article also appears as an invited chapter in *Creative Psychotherapy, A Source Book*, edited by Anthony G. Banet, Jr. (La Jolla, California: University Associates Inc., 1976), 38-51.
2. "Transpersonal Being: The Unchangeable Core." *Voices: The Art and Science of Psychotherapy* 10, no. 4 (Winter 1974-75): 40-46.
3. "Misconceptions of Transpersonal Psychotherapy: A Reply to Ellis." *Voices: The Art and Science of Psychotherapy* 8, no. 3 (Fall 1972): 21-26.
4. "Quiet Mind Therapy." *Voices: The Art and Science of Psychotherapy* 7, no. 1: 52-56.
5. "The Hopelessness of Hope." *Voices: The Art and Science of Psychotherapy* 6, no. 3 (Winter 1970): 15-17.
6. "A Therapy for Loneliness." *Voices: The Art and Science of Psychotherapy* 8, no. 1 (Spring 1972): 24-29.

The following article is reprinted with permission from: *Psychotherapy: Theory, Research, and Practice.*
"The Essence of Personal and Transpersonal Psychotherapy"

> Sail forth, steer for the deep waters only . . .
> I with thee, and thou with me.
> —Walt Whitman

Through the influence of Eastern philosophy upon Western psychotherapy, as expounded by writers such as Watts (1961), Assagioli (1965), Maslow (1969), and more recently by this writer (Hammer, 1971, 1972, a & b), the interest of psychotherapists in the transpersonal or transcendent aspects of human consciousness has been increasing enormously, and one function of this paper is to help provide the reader with a more basic realization of the nature of the Transpersonal [aspect of the human psyche]. However, what has been less recognized and understood, and what this paper also seeks to demonstrate, is that the process that most expeditiously leads to the awakening of consciousness to its Transpersonal or Transcendent essence is also the same process that most expeditiously leads to the transcendence of personal psychopathology. This growth process is what is here referred to as "Transpersonal Psychotherapy." Transpersonal psychotherapy is not so much a technique for doing psychotherapy as much as it represents the essential threat [thread] that underlies all psychological growth and therapeutic effect whenever they occur.

Transpersonal psychotherapy concerns itself, ultimately, with helping consciousness transcend its identification with the various limiting and relative self-defined personal labels, concepts, or images which comprise the apparent and illusional [illusory] ego, and awaken to itself, in what is referred to as the Transpersonal Awakening experience, as the real "I-Principle," or "Transpersonal Self," which is what

Consciousness is when It is in Its most essential and natural condition of being a perfect Unity, i.e., an unlabeled, indivisible, unbounded, Whole, which is not a sum of labels or parts, but an absence of parts. The Transpersonal may also be alluded to in other ways as well by saying that it is that absolute Truth, which is the perfect Silence of pure Consciousness, which serves as the essential [underlying] background, support, or substance, which composes [comprises], and from which arises, all personal forms and objectifications of consciousness, such as, thoughts and feelings, and which underlies all of the various states of consciousness, such as wake, dream, and deep sleep; It is that pure Subjectivity or most subjective Subject which is beyond all subject-object duality and relativity; It is that true and intrinsic nature of Consciousness which comprises, as a unity, the triune of absolute Peace-Love-Joy, (which shall here be subsumed under the single unifying term of "Bliss"), and from which source arises their corresponding equivalents on the relative, objective, or personal plane of consciousness in the form of sensations of calm, eroticism, and elation or pleasure.

Because Transpersonal Consciousness is pure [undifferentiated, objectless] subjectivity, and cannot be objectified or made into something known by some more subjective subject or knower, the terms used above in the discussion of the nature of the Transpersonal are meant only to focalize psychological vision to point in Its direction, and are in no way meant to suggest that the indefinable Reality pointed to, from different points of views, through the words and labels, is something which can be limited and grasped cognitively or conceptually, for It clearly cannot. In truth, nothing at all can be said or known about that Reality. Only labels can be known or experienced, and the Transpersonal cannot be objectified or labeled [or defined]. It is for that reason that those Masters, in whom consciousness has become fully Awakened, when asked about the nature of the Transpersonal, quite often "respond" only with their own Silence of Consciousness, and do not offer any verbal response at all, which is the only really correct "reply." For the same reason, the reader must understand that the Transpersonal is not something which can be reduced to a feeling, and can be experienced or known in the conventional sense of the term "to experience," which means as the dualistic and relative subject standing outside of something labeled and objectified. There is another form of "knowing," which is by *being* that Reality, i.e., by being one with, or in unity or identity with, that Reality in its self-luminous state. That which is self-luminous does not require the help of anything else in order to be known. This is the only way the Transpersonal can be "known." It is only through one's own direct realization of this Silence or Bliss Consciousness that brings a permanent end to the false identification by consciousness with the personal ego, [or the conceptually defined, illusory, separate, divisive, sense of self].

There are two fundamental aspects to the Transpersonal Awakening, which help to explain how it leads consciousness to the complete surrendering and transcending of its identification with the personal ego. One basic aspect of Transpersonal Awakening is the direct realization that the "all" of diversity is not a reality, as such, but has only apparent and illusional [illusory] existence, and is supported, as its essential substance, by the one Reality which is the Unity of pure Consciousness [beyond all of the multiplicity and diversity of objects of knowledge that temporarily arise within consciousness]. There is the direct realization that objects, as such, are never really directly related to, or known, [as independent, self-existing, entities], but, rather, it is only the knowledge of objects, as it takes place within consciousness, that is ever experienced or known. Therefore, all objects are essentially only objectifications of, and reducible to, pure Consciousness, the one and only Reality. In other words, what is known is not essentially different from the process of knowing or awareness of the known, and knowing is not essentially different from the knower, so that one realizes that the world, is, essentially, the knower himself, or pure

Consciousness, and so all is One. Therefore, all objectivity and diversity is realized as being merely a thought-form.

The capacity to recognize and experience what is referred to as the duality of the self and the world depends upon labels [differentiating interpretations, or contrasting definitions]. Both are essentially only objectifications (or modifications) of the perfect Unity of pure Consciousness, and gain apparent existence only through the superimposition of labels [or definitions] upon that one Reality. With the application and experience of a label, both the external world and the sense of self arise simultaneously as relative and mutually interdependent realities, with the world serving as the object and the personal self as its subject. If one or the other of these mutually interdependent relative realities [presumptive constructs] drops out, then the other also drops out.

There are actually three basic ways in which the ego or sense of self tries to affirm its illusional personal existence. The first, as discussed above, is as a *subject*, in its role as the thinker, perceiver, doer, knower, or experiencer of its relative labeled experiences, which include not only the experiences of the world, but also of his own experiential and conceptualized self. The second is as an *object*: by constructing (defining) and identifying itself as being some labeled and objectified physical, experiential, or conceptual self; it relates to the world and itself as that object, and seeks to absolutely affirm, enhance, and protect the particular objectified self through the validating or affirming responses of others. The third basic means by which the personal sense of self tries to affirm itself is through its identification of itself with desire, or the *will*, and its potency or capacity to control or influence what it puts itself on the line to influence. The operations and yearnings of egoistic consciousness will be discussed in more detail throughout this article, because only by a complete understanding of the nature and function of the ego, can its relative and illusory nature be realized, which ultimately enables consciousness to come to dis-identify from all of the ego's many manifestations, and, thereby, transcend it, and awaken to its own Transpersonal nature.

Another basic aspect of Transpersonal Awakening involves the direct realization that Conscious awareness is already [intrinsically being] what egoistic desire seeks to fulfill through its pursuit of various objects. Regardless of what objects the ego desires and pursues, it is ultimately for their capacity to yield a sense of peace or joy that the object is desired. Consciousness is, intrinsically, [being] that absolute Peace and Joy already when it is Transpersonal, which it is when it is totally free of egoistic desire. Desire only takes consciousness away from its realization of itself as Paradise or Bliss. Thus, a real and lasting sense of gratification and fulfillment can never come from any desired object. The only true fulfillment of desire is the ending of desire.

Thus, Transpersonal psychotherapy recognizes that the most basic yearning of personal consciousness is to discover the ultimate answer to the question, "Who am I?" not in the relative or egoistic plane, in terms of an objectified personal identity, [or a conceptual self-definition], which, because of its relativity [exclusivity, and partiality], is never real, but, rather, in the most subjective, essential, or Absolute sense. The thwarting or frustration of this most basic of all psychological yearnings is the basis for the development of all forms of psychopathology. Psychopathology begins with the rejection of the unity of consciousness for which is substituted the identification by consciousness with the various labels or fragments that comprise the dualistic psychological ego. Duality of consciousness arises in man because he is not content just to *be* himself, he wants to *know* himself, so as to be able to assuage his fear that he is truly a nothing void. Man, being essentially a unity of consciousness, or pure subjective consciousness, cannot make an object of himself as he truly is, and, therefore, cannot really experience himself. So, man proceeds to make himself an object, or something known through the identification, by his consciousness, with the various labels by which he defines himself. By objectifying, (identifying with), and experiencing, these labels of himself, he then believes that he has created a self, and is now able to experience himself as being both this objectified self as well as the subject or experiencer of those objectified labels. This is, essentially, what is meant by the dualization [division, fragmentation] of consciousness.

When consciousness becomes identified not only as being the self which is the experiential reality (e.g., emotions, feelings, desires, impulses) that arise from moment to moment in consciousness, but it also identifies itself as being the self which is the [dualistic, detached, reactive] observer, judger, or censor of that feeling from the standpoint of some apparently fixed and conceptualized or idealized entity—that is the beginning and essence of duality and the pathological process.

The essence of Transpersonal psychotherapy involves helping the patient to live in the desireless state of Being, or Unity of Consciousness, which means making no [exclusive] identification of self with any labeled thing, but, rather, centering oneself between all pairs of relative opposites, such as, strong-weak, worthy-worthless, male-female. This puts an end to the dualistic contradiction of making consciousness both a subject and an object, and also puts an end to the egoistic drives for an absolute sense of self-enhancement, self-protection, and self-affirmation, and, further, puts an end to the chronic states of anxiety and frustration, and their consequential negative experiential states, such as, hostility, depression, loneliness, and tension, which accompany the continuous threat of the non-fulfillment of these strivings for absoluteness. One is then not nothing, but only no-thing [i.e., one is no definable or knowable thing], for one is still that something which is pointed to, and represented by, the label of "pure Consciousness," which is also one with pure Being.

To establish that perfect [internal] Unity, consciousness must first unify itself in terms of all of its personal aspects by rejecting nothing which is experientially real in itself. In order to accomplish that, consciousness must first disidentify from all fixed conceptual selves [or preconceived, exclusive, self-definitions] with which it has identified itself, because, if it holds to being some fixated and enduring conceptual self, there will be no tolerance for those experiential realities which are in contradiction with that fixed [and exclusive] conceptual self. Thus, for example, if I hold myself to be a "kind" person, I will not be able to permit myself to recognize and accept angry feelings when they arise in consciousness because kind people just do not get angry. Therefore, to bring about a personal unity in consciousness, I must first take my stand as being nothing fixed or enduring [or exclusive, or predetermined], but (instead) hold myself to be only the moment-to-moment experiential reality which arises in consciousness. Thus, some moments, I am anger, then sadness, then elation, then tenderness, etc.

In helping the patient [psychotherapy client] to quickly identify his rejected experiential realities so that he may be in the position to unify with them, [by fully uniting one's conscious awareness and feeling-energy with them], it is helpful for the therapist to identify the patient's psychological needs and strivings, or the things that he is trying to prove about himself, and to be aware of the fact that psychological needs are not real, as such, and, therefore, cannot be filled, but only represent escapes and compensatory opposites for those negative experiential realities which the concept of self rejects and disowns, and tries to pretend do not exist by trying to actualize [achieve and validate] their more positive compensatory opposite. For example, the striving or need for power compensates for the need to escape from feelings of impotence, weakness, helplessness, or vulnerability; the need to secure from others a feeling of being loved or valued often compensates for, and seeks to deny, one's more basic conviction and feelings of worthlessness or unlovableness; the need is not for independence, but rather, the need is to deny or compensate for one's more basic rejected feelings of insecurity, etc.

The therapist must help the patient to confront and integrate with those rejected experiential aspects of self which he actually is [being], at any given moment, instead to trying to help the patient actualize [achieve and validate] its compensatory opposite [positive ideal self-image], or what the patient feels that he *ought to be*, or that which he is trying to protect, enhance, or affirm about himself. As peculiar and contradictory as it may sound, [inner] peace is to be found only in the midst of (i.e., in communion, non-duality, or at oneness with) pain, and never by struggling against or running away from what is considered to be the negative or painful. *Only communion with psychological pain opens the door for its liberation and transcendence*; only a yielding, letting be, or full acceptance is its ending. Psychological pain does not exist just because of the mere presence alone of some stimulus or reality which is termed "painful." Rather, the pain is produced by the interpretation of that fact or reality which produces the tendency to avoid or resist that fact. Only when the mind recoils from a fact or reality is there pain. *Psychological pain is part and parcel of the process of escape and resistance.* Pain is not inherent to any feeling [per se], but arises only after the intent to reject it arises. Essentially, the feeling of psychological pain is created by the attempt to fragment or separate consciousness from itself; the splitting of the unity of consciousness into the duality of a conceptual observing entity which tries to run from, distort, or overpower the rejected feeling, and the observed feeling itself. *If consciousness in duality is the cause of the pain, then only consciousness in unity can be the elimination of the pain.* Therefore, it is only in full communion with the formerly rejected feeling, in which conscious awareness is fully accepting and totally merged into it, so as to re-establish a non-dualistic reunification with it, that there is the ending of [psychological] pain.

Thus, for example, the patient reports that his girlfriend caused him [emotional] pain by rejecting him. However, that rejection is only a fact; intrinsically there is no pain in it. But the patient's mind recoils from that fact, and he feels psychological pain because his consciousness is recoiling from the interpretation that he has applied to the rejection, which is related to some kind of threat to his sense of self, as reflected in his need for self-enhancement, self-protection, or self-affirmation. Thus, if his need for self-enhancement has been threatened, then likely, he has interpreted the rejection in such a way as to arouse and confirm feelings of worthlessness in himself, which already existed there as a basic conviction. Because total lack of self-esteem and worthlessness tends to be equated with nothingness, his sense of being a psychological self becomes threatened with extinction, and so he rejects this feeling in himself, and [psychological] pain ensues. If, however, he lets be that feeling, which he is labeling as worthlessness, and does not try to strive to gain a compensatory sense of worth, but, rather, just yields and merges with the feeling, and lets it speak for itself totally, then he will find that both the feeling and the pain related to that feeling have been transcended. *Thus, the therapeutic rule is, always help the patient unify with what he actually is experientially [being] from moment to moment, but never encourage him to pursue some compensatory ideal of what he believes he ought to be.*

Ultimately, the therapist will discover that all of the patient's compensatory needs are reducible to, and merge, essentially, into the one most basic compensatory need, which is to affirm oneself as being absolutely something, which serves as the compensatory opposite and defense that attempts to help consciousness avoid that one most painful experiential reality and fearful realization—that one is essentially no-thing (i.e., no labeled thing), which is equated with nothingness, or psychological extinction. Thus, consciousness attempts to avoid the recognition of itself as a void by identifying itself with various labels which serve to define itself, and, thereby, pretends to give itself some personal reality [or inner self-knowledge]. Consciousness then becomes totally devoted to the service of making this conceptualized labeled self some kind of absolute something instead of the relative something that it really is.

Egoistic consciousness, because it is totally devoted to making and proving itself as being something absolute, which is referred to as living in Becoming, is invariably in a state of discomfort because it is always operating within a framework of threat and frustration in regard to its needs for protection, affirmation, and enhancement, and so negative experiential states such as, anxiety, tension, hostility, depression, and loneliness are always a part of a consciousness when it is living in Becoming. The constant devotion and desire of egoistic consciousness to actualize what can never be in its grasp, because the personal self, composed of relative labels, [or exclusive self-definitions], can never [actually] attain absoluteness, guarantees that frustration, tension, and unhappiness will be chronic, whereas a consciousness that lives in Being is free of all the negative experiential states, and finds that peace, love, and joy are naturally intrinsic to itself. In essence, then, *the greater the degree of self-preoccupation*, caused by threats to, and the frustration of, the ego and its drives for an absolute sense of enhancement, protection, and affirmation, (which is related to the perceived tenuousness of the ego's sense of existence) [as a conceptually defined entity], *the greater is the degree of psychopathology*.

Transpersonal psychotherapy recognizes that the various negative experiential realities are all related to threats to the sense of self, and frustrations of its ambitions to make itself absolutely validated, thereby reflecting its basically illusory nature. Therefore, the treatments of these symptoms alone is superficial, and in the long-run ineffective, because they must ultimately return in view of the fact that the identification with the illusional ego, which is their basic cause, still exists, and, therefore, is a threat to it, and frustration of its drives is inevitable. Transpersonal psychotherapy takes the position that the *identification, by consciousness, with the ego must be transcended, and then all of the negative experiential states and symptoms will also immediately be transcended,* because there is then no longer any labeled or personal self to be threatened with frustration and extinction. If transcendence of the ego is to be the end [basic goal] of *psychotherapy,* then the process itself, as its means, must also involve the transcendence or surrender of the ego, which Transpersonal psychology does accomplish through the process of non-dualistic awareness, or self-communion, which *involves consciousness being in a state of at-one-ness with its moment-to-moment experiential realities.*

Another way to quickly identify what experiential realities you are rejecting in yourself is to sensitively observe what aspects of the world you are rejecting or finding absolutely intolerable. If you cannot accept some aspect of the world, then what you are really saying is that you cannot accept what that thing does to you, which means more basically that you cannot accept being that experiential reality or response to that aspect of the world. You [feel that you] cannot accept the experiential self that you are [actually being] that moment. When I am totally self-accepting and self-communing, I am free to let the world be whatever it has to be, because I am prepared to be, and accept [the emotional experience of], whatever it is that the world may trigger in me. I no longer disown, but, rather, call all my responses my own, and therefore, my world and my ability to make contact with it is significantly broadened and enhanced. Thus, *psychopathology begins with the first self-rejection of anything that is experientially real [in oneself], which produces a sense of division and duality to consciousness; whereas what may be called psychological health is that state of consciousness in which it is free of a judgmental self-concept, and, therefore, is a totally self-accepting or self-communing unity.* Therefore, until the patient has learned that only he, alone, and not the world, is responsible for his own experiential state of mind, he cannot be considered as being psychologically healthy.

To discuss the process of self-communion or non-dualistic awareness in greater detail, it is first essential to understand that when the dualistic self-concept entity is silent or inoperative, then the mind is without movement on the surface, and the process of imagination is stilled, and there is no distracting opposition to prevent the clear contact, hearing, and understanding of what arises spontaneously. In that state of non-duality, consciousness is in its [original, intrinsic] Transpersonal condition, or the state of Being, which is the natural self-healing and creative condition of consciousness. In that state, there is no dualistic entity operating as the judger or controller of the spontaneously arising contents of consciousness and so, being unimpeded, the rejected aspects of consciousness are free to arise spontaneously and [thereby] creatively reunify themselves into the unitary whole that consciousness naturally is.

In self-communion or non-dualistic awareness, one makes no conceptual reaction or interpretation of any kind to the experiential reality that arises spontaneously, but rather, one should adopt an attitude of silent witnessing or quiet mind observation, or listening to that which arises, and, therefore, consciousness is then in a non-dualistic state of being one with what is, and not pursuing some imaginal [imaginary presumption of] what ought to be. Consciousness is then in the Transpersonal state of Being, instead of the egoistic state of Becoming. Letting be and being one with what is the moment to moment spontaneously arising experiential content of consciousness is the immediate end of duality and conflict within consciousness.

Thus, to be in this non-dualistic state of consciousness, one must not label, judge [as] good or bad, or have any kind of desire or goal in regard to what arises in consciousness. There must be no sense of avoidance, resistance, condemnation, justification, distortion, or attachment in regard to what arises, but only a *choiceless awareness* because any such reaction is a response of a self-concept entity which puts consciousness into the pathological state of duality, and, therefore, consciousness is no longer in the non-dualistic state, which is the only condition of consciousness in which real therapeutic effect can take place. Without the full integration which non-duality yields, the rejected [feeling or experiential state] still remains short of being fully assimilated. Without the occurrence of self-communion, consciousness is still in the pathological state of duality, division, and conflict, so self-unification or self-healing cannot take place. The rejected painful experiential realities are not free to spontaneously arise and creatively be integrated, and so no healing effect or growth is possible.

Therefore, one need only yield to and merge with the experiential reality just as it [actually] is, letting it pervade one's awareness entirely, and permitting it to speak for itself to completion. Sometimes closing the eyes may assist the complete focusing of attention on, and its total absorption into, full identity with the feeling that is arising. The therapist can help the patient to understand and establish himself in the state of non-duality by encouraging him to speak as though he were the feeling itself. This can be done by simply asking the patient, "What would the feeling (e.g., anger, fear, depression, loneliness, etc.), say if it could speak?"

To achieve the creative and self-healing state of self-communion most expeditiously, it is also helpful if one takes the creative stance in consciousness that consciousness is a natural unity [as an indivisible wholeness], and not a duality, and, therefore, there is only one self, and not two. Because there is no real enduring or conceptual "me" that operates as the entity which is the [dualistic, detached, reactive] observer-controller-judger of that which arises in consciousness, one should, therefore, take the stand that one is only [being] that varying experiential reality that arises in consciousness and changes from moment to moment. Some moments, it may be elation; other moments, it may be sadness, tenderness, destructiveness, fear, loneliness, etc. Thus, for example, one should not say that this moment, "I am hostile," or "I have hostility," but rather, "I am hostility" because the first two statements imply a second, dual, or additional self to which the experiential reality of hostility belongs. In reality, *there*

is no other self to whom the particular feeling is happening.
There is only the feeling itself. All other selves are only conceptual and illusional ideals of what [presumptively] ought
to be. Thus, nothing can be done about what is experientially arising this moment. One can only adopt an attitude of
choicelessness in regard to what is [i.e., take an attitude of
natural, nonselective, nonjudgmental, "letting be" of whatever experiential states arise in one's consciousness], and
therefore, there is nothing else to do but just let it speak for
itself and tell its own whole, complete, story or message.

Thus, two basic forms or degrees of duality and pathology have been implied. The first is that duality and pathology are necessary to give birth to and affirm the ego. What
may be referred to as the universal pathology is the initial
or *fundamental duality* common to all non-Transpersonally
Awakened people, and that is the duality which involves the
separation in consciousness between self as subject and self
as object in its various forms, such as the observer and that
which is observed, the experiencer and that which is experienced, the judger and that which is judged, the controller
and that which is controlled, or the conceptual self and the
experiential self. The *secondary duality*, which follows after
the establishment of the fundamental duality, and which is
the more severe or advanced degree of duality or pathology,
is the personal or diagnostic pathology that relates to one's
personal repressions. It is that duality within consciousness
between what is [deemed to be] personally acceptable and
unacceptable, or between what is conscious and unconscious, and is based upon what threatens the ego's sense of
existence, which is related to the ego's needs for a sense of
potency, worth, integrity [self-consistent cohesiveness], and
affirmation of its labeled identifications [or conceptual self-
definitions]. This determines the particular form and severity
that the individual's pathology will take.

These various forms and degrees of duality and pathology may be most efficaciously and expeditiously transcended through a process referred to here as *transpersonal*

*psychotherapy. Transpersonal psychotherapy may be suc-
cinctly defined as the attempt to restore consciousness to its
natural state of being a unitary whole through the process of
self-communion. Self-communion is the essence of all therapeutic effect* regardless of the system of therapy under which
it occurs. It is the essence of what is meant by integration
or reunification. It is the whole-ing process of consciousness, which is essentially what is meant by healing. In most
systems, when self-communion does happen to occur, it is
usually rarely and most fortuitously achieved; whereas in
transpersonal psychotherapy, the achievement is deliberate
and most direct.

There is no real psychological healing without self-communion, and whenever any process of therapy has been
successful, it is only and always because, in some way, the
patient has been helped to be in a state of communion or unity
with whatever painful experiential reality he was formerly
rejecting. If the ego, as the [dualistically separate, reactive,
interpretive] observer, is surrendered, and consciousness
takes its stand as being one with the observed, then in that
moment has integration or growth occurred. No more expeditious or effective form of therapy is possible than that.

At times, it is possible that intellectual interpretations by
the therapist may facilitate the arousal of some particular rejected experiential reality in the patient, but that alone is not
sufficient to guarantee that the patient will then go ahead
and fully accept and permit himself to merge and integrate
his consciousness with that particular aroused experiential reality, which is essential if psychological healing and
growth is to occur. Intellectual interpretations by the therapist which lead to the patient perceiving his experiential self
from the point of view of some distanced and dualistic observer, or having just an intellectual grasp or set of theoretical explanations of his psychodynamics, still maintains
the patient's consciousness dualistically outside of himself,
and, are, therefore, not sufficient of themselves to produce
the condition of self-communion or integration [with painful

feelings or experiential realities], which is necessary to yield a therapeutic effect. In fact, in the long run, such intellectual interpretations may be permanently inhibiting to growth because they only serve to teach and condition the patient to look outside of himself for the truth of himself, and thereby, maintain the patient's consciousness in a state of duality [or self-division]. Strangely enough, there are some systems of therapy currently in vogue that actually set out deliberately to encourage and intensify dualism in consciousness by enhancing the capacity of the patient's ego, as observer, to control, suppress, and dominate its dualistic observed experiential realities which the patient feels are objectionable or painful to him. It is extremely questionable whether such systems can legitimately be called therapeutic.

Therefore, the only really essential therapy for the patient is that he comes to learn how to convert the pathological duality of consciousness into a unitary whole, by himself. When he is able to accomplish that consistently, then he no longer needs the therapist, nor does he require any further therapy. He no longer disowns any of his own experiential realities. He knows how to unify and heal himself. He knows how to be his own therapist. Every successful therapeutic process should, at the outcome, always leave the patient capable of being his own therapist. [According to Maurice Friedman's interpretation of Martin Buber's views on psychotherapy, "What is necessary is the conscious liberation of the patient from this unconscious imposition of the therapist—leaving the patient really to himself, and seeing what comes out of it. The therapist approaches the patient, but he must try to influence him as little as possible, i.e., the patient must not be influenced by the general ideas of the school."[1] In the words of Buber, himself, 'It is much easier to impose oneself on the patient than it is to use the whole force of one's soul to leave the patient to himself and not to touch him. The real master responds to uniqueness.'"[2]]

At this point, the reader may be wondering why the patient, prior to coming in for therapy, does not naturally and easily achieve self-communion through his own efforts. There are two fundamental reasons why the patient makes no attempt on his own or prevents himself from establishing the self-healing, self-communion with his rejected painful feelings. In some cases, the ego is convinced that the repressed feelings are more powerful than the ego's capacity to contain or control them, and so it fears that the full contact of communion with the feelings will lead to the uncontrolled acting-out or overt expression of those feelings in inappropriate behavior which will lead to the ego's destruction. This may occur either from the psychological point of view, in which the feelings or related behavior are interpreted as being in direct contradiction with his identified concept of self, and, therefore, is a threat to its existence; or from the physical point of view, in which he is frightened that the acting-out of those feelings will bring a returned retribution from others that could be a threat to the ego's existence, as would be especially true, for example, in the case of repressed destructive or sexual feelings. However, in fact, *self-communion with repressed feelings actually removes the cause or need for acting-out rather than facilitates acting-out*. The repressed feelings constantly push for expression into conscious awareness, not behavior, because they are obeying the basic principle of consciousness, which is to restore itself to its natural condition of being a unitary whole by making conscious all that is itself [i.e., consciousness naturally seeks to reunify itself by making conscious, and, thereby, reintegrating, all experiential states that have previously been repressed into the subconscious]. Therefore, those feelings are not really pushing for acting-out or discharge through expression into behavior, but, rather, they are pushing only for reintegration and complete drainage of their repressed energy which occurs once those feelings are fully acknowledged into consciousness as self, instead of being kept outside and treated as not-self, and are permitted to speak for themselves to completion [without any kind of censorship or interference by one's consciousness].

In other cases, self-communion is resisted because the ego, which is identified with the observer or controller of those painful rejected feelings, equates loss of control of those feelings with total impotence of will, on its part, which is further equated with the extinction of the ego. From another point of view, the patient has a firm conviction that confrontation with those painful experiential realities would be more than his ego would be able to bear, and would overwhelm his ego, and so he fearfully concludes that it would lead to his psychological destruction. This conviction comes about because he has learned that the closer his conscious awareness comes to having full contact with his psychological pain, the more intense is the experience of the pain, and, therefore, he concludes that full contact with the pain would be overwhelming and self-destructive. However, he fails to recognize and understand that proximity is not communion. Being with your pain is not the same as being your pain [i.e., being fully, non-dualistically, unified with your pain]. Communion does not exist until there is not the slightest trace left of duality and separation between the pain and its observer. As ironical and paradoxical as it sounds, *communion with pain does not bring greater pain, but actually yields liberation, and joy.* In fact, consciousness in communion with anything, not just with psychological pain, of course, yields peace, and joy.

It should be clear from this discussion that consciousness can never really *be* anything personal, it can only *know* the personal. It can only label and dualistically know or experience that particular label that it has applied to itself from a standpoint outside of it, as its relative and interdependent experiencer [or interpreter]. The instant that consciousness tries to *be* anything *personal*, by merging the observer or experiencer into a state of unity, and, thereby, standing in identity with that personal experiential reality, one finds that the personal immediately dissolves, leaving consciousness in its natural Transpersonal condition, which is intrinsically Peace-Love-Joy. Therefore, all psychological pain is an illusion. The only Self that is real, and the only Reality that consciousness can ever *be,* is Peace-Love-Joy. Whatever consciousness knows of itself is never real, and never Itself, but is only that labeled objectification or conceptual illusion which is only apparently outside of itself. Thus, consciousness can only be what is real, and can only know of itself what is unreal. The real can never become the unreal, and, therefore, Consciousness is [intrinsically being] the Transpersonal [Reality] already, and so It is nothing that can be pursued, for It is not something which is outside of oneself, but, rather, One is That already, and one can realize That directly when all pursuing or living in Becoming ends.

Thus, through the process of self-communion, as each rejected painful experiential reality creatively and spontaneously rises to consciousness and is totally accepted, embraced in non-duality, reunified, and transcended—then in that moment is consciousness Silence. Continuing in this way until all of the rejected painful experiential realities are retrieved and reunified, and consciousness is no longer identified as being any relative or personalizing label, then consciousness is quiet and still to its depths and is once again in the natural condition of being a perfect Unitary Whole as the Silence and Light of pure Consciousness. Then out of that Silence of Consciousness occurs what is referred to as Transpersonal Awakening, which has also been called by other names, such as Self-Realization, Cosmic Consciousness, Kingdom of Heaven, Liberation, Enlightenment, Nirvana, etc. This is the only true fulfillment for consciousness. That is Home.

In essence, transpersonal psychotherapy is just a sophisticated form of the scriptural [sic] declarations, "to thine own self be true" [William Shakespeare, *Hamlet*, Act 1, Scene 3], or "see the truth and the truth will set you free" [John 8:32: "You will know the truth, and the truth will set you free"]. For in being the moment-to-moment [experiential] truth that arises in consciousness, and nothing else but that, then consciousness is in unity, and is liberated from the dualistic ego.

If you have the direct realization that you are only one self, and not two, and that self is only what is, or that which is your moment to moment [experiential] truth that arises in consciousness, then you *are on your "way"* Home. Thus, to realize non-duality is to realize that you and the universe are one, because there is no universe until your awareness of some element of it arises in consciousness. At that moment, you and that element of the universe are one because you are one or in unity with whatever arises in consciousness from moment to moment. Therefore, for example, if this moment, your consciousness is confronted with a barking dog, and you do not have the immediate realization that you and the barking dog are one, then you will realize that you and the universe are one, and the self-discovered realization will eventually occur that you are the all, and, also, the One Consciousness which underlies the all. Finally will come the realization that there is only the One, and being in perfect Unity with That, you are Home. ". . . and he who loses his way a thousand times shall have a Home-coming."[3]

References from the Original Article

1. Assagioli, R. *Psychosynthesis: A Manual of Principles and Techniques*. New York: Hobbs, Dorman, & Co., Inc., 1965.
2. Hammer, Max. "Quiet Mind Therapy." *Voices* (Spring 1971): 52-56.
3. Hammer, Max. "A Therapy for Loneliness." *Voices* (Spring 1972): 24-29.
4. Hammer, Max. "Misconceptions of Transpersonal Psychotherapy: A Reply to Ellis." *Voices* (Fall 1972): 21-26.
5. Maslow, A. "Theory Z." *Journal of Transpersonal Psychology* (Fall 1969): 31-48.
6. Watts, A. *Psychotherapy East and West*. New York: Pantheon Books, 1961.

Comments on "The Essence of Personal and Transpersonal Psychotherapy"

By Barry Hammer

My late father, Max Hammer, changed some of his views with regard to the true nature of the self, reality, and therapeutic healing of psychological pain, after he published the preceding article, "The Essence of Personal and Transpersonal Psychotherapy." He later came to view the reality of consciousness, and the true self, as a relational reality, involving loving, unselfishly caring interactions between the distinctive particularity of oneself, as knower, and the distinctive particularity of other individuals and phenomena in the world, as related and not dualistically separated objects of knowledge. This was a marked departure from the views presented in the preceding article, of the reality of consciousness basically being a monistic undifferentiated unity, devoid of diversity, objectivity, and individual particularity. In the article, my father describes diversity as an illusory modification of undifferentiated, objectless, pure consciousness, "One basic aspect of Transpersonal Awakening is the direct realization that the 'all' of diversity is not a reality, as such, but has only apparent and illusional existence, and is underlied, as its essential substance, by the One Reality which is the Unity of pure Consciousness . . . Therefore, all objects are essentially only objectifications of, and reducible to, pure consciousness, the one and only reality . . . Therefore, all objectivity and diversity is realized as being merely a thought-form" (203). However, Max Hammer later came to distinguish the ego as a false sense of individuality, i.e., a presumptive, illusory, sense of detached, recoiled, continuously self-aware individuality, involving a conceptually defined sense of exclusive identity, with an extreme sense of dualistic separation from other individuals and the objective world, and a continuous inner monologue, which he called the "personal life story daydream fantasy," in contrast to our real individuality and its genuine natural particularity, differentiation, or personal qualities, consisting of our intrinsic individual natural inclinations, temperament, mannerisms, interests, potentials, talents, skills, preferences, aspirations, values, attitudes, and life experience, developing optimally through heartfelt, loving, deeply invested, relational encounters with other individuals, phenomena, and activities in the world. This is a distinction between the ego as a false sense of individuality derived from presumptive conceptual self-interpretations, in contrast to the real individuality as an experiential sense of particularity, consisting of openness to the full range of our spontaneously arising reactions to inner and outer experiences. In his later reflections, verbal comments, and written notes, Max Hammer came to view psychological health, well-being, and freedom from unnecessary psychological pain, as involving developing individual creative potentials, productive capabilities, natural inclinations, and other distinctive, constructive, predispositions, to the fullest possible extent, while letting go of identification with conceptual self-definitions, as an illusory, preconceived, sense of individuality, involving a conceptually presumed, rather than experientially authentic, sense of overly extreme differentiation from other individuals, as a self-defined exclusive sense of identity.

Those later discussions and written notes dictated to me by Max Hammer took the position that the basis of psychological health involves recognition of the true nature of reality as a relational principle of distinctive particularity of individual life forms, all sharing the same universal or collective consciousness or conscious-love-life-energy substance, like individual cells and organs abiding within the same seamless whole human body. This principle of unity-in-diversity, or diversity-in-unity, brings to mind the Latin phrase, *"E Pluribus Unum"* ("In the many, one"), the African term *Ubuntu* (or fellow feeling), the German concept *Gemeinschaftsgefühl* (fellow feeling, or "social interest," as described in the psychological writings of Alfred Adler)[4], as well as I Corinthians 12:12: "The body is a unit, although it is made up of many parts, and although its parts are many, they form one body." That natural, intrinsic relatedness of being makes non-dualistic, harmonious, loving, empathic, communion between individuals possible, *without* effacing their distinctive individual particularity within a greater monistic undifferentiated unity of pure consciousness, like the distinctive particularity of a drop or molecule of water being lost when it falls into a larger body of water, such as a river, lake, or ocean.

Another significant clarification that should be pointed out is that, whereas in "The Essence of Personal and Transpersonal Psychotherapy" Max Hammer presented the view that, "In reality, there is no other self to whom the particular feeling is happening. There is only the feeling itself" (207); in later spoken remarks and typed notes, he suggested that people should not personally identify with negative or disturbed feelings, such as non-constructive anger or destructive hostility, so as to not be tempted to inappropriately, impulsively act it out, but instead be aware of the difference between the intrinsic peace-love-joy of their permanent being and temporary feelings that may occasionally cover over and thereby prevent the conscious experience of the true nature of their permanent being, just as the temporary arising of dark clouds and storms do not change the nature of the permanent pure clear sky, sun, and sunshine.

The following article is reprinted with permission from *Voices: The Art and Science of Psychotherapy.*

"Transpersonal Being: The Unchangeable Core"

Consciousness, as is the case with all manifest realities, is ever-functioning at two levels simultaneously, as both *form*, and also as its underlying *background*, substance, or essence.

At the level of form, consciousness is personal or egoistic; which means that it is dominated by a persona or self-concept composed of a sum of traits, and it is this personal entity self which attempts to become or establish itself as being *absolutely* something rather than the *relative* something that it actually is, because all labels and traits are only relative in nature, and never absolute. By this means, the conceptual personal self hopes that it will establish itself as the unchanging or permanent core or center of consciousness. It is this process to which the term "living in becoming" has been applied, and because of its extensiveness, [it] may be characterized as the "Universal Pathology."

At the level of substance, essence, or background, Consciousness is pure or unobjectified as personal thought or feeling; it is pure Subjectivity. In that condition, it is Transpersonal or pure Being, which is the *true* Core of every person's being, in the same way that ocean water is the transcending or transpersonal substance or background reality underlying the constantly changing individual form of every wave, bubble, ripple, within it. Because water can exist independent of the wave, but the wave cannot exist independent of water, then [therefore] the water as background substance is the more essential reality than the form appearing out of it, which has only apparent or temporary reality. Whatever is dependent upon something else for its existence cannot be considered as being essentially real, but is only appearance, or Reality appearing-as, just as wave and bubble are only water appearing-as. It is the Transpersonal [Being], as pure Consciousness, which is the Reality background or substance of which one's personal thoughts and feelings are composed. Thus, the Transpersonal is not an opposite of the personal, or Being an opposite of becoming, but, rather, the former is the true Reality and background substance underlying the appearance of the former.

That which is ever-changing or becoming cannot be considered to be one's real core because it is always in the process of becoming something else. That which changes always changes, and that which is changeless remains changeless. That which changes or is becoming is in the realm of time, space, and causality, each of which is dependent upon thought for its existence; but that which is changeless is in the realm of Being, the realm of the timeless-spaceless or Eternal Now. Only what is changeless really is, and what really is always is. Only the Now really is, and the Now never ceases to be the Now. What is always is, but that is not true for what seems or appears to be. What really is does not become what is not. Life never becomes death. Only that which seems or appears to be becomes that which no longer appears to be. Thus, it is only the form, the manifest, that changes, and constantly changes, but the changeless Transpersonal background is unmanifest [undifferentiated, and indistinct], and so Transpersonal Consciousness comes to be equated with a void, and, therefore, the loss of sense of the personal entity self, or the end of the objectification of consciousness becomes equated with psychological death. In reality, the Transpersonal Consciousness is pure Being or pure Life Itself.

Thus, as is true with the ocean water forms of waves and bubbles, constant change or becoming is intrinsic at the level of form. Here nothing remains the same in spite of the label that we may apply to a particular form in the attempt to make to appear to be static, permanent, and separate that which is truly ever in omnidynamic flux; and so, because individuality of consciousness or personality is at the level of ever-changing form, one cannot [realistically] speak of an unchanging core at that level. Nevertheless, everyone does attempt to validate the illusion that the conceptual or object self is an unchanging, permanent self. But, since the concept of self, composed of labels or traits, basically is relative rather than absolute in nature, at this level, one is constantly in movement or change between the two relative opposites, since every trait has an opposite intrinsic within it; e.g., potent-impotent, secure-insecure, worth-worthless, elated-depressed, intelligent-ignorant, attractive-unattractive. In addition to a trait being relative to its relative opposite, it is also relative to whom or what standard of comparison one relates oneself to. Thus, for example, if I use an intellectually impaired person, of very low IQ, as the standard of comparison in regard to my trait of intelligence, I will consider myself to be relatively more intelligent, and may even label myself as being a genius; but if I go to the other extreme, and use Albert Einstein as the standard for comparison, then I would consider myself to be considerably more ignorant in general than he, and therefore, label myself as stupid or an idiot. No one can assume any trait without some kind of standard of comparison. Finally, every trait is dependent upon subjective judgment and interpretation; therefore, the same reality that you label as tenderness, I might label as weakness; what you might call inner peace, I might call boredom; what you call assertiveness, I might call aggressiveness or viciousness; what you call trusting, I might call gullibility; what you call independence, I might call fear of commitment. Therefore, no one can ever [realistically] stand as being anything [as a conceptual self-definition that one holds to be exclusively, always, permanently, or totally true of oneself, at all times, and under all circumstances].

The self-concept or personal entity self, being relative in nature, is constantly devoted to becoming or making absolutely protected, affirmed, and enhanced that set of relative traits with which it is identified. Because the relative can never become the absolute, that task is a hopeless one; therefore, frustration, tension, hostility, and anxiety are constant companions of one who lives in becoming. That which is formal [existing at the level of surface form, rather than the deeper substance and essence levels of reality], objective, or personal always operates within the realm of becoming, which is a condition of constant change, or omnidynamic flux, and so the realm of form or personality can have no real core, no real unchanging being, at that level. Its true Core is at the level beyond, at its transcendent or Transpersonal level, the level of essential or pure Consciousness, which is one with uncreated, uncompounded, unconditioned Being; Consciousness as an unlabeled, unfragmented, indivisible unitary whole. Therefore, the true Core of one's being can only be at the Transpersonal level, or level of Being, and never at the personal level or level of becoming.

Thus, one's real Core is Transpersonal Being, and because, in reality, one is That already (albeit unrealized in most), it is meaningless to talk about how close one can get to that Core. Who [else] is it that is to get close? The personal self is basically an illusion anyway. The question would be the same as asking how close the wave can get to the water. The personal self can operate only at the personal level of consciousness, or the realm of becoming, and so can never really get close to, or know, the Transpersonal, which is the realm of Being. The one cannot know the other. When one stands as the Transpersonal, there is no personal self-awareness present. One cannot get close to that Transpersonal Core in progressive degrees, because Being cannot be an object of becoming. Becoming never becomes Being. Becoming implies time, and Being is not in time, but in the timeless Now. One does not get from time to timelessness over a span of time.

Looked at from another point of view, becoming cannot become Being because it is only the fragment, never the whole that is becoming, because the whole already is what the fragment is trying to become. The personal self, which is only a fragment arising out of the whole of consciousness, cannot become the whole, because the true whole of consciousness is without any fragments, but, rather, is an indivisible or unfragmented unitary whole rather than a [composite] whole which is the sum of fragments. An analogy for becoming trying to become Being would be like an individual wave trying to become the whole ocean of water, which in its non-personal dimension, it is already but can realize that only when it surrenders its stand or identification with that limited definition of self. The personal self, who is fragmentary, limited, and relative in nature, tries to expand itself to become the unlimited and absolute Self, which is the whole of consciousness, which is not possible because the finite cannot incorporate the Infinite within its own limited boundaries. What is possible is to realize one's true wholeness by disidentifying from the illusory [self-divisive, self-fragmenting] boundaries imposed by self-defining labels. Then one stands in realization of the wholeness which one has always truly been, [naturally, intrinsically], and which is one's true Core.

Those who live in becoming continue to live in becoming, come to value it, and fear its loss, because they come to associate the striving and tension of becoming with a sense of vitality, aliveness, or sensation of life itself; therefore, they come to interpret the end of the striving, desiring, and goal-setting of becoming as stagnation, which has become synonymous with the death of the personal entity self.

Consciousness can transcend the state of becoming, and live in the state of Being, only when all desire and striving to become something absolutely protected, affirmed, and aggrandized ends. This occurs when consciousness is no longer identified with any personalizing label or trait, and therefore, is no longer in polarity [i.e., no longer selectively, divisively, taking sides between various pairs of desired/pursued and rejected/avoided opposite objects of knowledge, as opposite extreme poles of experience and conceptual self-definition], but, rather, is centered at the point of neutrality between all pairs of relative opposites, which is transcendent of all points along any such continuum, and, also, when consciousness is no longer in duality. Consciousness is in duality [or unnaturally self-divided] when it takes its stand as being two interdependent fragments, both the self which is subject, and the self which is the interdependent object [i.e., the interdependent object of knowledge, or the objectified sense of self-knowledge, of the subjective self as knower, as conscious awareness]; such as, the I and the me, the knower and the known, the observer and the observed, the experiencer and the experienced, the judge [judger] and the judged, the controller and the controlled, or the conceptual self and the experiential self. The real transformation of consciousness, which is healing, takes place when duality is surrendered in non-duality, which occurs when one clearly sees that the observer is really one with the observed.

When the dualistic conceptual self, standing as some kind of permanent entity self, is surrendered, so that consciousness stands totally content to be nothing other than the moment to moment experiential reality (e.g., emotions, feelings, desires, needs, impulses, sensations) that spontaneously arises [in a given moment], then consciousness is no longer in duality [i.e., in an unnatural state of self-division and consequent psychopathological self-conflict between various polar opposite forms of conceptual self-definition and experiential self-knowledge, as the basic underlying source of psychological pain], which is the state of becoming, [or striving to become something other than what one is currently being], but, rather is in non-duality [or natural self-unification of one's pure conscious awareness with one's actual experiential states], which is the state of Being. Spontaneous consciousness refers to that condition of consciousness that is totally free of any kind of pre-commitment or expectation as to what the content of consciousness should be [or should not be]. There is no purposeful effort to initiate, create, or tell oneself what the topic ought to be for consciousness to consider; rather, one adopts a stance which is a passive receptive waiting for what arises of its own. If nothing arises, then one is content to be [inner] Silence.

In the state of Being or non-dualistic awareness, there is a yielding or a letting-be attitude that exists, so that whatever experiential reality arises spontaneously to conscious awareness is felt to be sufficient [and, therefore, is fully unified with by one's non-reactive, nonjudgmental, pure conscious awareness]. There is no rejection of what is or what arises for the preferred pursuit of what one believes *ought* to be in consciousness. There is no conceptual judgment or interpretation raised in regard to what is, but only a quiet mind, or non-reacting state of consciousness, in which there is the total absorption of attention in the choiceless, non-dualistic, listening to that experiential reality speak for itself to conclusion. In contrast, in the state of becoming, one stands as the dualistic [self-divisive] self-concept, which rejects what is the moment-to-moment [actual] experiential reality, and instead, pursues the absolute ideal of what it feels that it ought to become.

Thus living in becoming is transcended when consciousness is no longer in duality, and consciousness is no longer in duality, when the self-concept, as the dualizing [self-divisive] observer-judge-controller [and censor] of the observed contents of consciousness is absent; and that conceptually reacting and interpreting personal entity self is absent only when one no longer labels, judges good or bad, controls, or has any kind of desires, goals, or objectives in regard to the moment to moment spontaneously arising experiential reality. These are all forms of splitting, separation, distanciation [distancing], [avoidance], or movement away from that [actual] experiential reality, and therefore, create a self-division or duality in consciousness between that experiential reality and the judging or controlling entity which is trying to move away from that experiential reality, which is a state of intrinsic division, conflict [i.e., painful inner self-conflict], and pathology.

Therefore, with the absence of the self-concept entity, one is then in a non-dualistic choiceless condition of letting-be and being one with that spontaneously arising

moment to moment experiential reality, and therefore, one can do nothing but let it speak for itself, and tell its own complete story until totally drained. In that state of Being, or non-dualistic awareness, the creative understanding that liberates consciousness from that painful experiential reality then comes of its own *in a sudden flash.* When the painful feeling has spoken for itself until drained, then the fragmented and encapsulated psychic energy contained within it is totally discharged, which is to say totally integrated and reunited into the whole of consciousness; which is the only [meaningful] transformation of consciousness and criterion of therapeutic integration, healing, [psychological] growth, or liberation, and is the essence of what is called Transpersonal psychotherapy.

Thus, the "Way" of self-healing or whole-ing the mind is through non-dualistic awareness, which is a process of letting-be. Letting-be is not to be confused with the often used notion referred to as self-acceptance. Self-acceptance is really a [disguised] form of self-rejection because it still involves a condition of duality in consciousness, in which the self-concept, standing as the dualistic judge, is still operative, and making the judgment that its judged experiential reality is acceptable; but really meaning that it is to be tolerated. Therefore, what is called self-acceptance is really only a [conditional, superficial] state of self-toleration, which is that dualistic [self-divisive] condition in consciousness in which there is in conscious awareness the co-existence and pretended state of compatibility of two basically contradictory or conflictual [conflicted] fragments of self as judge and the judged. The act of judging is, itself, a form of rejection of what is because it involves moving away from and standing outside of what is, as something else, in the form of some additional judging entity. If what is were truly acceptable, then no judgment of it at all would be necessary, and one would then stand as being no judger or nothing other than what is [actually arising as experience, in the here and now present moment]. Thus, no real healing can take place in consciousness until the judge and duality is surrendered and consciousness is in non-dualistic awareness.

In non-dualistic awareness, consciousness is in a true condition of openness, and so the mind is able to heal or integrate itself because the dualistic self-concept is not present to operate as a judging, censoring, or repressing agent. As a result, all the previously painful or negative experiential realities rejected or repressed from conscious awareness are now free to spontaneously arise to conscious awareness and be fully integrated under the impetus, basic drive, or yearning on the part of consciousness to restore itself to its natural condition of being an indivisible unitary whole. Awareness naturally yearns to flow to its Core or Source as pure Consciousness, as a river naturally flows to the sea, and will do so if one surrenders the inhibiting agent which is the self-concept or personal entity self which attempts to control the free flow of consciousness in order to be protective of itself, by preventing itself from becoming consciously aware of the presence of contradictory fragments within itself, which would threaten its integrity-feeling [feeling of cohesiveness], sense of wholeness, or sense of internal consistency, and, thereby, threaten its sense of [psychological] existence. When that self-concept is surrendered, then there is nothing within consciousness to feel threatened, and then awareness is free to flow to its Source—healing itself along the way by integrating with all its rejected and repressed relative opposites.

Healing the mind is essentially a process of whole-ing the mind—which basically involves the transcending of identification with all polarities and relativities, and resolving them in their Source as pure Being. This is achieved through the process of non-dualistic awareness—by which means, there is the retrieving and integrating of the various repressed painful negative experiential realities, which are the relative opposites of those [positive or desired] traits with which the sense of personal self stands identified, and which would be extremely threatening were they to be fully experienced because they have been labeled and judged in such a way as to connote a sensation of nothingness, and so [they] are repressed and lost to conscious awareness. As each painful or negative experiential reality is retrieved and stands in conscious awareness opposed to its relative opposite trait, with which one is identified, then each is cancelled out because to stand as both relative opposites at the same time is to recognize that one can never be either one. One comes to recognize that one can never [realistically, or exclusively] stand as being any labeled trait or anything personal because all such are relative in nature, and so one then stands as being nothing, a Void that is no real void, but only pure Being, or pure Consciousness, void only of objectivity and the mind movement of becoming. All living in becoming is an attempt, in one form or another, to escape from the experience of the sensation of oneself as a void by trying to affirm its compensatory relative opposite that one is absolutely something.

To illustrate, one may pursue experiential realities related to feelings of worth, potency, or intimacy, each of which provides the sensation experience that one is really something, and are compensatory opposites for experiential realities from which one is trying to escape—which reflects a sense of worthlessness, impotence, abandonment, or vulnerability, each of which is unconsciously equated with an underlying sensation of being a nullity. Therefore, in transpersonal psychotherapy, if a patient reports a great need for intimacy, he is asked to let be that feeling that would arise if this need were not gratified. In other words, the patient, through his need for intimacy, is pursuing that experiential self that he feels that he ought to be—which is his living in becoming instead of living in Being and letting-be what is. If intimacy is what ought to be, then what [actually] is? If a feeling of intimacy, protection, security, or worth is what [presumptively] ought to be my experiential self, then what experiential self am I actually being, this moment, that I am trying to run away from? The patient then may report a feeling of loneliness, abandonment, vulnerability, impotence, or worthlessness, each of which is only a different label for the same underlying painful sensation of feeling oneself to be unaffirmed as a particular self, which is experienced as a threat of extinction of that conceptualized personal entity self. The patient [client] needs to be in a state of non-duality with that painful experiential reality, equated with his being a[n inner] void—which means that he must not label it, judge it as being good or bad, try to control it, or have any desire or goal in regard to it; but rather, with a non-reacting, non-interpreting, non-concept arousing, quiet mind, he must just let the feeling be, and let it speak for itself to conclusion. Ultimately, there will arise spontaneously to the patient the realization that being nothing is not a condition of nullity, but only the Silence of pure Being.

When one comes finally to understand the inter-relationship between every thought of becoming, and its underlying desire, and the feeling of deficiency underlying that [compensatory] desire, which is related to being [experiencing oneself as] a[n inner] void, then all objectivity is resolved in its Source, and one stands as being nothing but pure Being, liberated from all limitations imposed upon consciousness through fragmenting definitions of self. Then all mind movement ends, and consciousness is Silence to its depths, and is then in its natural condition of being a Perfect Non-Duality, or unlabeled, indivisible unitary whole. Out of that Silence of pure Consciousness, which is a brilliant Light, in an intuitive flash, Transpersonal Awakening or Fulfillment Realization occurs.

Essentially, Transpersonal Awakening involves the direct realization that one's Real Self is Eternal or Transpersonal Being, the true Core. The direct realization of that Transpersonal Self which is pure Consciousness-Existence is intrinsic Fulfillment because it is one with absolute Peace-Joy-Love, which may be subsumed under the one unifying label of Bliss.* Bliss Consciousness is Fulfillment Realization because It is the object of all desire, and all psychological desire is only for a sense of peace, joy, or love, in one form or another. Therefore, it is the end of all desire, which is also the end of all sense of deficiency from which desire arises. Desire reflects the attempt to become whole, which prevents the direct realization that one is already [intrinsically being] whole. Desire is the affirmation of the conviction of one's deficiency. Desire assumes deficiency, and therefore, one cannot ever realize that one is [inherently being] Fulfillment already until all desire and becoming subsides. Free from all sense of deficiency and [compensatory] desire, Consciousness is then truly Perfection, which is Fulfillment; not the perfection that is some relatively positive conceptual trait become absolute, which is not possible anyway, but rather, the Perfection [or the intrinsic flawless wholeness] of Consciousness, which is the absence of all conceptual ideals of self and strivings of becoming—which is the Perfection of Consciousness in its true fullness, or natural condition of being an unlabeled, indivisible unitary whole, a perfect Non-Duality. Only That is the true unchangeable Core.

---

*The various labels used here to refer to the nature of Transpersonal Being are not meant to evoke anything conceptual in the reader's mind, but rather, on the contrary, are meant to convey the impossibility of conceptualizing that Perfect Non-Dualistic Void. In truth, nothing at all can be said about that Reality because all labeled things have their relative opposite, whereas It is beyond definition and relativity. At best, words can only serve as pointers to that Truth, but the concept of the Truth is not to be confused with the Truth Itself, just like a finger pointing to the sun is not the sun [itself] nor is it the means of arriving at the sun.

Comments on "Transpersonal Being:
The Unchangeable Core"

By Barry Hammer

After "The Unchangeable Core" article was published, Max Hammer came to distinguish between a basically unreal kind of becoming, as a sense of inner deficiency striving to conditionally achieve or become a greater sense of proficiency, well-being, or self-enhancement, in some way, in contradistinction to "real becoming" involving a dynamic process of deeply invested attunement to the flow of changing experience in the here and now, as well as genuine experiential self-enhancement through a dynamic process of actualizing the limitless, never-ending, unfolding, seed-like potentials of one's permanent being. Although our permanent being is an essentially unchanging, unalterable, unconditional, intrinsic wholeness, and fulfillment of pure conscious awareness in self-realization as the greater wholeness of peace-love-joy, or bliss, which does not conditionally become a contrary, deficient nature, it does become the spontaneously unfolding experience and expression of the limitless variety of dynamically changing nuances, indivisible whole spectrum, or "many splendors" that permanent being nature can spontaneously take from moment to moment. Max Hammer sometimes used the metaphorical analogy of a visible fruit-bearing tree or flower growing or unfolding from its invisible, immobile, underground roots to represent the process by which our essentially changeless, permanent being nature unfolds, actualizes, manifests, or develops its limitless creative potentials, as well as expressing our other natural inclinations, interests, skills, and preferences, which enable us to become dynamically enhanced in a real, experiential way, by developing higher levels of creative fruition or greater levels of enhanced functioning without thereby engaging in a conceptually presumed, illusory sense of becoming or striving to overcome some purportedly deficient nature other than our intrinsic, unalterable, unconditional, wholeness of being as peace-love-joy.

According to Max Hammer's later views, optimal psychological health, inner peace, and well-being involve being open to a natural, intrinsic, holistic integration between our essentially changeless, permanent being, as an inherent, unconditional, sense of wholeness and fulfillment, indivisibly united to our dynamically changing becoming nature, such as the flow of spontaneously arising experience; responsive, creative, self-expression; and related insightful self-discovery, not mediated by a conceptually presumed, illusory sense of deficiency conditionally striving to become enhanced in some way. The holistic unity of permanent being united to real becoming, as a process of proficiency rather than deficiency, was also metaphorically depicted by Max Hammer through the analogy of two distinct sides of the same indivisible whole coin, both sharing the same unitary metallic substance, representing the indivisible, holistic, integral nature of consciousness, life energy, or reality intelligence. He also used the metaphorical analogy of traveling from place to place in a mobile home to depict the basis of optimal psychological health and fulfillment as involving the ability to feel unconditionally secure in our intrinsically whole, permanent being nature, but bringing that unalterably relaxed, secure, joyful nature into the changing hustle and bustle of everyday life in the world. In contrast, dualistically resting in changeless, permanent being apart from the dynamically changing flow of real becoming experience and responsive self-expression is not true wholeness, optimal psychological health, and fulfillment, but is basically static, overly restrictive, and deadening. True wholeness and fulfillment also cannot be found in the process of functioning exclusively in the stressful, disturbing, sometimes chaotic, turmoil of becoming or continuously changing circumstances, divorced from the calming influence of changeless, permanent being. Only functioning consistently with the reality of our timeless, changeless, permanent being indivisibly united with and unfolding as our dynamically changing, evolving, progressively developing, becoming nature, or our responsive life in the world, provides the experience of true wholeness and optimal psychological well-being. According to Max Hammer, optimal fulfillment, psychological health, creative insight, and productive functioning come from accepting the natural holistic integration of our changeless, permanent being and our spontaneously ever-changing, becoming nature, which draws its creative, productive, and transformational potentials from our changeless permanent being, metaphorically similar to a plant above ground deriving sustenance and stability from its roots which are hidden below ground.

Max Hammer's later view was that the ability to recognize and function consistently with the indivisible wholeness of reality intelligence as changeless permanent being, paradoxically, indivisibly united to continuously changing real becoming, is the only true basis of enduring psychological health, happiness, and harmonious living. He recognized that developmental growth of creative self-understanding involves the process of being continuously open to discovering new insights, creative potentials, and transformational breakthroughs coming from staying in communion with the dynamic flow of actual experience and spontaneously arising responsive self-expression, in the present moment, while also remaining continuously rooted in the intrinsic, unconditional, indivisible wholeness, relaxed peace, contentment, and fulfillment of our basically changeless, permanent being nature.

Openness to the core integrity level of our own being, as the juncture or holistic integrating nexus point of our whole individuality, where being-becoming and all other relative polar aspects of our being are indivisibly united together, that core integrity level of our holistic being-becoming individuality, dynamically unfolding through the "still small voice" of intuition, and also arising from our deeply invested, heartfelt, caring, loving, responsive, empathic communion with the relational flow of inner and outer experience, in the here and now, that is most essentially the supreme inner creative energy power source within us, from which many creative insights and productive, transformational, innovative break-throughs arise, like an underground reservoir from which limitless waters of life unceasingly flow, or the underlying root level of our unchanging permanent being united to our unfolding real becoming development in the world, functioning like a vast repository of hidden, seed-like, archetypal patterns or blueprints from which limitless new possibilities can be developed and explicated in more tangible form in the world.

Psychotherapists, counselors, life coaches, clergy, spiritual teachers, social workers, and other people in professional or unofficial "helping" or mentoring roles would do well to not impose their own views as a process of indoctrination, but to help clients more clearly discover what is already abiding within them, as their own natural individual and relational potentials, abilities, talents, inclinations, aspirations, insights, values, and other inner resources. This involves mentors functioning as empathic, clear reflecting "mirrors" and warmly caring elicitors in a nondirective, alertly attentive, clarifying way, thereby helping their clients, friends, or others they are advising to discover and develop their own inner source of authenticity, creative insight, transformational development, and energy-power. Such a caring, nondirective mentor encourages clients to tune into the unfolding experiential truth of themselves, so that they may learn and grow transformed from discovering or uncovering their own real inner voice, their core integrity, the unfolding unmarked "winding trail," "song," "dance," and "story" of their own energy of heart, soul, mind, and body. Sometimes this process may involve the therapist, counselor, or mentor alerting clients when they seem to be wandering away from the actual experiential truth of themselves, by pursuing and being sidetracked by some kind of presumptive egoistic ideal that does not seem to "ring true" or apparently lacks a clear vibratory energy tone of authenticity, wholehearted conviction, sincerity, integrity, and true self-responsibility or accountability.

The following article is reprinted with permission from
Voices: The Art and Science of Psychotherapy.

"Misconceptions of Transpersonal Psychotherapy: A Reply to Ellis"

I appreciate the invitation to comment on the article by Ellis. I feel his is an important article and worthy of publication, for it raises many of the questions and concerns, as well as illustrates many of the misconceptions, that many readers hold in regard to transpersonal psychotherapy. In the very limited space allotted me for this reply, I will not be able to respond to all of the issues he raises; but perhaps through the use of several analogies, I may be able to clarify those issues which have concerned many other readers with whom I have had contact. Some other issues that I cannot cover here have been dealt with in my article, "A Therapy for Loneliness"* (*Voices*, Vol. 8, No. 1, Spring 1972, 24-29). Still others are clarified in another paper, "The Essence of [Personal and] Transpersonal Psychotherapy." (*Psychotherapy: Theory, Research, and Practice*, Vol. 11, No. 3, Fall 1974, 202-210). In the main, however, most issues can be resolved only by the reader himself going through the process of transpersonal psychotherapy.

The issue of the existence of the Transpersonal Self is not really a debatable one because there cannot be a personal consciousness without a Transpersonal Consciousness any more than form can exist without substance. Can there be a wave without water, or a candle without wax? It would be tantamount to saying that various forms of thought and feeling could exist without the presence of their substance or background, consciousness. So there is nothing magical about the Transpersonal, as Ellis insists there is, because, quite naturally, no form can exist without being supported by its more essential background. What would be truly magical is if Ellis's intimation were true; that the personal ego [or the conceptually defined, delimited, objectified, sense of separate identity] could exist separate and apart from the Transpersonal [reality of objectless pure consciousness] which comprises it, and is its most essential reality. As every psychologist knows, there cannot be a foreground without a background to support that form. So all form can be clearly understood to be nothing more than the superimposition of appearance upon the more essential reality of its background or essence. The Transpersonal is nothing more than the background, support, or essence (which is pure consciousness) *out of which* arises those personalizing objectifications in the form of what we call thoughts, feelings, desires, sensations. So Transpersonal *psychology* asks the fundamental question: What is the source, essence, or supporting background of one's personal consciousness?" Transpersonal *psychotherapy* asks: "What is the most expeditious means of helping the limited personal consciousness awaken to its most essential and unlimited nature? *The basic challenge for Transpersonal psychotherapy is how to reduce or merge all of the objectifications [objects of knowledge] of consciousness [the knower] back into the background and source from which they all arise, so that there can be an awakening to that Reality.* Just as it is difficult to see the water for the wave, or the wood for the tree, or the pure, [clear], white movie screen for the superimposed images projected upon it, so, too, is the Transpersonal Consciousness clouded from awareness as a function of objects of personal consciousness which are superimposed upon it. Ignorance of the awareness of the Absolute background of pure Consciousness is not proof of its non-existence. The declaration, "I don't see God or anything Transpersonal anywhere," is very similar to the analogy of the ocean community of waves, ripples, bubbles, foam, talking to each other and affirming each other's personal existence, and stating that they have heard some talk about their being some more essential reality than their own limited entities called Water. But as one such wave was heard to say, "It must all be nonsense, because wherever I look, all I see is us waves, bubbles, ripples, and foam. I don't see any water anywhere." It is ironical that the consciousness that asserts that pure consciousness is not to be found anywhere, and that all that exists is only our own individual thoughts and feelings, is, itself, the essential Consciousness that is being denied existence.

Ellis wonders whether Transpersonal psychotherapy might not end up dehumanizing man. Man is not fully humanized until he is fully himself. To be acquainted and identified only with his more superficial personal consciousness is his true de-humanization, and origin of his psychopathology, for man is not truly human until he has awakened to the totality, fullness, and depth of what he is as Consciousness—which requires that he awaken to the Transpersonal. Just being that part which is one's personal or egoistic manifestations is not sufficient for human consciousness. There is an enormous hunger for it to be awakened in its entirety and limitlessness, and nothing but full Enlightenment and Liberation will do. The defeat or denial of this most basic yearning of consciousness is the true origin and basis for all psychopathology. In the same way as the wave awakens to the realization that it is both wave and water, so too when Jesus [metaphorically] asserts, "I am the Father and the Son" [John 14:11. "Believe me when I say that I am in the Father, and the Father is in me."] He is asserting [for everyone, not just himself], "I, as consciousness, am both the background and its objectifications [i.e., our pure consciousness comprises its knowable objects of knowledge, but is also beyond its objects of knowledge, and should not exclusively identify with them. Our individual pure conscious awareness is intrinsically united to the Divine or Transpersonal Reality, and, therefore, is an inherent wholeness, fulfillment, or bliss]." It is from that stand that he asserts to his listeners, "The Kingdom of God is within thee" [Luke 17:21], and "Seek and ye shall find" [Luke 11:9]. But man still refuses to take up the challenge [of discovering our own Transpersonal or Divine nature by ceasing to exclusively identify with limited objects of knowledge, and by expanding and awakening our consciousness to its true nature by being open to the experiential truth of ourselves and to loving communion with other individuals]. Transpersonal psychotherapy is one attempt to assume that challenge. It should also be noted that man is his most human and real self when he is love, and to be love, man must be his Transpersonal Self and not his egoistic self. What is referred to as "peak experience" is only and always the result of momentary ego transcendence. There is no other natural way to be high.

It is quite understandable that the ego resists the surrender of its identity and glory with all the intensity it can muster, and that, therefore, the Transpersonal is perceived as being a great threat. One can [almost] hear any reader's ego shouting as it is confronted with the possibility of its more basic and real transpersonal nature: "You want to destroy me, but I shall destroy you. I have worked all my life to get, finally, where I'm at, and now you are telling me that my personal life and efforts at my own aggrandizement have been for nothing. I finally am beginning to feel like a somebody, and a somebody of worth. Now you are asking me to throw it all away and accept the fact that I am no better than anyone else. Never!" One cannot say to a child who is dearly attached to his toys that when he is more mature, he won't even miss not having his toys. The child will only assert to the parent that if growing up means no longer loving [and having] his toys, then he would rather not grow up. In the same way is consciousness, in its stand as ego, devoted to its toys—the mind and senses, and the various sensations and experiences that it enjoys. So, too, it resists its own maturity and development, and the surrender of its toys, for it has no understanding or realization of what full maturity can bring. But from its stand as Transcendence, Consciousness feels no sense of deprivation at the loss of its [conceptually defined] personality and of its personalizing sensations and experiences.

For this reason, communication, the sharing of experiences, and making oneself understood to another [individual] who is at a less mature level of consciousness is extremely difficult, if not impossible. But most of all, Transcendence is difficult to communicate because it represents that "state" [or inherent, unmodified, original nature] of Consciousness in which it is Silence. A Consciousness no longer objectifying [or defining] itself in the form of thoughts, feelings, desires, and sensations, is Silence. What words or thoughts can ever describe or take one to Silence? At best, words only can be pointers to that Truth, and some words may be better than others, in this respect, but the word is not to be confused with the Truth or Silence itself. Any word or thought is really mental noise or sensation, which is the antithesis of Silence. A finger pointing to the moon is not the moon, and it's not the journey to or landing on the moon. Each person must make his own trip through his own consciousness by himself, or if he is fortunate with the help of a guide who has himself completed the entire voyage, and whose words can continue to point to the Truth until the journeyer's consciousness lands there itself.

The issue of the resistance by the ego to the loss of its personal identity and the yearning for superiority relates, also, to Ellis' contention that he finds it quite possible to be a personal self without comparing himself to others. However much this may appear to be true, it really cannot possibly be so because any trait with which the ego is identified is never anything enduringly inside the psyche of the individual, but is based only on a momentary judgment, and *arises only out of some relationship*, and as a function of comparison in that relationship. No trait can be held to exist without comparison, because a trait is only a *relative* reality, and not something *absolute*. Thus, whatever [conceptually defined trait] you hold yourself to be is only something that is relatively more or less than someone else in this moment, and also relative to its relative opposite, which one must also be in some moments. For example, at first glance, I may hold myself as being a particular fixed identity such as, kind, intelligent, independent, angry, or evil. But in reality, I cannot say that I am always the same particular trait, because from moment to moment, my response or experiential reality changes as my relationships change; the other person to whom I am necessarily comparing myself is also a changing thing. So, I cannot really label and identify myself as *being* an angry person as though it were some kind of enduring trait, because I am not angry at all times, [and] with all people. I may hold that I *am* anger only as confined to this moment in my relationship to you, regardless of whether you are physically present, or if the relationship exists only in my memory. Compared to you, I feel worthless relative to the particular task in which we are currently engaged, and this makes me angry. However, at other moments in my relationship to you, my experiential reality may be one of warm and tender feelings, and no anger at all. Therefore, Ellis cannot legitimately conclude that it is possible to be some trait without making comparisons [with other individuals], nor is it possible to really hold that one is any trait at all, because all traits are only relative realities, and not absolutes, and, therefore, one is always its relative opposite as well, and, therefore, one is really neither. Therefore, one is, in essence, really never anything other than one's transpersonal nature [as indefinable, undifferentiated, objectless pure consciousness].

As long as one is devoted to the egoistic and irrational goal of absolutely affirming one's identity, love is not possible. The attempt to establish that one is a particular thing or identity demands continuous affirmation of that identity, which requires that one be constantly in a state of comparison, competition, and one-upsmanship with others. This produces a sense of combat, hostility, conflict, and separateness, which makes love or the establishment of a communion relationship impossible. All of life is perceived as being a chronic set of hurdles to be overcome. That is essentially what living in the egoistic state of "Becoming" feels like. Love, on the other hand, exists only in the state of "Being," which is that state of consciousness when it is contented to be in full contact or communion with what is, and not involved in the pursuit of the imaginary goals of what [presumptively] ought-to-be. For a particular identity to be affirmed, it must be able to apply its influence to produce an effect consistent with and affirming of its identity; whereas love demands a surrendering of that sense of identity, will, and all aspects of self-awareness which keep one feeling distinctive and separate from the other, so as to produce the full contact of communion. Love is a surrendering of the subject-object duality, and, therefore, it is not something that can be objectified, experienced, or enjoyed, which is in contradiction to what Ellis implies. Whatever is being *experienced,* as love is not love, but only some feeling of ego-enhancement.

In regard to the Transpersonal experience of being one with the universe, Ellis also reflects a misunderstanding when he asserts that he does not want to be one with the universe if it means that he has to be a tree, or his [own] excretions. Being one with the universe means being the *universe*, or the universal, not the particular or personal objects manifested out of it. The wave in communion with the bubble does not become the bubble, but, rather, loses its individual identity and becomes one with the universe which underlies both the wave and bubble, which is its essence as water. To say that I am one with the universe, therefore, is not to say that I become [one with] each particular object of the universe, but, rather, I become the background of all the manifested forms of the universe, which is to become one with the universe itself.

Another major misunderstanding relates to the transcendence of the ego. Transpersonal psychotherapy is concerned not with the *permanent* destruction of the ego, but, rather, with the transcendence by consciousness of its *identification* with the ego. In some ways, it is like the adult who has transcended his identification with his child self, even though the child in him may be activated from time to time. Transcendence of the [exclusive] identification with the ego just means that consciousness has transcended or gone beyond its false identifications with various aspects of the body, senses, and mind, which previously made consciousness feel itself to be personally separate and distinct. When transcendent, consciousness yields the ego's drives for self-enhancement, self-protection, and self-affirmation; it recognizes itself to be fundamentally, just *Being*; that pure and most subjective Subject which is of the nature of pure Consciousness, the essence and background of all individual personalities. As soon as consciousness knows its depths and "knows" its true essential transpersonal nature, then the ego is recognized as being only an illusional and apparent identity, like a dream or image in a mirror, and then consciousness wears its ego as though it were a [disposable] suit of clothes. One never confuses the suit of clothes with the real being behind it. The ego can certainly sometimes serve a relatively "useful" function, especially at those times when verbal communication and physical self-preservation are necessary. The body and senses do, at times, make for a sense of physical boundaries, or a physical ego, but after Transpersonal Awakening, there is no longer a sense of being a bounded psychological entity. Consciousness no longer feels itself bounded, separate, or divided. During the Transpersonal Awakening, consciousness recognizes that the world of objects is nothing more than the result of the objectification of pure Consciousness as that Light of pure Consciousness passes through the prism of mind and senses, just as a world of various colors is created when light is passed through a glass prism. Thus, in a real sense, the mind and senses do not really perceive the world; they *create* the world of objects by superimposing dimensionality onto pure Consciousness in the form of space, time, and causality. In the same way, when the prism of mind and senses are silent or inoperative, then consciousness is no longer objectified and diverse, and It shines in all of Its Self-luminous glory as the Transpersonal "I-principle." Thus, when Consciousness knows Itself to be unlimited and absolute rather than just contained within the mind; knows It shines in Its own glory even when mind, body, and senses are inoperative; knows It is beyond time, space, and causality; then It recognizes that It is deathless because It is beyond the relative opposites of what are referred to as life and death, and is, rather, the basic Reality which underlies both of these superimposed appearances. The awakening of consciousness to its identity with the Transpersonal is not something that the ego can take personal credit for, because in the transpersonal plane, the ego is non-existent, and is clearly recognized as being illusional. So it is not, as Ellis assumes, a matter of Hammer asserting that he is God, but, [rather], that God asserts that He is Hammer, Ellis, and "all the rest"; just as when the wave knows itself to be essentially water, it has seen through the illusion of its own personal identity, and, therefore, it is not wave that takes credit for being water, but it is water that asserts that it is wave, bubble, ripple, foam. As water, it can say, "All forms rise up out of and set in Me, and all are brothers born of the same Father." So, too, is it with Consciousness.

As far as the issue of whether or not Transpersonal or Quiet Mind psychotherapy is scientific or not, one can only say that it may or may not be, depending upon one's definition of the term "scientific." However, this issue is not the most germane for the field of psychotherapy. It seems to be rather irrelevant to the more essential issue of whether it is most expeditiously therapeutic or not. As e. e. cummings* puts it:

"While you and I have lips and voices which are for
kissing
and to sing with
who cares if some one-eyed son of a bitch invents
    an instrument
to measure Spring with."[5]

It is my conviction, and I leave it to the reader to determine its validity for himself, rather than debate the issue from the outside, that the most expeditious process for [psychological unrest] symptom removal and for reaching the Transpersonal is the same. If one learns not to label or make judgments in

regard to his symptoms, but, rather, totally merges the dualistic ego, operating as the observer, into the observed symptom, [then], in that state of unity of consciousness called
living-in-Being (or "letting-be"), there can *be* no symptom.
There can be no more expeditious therapeutic process than
that. All symptoms are caused by the ego contesting [resist-
ing] or trying to run from the experiential reality which consciousness is [being] that moment. When the ego (as subject
or knower of the symptom, which is the object or the known)
is surrendered and merged into the known, then the known
[symptom of psychological inner conflict] also disappears
because the subject and object are mutually interdependent
upon each other for their existence.

Another way to understand why this process is effective is
to recognize that one cannot know what one really is at the
moment one is [being] it, for one is then standing in identity
with it. One can only know or experience what one labels as
being outside or objective to the self as subject. Therefore,
by being one with the symptom or standing in identity [non-
dualistic full unification] with it, then it cannot be known,
and so it is gone. It is like an eye that sees [objects that are
outside of itself], but cannot see itself. The eye can see only
what it is not [being], but cannot see itself. All that it sees
is the seen, which is always outside of the seer, and never is
the seer himself. In the same way, whatever the "I" knows,
is outside itself; whatever it is in identity or unity with, it
cannot know [because objects of knowledge must be dis-
tinguishable from the knower in order to be objectified, and
thereby known, rather than being hidden within the knower];
therefore, all symptoms [of psychological pain or pathology]
are transcended just by being in unity with them instead
of being the dualistic observer who stands outside [of the
symptoms of psychological disturbance]. That observer is
nothing more than the conceptual self, and is nothing real. If
consciousness persists in this self-integrating state of unity,
one day when all that has been [previously] rejected has
been welcomed back home, and then the mind will be totally

quiet. And if consciousness persists in being in unity with that Silence, it will awaken to its own transpersonal nature [which heals all psychological pain and pathology, because the Transpersonal nature is an inherent wholeness, free of all self-conflict, as well as Being an intrinsic unconditional peace, well-being, and fulfillment].

Comments on "Misconceptions of Transpersonal Psychotherapy: A Reply to Ellis"

By Barry Hammer

After this article was published, my father came to view individual particularity as real rather than illusory, consisting, for example, of an individual's distinctive natural mannerisms, potentials, abilities, talents, inclinations, preferences, values, aspirations, and other inner resources inherent to his/her being or life energy force. He came to view every individual as epitomizing a relatively unique, distinctive, archetypal, permanent being pattern, prototype, blueprint, texture, or "grain" of the universal, connective, relational energy field, or the Transpersonal/Spiritual/Divine Reality Intelligence. This view differs from the focus in this and other published articles authored by Max Hammer earlier in his development on the transpersonal reality as transcending and essentially nullifying or at least minimizing, rather than including, and thereby maximizing individual particularity or diversity.

Max Hammer's later view of the individual's intrinsic, natural, real individuality should also be carefully distinguished from the ego's illusory sense of identity, primarily based on presumptive conceptual self-definitions. The ego's conceptually defined sense of identity usually tends to be rather static, rigidly self-confining, narcissistically self-preoccupied, and viewing itself as existentially and experientially unrelated to other individuals, as a divisive principle of exclusivity, whereas the real self or soul is inherently relational, connective, responsive, dynamically developing, and experiential, rather than conceptually defined or presumed and self-isolated in orientation.

My father gradually shifted from viewing the spiritual reality as an undifferentiated monistic unity, exclusive of multiplicity, to viewing it as a relational reality of love that includes diverse individuals and phenomena and connects them to one another. Diversity is naturally joined together in an indivisible web or network of relations by the cohesive relational energy of life as love or loving warmth. The holistic relational energy field, the universal reality intelligence, naturally balances and integrates the predominantly centripetal connective or cohesive force with a more polarizing, diversifying, centrifugal energy force. The centrifugal energy force would likely eventually lead to divisive, antagonistic, chaotic, toxic, disintegration of the individual person, human community [society], and world ecosystem if it were not balanced by the integrating, unifying, harmonizing, centripetal energy force of reality intelligence.

We each glorify the Universal Creative Source Intelligence and other living beings as our natural relations, by developing what is real in ourselves to the fullest possible extent and contributing that to others around us, as well as to the connective relational whole energy field. We each contribute to the never-ending process of the transpersonal or relational reality of love's advancing self-discovery by developing what is truly real, natural, and therefore, genuinely lovable, lovely, and loving in ourselves, as well as by finding, appreciating, and eliciting truly lovable, lovely, and loving qualities in other individuals and phenomena around us. The notion that the spiritual, Divine, or transpersonal reality of life as love has endowed everyone, at least subliminally, if not necessarily fully consciously, with a natural purposive (telic, ontic) urge to glorify, reflect, or contribute to the growing self-exploration and self-discovery of reality by discovering and developing what is real in ourselves, exploring truth, actualizing natural real potentials in ourselves that is inherent to our own being or life energy force, and eliciting what is truly real in others is epitomized, in our view, in the sacred wisdom teachings of many diverse spiritual and religious traditions and ethnic cultures. Examples include scriptural declarations such as, "My word that goes out from my mouth: It will not return to me empty, but will accomplish what I desire, and achieve the purpose for which I sent it" (Isaiah 55:11) and "They will be called oaks [or trees] of righteousness, a planting of the Lord, for the display of His splendor" (Isaiah 61:3, cf. Isaiah 60:21), as well as songs such as "The Battle Hymn of the Republic" ("Glory, glory, hallelujah, His Truth is marching on!") and "To Dream the Impossible Dream."

Excerpts reprinted with permission from *Voices: The Art and Science of Psychotherapy*. Some paragraphs that have already been covered in chapter 1 of this book are omitted from the following reprint of this article.

"Quiet Mind Therapy"

Quiet Mind Therapy (QMT) is a derivative of Eastern forms of meditation and is designed to lead to the elimination of individual [inner] conflicts and more basically, the elimination of the conflict-maker, the ego.* (*The term ego is used in this paper to connote one of several different aspects of the sense of self, e.g., the feeling of being the conscious and permanent subject of all experience; the nucleus and center of consciousness, which organizes, stabilizes, and helps one understand one's experiences; the feeling of being a separate and particular and circumscribed personal entity self; the feeling of being an objectified, imaginal [imaginary, presumptive], conceptualized, "me").

There can be no sense of real peace of mind as long as the ego exists because the ego is synonymous with [inner and outer] conflict. How can the ego ever be really happy when it must rely on anger, fear, cravings, contrast, comparison, competition, opposition, defiance, influence, conflict, tension, and separation for its very existence? For without these, there would be no sense of self [or continuous separate self-awareness and self-definition]. Just reflect for a few moments, and you will clearly see how each of these serves to personalize [define, differentiate] and separate the self. The ego feeds and grows on conflict, for conflict affirms its separateness [from other individuals, as well as reinforcing one's sense of separate self-awareness]. The self is an affirmation of separation [as a continuous sense of separate self-awareness, by the conscious knower, defining itself and distinguishing itself from others through its various reactive conceptual interpretations of itself and others. That separate sense of self-awareness, self-will, and individual distinctiveness, is defined by a sense of differentiation and dualistic psychological distance from others, which is particularly heightened or enhanced by reacting to oneself and others in some kind of oppositional, resistive, conflicting, antagonistic, divisive, contrasting, comparative, or competitive, manner.

That kind of oppositional and interpretive reactivity also functions as the ego's sense of self-knowledge-identity, and inner animation, or sense of psychological aliveness, as a continuous process of conceptual mind-movement. That inner flow of reactive conceptual thought can sometimes function like a continuous inner monologue, which often divorces the knower from making direct contact with the actual experiential truth of oneself and other individuals, in a given moment, by interposing the barrier of a continuously self-aware knower, as a psychological sense of identity, or an overly reactive "I entity."] The self has existence only relative to its distinction from something other, which is experienced as not-self. There is no experience of self without the experience of something else as not-self standing in opposition to the self [as a basis for a differentiating sense of continuous self-awareness and conceptually defined self-knowledge].

Therefore, love, which is union, is not possible for the self. In union, there must be the loss of the sense of self; there cannot be separation [because continuously maintaining separate self-awareness, with the mind frequently recoiled in its own self-absorbed inner monologue, blocks deep investment of one's conscious attention and energies in another individual, as the basis of engaging in empathic communion and good communication with them, and, thereby, being able to contact and understand the actual experience of the other individual, as the basis of feeling closely connected to them, at an experiential and energetic level. As long as the mind is absorbed in excessive inner chatter and egocentric motivations, one cannot empathically "stand in the shoes" of another individual, and understand them from their own frame of reference, as a basis of feeling inwardly closely connected to them, which is what true love or genuine friendship involves]. Because real love is not possible for the self, there is no real happiness, peace, or beauty in life as long as one clings to the sense of self; for is not love the mother [source] of all these offspring?

[Furthermore, as long as one remains highly invested in conceptual self-definitions, as a basis of maintaining egoistic self-awareness, there will be no way to effectively resolve inner conflicts arising between positive ideas of oneself that one seeks to validate about oneself, and negative ideas of oneself that one rejects and seeks to disprove about oneself. That incessant process of inner conflict between the ego's positive and negative ideas of itself can never be conclusively resolved within the ego's intrinsically divisive train of thought, which prevents oneself from experiencing the indivisible wholeness and inner "peace of God that passes all understanding" (Philippians 4:7) that is intrinsic to the Real Self, as an intrinsic wholeness of Being, which one is Being prior to, and after the cessation of, all presumptive, self-divisive self-definitions and self-interpretations. The ego's presumptive conceptual self-definitions can also function as a barrier between one's conscious attention and the actual experiential truth of oneself, further exacerbating inner conflict, whereas the basic goal of psychotherapy is to enable clients to experience inner peace, fulfillment, and contact with what is actually real for themselves].

QMT recognizes that man's basic problem is related to the fact that because he identifies with his ego, he lives in a sense of *duality*—that is, always *outside* of his experience, rather than being *one* with it. He sees himself as the experiencer of his experience, the observer of the observed, the knower of the known, the thinker of the thought, and the doer of that which is done; when, in fact, there is no such real separation. There is [are] only the states of experiencing, observing, knowing, thinking, and doing. Both the subject and the object that produce the state of duality come into apparent existence only after the fact of experiencing, and are basically illusory, but necessary in order for the ego to affirm and enhance itself. Otherwise, the fear would set in that one is basically just a nullity, a void, and this is tantamount to a fear of non-existence, a [psychological] death anxiety. For all of one's conscious life, all of one's thoughts and feelings have repeatedly assumed and confirmed but one affirmation; that is, the existence of the separate self. To surrender the false belief that one is a separate ego is to surrender all that has seemed to constitute one's very existence [as a psychological entity or identity with clearly demarcated self-definitions differentiating oneself from other individuals].

The sense of self, [as separate self-awareness and conceptual self-definition], creates a state of duality not only between itself and the not-self world of [objective] reality, but also serves as the censor and wall of division within itself between the known and the unknown, between consciousness and unconsciousness [such as, by interposing a presumptive "ought to be" as a barrier to letting one's conscious attention make direct, non-interpretively mediated, contact with the actual experiential truth of oneself, in a given moment. *Defining oneself in some preconceived way blocks one's conscious awareness from contacting experiential aspects of oneself that can be found only outside the parameters of such predetermined self-definitions.* That is why authentic self-understanding or insight into the actual experiential truth of oneself is most likely to be achieved when one's conscious attention is not self-absorbed in any kind of predetermined egoistic self-definition and self-divisive inner conflict between approved and disapproved ideas of oneself, which prevents one from being open and sensitively alert to the actual flow of experience, in the here and now moment. This may not necessarily conform to those preconceived conceptual categories and may reveal new insights about oneself beyond the scope of one's previous conscious understanding].

The only way for there to be the true understanding of a [psychological] problem or conflict is when there is an integration of the known and the unknown. The sense of self prevents such integration, and maintains the duality and separation of the known and the unknown. When the sense of self is absent, then duality is eliminated. The thinker and the thought merge into the state of just *thinking*, which is also the state of true integration [or wholeness of conscious awareness, beyond all presumptive distinctions between the thinker, its thoughts, as well as inner and outer phenomena that are being interpreted through those thoughts, or between the actual experience of one's feelings and the reactive, partisan, conceptual interpreter of one's feelings]. This [non-dualistic unity or unmediated direct contact with one's actual feelings and other experiential states] is the *basic therapeutic state*. It is only in this state that true growth [of self-understanding, self-transformation, and therapeutic self-healing of inner conflict] can take place, for growth necessitates integration [because genuine growth, or psychological healing, occurs only when one's conscious attention makes unmediated, non-interpretive, nonjudgmental, non-dualistic, contact with previously rejected or unknown experiential aspects of oneself]. This is the state that may also be referred to as the state of creative understanding* (I'm sure that everyone, at one time or another, has observed in his own life how creative insights come of their own, early in the morning, just after barely awakening, when the sense of self is not yet fully intact) or the state of creative healing, depending upon one's particular interest and emphasis. Healing, understanding, creativity, integration, and growth are all essentially the same [process]. In each instance, there is the absence of the sense of self. With no censor or controller present, then there is no interference with the free-flowing process of thinking [or in-sight-full contact with the actual flow of experience, spontaneously arising in the here and now present moment]. Then, in this state in which there is just thinking, [or just unmediated, un-interpreted, experiencing], without the presence of the thinker; that is, when the observer has become one with the observed, consciousness and unconsciousness become momentarily integrated, and the totality of the problem becomes readily apparent, and the problem, with all of its ramifications, is then free to unravel itself to its resolution [in one's quiet, nonreactive, nonjudgmental, non-interpreting, non-interfering, pure conscious awareness]. Thus, the patient [psychotherapy client] is in the state of Quiet Mind when he comes to recognize that he *is* [actually being], for example, his anger, his fear, his depression, and not just the observer from the outside. Then the basic pathological state of duality is transcended [which enables one's conscious awareness to deeply contact, and thereby, gain significant transformational insights into, previously rejected or unknown aspects of oneself that were incompatible with, or beyond the scope of, the ego's predetermined self-definitions, and, therefore, were, consciously or unconsciously, excluded or selectively blocked by the ego from being recognized and considered by one's conscious attention].

QMT, unlike any other therapeutic approach, deals directly rather than indirectly with the attempt to integrate and unify the mind. Most other approaches attempt to achieve unity for the patient's fragmented psyche through the medium of the relationship with the therapist in what is typically referred to as [the process of] transference. But this process is indirect, and subject to considerable distortion and misinterpretation by both the therapist as well as the patient. This problem is eliminated in QMT because the patient integrates his own mind [by letting go of preconceived self-definitions and self-interpretations that automatically, divisively, exclude aspects of one's actual experiential dynamics that abide beyond the scope of those preconceived ideas of oneself].

QMT is also not to be confused with the process of self-analysis because in QMT there is no analyzer separate from that which is to be analyzed, and acting upon that which is to be analyzed. In QMT, the mind learns the means by which it can liberate itself by itself [by permitting one's actual feelings and other experiential states to freely speak for themselves, rather than speaking for them, in a predetermined, controlling, analytical, interpretive, manner, which prevents those feelings and experiential dynamics from spontaneously and creatively revealing their own insights, or self-understanding, when one's conscious attention has no preset interpretive agenda, but, instead, is open to making unmediated direct contact with previously unknown experiential aspects of oneself. Encouraging clients to let go of restrictive predetermined self-definitions enables them to experience a liberating, expansive, sense of freedom from self-confinement and free flowing contact with previously unknown, unconscious, or rejected, aspects of their experiential being, like being able to breathe freely once the stultifying psychological and social masks, or restrictive personae, of egoistic self-definitions are removed]. The involvement of the therapist is necessary only until the patient learns and understands what is involved in accomplishing this for himself.

Now the basic question arises as to what is the means by which the [separate] sense of self can be eliminated so that the thinker-thought integration can take place, and the mind can come to the truth and understanding of its own conflicts and thereby heal itself? In truth, there is no method, no formula, no system, no technique, no discipline [by which means that can be achieved]. For any such [preconceived] path involves movement in a predetermined direction, and any effort made to direct the stream of consciousness only activates the sense of self as the director and controller of consciousness, [which blocks one's conscious attention from contacting, with alert sensitivity, and, thereby, gaining insight into, experiential dynamics of oneself that do not abide within the scope of that preconceived path or agenda]. When one clearly and deeply understands that nothing, as such, can be done (that is, nothing purposeful or intentional, for any such doing only activates the sense of self in the form of the doer), then all that is left is for one to be content just to observe, without [any predetermined] motive, the [spontaneously arising experiential] contents of consciousness from moment to moment. One need only permit the contents of consciousness to rise and fall without making any effort of any kind to interfere with it [or interpret it, in some preconceived manner]. There should be no labeling, condemning, justifying, resisting, controlling, or directing the contents of consciousness, for any of these can activate the sense of self in its role as discriminator, censor, and image-maker [so that one's conscious awareness is cluttered or preoccupied by that predetermined interpretative agenda, preventing one from alertly noticing experiential dynamics, spontaneously arising in oneself, that do not conform to any restrictive, selective, preset agendas].

One can understand the truth of these statements only by undergoing this creative process himself. If one self-discovers the [experiential] truth of himself, then that truth does set him free, rather than [obtaining liberation from psychologically painful inner conflict through] any effort on the part of the self to liberate itself. Truth is not something that one can give to another, for it is not a constant and static thing. It is whatever we are [actually experiencing] from moment to moment, and only one's own mind can be sufficiently swift and alert to be with that moment-to-moment [actual experiential] truth [of oneself]. Truth is to be discovered and understood in every action, in every thought, in every feeling, in every motive, in every desire, however trivial or transient.

In essence, then, if one can just "let be" and observe whatever thought, feeling, motive, or desire arises in awareness, then he will find that those conflicts and problems invested at the moment with the most psychic energy, will [spontaneously, effortlessly] present themselves to awareness until all the layers of the self are so confronted, understood, and transcended. Finally, one confronts the Void, or inner feeling of emptiness and nothingness which these layers of conceptual self were designed to cover and fill [by providing oneself with presumptive, conceptually-defined, self-knowledge, so that one does not experience oneself as a mystery unto oneself]. If, in the same sense of integration and unity, one is content just to be with this [seeming] Void, and be one with it, then, lost in union with the deep "Sound of Silence" of the Void, a moment may come in which the mind will be freed of its sense of being a personal ego [as an overly restrictive, confining, burdensome, artificial, illusory, presumptive, conceptually-defined, sense of identity, in contrast to the liberating, expansive, feeling of having no predetermined sense of identity, and no longer interpreting being a mystery unto oneself as a frightening sense of inner emptiness, but, instead, recognizing its true experiential nature as intrinsic wholeness of being, inner peace, and unblocked, free flowing, regenerative, joyful, life energy].

One then awakens to oneself as a new self, which may be referred to as the True Self (for one clearly recognizes the illusional and false quality of previous identifications) or the *Transcendent Self.* (This is not to imply that one has become something new, or that one has really achieved anything; rather, one awakens to the recognition that one has always been this Transcendent Self, but has only now awakened to that realization). This Transcendent Self is a limitless, non-conceptual, non-personal, non-entity Self. It is duality transcended. It is "Paradise" regained. It is Death transcended, for in a sense, one has already "died" psychically [psychologically], and been resurrected to a Life and Reality heretofore only imagined. Death, like Time, is clearly understood as a fiction. Life, in truth, is Eternal. There is also the recognition that Consciousness is One [in contrast to the ego's intrinsically divisive sense of identity and interpretation of other individuals, defined in terms of dichotomous, exclusive, static, deadening, conceptual categories]. One now stands as the Unity of Love, Peace, Bliss, and Beauty. There is a surge of free-flowing creative energy that brings a rapture to which only tears can give full expression.

For this [process of letting go of false, limiting, conceptual self-definitions and self-evaluations, and reclaiming our real nature as undivided pure consciousness, contented to be a mystery unto itself, without divisive, conflicted, self-definitions and self-evaluations], psychotherapy has no system. There can never be such a [preconceived] system, for a system initiates, directs, and controls the contents of consciousness, and only an untracked, unpatterned, creatively free-flowing consciousness can ever come to its own Source [or essential ground of being] and liberate itself [from illusory inner conflicts and psychological pain, most essentially grounded in the ego's conceptually defined, preconceived, divisive, conflicted, sense of identity]. The attainment of the truth that can liberate [the psyche from self-divisive self-conflict] can only be self-discovered, and that must involve the risk of making an uncharted journey. It is inevitable that psychotherapy will one day come to this.

Reprinted with permission from *Voices: The Art and Science of Psychotherapy.*

"The Hopelessness of Hope"

When working with a patient who is in a state of despair, many therapists are prone to offer hope to this patient in the form of some kind of supportive statements, or some kind of philosophical or religious doctrine in the attempt to comfort the patient and allay his sense of despair. I would like to point out that the offering of hope as a therapeutic device is not only a hopeless means of ever freeing anyone from his misery and suffering, but is actually detrimental, and serves only to enhance delusion and psychopathology. We are encouraging a pathological process when we encourage a person to reject and deny the reality of what *is*, and, instead, encourage him to pursue what [presumptively] *ought to be.* It is only a mind that cannot deal with the truth of what is that turns reality into despair.

The healthy pattern of living which patients should learn is the pattern of living in the reality of what is, and never the avoidance and denial of reality. The encouragement of hope only serves to teach the patient to live in the illusory and in the promissory. Therefore, the offering of hope should be more the domain of religion than of psychotherapy. Religion promises hope, for example, in the concept of Paradise, basically in order to help people disguise and avoid the recognition of what they feel to be the insufferable conditions of their lives, and, also, to help people deal with the fear of their finality or non-continuity which we label death. Psychotherapy, on the other hand, should encourage confrontation with reality and not its avoidance. It should recognize that fear of non-continuity is a problem for the mind, and, as such, can be dealt with and resolved or transcended like any other such problem.

Hope encourages the practice of self-deception. It confirms for us that some aspect of reality is really intolerable, and invites us to escape. It encourages us to turn our backs on the reality of our despair, and makes us delude ourselves to the effect that "where there is now darkness, there will one day be light." Inherent in hope is the suggestion that it is possible for light to come even if it involves the circumventing of the recognition of the darkness. Psychotherapy, on the other hand, suggests that it is only through the door of darkness, and its exploration and understanding, that light can ever come. Only by dealing with despair itself can we ever be led to liberation from it. The solution to a problem lies only in the problem, and never *away* from it. When the patient confronts himself with why he is committed to making himself unhappy if he cannot have in life what he so badly longs for, and when he finally comes to understand the truth of the source of his despair, only then is liberation possible.

Hope must always be shadowed by the darkness of despair. Hope does not eliminate, it only disguises or camouflages despair so it is not so readily recognized. Hope provides a kind of stupor for the person in despair in the same way as does an intoxicating drug. But though the prisoner may have forgotten the prison, he has not escaped from it. Religion, philosophy, and pharmacology tend to contribute, for the most part, toward helping man forget his mental pain. The kind of therapy they offer for despair is basically one of camouflaging and distorting the reality of what is. The role of psychotherapy, however, should be one of helping the person become liberated from his mental suffering. All too often, psychotherapists have served as camouflage providers rather than as liberators. It is liberation rather than camouflaging that is essential in dealing with despair, and this liberation can only be achieved through the door of the reality of what is. Therefore, in psychotherapy, there can be no legitimate role for the use of hope.

Essentially, hope is desire, and as such, leads one to live in a state of constant frustration. The legacy of hope is unhappiness, for unhappiness is basically unfulfilled desire. Thus, hope puts one in the state of "Becoming", which itself is a contributor to mental suffering, for there must always be pain involved in the struggle to become what one [presumptively] ought to be, or achieve what one ought to attain. The distance in time between what is and what ought to be, of necessity, must always be filled with struggle, conflict, and tension. Freedom from mental anguish must involve a freedom from living in the state of "Becoming." It must rather involve the living in the state of "Being," which is the living in the reality of what is.

Clarity, which is the fundamental ingredient in producing understanding and liberation, is lost when hope is involved. The understanding of what is does not demand hope, but, rather, direct perception, which is to be directly aware without the interference of desire. It is desire that makes for confusion, and hope, like belief, is an extension of desire and a distorter of truth.

Hope only serves as a distraction, which prevents one from easily looking at and ultimately coming to understand the nature of one's despair. It is only truth, and the understanding of why one suffers, that can liberate one from sufferings, for that which is understood leaves no residue in the mind. However, if one is committed to fleeing from [psychological] pain, then one can never be in the position of coming to understand, and, thereby, be liberated from, that pain. Any aspect of life is painful only when it is resisted. Peace comes not with the flight from pain, but, rather, from the cessation of struggle against it, not through resignation, but as the result of a deep understanding of the nature of mental suffering. In this regard, I am reminded of the soliloquy from the movie, "The Night of the Iguana" in which the mental suffering is analogously compared to the behavior of the iguana that is tied to a tree with a tight rope around its neck. The more the iguana tried to escape from its predicament, the tighter it pulled the rope, and the more it choked itself. In the same vein, despair is to be understood not as being the direct result of life's events, but, rather, the result of our attempt to escape from the consequences of those events.

Hopelessness is intrinsic to hope. Hope has in it the implication that there are some conditions in life which are bad, in an absolute sense, and which produce mental states that therefore have to be denied, rejected, and camouflaged. Thus, basic to hope is the concomitant implication that liberation from one's current negative circumstances is hopeless, and, therefore, this event has to be absolutely avoided and denied. In truth, no event, circumstance, or condition is bad in an absolute sense. When the patient's mind interprets it as such, then he has to come to understand why he has done so. Even the imminence of death is not to be interpreted as bad in any absolute sense, but, rather, as an event of life that has been given all kinds of negative and fear-producing connotations and labels. When the mind tries to escape from the reality of this event by retreating into the state of hope then, in a sense, one has already "died" [in a psychological sense]; for in imagination, reality is lost, and [then] the time that one does have left to live cannot be lived in any creatively full or real sense. To really live, one has to be fully attuned to and in communion with the reality of what is. Hope makes this impossible.

The psychotherapy that helps the patient deal with the reality of what is and helps him to understand that he is in some way responsible for his own mental state in regard to that reality is, then, in a position to offer the patient liberation rather than escape.

Reprinted with permission from *Voices: The Art and Science of Psychotherapy.*

"A Therapy for Loneliness"

Loneliness is not a real thing, but only a label, which is superimposed upon a more basic struggle and problem. Contacting, acceptance, and resolution of this more basic universal problem are both Man's and psychotherapy's most essential challenge.

Loneliness is the central problem for psychotherapy because the reality underlying it underlies all pathological symptoms. At the core of loneliness and every other negative psychological state lies some form of egoism, the ego's drive for self-affirmation, self-protection, and self-enhancement. These forms of self-preoccupation serve essentially to distract consciousness from recognizing the more basic reality, that one is really nothing but an inner void [of undifferentiated pure consciousness, the knower, as a mystery unto oneself, with no intrinsic self-knowledge], and *that the ego, like a dream, has only apparent rather than actual existence.*

Loneliness is obviously more than just the fact of the physical state of aloneness but also, represents the mind's rejection of that fact, and the psychological interpretation of this state of aloneness as offering a threat of extinction of the psychological self. We have all come to recognize that loneliness represents more than just the desire to flee from the state of aloneness, and that the therapy for loneliness demands more than just the physical presence of other people. Rather than just the escape from being physically alone, the lonely person is seeking a particular kind of relationship in which he longs to have recognized and affirmed, by the other, that most basic self that he holds himself to be. The experience of loneliness tends to become exaggerated when one's major source of ego affirmation has been lost, and no other seems to exist in the current environment. However, more than an alienation from others, loneliness reflects a more basic self-alienation, for no one who is really in close contact or communion with what is experientially real in himself ever feels lonely even when physically alone. It is only the person who needs to use other people as the primary means of preventing his consciousness from having direct contact with what is experientially real in himself who suffers from loneliness.

There is, essentially, a three-fold aspect to loneliness. The label of loneliness represents an *underlying fear*, an *inner ache* or hollowness feeling, and a *deep yearning to be loved*. The fear is that, psychologically speaking, one is nothing, as in being psychologically extinct unless that self which one holds oneself to be is recognized and affirmed by someone that one particularly values. The inner ache or hollowness feeling is related to the combination of the oblique perception of one's inner emptiness [or lack of intrinsic, enduring, definitive, self-knowledge], plus the immediate rejection of and struggle to escape from that realization. Therefore, the yearning aspect of loneliness represents that attempt on the part of consciousness to find a someone who will affirm its own self-defined labels of itself, and, thereby, remove the fear [fearful insecurity] and hollowness [of recognizing, mostly at some deep subconscious level of awareness, that one's own being is really a mystery unto itself, because those conceptual self-definitions with which one is identified are only acquired presumptions about oneself, that have no intrinsic experiential validity or substantiality, as an actual inner presence, and which quickly fade from one's conscious awareness unless they are frequently reaffirmed through continued conceptual interpretation of oneself].

More specifically, the yearning to be loved represents the ego's attempt to deny the illusory nature of its own existence by finding a *particular* person who will provide the illusory feeling of the absolute affirmation of one's own personal existence and worth through that person's recognition and valuing of those [conceptually] self-defined attributes with which one has become identified. Feeling intensely valued for what he holds himself essentially to be, which the lonely person terms "being loved", he then is able to conclude that his personal existence has achieved some kind of absolute recognition and affirmation because out of the universe of all eligible people, he has been chosen, because of what he is, to be loved [or valued] by this very valuable other.

The truth is that because Man is identified with his ego, we all suffer from what we term loneliness, although there are short respites from that awareness through the use of various forms of sensory and intellectual distractions and short-lived interpersonal attachments. We are all struggling to escape from the awareness of the reality that we are nothing [because any particular conceptual self-definitions that we hold as a sense of self-knowledge are only acquired presumptions about ourselves that have no intrinsic validity, or definitiveness, but rather, are always disputable and capable of being challenged and possibly invalidated or disproven].

We are all essentially nothing, for to be something, one has to be that thing *absolutely*, [or exclusively, totally, and permanently], which is impossible, for no one is omnipotent, and, therefore, we are only relatively something. We are also its relative opposite, [to some degree], and, therefore, we really are neither [self-defined quality exclusively, permanently, and completely]. Therefore, the problem of discovering one's identity, which has become the primary focus of many contemporary therapies, is really a false issue for no one has a [indisputably valid, unchangeable, exclusive] personal identity, [as some kind of definitive conceptual self-definition]. Any "who" or "what" with which one has identified oneself can only be relative, and never absolute, [as well as only conceptually presumed, rather than actually experienced as intrinsic to one's being] and, thus, one can never [really] be that thing at all.

Loneliness is basically a manifestation of egoism, and the ego [or the conceptually defined sense of separate self-awareness] is the big problem-maker and central problem for psychotherapy to deal with. The greatest obstacle to enhancement of the more positive experiential states is the ego and one's identification of self with the ego. The ego has only apparent existence, and is nothing real, but borrows its apparent reality from the self-defined labels with which it identifies. The ego is essentially an illusion, and one's devotion to the basic ego drives (for self-aggrandizement, self-protection, and self-affirmation) only intensifies that illusion, which makes the arousal of negative experiential states a much greater likelihood. Threats to the ego, and its labeled attributes, and frustration of its basic drives, are responsible for producing symptoms, such as anxiety, tension, hostility, depression, and loneliness. For example, *anger* occurs as a reaction to the frustration of the will and represents an assertion of the self to deny the feeling of impotence or nonexistence of the will through its capacity to produce an influencing effect on the other. *Anxiety* represents the perception of the threat of possible disaffirmation of the self. *Depression* represents the reaction to the recognition that the self already has been disaffirmed, and now feels diminished in esteem, and is moving in the direction of total worthlessness and nullity. *Loneliness* represents the feeling of loss of the physical object that was [formerly] used for self-affirmation and the yearning for the return of such an object. Therefore, when reduced to basics, it may be seen that the various negative psychological experiential states are really heightened forms of egoism. In these negative states, psychological threat to the self-defined ego has produced an intensification of self-awareness through interpreted feelings of vulnerability; the particular symptom that results represents some form of attempt to escape from the direct awareness of the feelings of vulnerability and the threat of extinction to the ego.

Transcendence of one's identification with the ego is, therefore, the elimination of all negative [painful, unhealthy] psychological states, and the awakening to oneself as a new reality, which, for want of a descriptive label, may be called *love*. Love is the antithesis of egoism. Love is the state of selflessness and desirelessness. In the state of love, there is total surrender of the sense of [separate] self-awareness, which is absorbed totally in the awareness of the object of our love. Love comes into being within us as an experiential reality not when we are being loved or valued by another, but rather, when our own consciousness is making [deeply invested caring] contact and is in a state of [non-dualistic, empathic,] communion with the experiential reality of the other person, outside the boundaries of our own ego [or sense of separate self-awareness]. When conscious awareness has transcended the boundaries of one's own ego, and has lost itself totally in the state of communion with another person, then love becomes our natural state of being [as a relational energy presence dynamically flowing between oneself and other individuals who one loves, in contrast to the ego as an exclusively separate, self-preoccupied, narcissistically recoiled, sense of identity]. Love cannot be volitionally self-induced, for all such efforts are acts by the ego operating as the agent of those acts. Rather, love is something that one *is* [naturally, intrinsically, being, as a relational energy field] when one is not ego [as a separate sense of self-awareness, conceptual self-definition, self-seeking, oppositional self-will, and continuous inner monologue, recoiling the conscious mind upon itself, away from loving communion with other individuals in the world]. From love flows all the positive experiential states. Life without love is joyless, without beauty, and the inspirational feelings that flow from it, for love is the mother [source] of all of these offspring. Love also brings with it a deep sense of [relaxed inner] peace, for love is the full release from the tension that comes from maintaining self-defense and the striving toward some ideal of self-aggrandizement, [always feeling under pressure to validate, and further enhance, positive or favorable self-definitions, and avoid having them invalidated and replaced by opposite negative traits, so that one always feels "on trial," or continuously facing the possibility of being judged unfavorably by oneself and/or by other individuals whose assessments affect the ego's view of itself].

Desire is egoism, for the ego feeling [or separate self-awareness by the conscious knower] is absent when desire is absent. Love is egolessness and desirelessness. The egoist feels chronically bitter and hostile because all desires and attempts to find a profound sense of joy, beauty, and release from tension are constantly frustrated [as long as one remains identified with the ego, because the ego is rooted in a basic sense of deficiency, arising from rejecting being a mystery unto oneself as conscious knower because, usually not fully consciously, one interprets that lack of self-knowledge as a basic sense of deficiency or lack of inner substantiality. The ego is also a principle of intrinsic, irresolvable, chronic, tension and frustration, because it arises as a process of separate self-awareness by the conscious knower, which involves unnaturally contracting or recoiling one's conscious attention away from its base, ground, or underlying source, in one's own mystery pure being, and its experiential real energy, as well as from other individuals and phenomena in the world. Another related reason why the experience of tension arises is because the ego's chronic self-preoccupation blocks the natural, spontaneous, uncontrolled flow of experiential real energy within oneself, as well as between oneself and other individuals and phenomena in the world].

Love is not open to the egoist as the means of attaining these positive feelings because to love another person makes him feel too [psychologically] threatened. To the egoist, love connotes a sense of openness, penetrability, and vulnerability of the self to being hurt or possibly destroyed. Love also connotes a surrendering of the self—a self to which he has devoted his psychological life to protect, affirm, and enhance. Love is union, which involves the loss of the sense of self-awareness and loss of the feeling of separateness upon which the ego is dependent in order to maintain its individuality and integrity [self-consistent cohesiveness] feeling. Without those feelings, the ego fears it will be dissolved. Therefore, love must be rejected, and the egoist's life is consequently devoid of a real sense of joy, beauty, and peace, and as a result, negative experiential states predominate [which the ego tries to cover over, disguise, and compensate for by superimposing more positive or gratifying experiential states and conceptual self-definitions, which are, essentially, artificially contrived, unreal, and, therefore, not deeply or enduringly satisfying]. Thus, one must either love or be in psychological hell.

In essence, then, man is a two-fold being. At one time or another in his relationships, he is either ego or love. When he is *ego*, he lives in the state of Becoming, in which he is ambitious and continuously and totally devoted to the goals of self-aggrandizement, self-protection, and self-affirmation [as an attempt to *become* enhanced in some way in order to undo the ego's underlying sense of basic deficiency, inner emptiness, or lack of definitive self-knowledge]. (In fact, *all* psychological drives are forms of egoism, and are essentially reducible to one of these basic ego goals). Because of the illusory nature of these goals and their demand for absolute fulfillment, he constantly feels threatened and frustrated, and the negative experiential states (loneliness, anxiety, tension, hostility, depression, and inner feelings of coldness, worthless, and ugliness) are his constant experiential realities. When he is *love*, he lives in the state of Being, in which he is content just to be an unlabeled, indivisible, whole; in that state, his experiential realities are marked with warmth, joy, sensitivity, beauty, inspiration, creativity, and peace, and he is free from all psychopathological states.

[Love, as the deepest, relational, core level of one's own real being or life energy force, undoes the experience of loneliness, or inner emptiness, arising from the ego's estrangement from what is experientially real in oneself and other individuals, by undoing the ego's self-contracted recoil away from one's own relational energetic being, one's real self, through openness to the moment-to-moment experiential states actually arising within oneself, and also through deeply invested empathic communion and energetic connection with other individuals, as well as with other kinds of phenomena or activities in the world. That is, the energy of love, arising from various kinds of genuinely caring relationships, undoes the ego's basic sense of loneliness, or inner emptiness, by reconnecting one's conscious attention to the relational energy flow that is one's true ground or foundational level of being, and which can be experienced only when one is forgetful of the ego's continuous inner monologue or contrary counter-flow of reactive, presumptive, imaginary, conceptual interpretation. This functions as an intervening barrier divorcing one's conscious attention from direct, non-conceptually mediated, non-preconceived, contact with what is actually experientially real in oneself and in other individuals who one encounters, in a given moment. Superficial kinds of personal human relationships, or social interactions, that do not involve empathically contacting what is experientially real in other individuals, and disclosing what is experientially real in oneself, do not really dispel the experience of existential loneliness, or the sense of being "lost in a crowd" of people because one continues to feel inwardly empty when disconnected from the relational energy of love flowing between oneself and other individuals through connecting to one another's genuine experience and to one's own actual experience, even if one is in the physical presence of other people].

The greater the degree of egoism, in terms of one's preoccupation with and devotion to the goals of self-affirmation, self-aggrandizement and self-protection, the greater is the severity of one's pathology. Pathological symptoms basically represent the danger signal that one is becoming too far removed from what is most essentially real in oneself. Because of the prevalence of this condition, the state of egoism and the drive to absolutely affirm the ego may be referred to as the "Universal Neurosis," and, by the same token, the state of love may be referred to as the "Universal Psychotherapy," or the state of psychological health, when the labels of pathology and health are reduced to their most basic elements. Therefore, in essence, psychopathology in general, and loneliness in particular, as a manifestation of the relatively exclusive living in the egoistic state, is a reflection of that person's inability to love [or to relinquish separate self-awareness in deeply invested, caring, non-dualistic, empathic communion with other individuals, phenomena, and activities in the world.

This view that egoistic self-preoccupation is the basic underlying source of all kinds of psychopathology, painful inner conflict, and unhappiness, whereas love, or surrendering separate ego self-awareness in deeply invested communion with other individuals, is the basic psychotherapeutic undoing of that pathology, coincides with the views of Alexander Mueller, an associate of the prominent psychologist Alfred Adler. According to Mueller: "Community feeling should be compared to health. A state of health is considered normal, and a state of illness is considered abnormal. In this same sense, the possession of community feeling is normal, and its absence is abnormal, according to the opinion of Individual Psychology."[6]

Similarly, Adler, himself, points out that caring human relationships can undo unhappiness and psychopathology rooted in egocentric self-preoccupation:

> And since true happiness is inseparable from the feeling of giving, it is clear that a social person is much closer to happiness than the isolated person striving for superiority. Individual Psychology has very clearly pointed out that everyone who is deeply unhappy, the neurotic and the desolate person stem from among those who were deprived in their younger years of being able to develop the feeling of community, the courage, the optimism, and the self-confidence that comes directly from the sense of belonging. This sense of belonging that cannot

be denied anyone, against which there are no arguments, can only be won by being involved, by cooperating, and experiencing, and by being useful to others. Out of this emerges a lasting, genuine feeling of worthiness.[7]]

To eliminate the problem of loneliness, the patient's capacity to love is what has to be enhanced. In Buber's terms, one has to move from exclusive living in I-It relationships to living in the I-Thou relationship.[8,9] The I-It relationship involves defining oneself as some labeled attribute or part, and bringing only that [exclusive] *part* to a dualistic relationship—in which the other is also related to as a labeled part, and as an object to be experienced, manipulated, and influenced, as the means of affirming, protecting, or enhancing the ego. In contrast, in an I-Thou relationship, one comes to the other as an unlabeled, indivisible whole, and relates to the other as being an unlabeled whole, resulting in a relationship of unity and communion [in contrast to the ego interacting with others from a position of separate self-awareness, and avoiding direct contact with what is actually experientially real in oneself and others through the intervening barrier of distracting interpretive thought, dividing one's perception of oneself and other individuals between various positive and negative preconceived presumptive interpretations]. Only the labeled, the part [the partial definitions of oneself and others], can be experienced and manipulated; the unlabeled whole can only be communed with. It is a relationship free of egoism and selfish motive. If therapy does not help the patient to achieve this, then the patient is still operating in the realm of egoism exclusively, and the negative psychological states will continue to persist in one form or another.

The patient must be helped to understand that even though loneliness seems to suggest that his longing is for someone to love him, its real root lies in *his* fear and inability to love, and that this needs to be thoroughly explored. He needs to understand that his sense of isolation and encapsulation is basically self-imposed, the result of his fear of reaching out and making contact outside of himself; that the bridge for intimacy can be constructed only by his permitting himself to love another [individual], to reach out [in a deeply invested, caring, way] and [empathically] hear the other where that person's experiential reality really is at. Only when he is loving and making contact outside the confines of his own ego boundary does the experience of loneliness disappear. Being loved by another is not sufficient of itself to eliminate one's profound sense of loneliness. Being loved only provides the illusory feeling that one is of absolute value to another, and, therefore, one's personal identity and sense of worth seems to be absolutely affirmed. However, this is not the transcending of loneliness, but only the temporary forgetting of loneliness through distraction. It only serves to make one cling very dependently to the loved one as the means of escaping from the specter of loneliness and nothingness which closely shadow's one's awareness.

For loneliness to be transcended as a problem, one must no longer run from the reality of the inner void or state of nothingness that lies beneath the label of loneliness. The therapist needs to help the patient become aware of his particular connotation of loneliness to enable him to go beneath that label to the basic reality of the fear of the void which underlies it; rather than trying to treat the label of loneliness itself, for example, by advocating some form of distraction and escape from that state through the increased preoccupation with superficial external relationships. Loneliness, as an attempt to run from the reality of one's own inner emptiness, is very much like its cousin, boredom, which seeks to avoid that inner emptiness with a distracting activity; whereas loneliness is a reaction to the same danger signal that one is perilously close to awareness of the illusory inner emptiness. But loneliness utilizes a person rather than an activity as the distracting agent.

Psychological health and healing basically involve ending the struggle against what is real in oneself. Struggling against what is experientially real and painful in oneself produces an internal state of [self-divisive] dis-integration, which is the essence of psychopathology. Therefore, the therapist should in no way encourage the patient to run from the reality of his own inner emptiness or state of being no labeled thing. The patient must face and live with this emptiness, and not escape in any direction. Any attempt to escape brings fear. There is never any fear in just being with what is. Only when there is not the slightest semblance of escape or avoidance from the reality of what is called the void or nothing state can the universal problem of loneliness and egoism be permanently transcended.

If the patient permits himself to merge and integrate himself totally with that inner void, only then will he discover that being nothing is not psychological extinction or any other negative connotation which he may have held to, but, on the contrary, that nothing state of being an unlabeled, indivisible whole is the essence of consciousness and man's true nature; that state is the Unity of Absolute Love, Joy, Beauty, Peace, and Freedom [as an inner fullness of being rather than actually being an inner emptiness or void, as the ego presumes lack of conceptually defined self-knowledge or separate sense of identity to be]. That is one's Real Self. Then one is just I AM and nothing more. One is Consciousness, pure, [undifferentiated], the stuff or essence from which all forms of the ego arise [without holding any conceptual self-definitions, but, rather, being contented to experience oneself as the energy-feeling of love, and its related qualities, mentioned above].

To be free of its identification with the ego, the patient's consciousness, ultimately, has to dis-identify from all of the concepts and self-defined labels with which it has falsely come to identify itself, and from the objectifications with which people typically become identified (such as the body, intellect, emotions, senses, will), of which the ego feels itself to be the hub and integrator. To be free, one has to permit oneself to be the unlabeled, indivisible, whole, the

Silent Witness, the pure Subject that one really is, identifying with nothing objective to that Subjective Consciousness. One then awakens to the realization that one's sense of
loneliness was only the result of superimposing a sense of
personal egoism upon one's essence or natural state of Being, in the same way as unformalized [formless] ocean water
comes to be identified with its manifested, labeled, form of
wave. Then one will see that there is no real threat of extinction of one's Real Self any more than the wave really dies;
for in a real sense, it has never existed, but only had apparent existence through the label with which it has become
identified. It has never been other than its essence, unformalized water, nor will it ever be anything else but its essence.
A form or a labeled thing never arises out of nothing, but,
rather, arises out of its essence or stuff of which it is composed. Therefore, contrary to the fear of most people, when
form dissolves, it does not dissolve into nothingness, but,
rather, dissolves back into the [underlying substratum or] essence from which it arose. Thus, dissolution [of the ego as a
sense of separate self-awareness, conceptual self-definition,
and self-evaluation] is not extinction but rather, a return to
its most basic [underlying] reality. The same is true for the
manifestation of the formalized [clearly delineated] personal
ego and its dissolution back into its essence [undefined] pure
Consciousness, which is the Unformalized Self or Real Self.

Having transcended one's identification with the ego, one
then also has transcended all of the ego-related problems
and negative experiential states. Strictly speaking, there can
never be a therapy for loneliness as such, or for any of the
other negative experiential states, for they all have the same
root cause. *There can only be psychotherapy for the transcending of egoism. This will be the ultimate psychotherapy.*
**The painful truth that many therapists will have to
face** is that they use their relationship to their patients as a
means of running from their own loneliness and inner emptiness; [and] that they encourage the patient, in one form or
another, to do the same. Through various forms of influence

and manipulation, the therapist uses the patient to affirm his own ego, and, also, tends to use the therapy process as the means of affirming the patient's ego. Most therapists have correctly come to recognize that the arousal of threat [anxiety, emotional insecurity] and symptoms [of psychological distress] are the result of the ego's need for affirmation and preservation, so they have therefore assumed that affirming, protecting, and enhancing the patient's ego must be the essence of the therapeutic process. But that assumption is not valid because they have not correctly understood that ego affirmation only temporarily relieves [perceived] threat[s] to the ego, and, therefore, symptoms of one type or another generally reoccur. Symptoms must continue to arise because the patient is still basically irrational. The patient's prime irrationality is that he is trying to make absolute that which can only be relative. He is trying to prove the absolute existence of a thing that has only apparent or conceptual existence [because the ego's sense of identity or self-knowledge basically consists of presumptive, conceptual self-definitions, or rather arbitrary self-interpretations]. The ego can never really ever be permanently affirmed [permanently validated] because it cannot be absolute [or exclusive of its rejected relative opposite qualities]. Therefore, by encouraging the affirmation and preservation of the ego, the therapist has only served to ultimately preserve the continuance of all of the patient's negative experiential states rather than their transcendence. That transcendence can occur only with the transcendence of one's identification with the ego.

In order for it not to be a matter of the blind leading the blind [into a ditch of illusory conceptual presumptions, not grounded in directly observing the patient's or client's actual experiential dynamics], the therapist has to deal with this problem of loneliness and need for ego-affirmation within him first. Only then will he be in the position to really help the patient. Only when Man understands and resolves this most essential problem will he really fully be able to love and realize his fullest potential as a human being, and only then will the world move in the direction of really being a place in which joy, beauty, and peace are optimized. Only as the individual changes can the world change, for the world is not more than the composition [composite] of the individuals [that inhabit it]. The nation is the collective ego, and has the same ambitions for ego-affirmation, protection, and enhancement, as does the individual ego. Therefore, the absence of friendship and love, and the same negative experiential states of fear, hostility, and alienation exist among nations [and other social groups] as they do among individuals. To be reformed, the world does not require an external revolution, but, rather, its individuals require an internal revolution in which the ego is overthrown and supplanted with love.[10]

TYPED NOTES DICTATED BY MAX HAMMER TO BARRY HAMMER DISCUSSING THE RELATIONSHIP BETWEEN PSYCHOTHERAPISTS AND CLIENTS

I. Psychotherapeutic Healing through Love or Empathic Communion and Warmhearted Caring of the Psychotherapist for the Client

Our advice to psychotherapists is that there is nothing else that produces psychotherapeutic healing but love, especially the expression of warmhearted caring, empathic understanding, and nonjudgmental unconditional acceptance by the psychotherapist or counselor to the client, arousing that experience of warm caring or love in the client. We are not using the term "love" to connote any kind of sexual or romantic feelings in the therapist or in the client, which would clearly be inappropriate within the framework of the psychotherapeutic relationship. Instead, we are using the term "love" to connote an energy of warm caring expressed by the psychotherapist or counselor to the client, and thereby aroused as an experience in the client. That kind of warm caring or love enhances the client's sense of emotional security and well-being by providing the experience of unification with life energy, which caring warmth most essentially is. The transmission of life energy from therapist to client undoes all kinds of psychopathology arising from the client's experience of absence of life energy, which is the essential underlying source of the experience of inner emptiness, fearful

205

anxiety, inner deficiency, dreadful feelings of the empty heart collapsed upon itself, and the arising of related processes of self-rejection of one's dreadful experiential states, producing self-division, self-conflict, and related forms of psychopathology.

The transmission of caring warmth or love from the therapist to the client produces a healing effect because the energy of caring warmth brings an experience of inner fullness, fulfillment, and wholeness of being, or being filled with a substantial life energy presence, so that the client does not feel inwardly empty, deficient, and dreadful. The transmission of the energy of caring warmth as wholeness of life energy also arouses the experience of relaxed inner peace, well-being, and emotional security in the client, which produces the client's greater self-love or sense of self-acceptance and self-unification, because the energy of love or caring warmth is a cohesive energy rather than a divisive energy. The psychotherapists' warmhearted caring for the client can also produce greater empathic understanding of the client, and that empathic insight can liberate the client from psychological pain and inner conflict, as well as motivate and enable the client to make constructive changes in his/her life. As the influential psychologist Rollo May suggests, when a psychotherapist engages in deeply invested, self-forgetful, empathic communion with a client, or when empathic communion occurs in some other kind of human relationship, that can produce greater understanding, liberating insights, and transformational breakthroughs.[11]

You, the therapist, have been sent by life to take loving good care of her children who cannot take good care of themselves, as they are unable to achieve psychological or emotional healing through their own unaided efforts, and are in great despair believing that life as love has abandoned them. You, the therapist, have to show them that that perception is not true. You have to be the living personification of the compassionate goodness of life as love or caring warmth which only presumptive conceptual interpretations makes appear less than its intrinsic true grandeur. If you learn to love deeply enough, strongly enough, you will love away the client's ego's unloving nature as a separate sense of self-identity and recoiled self-awareness, and when the client's false egoistic sense of self is undone by the energy of love or heartfelt caring warmth deeply invested in the client, then you, the therapist, will be, at least for the moment of the therapeutic encounter, nothing but a personified representative of the intrinsic goodness and grandeur of life, uncontaminated by conceptualization, and then you will have found your true home, and can help the client to discover it within themselves.

To be or express love, you have to find someone lovable, akin to your own nature as nonjudgmental pure being. You will find that nature in everyone if you are willing to look for it, and when you find it, you will recognize that the other individual is truly a related part of you, a true partner, and when that is experienced, then the egocentric sense of dualistic extreme separateness as recoiled self-awareness is undone, at least temporarily during the moment of caring communion. When the therapist becomes self-forgetful of the ego's illusory sense of separate self-awareness in deeply invested empathic communion with the client, then love, or genuine caring, as healing warmth, naturally arises in the therapist, flows to the client, and ignites the experience of that healing warmth in the client. That expression and transmission of warm caring from therapist to client produces a powerful healing effect in the client of a degree far beyond what just intellectual understanding alone can achieve.

Words and understanding, by themselves alone, do not have much psychological healing power. Understanding without the experience of love or caring warmth is rather cold, and that coldness leaves the client and the therapist still abiding in the mind, and does not undo the fearful anxiety, tension, dread, and sense of inner emptiness and deficiency arising from the absence of caring warmth as real life energy presence in the heart, which is the underlying source of all kinds of psychopathology. However, the expression of caring warmth from therapist to client can enhance the client's ability to experience that and begin to express that back to the therapist and to others in their lives, bringing the experience of inner fullness of life energy presence as an inherent sense of inner substantiality, security, worth, inner beauty, and joyfulness. Directly experiencing that truly divine nature of love within themselves, clients no longer need to be told by others that their nature is beautiful, lovable, truly grand, and of great intrinsic worth, which undoes all kinds of psychopathological inner conflict arising from self-rejection of their own being and uncomfortable experiential states.

If the therapist is truly interested in contributing to true substantial change in the client, that is usually better achieved through the expression of warm caring and non-judgmental unconditional acceptance, rather than through criticism of the client's apparent shortcomings, especially if that involves, or seems to involve, a sense of belligerent attack, which only increases the client's sense of insecurity, defensiveness, and lack of self-acceptance. Generally speaking, you cannot change others for the better by being critical of them. Unless their heart changes, they have not changed. Only when caring warmth comes into their own heart, as an experience of inner fullness and wholeness of a substantial life energy presence, have they truly changed for the better, and are then equipped to contribute to the positive change or psychological healing of others as well. If the therapist is able to generate that caring warmth in her or himself, it automatically has a rippling effect, and will naturally arouse the experience of that caring warmth in the client, through a process of sympathetic vibratory resonance. The cold cannot heal the cold; only the warmth can heal those who are cold.

Like Max Hammer, other compassionate psychologists such as Carl Rogers and Sidney Jourard understand that the therapist or counselor's genuine, sincerely expressed, warmhearted, caring for the client, rather than theoretical understanding of the client, and purportedly therapeutic techniques, is the key to true psychological healing. Hammer, Rogers,[12] and Jourard[13] as well as many other psychologists maintain that it is important for the therapist to respond to the client as an individual person, in a non-directive, non-judgmental, manner, and not relate to the client through the lens of a generic psychological theory or controlling theoretical agenda of whatever kind.

The expression of love or caring warmth need not necessarily arise as an effect of volitional effort, but it can be viewed as a natural, choiceless (involuntary) expression of recognizing that love or caring warmth is the intrinsic real nature of our being, which is naturally inclined to flow from us to others if we do not permit the ego or false sense of identity as a separate self to block it by perpetuating its recoiled sense of separate self-awareness and selfish self-concern. The ego is naturally uncaring, just as the soul or the real individuality is naturally caring, as an expression of being a relational individuality rather than a conceptually presumed sense of separate self-awareness and selfish self-concern. The ego's nature is to be willful, oppositional, resistive, combative, and divisive, whereas the soul's nature is intrinsically loving, caring, radiating, shining, glowing, giving, expanding, as the expression of our natural inclination to share our experiential energy nature with others, and to relate to them in a compassionate, harmonious, cooperative, manner, when it is appropriate to do so. The psychotherapist helps clients to heal psychologically by encouraging them to develop greater loving investment in contacting other individuals and the world of objective reality, instead of being narcissistically lost in their own conceptual subjectivity or continuous mental-emotional inner monologue, which recoils their conscious attention in subjective self-awareness, producing an impairment of investment in contact with objective reality in the world.

The ego, or sense of continuous separate self-awareness, cannot be healed because it is an illusion, not our intrinsic real self, and because it is the basic underlying causal source of psychopathology, arising from loss of investment of loving contact with objective reality in the world, produced by the ego's continuous stream of narcissistic self-awareness, recoiled inner monologue, oppositional willfulness, selfish self-concern, fearful anxiety, sense of inner emptiness, and deficiency of being and well-being. The ego cannot be psychologically healed because it is not our real self, and it is an intrinsically self-conflicted pathological nature, divided between conflicting positive and negative presumptive self-concepts and divided from rejected experiential states in ourselves as well as from other individuals and objective reality in the world because of its incessant self-preoccupation and self-judgments. Instead, psychological healing is achieved through transcending identification with the illusory ego-personality, functioning as a false sense of self, and awakening or developing an experiential awareness of the intrinsically relational nature of our real being as love or relational life energy presence. The ego is unreal, and its psychological suffering is unreal, arising from conceptual self-delusion.

The only effective way for the therapist to help the client heal psychologically is to help the client's real self as soul, or love, transcend its false identification with the recoiled ego, and awaken to the relational nature of the soul, the real self, our intrinsic real being. Only therapists who have awakened to the true nature of their being as love or caring warmth and its intrinsic psychological well-being can effectively contribute to the healing and growth of clients by arousing that nature in them. Thus, psychological healing is not really a matter of mastering a particular technique, but awakening or shifting individuals from identification with an illusory, separate, conceptual sense of self, to their real self, as the relational, connective, life energy nature of love or warmhearted caring. Otherwise, the psychological pathology must still continue, in some form, because we are still identified with the ego's continuous sense of separate recoiled self-awareness as an illusory sense of inner presence, rather than our intrinsic real conscious-life-presence, as caring warmth, which is our own unconditioned happiness, love, peace, and joy. The only thing real in us is love. Everything else is just idea, self-created illusion superimposed upon our real nature. We have to accept the oneness, the unity, the indivisibility of our being, and realize that consciousness, which is our intrinsic life energy presence as an indivisible unity, is always intrinsically being love and joy.

II. Psychological Self-Healing through Self-Love or Self-Unification with Your Own Painful Feelings and Uncomfortable Experiential States; How to Liberate Yourself from Painful Negative Feelings by Relaxing-Releasing Them Away

Be fully open to permit deeper and deeper levels of painful feelings and other uncomfortable experiential states that have previously been rejected and repressed into the subconscious or subliminal levels of your psyche to spontaneously flow into your conscious awareness. Listen, with warmly caring, compassionate, empathic sensitivity to the energy feeling tone arising in yourself, as the momentary experiential truth of yourself. Be consciously sensitive to intuitively distinguish between what feels experientially real and right in your bodily and emotional experience, especially in the region of the midsection, tummy, or "gut," functioning as your intuitively arising core integrity. Go deeply limp and relaxed, trusting that your own life energy force naturally has the ability to consciously retrieve and thereby drain, dissolve, and liberate itself from all painful feelings and experiential states, especially non-constructive, obstructing, distorted, perverted, antithetical forms of your own love-life energy force, all functioning as alien overlays, coverings, intruders, superimposed upon your pure love-life energy presence. Be totally serene even amidst the experience of intense inner and outer turmoil, trusting that your own love-life energy force has a natural capacity to retrieve and thereby drain out, dissolve, and dispel, all alien overlays, or superimposed dark, dense, opaque coverings at their foundational, root, or source level. Therefore, we should not block painful, turbulent feelings from arising to our conscious awareness, either because of our own false identification with those feelings, or by letting ourselves become affected by the negativity of other individuals, especially those with whom we are in close proximity.

Disassociate your own intrinsically pure love-life energy presence from the negative overlay by not identifying with it and holding it to be outside of you, but letting it spontaneously flow into and unify with your conscious awareness without controlling, evading, or blocking it in any way, so that it can be relaxed-released and drained out into your conscious awareness, layer by layer, until the deepest level of the painful negativity is fully relaxed-released away. Permitting painful negative feelings and experiential states to flow spontaneously and freely into your conscious awareness eliminates the sense of subject-object duality that produces the twisting and tension which comprises the underlying foundation of the negativity. That is, permitting the negativity to flow freely into our conscious awareness undoes the tension of duality between subjective knower and object of knowledge, and begins the process of untwisting deeper and deeper levels of negativity, so that it gradually gets fully untwisted, relaxed-released, and dissolved back into calm pure energy without any more association with pain and negativity.

The most important thing is to go totally limp, totally relaxed, without any resistive attempt to control, evade, or overcome the painful negativity in any way. That is what opens the door to healing love-life energy and liberating insight flowing, at deeper and deeper levels, from the core, center, or source of your being, whereas tension produced by resistive attempts to control, evade, overcome, or eliminate the painful negativity keeps that door closed. Identifying with negativity or struggling against it produces fearful anxiety and tension, which are like glue that keeps negativity stuck to us. That psychological glue is dissolved, enabling the alien overlay of painful negativity to automatically begin to peel off, like a false façade, persona, or psychosocial mask, when we no longer struggle against, identify with, own, or personalize negative feelings, such as fearful anxiety, tension, and frantic desperation. Instead, we must disassociate our IAM or our conscious love-life energy from it, and then it automatically, spontaneously, naturally peels off from our IAM or our conscious love-life energy presence, when the connecting glue of identification with it and struggle against it is removed. Engaging in slow, deep, rhythmic, breathing, at least at the beginning, may help our conscious love-life energy presence relax-release away, or peel off, the alien overlay of negativity, and may help us to more deeply spontaneously experience our unconditioned pure conscious-love-life energy, our unconditioned great heart nature of fully relaxed peace, and absolute or total security and well-being, which serve like a powerful light of divine intelligence, illuminating ever deeper or higher levels of the experiential truth of our being, and of our related realistic life circumstances. Deep breathing exhalation, deep sighs, will cast off a lot of the negativity.

If you love your psychological pain away, by unifying with it in the heart core of your being without identifying with it, that is what heals it. Metaphorically speaking, you are bringing the painful feelings home to the energetic heart core of your own being. By doing so, you are reunifying your whole inner "family," consisting of the various feelings or experienced object of knowledge forms that your conscious love-life energy presence can take, from moment to moment. Whatever painful feeling or experienced object of knowledge form of your conscious love-life energy spirit you have rejected from home, the heart core of your IAM, your source of origin, you have to totally welcome back home by non-dualistically reunifying with it in the heart

core of your being. When you welcome your painful feelings back home, back into the heart core of your IAM or
conscious love-life energy spirit, then you are also welcoming them back into the unifying wholeness of your being,
where they are healed and transformed from their painfulness back into their original pure love-life energy nature, so
that they are no longer painful and pathological because they
are no longer twisted in an unnatural sense of duality from
the wholeness of your conscious love-life energy force or
spirit. Therefore, love your fear, and love your pain, by welcoming it back home to the heart core of your own being.
That is the basic secret of transforming negative, painful, or
pathological energies, be they predominantly psychological
or physical, back into their original perfect purity of pure
conscious love-life energy presence, where the pain and pathology is relaxed-released and transformed by being reunified with the total goodness, total well-being, total love and
joy, fully relaxed peace, beauty, freedom, unconditioned inherent fulfillment, and wholeness of being of the core level
of our pure conscious love-life energy presence. Whatever
painful feelings or other experiential states you reject from
naturally, spontaneously flowing into your conscious awareness, and repress into the subconscious or subliminal level
of your psyche, you are dualistically or divisively casting
out of your inner home, the heart core, center, source level
of your being. That self-division of your conscious love-life
energy spirit from its rejected feelings or experienced object
of knowledge forms produces psycho-physical pathology
and suffering. Those rejected feelings and experiential states
have to be fully allowed back home again, into the heart core
or center of your conscious love-life energy spirit, if you are
to be made whole again, which enables the energy in those
feelings and experiential states to be untwisted and thereby
restored back to their original inherent purity, so that they no
longer have a negative, painful, or pathological quality. That
process of self-reunification with your previously rejected
painful feelings and experiential states is what produces the

healing growth of self-compassion, self-caress, empathic self-understanding, unconditional self-acceptance. This is the basis of the undoing or transformation of love-life energies that have become twisted into their antithetical nature of negativity, pain, and pathology, by being unnaturally dualistically divided from the natural wholeness of our conscious spirit love-life energy. Reunifying our conscious awareness with painful feelings, sensations, or experiential states enables them to be untwisted, relaxed-released, or transformed back into their original perfect purity, so that they no longer have any negative, painful, or pathological qualities. This process of self-reunification through unconditional acceptance of all of our spontaneously arising feelings and experiential states is also the "royal road to the unconscious" that psychoanalysts such as Sigmund Freud were seeking, as the most expeditious way of returning the repressed contents of the subconscious back to our full conscious awareness.[14]

If you want to be healed and whole, you have to love or reunify with your psychological pain, which you have previously rejected and cast out of the home of your heart core, the source of your being, your conscious love-life energy presence. That self-reunification of our conscious spirit love-life energy with its formerly rejected painful feelings and experiential states is what undoes the tension and self-twisting caused by unnatural self-division, self-conflict, self-rejection of the temporary object of knowledge forms of our permanent love-life energy presence, and when the unnatural dualistic self-division is undone, that is what untwists, relaxes-releases, and transforms the energy in our feelings and experiential states. Metaphorically speaking, this process of reintegrating previously rejected painful feelings, and thereby untwisting or relaxing-releasing the energy within them is like relieving ourselves of bodily tension by removing overly tight clothing that has been blocking the natural flow of our breathing and circulation.

PUBLISHED ARTICLES

BY MAX HAMMER

"The Essence of Personal and Transpersonal Psychotherapy"

The essence of transpersonal psychotherapy involves helping the client to live in the desireless state of being, or unity of consciousness, which means making no exclusive identification of consciousness with any conceptual label or self-definition. That absence of conceptual self-definition, self-evaluation, and desire puts an end to painful inner conflict with our actual experiential states, in the attempt to fulfill a presumption of what we "should be" experiencing or validating about ourselves. That is, having no predetermined conceptual self-definition puts an end to chronic states of anxiety, frustration, tension, depression, and other negative feelings, engendered by trying to absolutely, definitively and exclusively validate positive self-definitions and conclusively refute negative ideas about ourselves, which is not realistically possible. Having no conceptual self-definitions does not actually make you an inner nothingness, contrary to what the ego presumes. Unifying with and unconditionally accepting your actual experiential states is what restores the natural unitary wholeness of your being, which is what heals or transforms painful feelings and negative or disturbing experiential states. As peculiar and contradictory as it may sound, inner peace is found only through communion with psychological pain, and never by struggling against it, or avoiding it. Only communion with psychological pain opens the door for its liberation and transformation, only a non-resistive yielding, letting be, or full unconditional acceptance is its ending. Psychological pain is not inherent to any feeling, per se, but arises only after the attempt to reject it arises. Thus, the basic therapeutic rule is always help clients unify with what they are actually experiencing, from moment to moment, but never encourage them to pursue some presumptive conceptual ideal of what they believe they ought to be experiencing or validating about themselves. In that transpersonal state of unity wholeness of being, or undivided, nonreactive, pure consciousness, there is no dualistic entity operating as the judger, controller, or preconceived interpreter of the spontaneously arising contents of consciousness, and so, being unimpeded, the previously rejected experiential aspects of consciousness are free to arise spontaneously and reunify themselves with the unitary whole that consciousness naturally is. That non-reactive, non-judgmental, reunification dissolves the negative feelings and their painfulness. Thus, there is no true and enduring psychological self-healing without self-communion with whatever painful experiential states you were formerly rejecting.

"Transpersonal Being: The Unchangeable Core"

The transpersonal self, one's unmodified being as objectless, undifferentiated, pure consciousness, is the reality background, substance, or underlying substratum of which our personal thoughts and feelings are comprised. That is, objectless pure consciousness is the true core of every person's being, as well as the source and container of all changing personal thoughts, feelings, and experiential states. Consciousness can transcend the egoistic state of becoming, or inner turmoil arising from the attempt to become more than one is already inherently being, and abide in the inherent unconditional relaxed inner peace of changeless permanent being, only when all egoistic desire or striving to become something absolutely protected, affirmed, and aggrandized or enhanced ends. Ironically, the transpersonal self is already intrinsically, unconditionally, being all of the qualities of wholeness, fulfillment, and well-being that the ego (self-definition) is trying to conditionally achieve or become. When all self-definition ceases, then consciousness is no longer self-divided, which puts an end to psychologically painful inner conflict between positive and negative, or desired and undesired, self-definitions and self-evaluations. In the state of being, or non-dualistic awareness, the undivided wholeness of nonreactive pure consciousness, there is a yielding or letting be attitude that exists, so that we unconditionally accept and non-dualistically unify with whatever experiential states spontaneously arise to consciousness in a non-reactive, non-judgmental manner. This involves letting our painful feelings "speak" for themselves to conclusion, within our awareness, and "tell their own story," so that they can thereby drain out and dissolve into their underlying substratum of unmodified pure consciousness-feeling energy, without interpreting, censoring, or controlling our feelings in any way. The transpersonal self as undivided pure consciousness is intrinsic wholeness and bliss, or absolute peace-love-joy. That is the inherent fulfillment realization that puts an end to all sense of deficiency and compensatory desire. Desire reflects the attempt to become whole, which obscures the direct experiential realization that you are already intrinsically being whole.

"Misconceptions of Transpersonal Psychology: A Reply to Ellis"

The transpersonal reality is objectless, undifferentiated, pure consciousness, changeless permanent being, which is the underlying background, substratum, or essence from which arises changing objects of knowledge, including egoistic, personal, exclusive self-knowledge as thoughts, feelings, desires, or sensations. The transpersonal self is love, or a relational energy nature, a connective, warmly caring, expansive nature, which naturally arises without effort or volitional intention when we are self-forgetful of the separate ego pseudo sense of self. The basic objective of transpersonal psychotherapy is to help clients awaken their transpersonal being as love, or unitary wholeness, by unifying with their painful feelings and experiential states, but letting go of re-active identification with them, and acknowledging the relational nature of reality as love by connecting to others in a genuinely caring or loving way.

"Quiet Mind Therapy"

Quiet Mind Therapy is a derivative of Eastern forms of mediation, and basically involves eliminating the conflict-maker, the ego, or the conceptually defined separate sense of self, which blocks love or the psychological/energetic/ex-periential connection to other individuals. The ego's sense of separate self-awareness produces a sense of duality from our actual experiential states, which causes psychologically painful inner conflict. The only way to truly understand and resolve painful psychological problems or inner conflicts is to let yourself, as consciousness, the knower, be non-dualis-tically unified with your actual experiential states, rather than dualistically standing apart from them, as a reactive censor, controller, interpreter, or value judger of them. Only when consciousness is willing to be an undefined mystery unto it-self can it awaken or experience its intrinsic fulfillment na-ture. Letting go of predetermined systems of thought, goals, and conceptual self-definition liberates our life energy from restrictive confinement and self-divisive inner conflict, so that it can be naturally spontaneously free-flowing and an undivided wholeness again.

"The Hopelessness of Hope"

We psychotherapists are encouraging a psychologically un-healthy process when we encourage people to reject and deny the reality of their actual experiential states, and instead

encourage them to pursue a predetermined goal of what presumptively ought to be. Thus, psychotherapy should encourage confrontation with reality and not its avoidance. Hope
encourages the practice of self-deception. It confirms for us
that some aspect of our experiential reality is really intolerable and invites us to escape into an imaginary or hypothetical
alternative that is presumed to be better or more acceptable.
Only by dealing with despair or other psychologically painful experiential realities can we ever find a way to be liberated from it, through understanding the source of our misery.
Any aspect of life is painful when it is resisted. True inner
peace comes not from the flight from psychological pain, but
from the cessation of struggle against it. Psychological suffering can be resolved only through a deep understanding of
it, not through resignation or resistance.

"A Therapy for Loneliness"

The experience of loneliness is derived not from the state
of being physically alone, but from the ego's resistance to
surrendering its separate self-awareness in loving communion with others. When we are psychologically disconnected
from others through egoistic self-preoccupation, then we are
also disconnected from the relational core of our own being
or life energy force. This situation produces an experience
of inner emptiness, deficiency, and self-alienation from what
is experientially real in us, as well as alienation from others. Even if we are surrounded with the company of other
people, we can still feel lonely if others do not contact what
is experientially real in us, or if we use our interaction with
others as a means of distracting ourselves from what is experientially real in ourselves. The ego's sense of loneliness
also arises from anxiety about not having its sense of identity
and worth validated by others, and that lack of validation
threatens the ego with possible nullification of its sense of
psychological existence. We awaken the relational feeling-
energy of love as the intrinsic reality nature of our own being

only when we relinquish the ego's sense of separate self-awareness, continuous inner monologue, and selfish desire in communion with another individual. Love is the source of all genuinely positive experiential states, such as relaxed inner peace, emotional security, and fulfillment. Love, as the deepest, relational core of our own being, our life energy force, undoes the experience of loneliness arising from the ego's estrangement from what is experientially real in ourselves and others. Unselfish caring for others is the primary basis of psychological health, whereas becoming psychologically disconnected from others through egoistic self-preoccupation is the primary cause of psychopathology. True love involves Martin Buber's I-Thou relationship, in which we relate to ourselves and others as an undefined (unlabeled) indivisible whole, rather than relating to partial definitions of ourselves and others, as in Buber's concept of the I-It relationship, which involves selfish motivations and the retention of separate self-awareness. Effective psychotherapy necessarily involves both the therapist and client ceasing to identify with the ego's sense of separate self-awareness and its unrealistic psychological needs, rooted in the ego's basic sense of inner emptiness or deficiency. Similarly, meaningful societal transformation can be based only on a shift from egoism to love.

NOTES DICTATED BY MAX HAMMER TO BARRY

HAMMER, DISCUSSING THE RELATIONSHIP

BETWEEN PSYCHOTHERAPIST AND CLIENT

Expression of warmhearted caring by the therapist to the client significantly contributes to the psychological healing process by helping to gradually transform the experiential feeling-tone of the client's psychological heart or energy-feeling center. The therapist's warmhearted, empathic caring also helps the client to discover for himself that he feels better, and can generate an intrinsic sense of worth, inner beauty, inner peace, and emotional security by also expressing warmhearted caring to others.

Unifying with your painful feelings in the psychological or energetic heart core of your being is the key to psychological self-healing. This involves being non-resistive, deeply relaxed, and psychologically limp, so to speak. When you welcome your painful feelings back home to the psychological heart core of your own being, then you are also welcoming them back into the unifying wholeness of your being, where they are divested of their painful and pathological qualities by being reduced back to the natural original, indivisible wholeness of pure love-life energy.

CHAPTER 4

THE PROCESS OF NON-LABELING
AND LIVING IN COMMUNION
WITH ALL ASPECTS OF LIFE

This chapter deals with the problem of how labeling blocks our ability to live in communion with all phenomena that we encounter in the world, as well as with our own feelings, as a kind of communion with ourselves, and as a basis of psychological self-understanding.

We have a label, a conceptual definition, or a name for every aspect of what we call reality. Why is this so? Many insist that if we had no name for a thing, then it would not exist to us. We can "know" a thing, they believe, only by being able to label it. The sum of all of our labels then becomes the sum of the realities in which we live. Others feel that labeling is necessary for purposes of communication. They insist that experiences can be communicated only through the use of labels. However, in these discussions, we will see that not all knowing involves conceptualizing, and not all experience can be communicated with words. For example, is the reality of the experience of beauty communicated by the word "beauty?" Is the actual experience of love communicated by the word "love"? Is the sweetness of the scent of a rose communicated by the word "rose" or by the word "sweetness"? How do you communicate the taste of an orange? Will the word "succulent" do it? Will the word "tangy" do it? Will any adjective or word do it? Does the word *always* communicate the gist of a particular experience?

Let us observe what happens when we label. If you follow it closely, you will recognize that when you label something, such as a tree, then you put it in the category or grouping called "trees." I also immediately see that by labeling that object as a tree I am not relating to that particular tree, but to the generic category "tree" (i.e., to all trees). I also see that I have put psychological space between myself and that object, the tree, by relating to my conceptual image or definition of the tree, abiding in my own mind, rather than relating to the actual tree itself as a living energy presence, abiding in the world. I am now standing outside and away from the actual tree in the world and I can see now that I label the tree, or any other phenomenon that I encounter in the world, so that I can experience it, know it, as a concept in my own mind. I see that I have become the experiencer, and the tree has become the experienced. But is it the actual living tree that I am experiencing, or just the label "tree"? In other words, am I relating to the tree in its own particular suchness, its immediate experienced presence, or am I relating to my connotation of the label "tree?" At this point, the answer to this may still not be clear.

In any event, I recognize that part of the function of labeling is to set myself off and apart from the world, as a separate knower. When I label something, I am saying that the thing is a "not-me," that it is separate from me, a conceptually defined object of knowledge known by me, the knower. At the same time, I am also affirming myself as the "me" through my capacity to be separate from the known, and be the knower of the known. The "me" exists only relative to some "not-me." Therefore, in order for me to experience myself as a "me," it is necessary to separate myself from the world in which I live, and it is essentially for this reason, the need to affirm myself as a separate and unique entity self, that I label. Labeling always keeps you outside of and separate from the world in which you live, instead of being in communion with it, because you are relating to your own concepts, ideas, definitions, or labels of phenomena, as thoughts arising in your own mind, rather than relating to the actual phenomena themselves, in their non-conceptually mediated immediacy, or "suchness," abiding in the world. As long as you need to be a separate and distinct "me," you isolate yourself from reality instead of living in communion with it.

The more that the "me" labels, the more knowledge it feels that it has attained and accumulated, and the more expanded and affirmed it feels that it is. But, at the same time, it is also more separate from that which is experientially real, in itself and in the world, because our consciousness is focused on labels rather than on our actual inner and outer experience. The "me" itself is nothing more than the labels that the knower, the conscious attention, holds or applies to itself, and fearing itself to be basically nothing, or no knowable thing, when it has no labels, or self-definitions, it therefore applies all kinds of labels to itself, and as a result, lives under the illusion that it is really something specific and definable, and that it can truly know phenomena outside of itself by labeling or defining them. Therefore, the "me" is dependent upon labeling and experiencing as the means of affirming its own separate and unique sense of existence. But what is it that the "me" is experiencing? The major question still remains, which is, is the "me" really experiencing the reality in its own particular suchness, or is it experiencing just the label that it applies to the reality? Is the word the thing?

Have you ever looked at an object, such as a tree, without labeling it as such? When you label it as a tree, you classify it, put it in a generic category, and, therefore, you dismiss it, you never really look at it. But if you do not label it in any way, you find yourself looking at it very carefully, and discovering amazing nuances that you had never perceived before, such as all kinds of configurations in the bark, or insects and birds all living interdependently with it. This brings to mind Martin Buber's distinction between the I-Thou relationship and the I-It relationship, or relating either directly to the experiential immediacy of other individuals and phenomena, or to a conceptually defined label or indirect abstraction of them. The I-Thou relationship involves caring about others for their own sakes, or their intrinsic value as living beings, whereas the I-Thou relationship focuses on trying to use others to gratify our own basically selfish, egoistic goals, and defining them with our own preconceived conceptual interpretations. According to Buber: "The relation to the Thou is direct. No system of concepts, no foreknowledge, and no fancy intervene between Thou and I. The memory itself is transformed, as it plunges out of its isolation into the unity of the whole. No set purpose, no greed, and no anticipation intervene between I and Thou. Desire itself is transformed as it plunges out of its dream into its appearance. Every means is an obstacle. Only when every means has collapsed does the meeting come about."[1]

What you label, you destroy or distort by viewing it as a generic abstraction rather than an actual immediate presence with its own distinctive individual particularity—not static, as a conceptual definition, but dynamically changing from moment to moment. When you label a particular person as a Black, a Jew, a hippie, a Communist, a policeman, a Democrat, a Republican, etc., you are distorting your perception of the person as a person by disregarding what makes him what he is, as an indivisible whole living presence, beyond all of the partial, fragmentary, conceptual definitions that you project or superimpose on to him. The person, as such, is not real to you, in the immediacy of his actual living presence in the world; only his generic category is real to you, and you are implying, through the use of grouping, that all such people are basically the same. But if you do not label him in any way, then you will find that you look at him very closely, and he comes alive to you as a person. You see that he is one of nature's unique and artistic creations, but you also see that in many ways, he is just like you. He has fear, anger, and joy, just as you do. He is probably very dear to many people who love him. He may be capable of great cruelty, but he may also be capable of great tenderness. He is a real person whose moment-to-moment self may differ drastically. Therefore, which part of him are you hating and fearing, and which part do you want to hurt? This moment, he may seem to you to be very rigid or short-sighted or unkempt and obstreperous, but by not labeling him, you observe him very closely and carefully and you may discover that what motivates much of his behavior is the same kind of fear and confusion that motivates your behavior. He has his insecurities, just as you have your insecurities. When you observe him closely, you will feel *that* particular experience of fear and insecurity currently operating in him, and you will understand him, even if you do not necessarily agree with some of his particular views and behaviors. It is easy to hate a label, but you cannot hate someone whom you really understand. However, you cannot come to understand that which you label. What you label, you dismiss, and what you dismiss, you cannot be with or really make contact with in order to understand. What you label, you reduce to a static concept in your own mind, and thereby break off direct contact or unmediated communion with the immediacy of its actual living presence in the world, and its dynamically changing experiential states.

The same thing holds true in regard to your experience of yourself. You cannot understand yourself if you have labels for yourself. Can you understand your own feelings if you dismiss them with a label, which is only a presumptive abstraction that is divorced from the flowing energy of the actual feeling itself? The label that you apply to your own feeling separates you from that feeling by making you the outside observer of it. This is a form of escape from your actual feeling into your conceptual interpretation of the feeling, which is removed from the energetic flow of the feeling. It casts you outside of your own feeling, and all you are aware of is your conceptual interpretation of the feeling that you label, such as anger, depression, anxiety, etc., but you are not attentive to what it actually is, as a flowing energetic immediate experience. But when you do not label, you look at every feeling anew as it arises. When you label, you will see that the feeling is not different than the label. The label *evokes* and *intensifies* the feeling or actually produces the feeling in many cases. The feeling and the naming are simultaneous.

As an example, you feel afraid of being lonely. But what are you are really afraid of? Are you afraid of the actual *fact* of loneliness, or of your idea, interpretation, or *connotation* about that fact? Are you afraid of what it really is, or are you afraid of what you think it is? Because the word or connotation frightens you, it makes you avoid having direct experiential contact with loneliness as a fact, unmediated by any kind of preconceived conceptual interpretations or reactive approval or disapproval of that fact. You never look at the actual fact, or directly experience it in its immediacy without labels, and therefore you never come to understand the fact. The word "loneliness" with its memories and connotations of emotional pain, fear, isolation, and abandonment prevents your experiencing the actual feeling of loneliness, afresh, in the present moment, as a direct, immediate, experience, not mediated by preexisting conceptual interpretations. It is only when you are in direct and complete communion with the actual fact that there is no fear, such as the actual fact of feeling lonely or feeling uncomfortable with experiencing yourself as being physically and/or psychologically disconnected from other individuals. In communion, there is no psychological space, no sense of dualistic separateness between the observer and the observed. If you come to recognize that you are currently being the experience of fear, as a temporary modification of your pure conscious awareness and feeling-energy, then you realize that you are not some kind of separate entity that is trying to run away from the fear. If you are this moment nothing but the fear, i.e., not holding yourself to be anything other than the fear, then you will find that the fear disappears. Don't just take our word for it, do it yourself, and see for yourself. Likewise, various other kinds of painful, uncomfortable, or negative feelings drain out and dissolve when your consciousness no longer resists them, and is in non-dualistic full experiential unification with them.

It is only when you are in complete communion with the fact that there is no fear. If you are not in communion with the fact, then there can be fear; and there is no communion with the fact as long as you have an idea, opinion, theory, judgmental approval or disapproval, or any other kind of previous connotation about the fact. If you are face to face with the fact, then there is nothing to understand about it; the fact is simply there, as a non-conceptually mediated direct energetic experience, and you can deal with it, by letting it be instead of trying to avoid, eliminate, or control it in some way. But if you are afraid of the label or your interpretation of a particular experience arising within you in a given moment, then you must go into and understand the whole process of that label, and what the term implies to you. You labeled the feeling as loneliness. Why didn't you label it as aloneness, or simply the fact of being physically alone and/ or psychologically isolated from other individuals? What does "loneliness" really connote to you? Be precise. For example, does it mean to be empty, nothing, incomplete, bored, unprotected, or abandoned? Be with your feeling as a feeling, an unmediated direct experience, and not as a label, a mediated interpretation, and then you will understand why you are afraid of the fact of being alone or without the involvement of some significant other person.

Thus, psychological fear or anxiety is obviously the outcome of labeling—of projecting a symbol or presumptive interpretation to represent the fact; that is, the actual experience of fear is not independent of the word "fear." At least in some cases, the actual experienced feeling of fear is produced by words connoting psychological fear, although fear can also be engendered by conditions alerting us to potential physical dangers in the world, which then gives fear a realistic basis, in contrast to psychological fear, which may not necessarily have a realistic basis, but may be a habitual reaction to certain words, concepts, or labels that have a frightening connotation to us, consciously or subconsciously (subliminally). The label not only arouses the feeling, but also strengthens it and gives it continuity, as a habitual pattern of automatic emotional reaction to connotations that we associate with particular words, conceptual labels, and situations. Eliminating the label, and all of its connotations and associations, permits you to be in communion, direct, non-conceptually mediated contact with the actual feeling in its immediacy, and to directly experience what it really is; the self-understanding or spontaneous insight that is achieved in this way liberates you from the fear of it.

When you cease applying labels to yourself, you will be at peace with yourself because those feelings that arouse anxiety, anger, or depression cannot operate in you unless you label them, and thereby acknowledge them as being real for you. Another related factor that contributes to the experience of inner peace or relaxation is that when there is no labeling, then the acquisitive drive to expand the "me," or enhance our psychological sense of self is ended, or at least suspended for the time being. Most preferences are made for the personal advantage and affirmation of the "me," and so when the elimination of labeling puts an end to preference, it also puts an end to the "me," at least as a temporary suspension in a given moment, but not necessarily permanently. It is not necessary to permanently eliminate all personal preferences and conceptual interpretations because it is natural to have preferences in terms of selecting particular options that seem most consistent with our individual wishes and needs, and which seem likely to be most beneficial to us, such as selecting a particular person as a marriage partner and not other eligible individuals or selecting one particular educational program, career track, and place of residence, and not others, etc. Sometimes conceptual interpretations can also serve to illuminate rather than distort our understanding of certain feelings, situations, and other individuals. However, at other times, it can be helpful, appropriate, and illuminating to temporarily suspend our personal preferences and conceptual interpretations in order to view a particular feeling, situation, phenomenon, or individual from an unbiased perspective, and thereby be open to gaining insights about them that would not be possible if we were always completely, rigidly locked into a more biased, preconceived, judgmental mode of viewing.

In a related manner, we can make personal preferences, at times, without making absolute value judgments, or exclusive judgments of value. Thus, for example, we can still be open to recognizing the good points, the admirable or beneficial aspects of a particular person who we do not select as a marriage partner, or a potential career path that we decide not to pursue. We can make various kinds of preferences without making absolute value judgments, or positively or negatively assessing the intrinsic value of ourselves, other individuals, phenomena, or situations that we encounter, which is not realistically possible, but only a matter of presumptive interpretation. As Shakespeare suggests in *Hamlet,* "Nothing is good or bad, only thinking makes it (seem) so" (Act II, Scene 2, 250-251).

Furthermore, bringing back the self-aware "me" can be appropriate and illuminating, at times, as a means of exploring our own particular individual feelings, creative potentials stirring to be actualized, values, and life experiences, thereby developing enhanced self-understanding, self-actualization, and self-transformation. However, it can also be helpful, at times, to suspend the "me" concept, in order not to superimpose particular biased preconceived interpretations upon our immediate experience of ourselves, other individuals, or phenomena that we encounter in the world. Optimal living, including optimal relationship to ourselves and others, being true to what is experiential real in ourselves and in our encounters with others, involves a flexible process of being open to whatever perspectives and options seem most illuminating and appropriate, as well as most consistent with our own core integrity, in a given moment, rather than being exclusively, rigidly locked into a single predetermined viewpoint. No matter how valuable and illuminating any perspective can be at times, no exclusive perspective can be appropriate, illuminating, and useful all of the time. Hence, one of the factors that reflects a relatively high level of psychological maturity and constructive functioning is the ability to shift our perspective in a flexible manner, especially as a way of staying consistent with, or "going with the flow" of, our own core integrity (i.e., our intuitive sense of self-consistency) and whatever experience is actually arising in the here and now, in ourselves, other individuals, or phenomena that we encounter in the world. Along these lines, Martin Buber discusses the importance of aligning our actions and attitudes with a dynamic intuitive awareness of what is truly consistent with the core integrity or indivisible integrated holistic unity of our own being, as well as our relational discernment of what is truly real, life-affirming, and ethically responsible in our encounters with other individuals and situations:

> In spite of all similarities, every living situation has, like a newborn child, a new face, that has never be-fore and will never come again. It demands of you a reaction which cannot be prepared beforehand. It de-mands nothing of what is past. It demands presence, responsibility; it demands you. I call a great character one who by his actions and attitudes satisfies the claim of situations out of deep readiness to respond with his whole life, and in such a way that the sum of his ac-tions and attitudes expresses at the same time the unity of his being in its willingness to accept responsibility.[2]

Similarly, Abraham Maslow suggests that creative living is not restricted to particular activities, such as creation of artistic works, but is more broadly a process of moment-to-moment deeply invested, caring, joyful, self-forgetful com-munion with whatever reality you encounter in the world, which brings deeper appreciative insight into the truth of each encounter than would otherwise be possible, with a more superficial level of investment in relational encounters because of continued investment in egoistic self-awareness and your own inner thought-monologues:

> The creative person, in the inspirational phase of the creative furor, loses his past and his future and lives only in the moment. He is all there, totally immersed,

fascinated and absorbed in the present, in the current situation, in the here-now, with the matter-in-hand . . .

This ability to become "lost in the present" seems to be a sine qua non for creativeness of any kind. But also certain prerequisites of creativeness—in whatever realm—somehow have something to do with this ability to become timeless, selfless, outside of space, of society, of history . . .

It is always described as a loss of self or of ego, or sometimes as a transcendence of self. There is a fusion with the reality being observed (with the matter-in-hand, I shall say more neutrally), a oneness where there was a twoness, an integration of some sort of the self with the non-self. There is universally reported a seeing of formerly hidden truth, a revelation in the strict sense, a stripping away of veils, and finally, almost always, the whole experience is experienced as bliss, ecstasy, rapture, exaltation.[3]

Our view that the sense of natural response-ability or ability to respond consistently with what is real in ourselves, as well as responding with what arises from our attentive attunement to what is genuinely real in other individuals and situations that we encounter, is rooted or grounded in the sense of integrity or relational integrating wholeness that connects what is real in us to what is real in others, apparently coincides with Buber's and Maslow's view that meaning or ethical values are inherent to the intrinsically relational reality of being, rather than being arbitrarily invented or chosen by particular individuals and groups. According to Buber: "One can believe in and accept a meaning or value . . . if one has discovered it, not if one has invented it. It can be for me an illuminating meaning, a direction-giving value, only if it has been revealed to me in my meeting with being, not if I have freely chosen it for myself from among the existing possibilities, and perhaps have in addition decided with a few fellow creatures: This shall be valid from now on."[4]

Similarly, Maslow suggests that true values or Being-values are intrinsic to the reality of our own intrinsic being and of all being, rather than being arbitrarily selected as a matter of personal choice or preference:

> If my more biological interpretation of an intrinsic self is corroborated, then it would also support the differentiation of neurotic guilt from the intrinsic guilt that comes from defying one's own nature and from trying to be what one is not. But in view of what has gone before, we should have to include the intrinsic values or values of being in this intrinsic self. In theory, then, a betrayal of truth or justice or beauty or any other B-Value should be expected to generate intrinsic guilt (metaguilt), a guilt that would be deserved and biologically sound . . .
>
> *Many of the ultimate religious functions are fulfilled by this theoretical structure.* From the point of view of the eternal and absolute that mankind has always sought, it may be that the B-Values could also, to some extent, serve this purpose. They are *per se*, in their own right, not dependent upon human vagaries for their existence. They are perceived, not invented. They are transhuman and transindividual. They exist beyond the life of the individual. They can be conceived to be a kind of perfection. They could conceivably satisfy the human longing for certainty.[5]

In any event, the experience of inner peace and relaxation, as well as creative insight and inspiration, arises when the "me," in its role as judger of itself, is not active. Judging yourself and others will not help you become a better person, but only a more critical and unhappy one. He who is a critic will always find something to criticize, not only in others, but in himself as well. Even to judge approvingly is to keep the judger active. Many people are under the false assumption that the critic within himself or herself will be quiet if they can only do enough things of which it will approve. But this assumption is simply not true. As long as the inner judger of value or value judger is active or reactive, there will be continuous comparison, competition, and striving, which ultimately must bring fearful anxiety, frustration, and unhappiness. So the objective of optimal psychological health, fulfillment, and creative living (or what Maslow called the ongoing process of self-actualization) is not to try to live up to the judger's demands, expectations, and goals, as the means of quieting it, but to transcend the judger and its acquisitive drive entirely, including the accumulation of interpretive presumptions that recoil our conscious attention and energy investment in our own mind, thereby diminishing our ability to engage in insightful communion with or attunement to the flow of experience in the world. Therefore, freedom from psychologically unhealthy inner conflict and recoil into our own inner mind-monologue is accomplished only when reactive labeling and value judging ceases.

As you can see, labels only function to prevent you from being in direct contact with reality, not only in regard to the internal realities of your own feelings, but also the external realities of life. Applying labels makes you see the world in the same old way. Labels are a function of your interpretation of experience, and interpretation is often a function of memory of past expectations or habitual patterns carried over or projected into the present moment of experience. Therefore, you are always taking the new and interpreting it in the same familiar old way, in accordance with your previous experience, instead of directly experiencing the new as the new, as it spontaneously arises in the present moment, which makes life experienced as very boring indeed! Real living is always occurring in the present, but memory keeps you tied to the past, so in that sense, you are not really living; rather, you are *reliving*, i.e., you are repeating old habitual reactions and interpretations, again and again, like frequently replaying old cassette tapes, as habitual "mental tapes," metaphorically speaking. That kind of process of repetitively projecting habitual expectations and interpretations from the past onto the present moment of experience restrictively narrows our range of experience, by desensitizing us to new experiences and possibilities that cannot realistically fit within that preexisting framework. That process of force-fitting our present experience into preexisting categories of habitual interpretation makes our experience increasingly restrictive, boring, and stale.

But what happens when you do not label anything? Then you look at everything as though you were seeing it for the first time. You are in direct communion with everything because without labels, the observer is naturally united with the observed; there is no duality or sense of separateness between the two. You observe something *with your entire being*, with the totality of your energy investment and conscious attention, that is, with no contradiction, conflict, or resistive opposition within yourself, because part of you is not wishing to wander away to some other kind of experience that you presume "should be," instead of the "what is," or the actual experience that confronts you in the present moment. Then in that intensity of being contented to fully invest your conscious attention and energy in the present experience that actually confronts you, in the here and now, you will find that there is no separate, self-aware observer at all; there is only undivided holistic *attention*, or what may be referred to as the state or dynamic process of just *experiencing,* in which there is neither the reactive, recoiled experiencer nor the object which is to be experienced through a filter of preconceived interpretations and reactive value judgments. This is a process of non-dualistic *communion* with the experience that is actually arising in the here and now, unmediated by any kind of preconceived interpretations and judgmental reactions. This is a new way to contact life. This is what it means to really be living fully, by contacting your actual inner and outer experience directly, in all of its immediacy, with full investment of your conscious awareness and feeling energy, without being distracted by any preconceived interpretations, the pursuit of a presumptive "should be," or the avoidance of a presumed "should not be."

To contact life without labels is like being born anew. You are seeing everything fresh and new, as though you were seeing it for the first time. You are looking with *naïve perception*. The world is now fully alive, fully vivid and vibrant, and a real adventure, of which you can never tire or bore, because you are seeing it creatively anew each moment. It is as though your whole world had become a creatively alive art museum. When you go to an art museum, the objects of nature which you see there are all still-life, dead. You look at a painting of a pastoral scene, and you think that you are seeing a tree, but it is not an actual tree, it is only a picture of a tree, a lifeless imitation. And if you have the artist's experience of the tree in the painting, then that is *his* experience, and not yours, and every time you look at the painting, your perception is predetermined by what the artist wants you to perceive, and that is all that you can ever perceive in it. The living creativity of openness to new insight and new ways of encountering inner and outer experience is destroyed when perceptions become fixed and predetermined. How can that compare with the creatively alive experience of being in communion with a bird in flight or a rippling brook?

You have paintings that you love to hang on the wall and display to others because you believe that you can relegate beauty to being a possession, like all of your other possessions. You think that you are enriching the "me" by the beauty of your possessions, as though somehow that makes *you* more beautiful. But beauty, like love, cannot be possessed. In trying to possess it, you lose it, for where the self is, beauty is not. Possessiveness, including the conceptual definition as a kind of psychological possession or incorporation of objects of knowledge by the egoistic "me" as knower, labels what is known as a basically dead, static, conceptual definition, whereas true beauty arises as an experience of communion with dynamically, continuously, spontaneously, free flowing life energy, which cannot realistically be stopped or paused to be defined, controlled, predicted, or possessed. You cannot realistically reduce beauty to a memory, or to an abstract conceptual definition. You must be in communion anew with that live tree each time in order to "know" the beauty of "it," for it is only in direct communion that the beauty which is already abiding *within you* is released as well as abiding with and as other individual living presences and forces of nature that you encounter in the present moment. In communion, with its resulting loss of self-awareness, there is a vacuum or absence of reactive mental chatter and emotional clutter produced in you, and that vacuum is the "place" where beauty abides. When you don't label, you don't translate what you see into thought. Then the mind is silent, and in that silence beauty abides, as the inherent purity of joyful life energy beyond all interpretive abstractions and reactive value judgments. Ironically, in that moment of being nothing (i.e., being willing not to define yourself and others in any preconceived way), you are truly something; you are being beauty itself. Basically, then one "sees" beauty only by *being* beauty. As Gibran points out, "Beauty is eternity gazing at itself in the mirror."[6] Beauty is not something external to you that you see only with your eyes, or think about with your mind, but something of inspirational quality that fills your heart. Beauty is not something that comes through the senses, but is something that you *are being* when you are self-abandoned, or self-forgetful, in fully invested, heartfelt, caring, empathic communion with the actual experience that is arising within you or around you in the here and now. As Antoine de Saint-Exupery suggests, in his book, *The Little Prince*, "One sees clearly [or rightly] only with the heart. Anything essential is invisible to the eyes."[7] Beauty does not come as the result of comparison or approximation to some external standard. For example, some people insist that a particular sunset is beautiful because compared to other sunsets they have seen, it is more unusual or more colorful. One tends to equate the unusual or the extremely colorful as being the beautiful. But true beauty is not the colorful or the spectacular, and is in no way the result of comparison. It does not exist in anything external to you. When you are troubled and unhappy, then even the most impressive of sunsets will go unnoticed or unappreciated by you, whereas when you are deeply in love, you see beauty everywhere, even though the day may be dreary and cloudy. When the beauty in you is submerged in your own selfish preoccupation, then there is no beauty for you in the world either. *Beauty is the child whose mother is love, which is what you are in the selfless state of communion.*

You cannot cultivate love or beauty, through some kind of process of intentional effort, but if you are all the time alertly aware of what you are experiencing and doing, you can cultivate keenly observant sensitivity, and out of that sensitivity and attention will come communion with the intrinsic experiential beauty that underlies the entire world, and your own individual being or energy field. Beauty lives only in naïve perception, unbiased by any kind of preconceived interpretations, demanding expectations, and judgmental reactions. It is the seeing of what is actually present, in the here and now, with fresh and uncontaminated eyes, without preconceptions of any kind. When you are able to see any experience that is actually arising without the intrusion of labels, categories, groupings, or without the influence of past conditionings that is memory, then life is intrinsic beauty, wonder, and inspiration.

Life becomes experienced as a dull and repetitive bore only when you bring your past conditionings to it. And then you require some kind of artificial euphoric sensation or substance so that life won't seem like so much of a lifeless "drag" to you. But that is like putting on eyeglasses with distorting lenses in order to make the world *seem* different and interesting. The world does not become truly interesting by distorting its reality, but only by living in communion with its ever changing creativity, spontaneous flow of experience, or immediacy and sense of vitality. There is true euphoria only when the world is contacted with naïve perception. The world becomes more exciting as your awareness grows more alertly sensitive, penetrating, and open to contacting a wider range of potential experience, and only then may you be said to be truly living fully because you are then open to making optimal contact with actual life experience in the present moment.

It is not really living when you have contact only with the imaginary thought taking place in your own mind, as an extrapolation of memory or past experience, future expectations, and preconceived interpretations of the present moment, projected and superimposed upon what is actually present or actually happening in the current moment. The memory, future expectation, abstraction, or conceptual interpretation of the thing is not the thing itself, as it actually is arising in the present moment. The thing is known in its "suchness" or vivid experiential immediacy only through direct communion with it, and this requires the absence of filtering and screening memory, future expectations, and preconceived interpretive thought. Memories are the lifeless mental images that we carry about with us, and it is these stale images which meet this extraordinarily vibrant process or flow of experience called life instead of our meeting it directly, and as a result, the perception of life becomes distorted. *Living really begins when thought ends. Life is very real, vivid, and immediate; it is not an abstraction*, and, therefore, it is foolish to look for a philosophical or other abstract or conceptual meaning of life. Therefore, to say that life is not an abstraction, but something experientially real, means that the only genuine meaning that life can possibly have is to live it fully, in deeply engaged, receptive openness to and direct contact with it, unmediated by preconceived interpretations and selective, judgmental self-censorship of your experience. Therefore, exciting living does not come with pursuing "kicks," "thrills," or some kind of artificially contrived intense sensationalism, functioning as a predetermined, controlled, compulsively repetitive, addicting mode of experience that is basically designed to provide a distracting escape from what is spontaneously arising within and around you, but in an enormous sensitivity or attentive attunement to reality. When we commune deeply with our life experience, with loving heartfelt investment in the here and now, then occasionally, our consciousness can spontaneously penetrate into and thereby gain profoundly enriching experiential insight into the essential spiritual reality of love-goodness-beauty-joy that underlies the particular phenomena that we encounter, as well as gaining related insights into the broader reality and meaningful truths of life as a whole. This view that letting go of extraneous past memories, future expectations, speculative interpretations, and other egocentric psychological "baggage," in deeply invested communion with the "reality of the moment," is the key to creative and fulfilling living, is affirmed not only by the authors of this book, but also by other advocates of human potentials self-actualization, such as Abraham Maslow,[9] Eckhart Tolle,[10] and Brian Piergrossi,[11] among many others.

When the mind is quiet, and not in predetermined movement with thought, then it is one with the movement of life, and that is a great joy and beauty. Then there is no psychological space, barrier, filter, or veil separating you from life. You are actually being life, and only then are you living life as fully and completely as it can be lived. Only when you are one with it, fully immersed in the flow of actual experience in the present moment are you in full contact with life, and it is only in full contact that you are really living as fully and completely as it is possible to live.

When the mind is empty of any preset viewpoint or commitment to perceive in a particular predetermined way then it is open to being receptive to all kinds of things that may spontaneously impinge on it. You are then open to being aware of all kinds of realities that you may not have noticed before, when you were formerly locked into more predetermined ways of viewing and functioning. This is the only real way of expanding your consciousness. Memories, future expectations, and other predetermined interpretations are the selective conditionings or filters that function to close the mind to the ever new and ever changing reality. For example, when you go into the forest to look for something in particular, such as deer, birds, birch trees, etc., then that selective label is all that you will be open to perceiving, and you will miss everything else that could have impinged itself upon you had you been open and receptive and uncommitted in your perception. Therefore, as you walk with your head high, scanning the trees for birds, for example, the world of flowers, insects, and sky are all disregarded and do not exist for you. However, with naïve perception, the whole world is open to you, and there is no telling what you will encounter, which is what makes living so exciting. But to the "sophisticated" mind, there is only dull and endless repetition.

So be no expert at anything. If you feel like an expert, then you feel that you have no more to learn, but you approach life only seeking to use it as a means of confirming what you already know. But if you are simple and naive, then you can learn from everything. Even something considered as minor as a blade of grass moving and bending with the wind can have a message for you in terms of how to live your life. When you are in naïve perception, you are in communion with more than just the object, but with the principles of life that underlie it. For example, looking at a garden with naïve perception, you will see more than just the existing flowers and trees. In your openness, you will encounter the whole of the thing, and you will see universal principles in operation. You may see how nature lives in ecological balance. You may encounter and understand principles of life and death as some trees shed their leaves, and some flowers spring up after a winter's dormant sleep. You may see universal principles of brotherhood and interdependency as you observe how the same Mother Earth nurtures the roots of all of her various offspring that grow in her same soil, and how the sun shines on all the species alike, or how the rain drenches all the species also without preference. You may see the lilies of the field neither "toiling" nor "spinning" (Matthew 6:28;

Luke 12:27) toward any kind of becoming, i.e., not striving to achieve any predetermined objective, and it will "speak" its message to you, and you will understand because your mind, in not being pre-committed, is not closed and moving somewhere; therefore, you are open and receptive to seeing and understanding. You will recognize that you are inextricably a part of this whole event that you are perceiving, and not just an alien observing it from the outside, and this understanding will transform you.

To have this kind of holistic or total perception, you must know how to be aware, which means that in the process of being open and aware, the mind becomes extraordinarily sharp, sensitive, and penetrating, and it is that quality of sharpness and sensitivity, that quality of total attention and absorption, of seriousness which will produce or yield the greatest possible appreciative, penetrating, insight into the reality that you encounter in such an engaged, receptive, uncluttered, nonselective way. We haven't the eyes to see the whole thing at a single glance. This clarity of the eye is possible only if we can be in full contact with all of the details, and then let the mind take an intuitive leap.

Not all those who look can truly see what is actually present. In fact, to *look* is not to *see*. To look is to presumptively know beforehand, and to actively pursue that object for which you are seeking, and therefore to come to selectively perceive only that particular fragmentary, preselected thing. But to see is to be the passive recipient of the total understanding of life living itself out in its basic principles and relationships.

Some philosophies would have you live fully and intensely by having you live as though it were your *last* day on earth. But that only makes you fearful, grabby, and clinging. Living as though it were your last day makes you live in the sense of time, whereas in communion, there is timelessness. There must always be fear when you live in time. You want desperately to hold on to every moment of experience, to collect as much variety of experience as you can, and to preserve what you fear you will lose. Therefore, you cannot be with life and just watch it if you have a need to possess it and preserve it. It puts you in a hurry to gather and collect experiences, as though maximal living were equated with the accumulation of as many experiences as possible. In trying to do a great deal of living in a short period of time, you end up doing very little real living. You are too much in a hurry to gather or accumulate all kinds of available experiences, and you cannot be with anything long enough to make complete contact with it, contentedly, with full investment, not seeking any other kind of experience than what is actually present, here and now, and let it reveal itself to you, as it truly is, in your communion with it. Fullness of living does not abide in the *quantity*, or extensive variety, of experience, but, rather, in its *quality*, or depth of insight and appreciation, arising from depth of communion with whatever experience is actually arising in the here and now.

Living, truly, takes place only in communion, or, in the words of Martin Buber, "All real living is meeting."[12] Outside of communion, living becomes nothing more than just the pursuit of new and more intense sensations and presumptive conceptual interpretations, but then you will not know anything of what life really is. You can really "know" and understand only those things with which you have had communion. This can be with a person, with nature, or with any aspect of life. Then there is no sense of separateness between you and any aspect of life; therefore, you are then in the position of really "knowing" a thing without the element of time, or being in a hurry to move on and gather a wide variety of other experiences so that the possessive ego does not feel that it is losing, missing, or lacking anything, and experiences a sense of deficiency and lack of wholeness. Time brings with it fear and concerns around loss, gain, and possession, all of which destroy the capacity to really appreciate that with which you are making contact, in the here and now.

The reader should not misinterpret the importance of living in the timeless present to mean that you should have absolutely no regard for decisions that will affect your future activities. You can still make important decisions and plans, the necessity for which arises out of the creative present moment, which will affect your future life, without actually living in the future; that is, without actually being constantly absorbed in the state of anticipatory thought which keeps you removed from reality experience arising in the present moment. For example, if arising from your own self-understanding, achieved in the creative present moment, you discover clearly that you love children and would love to be a school teacher, then you might apply to a university that could provide you with the training that you would require to become a teacher, which means taking action now for something that will affect you in the future. But that kind of decision, or pragmatic planning, which arose out of the state of communion with what is actually arising as experience and appropriate as a responsive course of action in the present moment, is still part of the moment's reality, and not part of the "me's," "I"-thought, or the separatist ego's attempt to use predetermined thought as a means of aggrandizing and comforting itself or escaping from some reality.

The reader should also not confuse living in the timeless present with living in the present as an aspect of time (i.e., the current moment of time conceptually interpreted and defined rather than directly experienced in its immediacy, without conceptual mediation). The present as an aspect of time is meant to suggest a point or moment in time between the past and the future. That present is still within the realm of time and of interpretive thought, and is not the same as the timeless now, in which the concept of time and preconceived interpretive thought, as part of the ego's continuously reactive inner monologue, is absent. The "now" is not a point in time between the past and the future, but is that state of timelessness when thought is quiet. The "now" to which I am referring is reflected in this poem which I (Max Hammer) once wrote:

> Now is not now
> But Eternity
> Now is not remember when
> But ever-new
> Now is not toil and spin
> But lilies of the field,
> Now is not know
> But love,
> Now is not mine,
> But One,
> Now is not me and you
> But I and Thou
> Now
> Is

Many people prefer to live in the present time as a way of escaping the responsibilities of caring and planning for their own lives, and as a way of escaping responsibility toward others, and as a way of rationalizing their egoistic, selfish need to impulsively, recklessly indulge themselves with immediate gratification because they cannot tolerate frustration. Their philosophy is basically a hedonistic one: "Live for today, for who knows if tomorrow will ever come." Even though many of these people refer to themselves as the "now" generation, it should not be confused with the timeless "now" of communion.

Therefore, instead of living as though you were seeing the world for the *last* time, you should react to life as though you were seeing it for the *first* time, i.e., with a naïve perception, without the contamination of labels, preconceptions, expectations, or any kind of previous bias or conditioning. To really live, you must learn to die to yourself every moment, to die to that which is the past in you.

There is truly a lifetime in every day. When the sun comes up and you awaken, you are reborn anew, and when the sun goes down and you sleep, then the self of that day is gone. So why not bury it? Bring nothing of yourself forward from the previous day. That day has died; let the "you" that lived that day die with it. This is a new day and a new you. The world is not exactly the same today as it was yesterday and neither are you. You only pretend to yourself that there is some continuous and consistent self in order to try to feel secure by feeling some sense of permanence. You cannot accept your own finality. You are frightened of death. But again, is it death as a fact that you are afraid of, or the label and your connotation of it? This is another instance in which the label and its connotations so greatly overshadow the fact that the fact cannot easily be encountered and the fear understood. The connotations which you typically have of being in an eternity of nothingness and oblivion; the total extinction of the knower, and the inability to ever know anything again; the fear of being damned to eternal pain, and the inability to ever escape from it; a feeling of being totally lost and abandoned in total darkness with no means of ever finding your way back to the light; the fear of the painfulness of the process of dying and being unable to escape it, etc. All of these various kinds of frightening and painful connotations make you run away from having any contact and communion with the fact of death. But when you explore the problem of death, as a fact, you will inquire as to what it is that comes to an end in death. Is it life that comes to an end, or just the continuity of the "me," or the presumptive idea of yourself as a self-defined entity, viewing itself as being dualistically separate from others? Can that which is ever become that which is not? Does life ever stop being life? Can it ever turn into something different? When the continuity of the "me" ends, will you still be frightened of death, and will you not then know what death really is? When the continuity of the "me" is gone, what else is there for you to fear to lose? Explore the problem yourself and see. Get to the fact of death itself, and you will see what it is, and what you are really afraid of. See if it is really something to be feared or whether it is only the label to be feared. Is death really different from life, or must there be death for there to be life?

You are concerned about the continuity and permanence of the "me" but can there be renewal if there is continuity? And is not life continuous renewal? And must there not be death of the continuous and the familiar for there to be renewal? Thus, ironically, in trying to make yourself a continuous and permanent entity, you are living in a form of death, because there is no renewal in that which is continuous, and where there is no renewal, there is no life. Thus, in your own mind, you have believed that death is the extinction of continuity, but if you explore it, you may see that this is really what life is. You have also believed that life was the perpetuation of continuity of the "me," but if you explore it, you may find that that is really what psychological death is, because it offers no possible opportunity for renewal, or transformational growth, like a seed that cannot sprout and grow into a tree or flower, as a qualitatively greater level of transformational development, if it holds onto its shell, and its initial static identity as a seed. Therefore, in trying to make yourself into some kind of a consistent and permanent "me," as a conceptually defined sense of identity, you have, in a sense, committed psychological suicide by moving away from the reality of life as a process of unending new discovery and transformation. On the other hand, being willing to relinquish the ego's static sense of conceptually defined identity enables you to reach limitlessly higher or greater levels of qualitative transformation or creative renewal. As the Sufi poet Rumi suggests,

I died as a mineral and became a plant,
I died as plant and rose to animal,
I died as animal and I was Man.
Why should I fear? When was I less by dying?

Yet once more I shall die as Man, to soar
With angels blest; but even from angelhood
I must pass on: all except God doth perish.
When I have sacrificed my angel-soul,
I shall become what no mind e'er conceived.
Oh, let me not exist! for Non-existence
Proclaims in organ tones, "To Him we shall
   return."[13]

Similarly, the importance of letting go of our seed-like sense of self-enclosed static identity so that we can be transformed into a qualitatively greater level of openness to limitless possibilities and unrestricted dynamic development is metaphorically described as follows: "When one sows a single seed, it cannot sprout and produce many seeds until its existence is nullified. Then it is raised to its root, and can receive more than a single dimension of its existence. There in its root, the seed itself becomes the source of many seeds."[14]

That which always remains the same and becomes repetitive cannot possibly be truly alive, renewed, and transformed into a greater level of development. So to die to the "me" is to be reborn in communion with all of life, in every new moment, whereas to hold tight to continuity is to be in psychological "death," or to be inwardly deadened, numbed, by adhering to a basically static, predetermined way of viewing, functioning, and sense of identity. Without realizing it, you have been carrying the "me" over from moment to moment, as a static sense of identity and its static, predetermined interpretations of others. Never letting it die or fade from your awareness, you have never been able to really be with anything new, with anything really fresh and alive. When you are living fully and creatively, you are dying to the "me" from moment to moment. The "me" is constructed and composed of thought. It is basically the ideas, concepts, images, and memories that you have of yourself, as well as your preconceived interpretations of other individuals, situations, and phenomena around you. Thought is of time, and resides only in the past and future. Thought can never really be in the timeless present, now; and so the "me" can never really live, for true living takes place only in the present, only in full contact and communion with reality, and thought can never be truly present to contact in the present moment.

Changing the way you wear your hair or your clothes, changing your job, or the location in which you live, which is typical of the superficial ways in which many people attempt to affect change in their lives, is not really significant change at all. These are all just minor modifications of the ego's predetermined, habitual, basically static, stale, deadened ways of viewing and functioning. To really change is to be reborn anew and afresh every moment. Bringing nothing forward from the previous moment, it is as if you are being reborn every moment. You are new, fresh, creatively alive.

So, look at all your old hates, biases, and prejudices, and let them all die *now*—right this moment. Is there not someone you have made your enemy because you cannot die to the "wrongs" that you feel they may have perpetrated upon you? Look at your old enemy anew with naïve perception. Really look at him closely, and listen to him carefully and with your entire being. Don't just look at the memories, which remind you only of that aspect of him that hurt you in some way. But look at him as a totality and commune with him, and let come to you, from him, whatever understanding will spontaneously arise. Yesterday was yesterday; today is today. It's an entirely new him and an entirely new you. Be open and receptive for anything to make contact with you. Have no predetermined expectations about anything. Just make contact with all that confronts you, and let it affect you as it will. Don't predetermine what to react to or what to perceive. This is what is meant by living creatively, spontaneously, insightfully, flexibly, in dynamic responsive attunement to the flow of actual experience in every moment. Predetermination drains the life out of us, psychologically speaking, and makes all of living insipid.

So, let each moment be a lifetime unto itself. In truth, *reality has no continuity*. It is arising only from moment to moment, timeless and measureless. The only real living and the only true reality exist only in that timeless state of communion. Instead of celebrating a new birthday every year, learn to celebrate a new birthday every day, and a new birth moment every moment. Make all of life and every moment a celebration of joyful communion with whatever experience is actually arising as present, in the here and now.

Recommended Assignment or Contemplative Exercise

Write a journal or a report to one of your friends or loved ones at least once a week, describing your experiences with regard to non-labeling and communion. Even if your experiences are not positive or successful ones, describe what thoughts or feelings were dominating you that prevented you from being in fully invested direct communion with the here and now. Ask yourself why these particular thoughts or feelings intruded at that particular time. Thought functions as inner chatter, continuously recoiling the mind upon itself, preventing communion with whatever is actually arising as experiential reality, in yourself, other individuals, or phenomenon in the world that you encounter, in the present moment. Thought functions as a distorting filter between the experiencer and the experienced. You supply this inner chatter to yourself, subconsciously, so that you will have something to experience, and will therefore not have to surrender the egoistic sense of separate self-awareness. So don't attempt to force yourself to stop labeling by repeating to yourself, over and over again, "Don't label. Don't label." It is not subject to command, nor is the ability to commune subject to demand. It will come spontaneously with greater and greater self-understanding. That self-understanding will grow if you continue to be sensitive to what the chatter is saying in your mind, and when and why it comes. Then one day, the chatter will stop of its own accord, your mind will quiet, and you will be in communion with what is actually present, here and now, I and Thou.

SECTION B OF CHAPTER 4

THE ENHANCEMENT OF
CREATIVITY AND SPONTANEITY

Although all of the exercises are designed to contribute toward the development of your potentials for living spontaneously and creatively, this exercise is more specific, and concerns itself with the enhancement of your capacity to creatively and spontaneously do your own thing.

To live life as fully as possible and to realize your fullest range of natural potentials necessitates that you live spontaneously and creatively, meaning living responsively attuned to the actual experiential reality spontaneously arising in yourself and creatively arising in others around you from moment to moment. However, this exercise cannot teach you how to be creative and spontaneous. At best, it can only provide some clues or pointers in that direction. You must make the actual journey. You cannot be taught to be spontaneous and creative any more than you can be taught to be sensitively alert or to love, for these states exist only when the mind is not rehearsed or patterned in any way. So, no path, method, or formula can ever lead you to spontaneity or creativity.

No one can teach you the loss of the sense of self-awareness in the absorption of communion with the moment-to-moment actual experiential reality that is necessary if you are to be spontaneous and creative in living. It can never be the result of some deliberate or contrived act, for all such acts stem from the self as the one who acts as the doer. For that reason, the more effort you make to be creative, the less creativity and spontaneity can result. Genuine creativity is not something that can be realistically pursued, and thereby achieved, but it is something which spontaneously *comes to you* when all effort-making and pursuing ends, for only then is the sense of self-awareness put at rest. To live creatively and spontaneously is to live without the filtering and controlling process of the ego, the seat or center of the separate sense of self or dualistic self-awareness.

Prominent psychologists, such as Daniel Goleman, Abraham Maslow, and Charles Garfield, have described enhanced creative and productive functioning, or "peak experiencing" and "peak performing," as arising from an "egoless" process of "flow," where people are free of worry, self-consciousness and effortful control. According to Goleman: "Flow is a state of self-forgetfulness, the opposite of rumination and worry: instead of being lost in nervous preoccupation, people in flow are so absorbed in the task at hand that they lose all self-consciousness, dropping the small preoccupations—health, bills, even doing well—of daily life. In this sense, moments of flow are egoless. Paradoxically, people in flow exhibit a masterly control of what they are doing, their responses perfectly attuned to the changing demands of the task. And although people perform at their peak while in flow, they are unconcerned with how they are doing, with thoughts of success or failure—the sheer pleasure of the act itself is what motivates them."[1]

Goleman describes flow as a "glorious . . . feeling of spontaneous joy, even rapture," or "mild ecstasy."[2] Maslow is another psychologist who describes creative functioning (which he refers to as "peak-experience" or "self-actualization") as involving letting go of ego or separate self-awareness, selfish concerns, effortful control, value judgments, and predetermined expectations, replaced by greater spontaneity, relaxed ease, joyfulness, and fully invested, self-forgetful communion with "the reality being observed" or "the matter-in-hand."[3] Similarly, sports psychologist Charles Garfield describes peak performance as involving a "letting go" of worry, concern about possible outcomes of "success" and "failure," as well as relinquishing conscious control and calculating thinking, leading to deep relaxation of mind and body.[4] According to Garfield, peak performance involves a sense of joyful vitality and being in touch with or in deeply invested communion with the activity at hand, and with everything within and around you.[5, 6]

Spontaneity

Spontaneity is quite often confused with impulsivity, and many people who are really impulsive pride themselves on believing that they are spontaneous. The state of impulsivity exists when our impulses push for inappropriate, premature, reckless expression without the ego's consent, and are stronger than the ego in its role as the observer and controller of the impulses, with the ego in this case functioning as the aspect of the psyche that is concerned with making pragmatic, realistic, adaptive adjustments to the requirements of reality, so that behavioral acting upon impulses in inappropriate ways will not risk repercussions that could possibly endanger our continued survival or well-being. This aspect of the ego is consistent with Sigmund Freud's definition of the ego as a "reality principle" that is concerned with regulating the expression of impulses by delaying, frustrating, or redirecting inappropriate pleasure-seeking, sexual, or aggressive impulses. Freud referred to these kinds of impulses as the "pleasure principle," which, if gratified in their original form, might possibly endanger your individual survival or well-being.[7]

In the case of spontaneity, there is no predetermined sense of self present, acting as the controller of what we say and do. Genuine spontaneity is a process in which the self is absorbed in total communion with the challenge, and so there is no psychological space or predetermined agenda intervening between the awareness of the challenge and the response to the challenge. That immediacy does not necessarily mean that our response to the challenge is instantaneous, because a spontaneous response may arise after taking some time to observe and reflect upon a particular challenge, whereas responding instantaneously can, in some cases, reflect some kind of predetermined agenda or sense of fearful insecurity that goads us to respond prematurely, before we have had the opportunity to assess the realistic implications of the challenge and the appropriateness of our intended response. That kind of premature instantaneous response reflects impulsivity rather than true spontaneity. True spontaneity arises from an immediacy of attunement to the experiential realities of the challenge and to the appropriateness of our response, not mediated by any kind of predetermined agenda. A truly spontaneous response does not involve recklessly expressing impulses or impatiently seeking immediate gratification of perceived needs that are not appropriate within the context of a particular situation or circumstance. Impulsivity involves recklessly disregarding all possible adverse or even dangerous consequences that may, likely, result from our intended behavior, particularly if and when we feel that lack of immediate gratification would be intolerable, producing unacceptably uncomfortable levels of frustration, anxiety, and insecurity. Spontaneity is action without the filtering, censoring, or controlling process of the actor or doer. Spontaneity is the response to a challenge which has been perceived creatively, meaning that you are open to new creative insight (nonselective, unrestricted, uncontrolled insight) coming from direct, unmediated contact with the challenge or experience not mediated by any kind of predetermined agenda or presumptive bias. That is to say, when a particular challenge or stimulus is permitted to impinge upon you, and creatively elicit from you whatever response that it will without any interference from a controlling self, without impulsively acting out urges or desires that are clearly inappropriate or reckless, then the act or process of interaction is said to be *creative, involving a process of optimal openness and unrestricted, nonselective receptivity to new creative insight. Your perception of the interaction is not restricted to any kind of predetermined agendas, goals, expectations, or biased interpretations, and the response to this interaction is said to be spontaneous, not controlled by any predetermined plan of action or by any kind of overriding psychological needs that predetermine or control your response to the challenge or situation at hand,* because you are intolerant of having that demanding, impatient need frustrated or even postponed in any way. That is, if you are intolerant of having particular psychological needs frustrated, then your response to a particular challenge or situation will not be spontaneous or uncontrolled, and it will also not be truly creative or based on openness to unbiased, undistorted, nonselective insight, because you will not feel free to respond in a manner that does not provide immediate, impulsive, or controlled gratification of those particularly intensely, overridingly, demanding psychological needs.

Most essentially, functioning creatively and spontaneously involves responding with unbiased, nonselective, unrestricted openness to the full range of your available experience and intuitive insights because you are not restricted to any kind of preconceived agendas or selective interpretive frameworks. You are truly creative in the sense of being open to discovering new insights, appropriate adaptive responses, and transformational possibilities beyond the boundaries of what is already known or what the ego's preconceived agendas presume to be true, necessary, and worthwhile. Furthermore, the terms "spontaneous" and "creative" connote that your actions arise from alert attunement to or non-dualistic communion with the flow of actual experience, and discernment of whatever course of action seems most appropriate and authentic, genuine, or consistent with the truth of yourself, and the truth of the actual experience that you encounter, which you intuitively recognize as "the truth of the moment." Although spontaneity and creativity are closely interrelated processes, the term "spontaneity" refers primarily to responsiveness to current actual realities, whereas the term "creativity" involves openness to new transformational possibilities, internally within yourself, and also relationally in regard to your responsive encounters with other individuals, situations, and circumstances. Sometimes the term creativity also refers to unrestricted openness to the flow of experience and new insight, whereas the term spontaneity refers to responsive action that arises from that unrestricted openness to the experiential truth of oneself and the relational or contextual "truth of the moment." Such responsive action is usually appropriate action.

Genuine spontaneity and creativity are sometimes guided by intuitions or insightful "hunches" coming from your core integrity, the integrating or unifying relational core of your own being, which often functions relatively instinctually, subliminally, not fully consciously. Your core integrity naturally urges you to function consistently with whatever responsive options intuitively "ring true" or feel consistent at a vibrational energetic level of the psyche, with the integrated wholeness of your own being, experience, and the truth of the situation at hand, whereas predetermined, selective, partial, divisive, deficiency-oriented modes of perception and functioning reflect lack of integrity or lack of consistency with the intrinsic wholeness of your own being. True integrity has its source in the unifying center or integrating core level of your being, which naturally includes all other, extended aspects of your being and experience within itself, and provides intuitive insight into their essential underlying significance, perceived within a holistic relational context, like an indivisible hologram or an integrated, holistic, mode of perception. Being true to your core integrity involves responsively functioning in a manner that is consistent with and honors rather than violates the intrinsic value or preciousness of life, in yourself and others you encounter in a given moment. For example, at least in most situations and circumstances, violence would be an existential violation of your core integrity or natural inclination to affirm rather than violate the intrinsic value of life, and life-affirming qualities that are intrinsic to your own and everyone's real being or life energy force, such as, compassionate good-will, justice, as well as respect for the natural rights and freedoms of everyone. Integrity is naturally devoted to preserving and nurturing the continued developmental growth of what is truly real or life-oriented in yourself and in others, whereas egoistic lack of integrity often leads to the corrosive disintegration, fragmentation, distortion, violation, and degradation of what is truly real and life-affirming, replaced by defending and embellishing false presumptive ideas of yourself and others. Metaphorically speaking, caring for what is truly real, genuinely good, or naturally life-affirming in yourself and others is like nurturing the growth of a beautiful garden of flowers and trees, whereas constructing presumptive ideas of yourself and others is like making pictures or plastic figures that have no real life in them, which therefore cannot grow in a real way, no matter how much you try to embellish or aggrandize them.

Creative, spontaneous, wholesome ways of functioning arise from integrity or consistency with your intrinsic wholeness and rightness of being, rather than arising from the ego's basic sense of inner and outer division and deficiency, which reflect lack of wholeness and lack of attunement to what is truly appropriate or life-affirming in a given moment. Integrity is open to the spontaneously arising, creatively responsive, relationally connected, "truth of the moment," rather than following a static, predetermined, divisive view of "truth." Functioning creatively, or responding from your own sense of integrity means that you are functioning consistently with the totality or the indivisible integrated wholeness of what truly feels experientially real and right for you, in a given moment, whereas functioning inconsistently from what is experientially true for you would produce an unnatural sense of self-division, self-estrangement, lack of self-consistency, lack of integrated wholeness of being, or lack of integrity. True integrity means that our perception and actions are guided by the unifying core or center of our being, and its intuitive discernment of how we can best be aligned and move with, rather than move against, the integrated wholeness of all that is experientially real, rightful, appropriate, or life-affirming (regenerative rather than degenerative) within and around us, which reflects (not necessarily fully consciously) a self-consistent or sound vibratory energy pulse. Integrity is open to the whole flow of pertinent experience, rather than being selectively biased for or against any predetermined, exclusive mode of perception and action.

In some cases, genuine integrity may involve recognizing that you have ambivalent or contradictory feelings and motivational intentions about certain situations, but even when that occurs, genuine integrity is still naturally inclined to function consistently with our highest priorities, to the best of our ability, even if it involves sacrificing or at least postponing lesser priorities that are also part of but perhaps somewhat less essential to our holistic integrity. Similarly, integrity involves the natural inclination and the attempt to be true to or function consistently with the good-natured inclinations that are inherent to our real being or conscious-life-energy-field, whereas lack of integrity involves becoming self-divided from the integral or integrated wholeness and natural goodness of our own real being and experience by functioning in a manner inconsistent with it. The "goodness," virtue, or wholeness referred to here is a sense of goodness that is directly, energetically, intuitively experienced as the inherent nature of our own real being, and of all real being, rather than conceptually defined, ideally expected, or conditionally achieved as a value judged "should be," or merely presumed to exist. Integrity, an appropriate response to a given challenge, is a relational process that arises as your own authentic truth meets the experiential truth of the situation or circumstance at hand, as well as the interactive relational truth of the encounter between you and another individual or situation.

An authentic or creative response is consistent with the core integrity of your own real being because it keeps you unified with the integrated wholeness of your own actual experiential truth, rather than divisively moving you, as conscious knower, doer, and volitional will power, away from, against, or contrary to your own truth, or sense of authenticity, as a process of self-division, lack of self-integration, or lack of genuine integrity. Predetermined, selective ways of perceiving and impulsive, controlled, inflexible, exclusive, habitual ways of functioning involve a divisive split or discrepancy between the "what is" of our actual experiential truth and the "should be" that we try to substitute for the "what is," as a preferred replacement. That divisive split between our conscious attention and volitional intention, as knower, versus our actual experiential truth, as rejected object of knowledge, is the basic underlying causal source of most, if not all, forms of enduring inner conflict and related psychological disturbance. Some signals that we have moved away from alignment with the flow of integrity or self-consistency include feelings of tension, queasiness, inner conflict, lack of relaxed inner peace and easeful functioning.

Integrity also involves functioning in ways that respect, honor, and nurture rather than degrade the intrinsic, unconditional value of life in ourselves and others around us. The narcissistic ego sometimes follows a false, preconceived sense of integrity, involving asserting inflexible, dogmatic principles that are designed to enhance the individual's and group's conditional sense of value, worth, or idealized positive self-evaluation. This often involves rigidly following habitual, predetermined, inflexible, sometimes fanatical, extremist, absolutist, or exaggeratedly one-sided ways of functioning and viewing situations. This doctrinaire, egoistic, false sense of integrity should be clearly distinguished from true integrity, arising from nonjudgmental, nonselective communion with the relational flow of life experience, producing experiential insight into its intrinsic, unconditional, value, as well as the ability to function in a flexible, responsive, appropriate manner, grounded in openness to the spontaneously arising truth of the moment rather than following some kind of predetermined agenda. Superimposing predetermined egoistic agendas upon the natural flow of life experience and activity often degrades, distorts, and fragments the reality of life in a divisively partisan, biased, manner, by violating its indivisible wholeness or true integrity, as if trying to force fit the spontaneous, often unpredictable, winding flow of life into a preconceived mold or restrictive "Procrustean Bed." For example, the ego's false sense of integrity may involve judgmental stereotyping, belittling, scapegoating, or persecuting particular individuals or groups as being intrinsically inferior to its individual and group sense of identity or idealized self-definitions; as well as rigidly following certain preconceived political, social, or religious principles, sometimes defined in absolutist, authoritarian, or even totalitarian terms, even when those precepts are unnecessarily harmful and degrading to us and/or others. Sometimes this may involve trying to gratify the ego's idealized psychological needs for an exaggerated, grandiose sense of competitive superiority, worth, power, and excitement at the expense of others.

The ego's values often arise from a rigidly predetermined judgmental, "should be" or "should not be," whereas the true integrity that arises from our real being is guided by nonjudgmental, non-preconceived, flexible attunement to what is actually arising in us and others in a given moment. The core integrity of our real being can also sometimes value judge what "should be" or "should not be" in terms of intuitively recognizing which possible options are, or are not, truly appropriate, life-affirming, and psychologically growth-oriented in a given moment, whereas the ego's value judgments involve trying to force-fit ourselves and others into certain presumptions and rigid patterns that are often out of alignment with the natural flow of life energy and which block or undermine, rather than facilitate, the continued natural unfolding or greater developmental fruition of our own being, other beings, and the relational whole web of being.

Our integrity is our true conscience. In contrast to the Freudian superego conscience, involving feeling shame for violating internalized socially conditioned values, as well as the ego regretting doing something to violate and thereby invalidate its positive self-concepts and idealized self-images, our real conscience, our core integrity, alerts us to the importance of functioning consistently with the true reality nature of our being, so that there is no internal contradiction, division, or conflict. Functioning consistently with the true reality nature of our being produces self-unification of our conscious awareness with our whole energy field, and that inner integrated wholeness of unified conscious-life energy is our only truly effective and enduring healing of various kinds of self-divisive emotional inner conflicts rooted in functioning inconsistently with our core integrity. Whereas the integrity of our real self does not engage in self-judgment and self-definition, the judgmental superego, ego-ideal, or false sense of conscience is the idealized positive self-image of absolute proficiency that compensates for the absolute sense of deficiency or psychological inner emptiness and nothingness that the ego experiences itself as being at a deeper, mostly subconscious level of the psyche. In contrast to the ego and superego, or ego-ideal, our real being as love-wholeness is an experiential rather than conceptually defined, presumptive, value judged sense of goodness, grandeur, and natural true integrity.

Flexible ways of functioning that can be adjusted to reflect and facilitate continued new creative insight and transformational development in ourselves and in others, guided by our core integrity and our responsive attunement to changing circumstances, should also be distinguished from egoistic opportunism, which uses flexible, sometimes unscrupulous, even ruthless, Machiavellian means to gratify the ego's psychological deficiency needs at all costs, even if that involves violating the legitimate rights and freedoms of other individuals, as well as violating the good-natured qualities that are intrinsic to our own real being, life energy force, or core integrity.

Genuine integrity is constructive in the sense of having a natural or innate sense of responsibility to contribute to reality's ability to continue to construct, develop, grow, or build upon itself, in contrast to the ego's tendency to tear down, deconstruct, destruct, or distort reality in various ways, such as extreme nihilism, solipsism, and capricious, recklessly irresponsible ways of functioning, or by trying to force-fit reality into an unrealistic, idealized pattern, lacking a firm foundation in the enduring "ground of being" or the natural flow of life energy. The pursuit of imaginary ideals that are not rooted in the intrinsic reality of being or life-energy are metaphorically depicted in literature by the story of Don Quixote doing battle with windmills, or the novel *Gulliver's Travels* in which imaginary, dreamlike, castles were built on top of rootless, ungrounded floating clouds in the sky. This unrealistic, often unscrupulous attitude also typifies many ruthless authoritarian or totalitarian ideologies, which often try to justify cruel means that are purportedly designed to achieve "good" objectives, not recognizing that the results of our actions usually eventually reflect the good or bad (compassionate or cruel) means that we employ, sooner or later. Similarly, a particular kind of flower or tree can reflect only the particular type of seed from which it grew, and cannot reflect another type of seed; for example, an orange seed can produce only oranges, and not apples or bananas. Most essentially, values that are based on or grounded in genuine integrity come from attunement to the flow of being, constructive life energy, or actual experience, whereas egoistic values and devaluing usually involve trying to force-fit reality into some kind of idealized, despised, or other preconceived pattern that is not intrinsic to its actual being and its natural pattern of development, becoming, or realistic, workable, construction.

Consistent with our own view of integrity as involving self-consistency, or functioning consistently with the holistic, unifying, integrating center of our own individual being, and its natural authenticity, and relating to the wholeness of other individuals, rather than relating selectively or partially to oneself and others, Roberto Assagioli's psychosynthesis approach to psychotherapy seeks to achieve "harmonious inner integration, true Self-realization, and right relationship with others . . . **Psychosynthesis [involves] the Formation or Reconstruction of the Personality Around the New Center**. When the unifying center has been found or created, we are in a position to build around it a new personality—coherent, organized, and unified. This is the actual psychosynthesis . . . "[8] Assagioli suggests that developing greater awareness of the unifying center level of our individual being can help to calm down, transform, and harmoniously integrate turbulent emotions and desires that could otherwise induce agitation in us and push for inappropriate, possibly dangerous, outlets of expression:

> There are certain strong trends, certain vital elements that, however much we may disparage and condemn them, obstinately persist. This is true especially concerning sexual and aggressive drives. These, when detached from the complexes or diverted from their previous channels, create in us a state of agitation and unrest and may find new but equally undesirable outlets.
>
> These forces, therefore, must not be left to run wild, but should be disposed of in harmless ways or, better still, used for constructive purposes: creative activities of various kinds; the rebuilding of our personality, contributing to our psychosynthesis. But in order to be able to do this we must start from the center; we must have established and made efficient *the unifying and controlling Principle of our life*.[9]

Other prominent psychologists who maintain that unifying or integrating all aspects of the psyche brings psychological wholeness, healing, health, and harmony, involving the resolution of psychologically pathological self-division and self-conflict, include Carl Jung,[10] Abraham Maslow,[11] Ken Wilber,[12] Frances Vaughan,[13] Robert Augustus Masters,[14] as well as self-help and human potentials writers such as Debbie Ford.[15] These psychologists suggest, as did Max Hammer, that unifying the psyche, as the basis of psychological healing, health, and wholeness, necessarily involves integrating previously rejected, unknown, or unconscious feelings and urges, including seemingly "terrible" or socially unacceptable aspects of the psyche (called the "shadow" by Jung, Max Hammer, and other psychologists), by bringing an attitude of compassionate acceptance to them, and permitting ourselves to fully experience them, without identifying with them, and without inappropriately acting upon them.

The natural inner wholeness or self-unification that heals self-divisive inner conflict and psychological pain can be achieved only if we consciously recognize and patiently work through our inner conflicts rather than prematurely deny or escape them. Most people attempt to achieve a kind of immediacy of response which they refer to as "spontaneity" by arbitrarily rejecting inconsistencies or dualistic opposites in their concept of self, so that there remains an internal feeling of consistency, which then permits a kind of freedom to react without self-contradiction, delay, or hesitation. For example, if you were subject to internal contradiction in terms of sexual role, that is, if you saw yourself as being consistent with *both* a male and a female self-image, or *both* a psychologically masculine and feminine self-perception, regardless of your actual physical gender, then you would find it very difficult to respond to a stimulus that necessitates the expression of your sexual role. Inwardly, you would question, "Should I respond as a male or as a female?" or "I'm anxious to show everyone that I am a male, but that is not quite the natural feeling in me, so I must now ask myself, how would a psychologically masculine male respond in this particular situation?" Thus, a sense of internal contradiction or inconsistency makes it difficult to respond immediately and appropriately, if at all. As a result, you would repress the female or feminine component in yourself, and then you would feel the internal sense of consistency that all of you is male, completely masculine, psychologically as well as physically, and therefore your response would tend to be more immediate and consistent with your conceptually defined presumptive sense of gender identity.

But relative immediacy of response is not the kind of spontaneity to which we authors are referring here. A relatively consistent concept of self is not the same as responding without the direction and control of any self-concept. Spontaneity is action without concern about using the action as a means of being consistent with and affirming of our self-concept.

In spontaneity, there is true freedom of action and response. With no predetermined sense of self, or preconceived defined identity acting as a center or controller of our responsive behavior, which is concerned with organizing and trying to reconcile our behavior with our predetermined self-concept, there is then no sense of restriction, limitation, circumference, or automatic off-limits exclusion of possible options that are located outside of and would contradict and invalidate the parameters of our preset self-definitions and habitual ways of functioning. *There can be no center of a predetermined, exclusively restrictive, delimited sense of identity without there also being a circumference of a correspondingly restrictive way of viewing and functioning consistently with that self-definition.* As an illustrative diagram: draw or imagine a small picture of a dot or center inside of a small circle. The limiting circumference represents the entire repertoire of acceptable, permissible responses related to or controlled by the center, as the concept of self, or defined sense of identity, that you do not feel free to contradict, and thereby invalidate as a threat to the continued existence and plausibility of that sense of identity. Therefore, your responses are not free to be non center-related, or to be inconsistent with, and, therefore, invalidate your preexisting self-definitions and similarly controlled, habitual patterns of functioning. When a particular challenge is met by the center, or the particular preconceived self-definition that one is committed to validating (affirming), preserving, enhancing, or aggrandizing, then the center must choose from among its many possible responses one which will be appropriate for the challenge, but which must also be consistent with maintaining and affirming the particular self-concept with which you have become identified. Otherwise, if you behaved and viewed situations inconsistently with your preconceived sense of identity, you would have basically invalidated that sense of identity, and therefore become a psychological non-entity or inner nothingness, which is very frightening to the ego as a threat to its continued sense of psychological existence or self-knowledge.

In this sense, there can be no real freedom of response beyond or outside the parameters of your conceptually defined sense of identity, because to respond or function in a manner inconsistent with your predetermined self-definition is to invalidate, undermine, threaten, and thereby lose the sense of self with which you are identified. This makes you experience yourself as a "not-self," i.e., an unknowable, undefined, "nothing-ness," a nobody, a mystery unto yourself, with no sense of conceptually defined "somethingness" or identity, and no related sense of personal significance, importance, value, worth, and security. The response or way of functioning is conditioned, restricted, or predetermined by its necessity to portray and affirm a particular image of self, or exclusively defined identity, to ourselves, and to the others to whom we are relating. However, *when there is a center-less consciousness, or a conscious awareness knower without any predetermined self-definitions or preconceived sense of identity to uphold, defend, validate, or prove about itself, then there is true freedom to discover new realistic, transformational insights about particular situations, and to select the most appropriate options of responsive functioning in a given moment, guided by our core integrity, because then there are no correspondingly predetermined, exclusive, restrictive ways of viewing and functioning.* Only then is there true spontaneity, creativity, integrity, and authenticity.

This understanding that being free of predetermined social and psychological conditionings as the source of habitual, overly restrictive, ways of perceiving and functioning, as well as no longer trying to defend or validate preconceived self-definitions through such predetermined reactions, enables us to respond more appropriately, spontaneously, and flexibly to each new and unique situation or individual that we encounter in the here and now, as well as enabling us to gain new and greater authentic, unbiased, insights into ourselves, as a responsive, relational self, not an exclusively separate, isolated self, coincides with the following interpretation of Martin Buber's views by the prominent Buber scholar Maurice Friedman:

> When Buber speaks of the free man as free of causation, process, and defined being, he does not mean that the free man acts from within himself without connection with what has come to him from the outside. On the contrary, it is only the free man who really acts in response to concrete external events. It is only he who sees what is new and unique in each situation, whereas the unfree man sees only its resemblance to other things. But what comes to the free man from without is only the precondition for his action; it does not determine its nature. This is just as true of those social and psychological conditioning influences, which he has internalized in the past as of immediate external events. To the former as well as to the latter, he responds freely from the depths as a whole and conscious person. The unfree person, on the other hand, is so defined by public opinion, social status, or his neurosis that he does not "respond" spontaneously and openly to what meets him, but only "reacts." He does not see others as real people, unique and of value in themselves, but in terms of their status, their usefulness, or their similarity to other individuals with whom he has had relationships in the past.[16]

Similarly, Jiddu Krishnamurti points out that predetermined conceptual conditionings restrict and often distort our perception of ourselves, other individuals, and particular situations that we encounter to conform those perceptions to preconceived interpretations, expectations, agendas, and habitual reactions, preventing us from viewing ourselves, others, and various situations in a more realistic, flexible, appropriate, and insightful, manner:

When we condemn or justify, we cannot see clearly, nor can we when our minds are endlessly chattering; then we do not observe *what is*; we look only at the projections we have made of ourselves. Each of us has an image of what we think we are, or what we should be, and that image, that picture, entirely prevents us from seeing ourselves as we actually are.

It is one of the most difficult things in the world to look at anything simply. Because our minds are very complex, we have lost the quality of simplicity. I don't mean simplicity in clothes or food, wearing only a loin cloth or breaking a record fasting or any of that immature nonsense the saints cultivate, but the simplicity that can look directly at things without fear—that can look at ourselves as we actually are, without any distortion—to say when we lie we lie, not cover it up or run away from it.

Also in order to understand ourselves we need a great deal of humility. If you start by saying, "I know myself," you have already stopped learning about yourself; or if you say, "there is nothing much to learn about myself because I am just a bundle of memories, ideas, experiences, and traditions," then you have also stopped learning about yourself. The moment you have achieved anything, you cease to have that quality of innocence and humility; the moment you have a conclusion or start examining from knowledge, you are finished, for then you are translating every living thing in terms of the old. Whereas if you have no foothold, if there is no certainty, no achievement, there is freedom to look, to achieve. And when you look with freedom it is always new. A confident man is a dead human being.

Most of us walk through life inattentively, reacting unthinkingly according to the environment in which we have been brought up, and such reactions create only further bondage, further conditioning, but the moment you give your total attention to your conditioning you will see that you are free from the past completely, that it falls away from you naturally.[17]

The prominent psychologist Roberto Assagioli also supports our view that relinquishing exclusive identification with predetermined self-definitions enables us to be open to a broader range of experiences, illuminating insights, and options of flexible functioning than would otherwise be possible. According to the following interpretation of Assagioli's views, by John Firman and Ann Gila, dis-identifying from (ceasing to identify with) preset self-definitions, views of reality, and ways of functioning, can enable us to be open to the full range of all aspects of ourselves, all available observations and information, and all appropriate responsive options, but not to be exclusively locked into any particular paradigm:

One of the two functions of "I" according to Assagioli is *consciousness*. This notion is based on the observation that in disidentification from limiting structures of experience, your consciousness becomes free to engage a much wider experiential range. That is, when you are identified with a single part of yourself, your consciousness is controlled by that identification, almost as if you look out at the world through that single lens . . . In disidentification from such a role, however, your consciousness is free to engage these other parts of yourself, you become open to the full richness of your inner community, and can experience the world unshackled by the blinders of a single identification. Here it is clear that consciousness partakes of transcendence-immanence: it can be free to engage any and all experiences, any and all parts of ourselves. So as "I" disidentifies, the consciousness of "I" becomes free, and you find that an essential fact about who you are seems to be: "I have awareness (or consciousness)."

Another thing that occurs in disidentification is that you become increasingly free to make a variety of different choices—this points to the second function of "I," *will*. Trapped in a particular identification, you can only make choices from within the perspective of that single part of you . . . In disidentification, however, you find you can make choices from beyond any single identification, that you can make choices from the full range of who you are, drawing on the complete "palette" of your rich human potential.[18]

Assagioli correctly suggests that negative emotions and bad habits lose their ability to upset us and influence us to gratify them in inappropriate ways when we no longer identify with them:

We are dominated by everything with which our self becomes identified. We can dominate and control everything from which we disidentify ourselves. In this principle lies the secret of our enslavement or our liberty. Every time we "identify" ourselves with a weakness, a fault, a fear, or any personal emotion or drive, we limit and paralyze ourselves. Every time we admit "I am discouraged," or "I am irritated," we become more and more dominated by depression or anger. We have accepted those limitations; we have ourselves put on our chains. If, instead, in the same situation we say, "A wave of discouragement is trying to submerge me," or "An impulse of anger is attempting to overpower me," the situation is very different. Then there are two forces confronting each other, on one side our vigilant self and on the other the discouragement or the anger; it can look for their origin, foresee their deleterious effects and realize their unfoundedness. This is often sufficient to withstand an attack of such forces and win the battle. But even when these forces within ourselves are temporarily stronger, when the conscious personality is at first overwhelmed by their violence, the vigilant self is never really conquered. It can retire to an inner fortress and then prepare for and await the favorable moment in which to counter-attack. It may lose some of the battles, but if it does not give up its arms and surrender, the ultimate issue is not compromised, and it will achieve victory in the end.[19]

There can be no true spontaneity when the self is fragmented, that is, when it is divided up into different components, self-definitions, and levels of consciousness. The self becomes fragmented, or split, when you attempt to function relatively consistently with particular predetermined self-definitions and habitual routines, which divide, distance, and estrange you from any aspects of your own actual experience or experiential truth that are located outside of the exclusive selective parameters of that conceptually defined sense of identity. The ego tends to block or inhibit your consciousness from acknowledging and expressing any experiential truth or aspect of your own real being that seems to contradict, or be located outside the scope of, your conceptually defined sense of identity, which produces a fragmented split or sense of division between approved and disapproved, or accepted and rejected, aspects of yourself, as well as a dichotomy between the actual experiential truth of yourself, as revealed by your intuitive sense of core integrity, and what the egoistic self-concept would prefer to believe about itself, even if it sometimes contradicts that actual experiential truth. There is also an inevitable split between the conceptually defined self-images that you wish to be identified with, versus those that you wish not to be identified with, such as approving yourself or judging yourself favorably, only when you are able to validate certain positive traits, that make the ego feel a greater sense of worth and secure identity, as well as disapproving of yourself, or judging yourself unfavorably, when you seem unable to validate the positive traits, and, instead, experience yourself as having received some kind of evidence confirming the opposite negative counterpart traits that make the ego experience a diminished sense or lack of worth and secure identity, such as struggling to validate yourself exclusively as a "good" person rather than a "bad" person, strong rather than weak, intelligent rather than unintelligent, likeable rather than disliked, worthy rather than worthless, secure rather than insecure, etc. Frances Vaughan shares our view that filtering our experiences for the purpose of defending the ego's positive self-images or favorable views of itself can seriously restrict and distort our awareness of reality: "Ego defenses are coping devices used primarily to protect a self-image. They are learned early and used unconsciously in the belief that they are necessary for survival. During the early years of ego development, they protect the emerging egoist self-concept against whatever is perceived as threatening or unacceptable. Unfortunately, defenses also constrict awareness and distort perception, and tend to perpetuate the conditions that are defended against."[19]

Similarly, John Powell points out that people often suppress particular emotions and experiential states that contradict and threaten to invalidate their preferred self-definitions, and which they negatively value judge, assign an unfavorable value to, or disapprove of: "The final consideration that prompts us to deny certain valid human feelings is a 'value conflict.' For example, if 'being a man' has become an important part of my identity and self-image, a value upon which I place a high premium, certain emotions will almost certainly be considered damaging to this image. I will have to edit my emotions carefully to preserve my masculinity."[20] Powell also points out that other related factors that produce the unhealthy repression of emotions include being programmed or indoctrinated to reject certain feelings by disapproving parents, when you are an impressionable child, as well as "moralizing" or value judging some experienced emotions as "bad" or unacceptable to acknowledge as arising in us.[21]

When the self is fragmented or divided in this manner, then all of the fragmented and discrepant, contradictory aspects of the self, both conscious and unconscious, compete with each other in order to speak for or represent the self in its response to the challenge or stimulus. This internal competition and conflict makes spontaneity, authenticity, and inner peace impossible. In order to appear spontaneous, we may then permit the most immediate or dominant aspect of self to express itself in an impulsive, inappropriate way.

What makes it impossible to be spontaneous and creative is the fact that you run from surrendering the sense of self with which you are identified. It is a very frightening prospect for most people to consider surrendering the sense of self with which they are currently identified, and thereby experience themselves as being nothing, or lacking any particular conceptually defined self-knowledge. This is frightening not because it is so terrible, as an actual fact, but because the presumed connotation or label of being nothing is so disturbing. It tends to be interpreted as connoting psychological death, non-being, emptiness, extinction, worthlessness, insecurity, weakness, vulnerability, etc., because it makes the ego feel like less of a "something-ness" and more of a "nothing-ness." Because the connotations are so strongly negative and frightening, you assume that the fact is also something absolutely negative and intolerable, and therefore you make no attempt to discover what it really is.

However, with continued exploration, you may discover that, as an actual fact, being nothing, (i.e., being no particular conceptually defined sense of identity) is being ultimate simplicity, of pure being, beyond or prior to all conceptually generated sense of complexity, which brings a deep, liberating, sense of inner freedom, joy, and peace. This liberating experience of true fulfillment arises because in accepting the experience of being "nothing," meaning, no longer holding yourself to be a self-defined entity or a predetermined, exclusive sense of identity, in your own mind, with a preselected, controlled, restricted way of functioning, you are then one with the movement of life itself, rather than absorbed in the counter-flow or the contrary flow of thought, divorced from the flow of authentic life energy experience arising in the here and now. That reactive, resistive, contrary flow of thought is, metaphorically speaking, like a whirlpool twisted or recoiled back upon itself, and thereby divorced from the more expansive, spontaneously free-flowing, unpredictable, uncontrolled water of the indivisible whole ocean in which the whirlpool abides. Because you are so terribly frightened of being simple, by accepting being an undefined mystery unto yourself, as knower, you try to make yourself or define yourself as something complex, as a sense of identity, as a way of viewing yourself as more of a conceptually embellished "somebody" rather than being contented to be an inner "nothing and nobody" as an undefined mystery unto yourself. That conceptual self-enhancement sometime involves seeking to be highly conspicuous and unusual, in some way, as a means of drawing attention to yourself and your possessions, such as the way you dress, the car you drive, and the house you live in, or expressing outspoken opinions, even when it may not necessarily be appropriate or pragmatically advantageous to do so. The more inwardly empty or lacking in any enduring, substantial, intrinsic inner presence you fear that you are, the more complex, embellished, and showy you make yourself, and the possessions, opinions, and achievements with which you identify. That brings to mind the old saying, "Empty barrels make the most noise" as well as the metaphorical biblical maxim, "Who by taking thought can add even one single cubit to his stature?" (Matthew 6:27; Luke 12:25).

When you become bored and seek to change yourself, it is always keeping you exclusively locked into the same realm of the complex, but never leads you to a truly liberating progression from the complex to the simple. Change within the realm of the complex is not true substantive change at all, but only superficial alteration. Alteration is just a modified continuity of the same old psychologically immature, inauthentic, self-conflicted, inevitably frustrating level of psychological functioning, whereas real substantive change involves a true transformation into a qualitatively more authentic, liberating, relaxed, and fulfilling level of insightful self-understanding, experience, and functioning. For example, if you change from wearing a blue suit to wearing a brown suit because it will fit in better with adaptation to the particular demands of your external environment, then you have accomplished a rather superficial alteration but not a substantive change. The wearer of the clothes continues to be essentially the same inauthentic personality, or artificially contrived psychosocial mask, like a dead mannequin or statue, even with different attire and stylized poses. Therefore, there is only a modified continuity of the same egoistic personality that has occurred, even if presenting itself in somewhat different guises, because we are still functioning under the influence of the same basic psychological needs, seeking to enhance the ego's basic sense of worth, security, identity, and exciting inner vitality, as a way of compensating for the ego's deeper underlying sense of inner deficiency, nothingness, insubstantiality, inner emptiness, inner deadness, tenuousness, flimsiness, fragility, and insecurity. The ego, in its frantic drive for self-embellishment, as a means of denying and escaping deeper underlying feelings of inner emptiness and insubstantiality, is like a collapsible, hollow house of cards, outwardly embellished and seemingly impressive, but lacking a firm foundation in reality. Like a hot air balloon, it is puffed up with unrealistic grandiose pride, but easily punctured, deflated, and reduced to its more essential inner nothingness, insubstantiality, and insignificance. The same old contents have been packaged in somewhat different dress, so to speak, like "old wine in new bottles." (See Mathew 9:16-17; Mark 2:21-22; Luke 5:36-39). Changing your behavior, as well as changing your controlled self-image, which you present to yourself and others as a kind of psychological and social mask or persona, which is really external to you, is basically the same as changing your clothes, costume, disguise, or alias. For there to be a substantive, real inner change, rather than merely a superficial "cosmetic" rearrangement of your façade, the wearer of the clothes and the actor or doer of one's actions, (i.e., your inner conscious awareness), must in some significant way be transformed.

To translate this metaphor into its actual experiential equivalent, real change means dropping all acquired, presumptive, complex ideas and beliefs about yourself, by being content to be a mystery unto yourself, which is utmost simplicity or intrinsic purity of being. Thus, true transformation occurs only when the complex becomes the simple. Then your intrinsic being, content to naturally be a mystery unto itself, is no longer burdened by accumulated presumptive ideas and false embellishments of itself, like heavy psychological baggage or stifling dead weight. Thus, the real change (or genuine psychological transformation, maturational developmental growth, and healing of inner conflict and psychological pain), occurs not when there is an alteration in your concept or image of yourself, but rather *when identification with any and all preconceived concepts and images of self are transcended,* because you are now willing to be an undefined mystery unto yourself, letting the spontaneously arising, dynamically changing, responsive truth of the moment, or the unpredictable, relational, flow of life experience, be your only sense of self in a given moment, rather than fearfully clinging to a predetermined, static, permanently enduring, conceptually defined, exclusive sense of self, usually as a narcissistically self-preoccupied, non-relational, selfishly manipulative, uncaring ego-personality. Then you are said to be truly transformed, by being really simple, without any preconceived self-definitions or psychosocial images that you present to yourself and others.

Many people erroneously believe that being simple involves reducing the variability of their lives. Being simple is not necessarily the same as reducing the number of activities in which you engage. For example, a man who retires from his job may believe that he is simplifying his life, but all that he is really doing is altering the means by which he embellishes himself, as a conceptually defined sense of identity. Before his retirement, he used to embellish himself with business success, and now he embellishes himself with being a success at golf, bridge, fishing, or whatever.

To be really simple, *your motives must be simple*. You can live like a hermit in a cave and still be psychologically complex if your desires and your ambitions are to expand yourself, or enhance your sense of psychological identity, as a conceptually defined greater "something" or an important "somebody" in some way, such as gaining a greater degree of spiritual elevation or sense of peace, and then feeling superior to many other individuals who have not achieved that. *Thus, there is true simplicity only when the acquisitive drive to make the "me" more aggrandized is extinguished; this is possible only when there is contentment to be nothing but the spontaneously arising, uncontrolled, unanticipated, moment-to-moment experiential reality.* This is the only way to end continuous narcissistic self-awareness as a self-confining, self-imprisoning, psychological process, and the only way to be in communion with the moment-to-moment reality of dynamically free-flowing actual experience, as a liberating expansion of your conscious attention and energy beyond the confines of the self-absorbed ego in communion with other individuals and experiences in the world. Letting go of the ego's continuous sense of exclusively separate, recoiled, self-awareness through non-dualistic communion with someone or something beyond the ego also brings a cathartic release from the chronic tension that is produced by unnaturally recoiling your conscious attention and feeling-energy in continuous self-awareness.

When we let go of psychological clutter, false embellishments, and mind-chatter that serve to enhance or aggrandize the ego's sense of identity and importance, then our unencumbered awareness and feeling-energy are able to penetrate into significantly deeper levels of the reality of our own being and experience. That psychological simplicity enhances our true stature with enhanced levels of creative insight, inspiration, experiential wisdom, vitality, as well as the ability to appreciate true inner and outer beauty. Therefore, contentment with the natural simplicity of our own real being as an undefined mystery unto itself, or absence of egocentric psychological clutter, is how true greatness, inner substantiality, or genuine psychological maturity is achieved. When you are willing to be a mystery unto yourself, no longer seeking to enhance or embellish yourself in any way, it is only then that there is true simplicity, and therefore true spontaneity and creativity. Any other form of "spontaneity" or "creativity" is of a contrived, artificial nature, and that which is contrived is the antithesis of true creativity and spontaneity, which is that state where the contriving self is absent. This brings to mind the old Shaker song, "Simple Gifts:"

'Tis a gift to be simple,
'Tis a gift to be free.
'Tis a gift to go where you ought to be.
And when you go to the place just right.
You'll be in the valley of love and delight.[23]

Creativity

Creativity, more specifically, is an open, passive, and receptive state of mind in which consciousness meets a confronting challenge without a rehearsed or predetermined conditioning, expectation, or commitment in regard to how you will response to that challenge. It involves permitting the stimulus to operate upon you, and trigger in you whatever it will, without any interference on the part of the self to predetermine or control beforehand what its reaction or response should be.

When consciousness is uncommitted, or not put in a mental strait-jacket, then it is open and receptive to influences from the not-fully-conscious or subliminal levels of the psyche, and, as a result, you have available, to appropriately meet any challenge or problem, relevant observations from both consciousness and unconsciousness, so that you are functioning as the integrated wholeness of all levels of your being, awareness, or intelligence. However, when only your consciousness is brought to bear on a particular challenge or problem, then your ability to deal with it is always incomplete and fragmented. It would be as though a ship, traveling at night, were to consider only the visible part of an iceberg above the surface of the water to be a threat, but take no account of the often much larger, submerged aspect of the iceberg. Thus, when you are in a creative state of mind, you are bringing more of yourself than just your surface conscious awareness to every problem and challenge in life. You come to every situation that confronts you as a whole person, with an integrated whole psyche that includes openness to observations and insights about relevant factors arising from both conscious and relatively non-conscious levels of the psyche.

When the mind is committed to a particular agenda, then it is a closed mind, and unreceptive to what can intrude, from the unconscious, that could be relevant to the situation, especially if that input or insight is not consistent with your predetermined stance. The uncommitted mind is a consciousness that is not moving to get somewhere, as a predetermined agenda or goal. It is not committed to becoming or achieving any particular thing. Therefore, approaching a situation with the hope of attaining some kind of predetermined goal prevents a creative interaction with that situation, by blocking or summarily rejecting any relevant perceptions, observations, creative insights, or appropriate responses that are not consistent with that predetermined goal.

Likely, you have noticed, for example, that if you had to make a public speech, but did so extemporaneously rather than from a prepared text, that it tended to offer much more opportunity for illuminating illustrations and associations to enter your mind, which resulted in a much more interesting presentation. However, usually your feeling of insecurity makes you overly rehearse, and you use excessive prepared structure as a "crutch" for fear that without it, you might "fall flat on your face." You are invested in defending some kind of image or concept of adequacy, and you believe that over-preparation will guarantee your doing well, which will thereby preserve and confirm the image of efficacy with which you are identified. But inevitably, such a presentation turns out to be dull, boring, and lifeless. When there is no opportunity for creativity or unexpected insights to enter in, then, without that element of new possibilities and discoveries being present or potentially available what is being presented is sure to be perceived as without vitality or stale, and the almost automatic reaction to that realization is boredom, drowsiness, and inattentiveness.

Many psychologists, creative writers, and creative artists have recognized that the production of truly great creative works involves tuning into insights coming from the unconscious level of their psyche, or a subliminal level of their own being, deeper than their conscious awareness, which is possible only when the mind is willing to be, at least temporarily, relatively passive, still, quiet, relaxed, empty, and therefore receptive, not filled with irrelevant, preconceived, mental chatter, conscious willful effort to produce the creative product or idea, or the pursuit of other desires as a means of trying to assuage an underlying feeling of deficiency. For example, Carl Jung suggests that:

> Art is a kind of innate drive that seizes a human being and makes him its instrument. The artist is not a person endowed with free will that seeks his own

ends, but one who allows art to realize its purposes through him. As a human being, he may have moods and a will and personal aims, but as an artist, he is "man" in a higher sense—he is "collective man"— one who carries and shapes the unconscious, psychic life of mankind . . . The creative process has a feminine quality, and the creative work arises from unconscious depths—we might say, from the realm of the mothers. Whenever the creative force predominates, human life is ruled and molded by the unconscious as against the active will, and the conscious ego is swept along on a subterranean current, being nothing more than a helpless observer of events.[24]

Similarly, the poet Amy Lowell describes the creative process as coming into the conscious mind from the subconscious mind when the consciousness is "non-resistant" rather than exerting willful effort to achieve creative productivity:

It may seem that a scientific definition of a poet might put it something like this: a man of an extraordinarily sensitive and active subconscious personality, fed by, and feeding, a non-resistant consciousness. A common phrase among poets is, "It came to me." So hackneyed has this become that one learns to suppress the expression with care, but really it is the best description I know of the conscious arrival of a poem . . . How carefully and precisely the subconscious mind functions, I have often been witness to in my own work. An idea will come into my head for no apparent reason; "The Bronze Horses," for instance. I registered the horses as a good subject for a poem; and having so registered them, I consciously thought no more about the matter. But what I had really done was to drop my subject into the subconscious, much as one drops a letter into the mail-box. Six months later, the words of the poem began to come into my head, the poem—to use my private vocabulary—was "there."[25]

Learn to put your mind where your body is, and you will enter into every situation as a fully integrated and creative whole person. Usually, your mind wanders because you are too insecure and fearful to jeopardize an image or concept with which you are identified, so as a result, your mind is busily engaged in trying to control, anticipate, and be one-up on the situation. This, of course, prevents the potential for a creative reaction, drawing upon useful new insights, to occur. Fear and creativity are incompatible.

Fear yearns for authority to lead, direct, and protect. It is a well-recognized truism that dictators and absolute authorities of all kinds are more likely to come on the scene and be in public favor when the people are fearful. Insecurity insists on being given clearly defined, often rigid, direction and structure. This understanding of the psychological basis of authoritarian, repressive leaders and elite groups arising in society has been described by various social scientists, including Theodore Adorno[26] and Robert J. Lifton.[27]

Authority forces imitative and copying behavior, and imitation is antithetical to true creativity. To be creative, you must be free of both internal and external forms of authority. Externally, forms of authority such as parents, teachers, clergy, and political leaders are always designing prescribed blueprints for behavior and thought, which is detrimental to the process of true creativity. Internally, forms of authority such as, unrealistic conscience (arising from internalized societal norms rather than our own true integrity), ideal images, self-concepts, and various kinds of idealized standards, principles, values, and beliefs all demand conformity to predetermined patterns. *We can be truly creative or open to new and unexpected insights and more flexible ways of functioning only when thought is free of predetermined patterning and conditioning. Only when consciousness is free-flowing can it light where it will.* The egoistic, or predetermined sense of self-awareness, or the "me," is composed entirely of conditioned, habitual, or patterned responses, and so genuine creativity exists only when consciousness is free of the influence of its controlling center, the "me," or exclusively restrictive self-definition and predetermined, habitual ways of functioning and responding to particular kinds of individuals, situations, and circumstances.

The reader should not confuse the process of creativity being discussed in this book with the originality or uniqueness of some production. Being different or innovative is not necessarily the same as being truly creative. Creativity is a particular un-patterned, open, flexible, or non-predetermined, stance that we take toward all aspects of life. It may or may not eventuate in original or innovative productions, such as a painting, a poem, or a musical composition, depending upon the person's particular inherent talents or skills. Quite often, what is referred to as a creative production is really dependent upon an inability on the part of its "creator" to commune or relate intimately with others, which results in an intense drive within him for self-expression. But because he does not feel comfortable expressing himself in interaction with other people, he uses only an extension of himself to interact. The musical instrument, the artist's canvas, the sculptor's clay, or the writer's typewriter and paper and the imaginative process conveyed by such artistic mediums of expression all are extensions of the person himself, and he pours into it all of that pent-up self within him that he cannot share with others. Whereas, in contrast, the person who truly lives creatively is free of the tension and narcissistic self-absorption that so often serve as the impetus for the artistic production because he is constantly giving the self over in the fully invested absorption of constant communion with every confronting reality. For this reason, he is less likely to have the tension of a pent-up self, or imaginative energy, unable to surrender itself to anyone outside of himself, except his artistic medium, and he is therefore less likely to be driven to produce artistic creations. However, it does not necessarily mean that because you are not driven by an intense drive for self-expression, which is often termed creativity, that you will not contribute creative productions. You may do that, too, but the motivation will not be, primarily, that self-oriented preoccupation of most artists, but will stem from the love or sincere caring that you feel for others, and your unselfish desire to reach a large number of people in order to share and help others in some way to experience that which you are experiencing.

The basic motivational intention of genuine creativity is to serve reality by exploring some experiential truth, and sharing your insights with others, as an expression of unselfish caring for them, rather than seeking to gratify the ego through some process of imaginative fantasy that is primarily designed to entertain, comfort, gratify, or enhance yourself, in some way, but is not necessarily intended to illuminate the true nature of reality or to unselfishly serve the well-being of other individuals. Genuine creativity is not necessarily always realistic in a literal sense, but can also involve conceiving metaphorical ideas or imaginary stories that have no realistic capacity to come into physical existence, but which reflect and illuminate some significant experiential truths, such as *Aesop's Fables*, in which animals verbally communicate significant values and lessons about various aspects of human life. In contrast, imaginative fantasy does not necessarily arise from the intention to clarify some aspect of reality by engaging in a process of communion with or open, unbiased, exploration of experiential truth. Instead, imaginative fantasy keeps the mind self-absorbed in its own thought, as a kind of continuous inner monologue, which pulls you away from communion with the experiential truth of the here and now, inwardly and outwardly. In the process of imaginative fantasy, the conscious attention of the mind tends to wander away from communion with the actual flow of life experience, arising in the present moment as a process of openness to the actual experiential truth of oneself, and responsive communion with the objective reality of other individuals and phenomena or situations in the world, and, instead, drifts into a distracting, escapist process of presumption, pretense, make-believe, or unrealistic scenarios that may be highly innovative and unique, but do not necessarily provide authentic insight into the experiential truth of yourself, other individuals, circumstances, situations, or life as a whole.

Get Yourself Untracked

In order to live creatively, you must get yourself untracked, un-grooved, uncommitted to predetermined, habitual, egocentric modes of perception and behavior. Just as the grooves on a phonograph record permit only one song to be expressed, so too the tracks or grooves of your own conditioned thinking also permit you to sing only the one "song" of egoistic, narcissistic self-preoccupation. For example, if you are identified with your self-concept of being intelligent, then you will sing that same "song" over and over to everyone you meet; as if to say, most essentially, "Hey, everyone, look how intelligent I am." In contrast to the meaning of the terminology as many young people used it, in the 1960's and 1970's, if your life is "groovy," then you are truly in a bad way. Grooves and tracks lead only to the same predetermined railroad station, and over and over again you make the same "journey." Each time you make the journey to yourself, you pretend to yourself that your self-concept or idealized image has been so much more confirmed and enhanced. In a sense, the term "groovy" was probably meant to imply by young people that they are fitting in perfectly with the natural flow of life, but in truth, life is too unpredictable, multifaceted, and creative for you to be always able to follow its free-flowing movements. Only someone who is totally attuned to the spontaneous flow of life experience, because he is not restricted by the commitment to validate and enhance some preselected self-definition or sense of exclusive identity, can commune with life so sensitively as to be able to be with its every nuance and subtlety in the here and now.

So instead of being tracked and grooved like a phonograph record, learn to "sing your own song and play your own kind of music." However, to do so, you must not be the singer but the song, or the process of singing, metaphorically speaking. That is to say, be fully immersed in the flow of activity, without stepping back to try to know yourself as the doer and knower of the activity. Beauty is never abiding solely in the manifested object, per se, but, rather, comes from the beautiful flow of activity that leads to the manifested object being produced in a beautiful way, through a process of deeply invested, self-forgetful, loving communion with the creative process of production or activity, or through the spontaneous flow of life energy, which is intrinsic beauty. As Gibran puts it, "Where shall you seek beauty, and how shall you find her unless she herself be your way and your guide?"[28] Therefore, let your own spontaneously arising inner feelings be the guide for the song that it wants to sing.

All aspects of egoistic personality or preconceived self-defined identity are like a preset track, path, or direction, which predetermine your behavior, perception, or thinking. You must not permit any track to mold you and contain you, as a predetermined way of functioning and interpreting your experience, but only let the immediacy, creativity, or authenticity of the moment stir you and arouse you as it will. You have nothing to fear from the new liberation and elimination of guidelines. The mind with a free-flowing consciousness is one of great joy, relaxed peace, vibrant aliveness, as well as attunement to inner and outer true beauty. The patterned and tracked mind, no matter how successful it is in attaining its goals, will never find the psychological security it seeks, and even at its deepest roots, is so confined and restricted that it can never know real peace and joy.

However, pursuing your preferred or pragmatic goals need not necessarily be a problem as long as you are not exclusively locked into those goals, but are open to modifying and/or suspending them if it becomes appropriate to do so in light of new insights and changing circumstances. Some goals may be based on and serve as an appropriate response to openness to actual experience arising within or around you. Furthermore, an un-patterned or open mind is not to be construed as necessarily being the same thing as an anti-conventional mind. Many young people believe that they are displaying a sense of freedom and lack of habitual functioning or absence of patterning, through oppositional, non-conforming, and anti-conventional behavior and attitudes, but this is not true freedom, but just another predetermined groove, another habitual pattern that they have set for themselves. There is no creativity and freedom when any form of compulsivity, exclusivity, or predetermination exists. If there is a "must" or a compulsion to oppose and resist, then that is your new predetermined track, as a restrictive way of functioning, which may not necessarily be appropriate and an expression of your real being, authentic experience, developmental growth, and genuine intentions, in a given moment.

To go beyond and gain liberating insight into the habitual structured patterns of your mind, try to close your eyes and just let yourself be sensitive to what is going on deeply within you; let that reality manifest itself as a song without words, and just sing out loud, being one with that song, and not retaining separate self-awareness as the singer. That is, let the song arise spontaneously from the depths of your own being, as an expression of your full immersion in the immediacy of whatever you are actually feeling or experiencing, rather than standing back from the energetic flow of experience within yourself to try to compose a song through some kind of process of intentional effort or planning. Don't try to direct the process of singing, in any way, but let your experience, feeling, or activity spontaneously sing its own song. Usually, when you feel sad or in love, you turn to someone else's song and sing someone else's words that match your particular mood. However, this time, do not follow any song that you already know, but try to self-discover your own song in this particular moment. Do not construct one in a contrived, controlled, or effortful way. Just let your deep inner feelings in communion with your voice give expression to themselves, in a spontaneous, effortless manner. Conscious thinking is energy-draining, but just listening to what you are actually feeling or experiencing is energy-gaining. This is where true joy abides.

Don't be an imitator—make your own kind of music— each of us is truly being our own song. Discover what it is in this moment; the next moment, you may have a different song to sing. Let it express itself, without trying to formulate it or make it happen. As you attune yourself to the song within you—sad or happy, whatever it may be—you will find that at some point, the singer will merge and become one with the song, meaning that you will spontaneously lose separate self-awareness by becoming fully immersed in the process of singing, or expressing your energy or experiential truth in some other way. Then you will lose the egoistic separate sense of self and be immersed in the relational flow of real life energy experience, which will bring a profound sense of well-being. If you are partial to the dance, then let that inner song within you express itself through your body in non-contrived, uncontrolled, unplanned movements of your own dance.

If you like to draw or paint, try this. With brush and paint or some other drawing device, let your deep inner feeling guide your hand and draw a line on a sheet of paper. Do not hurry or rush, and do not have any predetermined purpose, direction, or goal to your drawing. The brush is drawn over the paper, never pushed. The shape of the figure drawn does not matter. Almost everywhere these days, we find that the drawing or product is valued, but its creator is neglected. Things have become of more value than their *maker*, and also more important than the process of production or creation. This kind of drawing or writing should proceed in silence. There should be no laughing or joking, for this is more than just play. Just continue to let the inner reality of what you are currently experiencing draw some kind of expression of itself. With such practice, you easily become an artist in everyday living, meaning that you engage in any kind of constructive activity, experience, or encounter as a heart-inspired work of art.

Another valuable exercise for enhancing creativity in any field of endeavor or gaining authentic insight into the experiential truth of yourself is to write poetry. It does not matter if the poetry rhymes or not. The important thing is to enter into communion with what is called the creative or intuitive unconscious. It involves "thinking" or perceiving with the heart instead of the mind. To write insightful poetry, in contrast to composing rather superficial or perfunctory poetry, you must adopt a very sensitively alert awareness toward directly contacting the immediate, non-conceptually mediated experience of what is actually arising in you and in the world in a given moment, and always ask, "What am I reacting to in this moment, and why am I reacting to it in that way?" You must learn to listen to every subtle whisper or faint glimmer of experience within you and others. Insightful, authentic poetry cannot be written when you are committed to defending against becoming aware of the actual experiential realities arising in yourself. The process of writing poetry heightens the sensitivities, which makes it possible to be closer to whatever is arising in yourself, especially if you write the poems from the heart rather than the head and express the energetic flow of whatever you are actually feeling or directly experiencing through your poetry, rather than stepping back from direct contact with that immediacy of experience to interpret it or speak for it, which removes your conscious awareness from the heart to the mind. Writing poetry brings you into very close and direct contact with your most subjective, intimate, experiential reality. To write about your depression, for example, you must dive right into it. You must soak or immerse yourself in it, very deeply, and only when it speaks to you clearly will you be able to put it into the words of a poem. You will learn how to creatively articulate your feelings by letting them express themselves spontaneously as a poem, and in this articulation, you will also be clarifying and understanding your true feelings. Writing poetry is also most essential for awakening the inspirational level of consciousness. The more it is exercised, the more vivid and intense it grows, and your capacity for experiencing great beauty and love will grow with it. But remember, don't purposely write the poem as an intellectually contrived act, but let it create itself and donate itself to your consciousness.

Recommended Exercise:

1. Write at least one report or journal entry each week, which you could share with a friend, loved one, counselor, or mentor, or read and reflect on it yourself. Your report should describe your experiences with spontaneity and creativity. Discuss, especially, the things that you are doing to get yourself untracked and the problems or successes that you are encountering.
2. Write at least one poem each week on your encounter and communion with a particularly significant internal feeling or emotion, or with some particularly significant or moving external event. You may make it as long or as short as you like, and it need not necessarily rhyme. After you have written the poem, write a short paragraph discussing what you feel to be the essential message or significance of the poem and how it has more deeply sensitized you to the truth of yourself or of the external event that you have expressed or communicated through the poem.

SECTION C OF CHAPTER 4

THE CO-CREATIVE MUSE:
A BLOG BY BARRY HAMMER

I find that the best kind of creative inspiration in any field of endeavor comes from communing deeply with other life presences, in heartfelt, open-minded, empathic attunement with them. The more deeply we invest our heart, mind, and senses in communion with other life presences, experiences, and activities in the world, the more the co-creative relational heart core of our own being becomes stirred, and reveals enhanced gifts of creative inspiration and meaningful insight, as the source of great artistic expression, heart-full living, and enhanced performance in any area of endeavor. When individual hearts resonate in deeply invested attunement with each other, they energize each other like magnets, releasing the co-creative process of synergy, like electricity flowing only when an electrical plug and socket, or positive and negative electrical poles, are connected to one another.

However, as long as the heart remains egocentrically, narcissistically, selfishly self-absorbed or self-possessed, we will be able to make only rather shallow contact with others, with only the superficial levels of our awareness. Without heartfelt communion, the mind and senses, by themselves alone, can contact, understand, and appreciate only superficial aspects of reality and provide only a relatively shallow, mechanical level of creative artistic functioning. That is why I agree with what St. Exupery wrote in his book, *The Little Prince*, "It is only with the heart that one can see rightly; what is essential is invisible to the eyes." I might add, what is essential in life is also not available to the analytical intellect, functioning independently of the deeper, relational, insight of the heart, because the analytical mind tends to be self-absorbed in its own thought, rather than making direct contact with other life presences, experiences, and activities in the world.

To make direct, deep, empathic contact with anyone or anything, and to tap into the relational source of co-creative insight and inspiration, we must let go of mental presumptions, preconceptions, and abstractions, which function like an opaque filter, barrier, or distorting mechanism, keeping the mind self-absorbed in its own thought and blocking direct contact and heartfelt empathic communion with actual life experience in the world, which the philosopher Martin Buber describes as the I-Thou relationship, in contrast to the I-It relationship. In Biblical terms, this is the difference between experiencing reality as though through a "poor reflection" or "a glass darkly" rather than "face to face" (I Corinthians 13:12), gaining deeper, undistorted, insight into reality through direct, non-conceptually mediated communion with it, in the here and now. Communing with the enduring living presence or living spirit that the author of any creative work has invested in that creative production can empathically reveal the meaningful intention and originating inspirational experience of that author or producer. The highest source of creative insight, inspiration, and production comes from relational communion because it is a relational reality nature, rather than a solo, divisive, dualistic, or separate individualistic nature. Therefore, introspective processes that produce greater self-involvement and break off heartfelt communion with others cannot reveal and release the highest level of creative insight and creatively inspired functioning.

Caring human relationships can also facilitate creative transformations of individual people and global society by enabling the power of love to gradually transform individual hearts, and the collective spiritual heart of humanity from selfishness, fear, and brutality to unselfish, compassionate, caring about others.

THE PROCESS OF NON-LABELING AND LIVING

IN COMMUNION WITH ALL ASPECTS OF LIFE

Not all knowing involves conceptualizing, and not all experience can be known and communicated with words. Predetermined conceptual labeling puts phenomena into static generic categories, which removes our consciousness from direct contact with the immediacy of changing phenomena in their distinctive particularity. That process of defining our experience puts psychological space between us and the phenomena that we encounter, which produces a psychologically disturbing sense of alienation from what is experientially real in ourselves and others, whereas non-dualistic, non-interpreting, nonjudgmental communion with actual inner and outer experiential realities connects us to the intrinsically vivid, joyful, beautiful flow of life energy, in the here and now. Life is experienced as a dull repetitive bore when we bring our past conditionings, memories, future expectations, and predetermined conceptual interpretations to it. The "me" as a conceptually defined sense of identity or ego-personality and its incessant inner monologue are primarily based on the labels that the knower, your conscious attention, holds or applies to itself. The ego fears itself to be an inner psychological nothing, or no knowable thing, as a mystery unto itself, when it has no labels or self-definitions. You cannot come to truly understand that which you label. Feelings can best be understood when we focus on the actual experience rather than on a predetermined label or conceptual interpretation of them. In communion, there is no sense of dualistic separation or psychological space between the

observer and the observed. Painful feelings, such as fearful anxiety, depression, and loneliness, disappear when we
are in non-dualistic communion or full conscious unification
with the feeling, and no longer resisting the feeling. Psychological anxiety and other painful feelings are basically the
outcome of labeling particular situations, and subside when
we no longer identify with or react to labels or words connoting those feelings.

We have also discussed the enhancement of creativity and
spontaneity, involving openness to new insights and options,
in contradistinction to egoistic imagination (or unrealistic,
escapist, fantasy) and reckless impulsivity. True spontaneity and creativity arise from an immediacy of attunement to
the actual challenge, or fully invested, self-forgetful communion with the actual situation, and responding appropriately, not mediated by any kind of predetermined agenda.
Genuine spontaneity primarily involves responsive attunement to currently existing experiential realities, whereas
creativity mostly involves intuitive insight into new realistic possibilities that may not have manifested yet. Our intuitively discerned integrity, coming from the core level of
our own being, is naturally related to genuine spontaneity
and creativity, and guides us how to function consistently
with the integrated wholeness of our own being, and of the
situation at hand, as our rightful or appropriate response to
it. In contrast to the socially conditioned and conceptually
derived Freudian superego, our integrity is our true conscience, intuitively alerting us to what possible options are
most or least consistent with the essential cohesiveness of
our own real being. Psychological health and maturity involve a flexible moment-to-moment attunement to the experiential sense of integrity or intuitive self-consistency arising
from the core level of our own being. Our core experiential
integrity is naturally, spontaneously, open and flexible rather
than predetermined, holistic rather than divisively selective
or partisan, guided by the intrinsic wholeness and fulfillment
of our real being rather than by deficiency-based needs and

presumptions coming from the more superficial, controlling, acquired, conceptually-defined ego-personality.

When our consciousness has no restrictive self-definitions or psychosocial conditionings, then we are able to function in a flexible manner, which produces greater insight and effective functioning, as well as greater harmony with all aspects of our own holistic being, and the ability to cope appropriately with all kinds of situations and circumstances. The ego seeks to embellish itself through accumulating conceptual self-aggrandizement and status symbols, whereas accepting the utmost simplicity of our being as a mystery unto itself enables us to intuitively experience its intrinsic grandeur, security, well-being, and fulfillment nature. Higher noetic capacities such as intuition, inspiration, creativity, and spontaneity arise from a process of relaxed openness, receptivity, non-striving communion with our actual inner and outer experience, not locked into any predetermined, exclusive, restrictive, mode of self-definition, perception, and functioning, letting the stimulus evoke in us whatever response it will, without having any controlled, preselected agendas. Genuine creativity and spontaneity involve openness to the full range of experiences and all levels of the psyche, including insights coming from not fully conscious or subliminal levels of the psyche. Creative insight and creative performance, in any field of endeavor or area of inquiry, are enhanced when we are in deeply invested, heartfelt, caring communion with our actual experience and with the task at hand, without separate egoistic self-awareness.

CHAPTER 5

DEVELOPMENT AND VALIDATION OF THE PSYCHOPATHOLOGY-HEALTH INVENTORY (PHI)

Abstract

The first part of this chapter consists of an abridged exposition of a new theory of the foundational aspects of the ego as a sense of personal psychological individuation and differentiation. From this theory, a new view of the essential nature of ego strength and psychopathology is derived, and a new experimental scale, called the Psychopathology-Health Inventory (PHI) is developed. Furthermore, this chapter presents a discussion of the interpretation and uses of the Psychopathology-Health Inventory, as well as the results of a series of studies investigating its statistical and experimental reliability and validity. The experimental data obtained to date describe the Psychopathology-Health Inventory as a highly reliable and valid measure of ego strength, and one with clear advantages over other such instruments in terms of superior discriminative validity, less susceptibility to the response set of social desirability, superiority in ease and speed of administration and scoring, as well as in terms of clinical utility. Its two equivalent forms make it an especially useful research and clinical tool for the assessment of changes that occur in ego strength and psychopathology as a result of psychotherapeutic treatment or other forms of intervention.

Theoretical Considerations

The gaining of a deeper understanding of the essential nature of psychopathology and health, and an understanding of the fundamental relationship between these two related states of psychological functioning, has been extremely slow to develop. This has been due in significant part to the fact that research and clinical assessment in these areas have been severely hampered because no truly adequate instrument has existed that was capable of including and measuring, within a single instrument, the entire quantitative range, or the whole continuum from relative pathology to relative health. A primary inhibiting factor impeding the development of such an instrument has been the lack of a consistent and meaningful theory that could demonstrate the existence of an operationally definable common dimension underlying both psychological pathology and health, so that they can be studied on the same continuum.

In this chapter, such a theory will be presented and will suggest that a newly-defined view of the nature of relative ego strength-weakness is the essential dimension underlying the continuum of relative psychopathology-health. Thus, relative psychological health is conceptually defined as referring basically to one's relative degree of ego strength, whereas relative psychopathology is the concept used to refer to one's relative degree of ego weakness. The Psychopathology-Health Inventory (PHI) has been designed to serve as the instrument by which the relative degree of psychological health or pathology (i.e., relative ego strength-weakness) can be operationally defined and quantitatively measured.

In order to better understand the new definition of ego strength and weakness that is to be presented in this chapter, the foundational structure of the ego-sense first needs to be discussed. The ego-sense, or self-perception of being a separate and distinct psychological individuality, entity, identity, personal self, or independent psychological existence, is not our real, inherent, or most essential being, but is only a conceptual, presumptive, psychological construct that is being created by and superimposed upon our inherent real being, similar to an image reflected upon a clear mirror. The ego-sense is designed to serve as an inner psychological entity, a conceptually defined sense of identity, or psychological body self-image, which is localized in physical space and time, and associated with a nonphysical personality self-image. Without such a personal psychological entity, or inner sense of self, we would feel inwardly empty of all sense of personality, and be without a means of being inwardly self-aware or self-knowing in the same way that the physical body entity, as our outer sense of self, enables us to be outwardly self-aware and self-knowing as a distinct individual.

The basic structure of the ego-sense or sense of psychological individuality is essentially founded upon or inferred from internalized outer sensations, as well as inner conceptual self-definitions, emotional reactions, familiar experiential states, distinctive personality traits, and personal willpower, which are combined together to comprise a personal sense of psychological individuation and differentiation, self-knowledge, or identity. All of these aspects of the ego-personality, functioning together as a composite process of psychological individuation, or individual self-awareness and distinctive particularity of self-knowledge, provide the ego with its sense of inner self-awareness or I-sense, as an I-entity, or sense of identity (i.e., its sense of personal subjectivity, or personal psychological self-image form, which enables the ego to feel absolutely separate and distinct from other psychological beings in psychological space). The sensations and concepts of differentiation provide the ego's absolutely separated sense of psychological individuation with a means of feeling absolutely or uniquely different from other psychologically individuated beings. The sensations and concepts of differentiation provide the ego with a sense of distinctiveness through a conceptually-created, or conceptually-defined, set of consistent and familiar personal qualities that contribute to its sense of being a finite, describable, particular, psychological entity or individuated personal identity. That conceptually defined personal identity serves to provide the subjective I-sense or separate self-awareness with a specific knowable content, distinctive self-knowledge, or sense of personal objectivity, me-ness, or knowable psychological inner substance, that enables us to be self-aware, and to know who we are as a distinctive personal psychological being or sense of particularity that is consistent and continuous over psychological time.

Later discussion will illuminate the characteristics of the sense of psychological individuation and differentiation in greater depth and detail, but at this point, it is necessary that we recognize that the process of individuation and differentiation enables the establishment of a sense of personal psychological form and substance,[1] subjectivity and objectivity, I-ness and am-ness, or knower and known aspects of our psychological sense of self or identity, enabling us to be self-aware of our psychological personality, and to experience ourselves as complete psychological entities, rather than an undefined inner emptiness and nothingness, lacking any kind of separate self-awareness and specific self-knowledge, which would arouse intense fearful anxiety and related feelings of deficiency and insecurity. When we then proceed to identify with those sensations, conceptual self-definitions, emotional reactions, and volitional intentions that provide and constitute a distinctive sense of psychological individuation and differentiation, the foundational structure of the ego-sense becomes established. Once that occurs, the potential for experiencing anxiety becomes pronounced, because it is now possible for our psychological being or existence to feel threatened with invalidation if those familiar sensations, concepts, emotional states, and volitional preferences are invalidated, thwarted, or interrupted in some way.

The ego-sense represents a sense of individuation and differentiation not only from other such psychologically-created or conceptually defined beings, but also from your own real, inherent, or essential being that you are always already intrinsically being prior to your conceptually-created ego-sense, which is really only an acquired, presumptive, sense of self-awareness and self-knowledge, as a conceptual construct that is not intrinsic to your being, as pure conscious awareness indivisibly united to your inherent vibratory feel-ing-life energy force. Your real being, energy field, or pure conscious awareness has no inherent enduring self-knowl-edge or self-awareness, and therefore is naturally a mystery unto itself prior to the formation of the ego as a conceptually defined psychological construct. As suggested earlier, the substance of our real being or awareness is intrinsically, orig-inally pure, like a mirror, totally free of all self-concept iden-tifications, which are like static, permanent images reflected or superimposed upon that mirror. Once the individual iden-tifies with those foreground forms or images of conceptual or psychological individuation and differentiation, then its background pure, clear being substance, as conscious aware-ness, the subjective knower, which was originally a mystery unto itself, is thereupon conceptualized and experienced as an inner void, because it is void of all sense of conceptual individuation and differentiation upon which the ego-sense is founded. Fear of experiencing the conscious awareness of that inner "void" is therefore the ego's greatest dread or threat, because it signals the ego's essential unreality and ex-tinction, which arouses feelings of psychological insecurity, anxiety, and deficiency that are deemed intolerable. Hence, it has to be repressed from conscious awareness and asser-tions of psychological individuation and differentiation have to constantly be superimposed upon it in order to cover the conscious awareness of the ego's basically void inner na-ture, as the subjective knower, pure conscious awareness, devoid of any intrinsic, enduring self-knowledge.

Therefore, if those sensations, concepts, emotional states, and volitional assertions, that comprise our familiar, dis-tinctive sense of self-knowledge or identity as a subjective, inward, psychological "I-am-entity" are not regularly gen-erated, validated, affirmed, asserted, confirmed, or protected from being disaffirmed, then the foundational structure of the ego-sense becomes undermined, and its essentially il-lusory nature or sense of being an insubstantial, tenuous, flimsy, inner void, becomes exposed, which we experience as a threat to the continued existence and credibility of our psychological sense of self. That is fundamentally what is meant by relative ego-weakness. The degree of the lack of development, affirmation, or validation of our sense of individuation and differentiation, or the degree of disaffirmation or invalidation of our sense of individuation and differentiation has received from others and/or from ourselves, basically determines how weak, diminished, fragile, insecure, insubstantial, tenuous, deficient, or how close to dissolution the ego-sense will feel, and how much psychopathology we will manifest or experience as a volitional, emotional, conceptual, and behavioral reaction to that basic sense of insecurity as a psychological entity or identity.

When the ego feels weak, helpless, insecure, or threatened with immanent nullification of its sense of psychological existence, which can sometimes involve a related loss of credibility of its sense of identity, it typically reacts with a sense of panic, disturbance, or frantic desperation, as well as obsessively trying to control the perceived source of the psychological threat to its psychological survival, resulting in attitudinal, volitional, emotional, mental, and behavioral patterns that evidence a relatively high level of maladjustment, inner and outer conflict, self-perceived deficiency, lack of well-being, as well as lack of realism or self-delusional ideation and inappropriate functioning. Some of these psychologically unhealthy patterns of inner conflict and outer maladjustment arising from a weak or insecure-feeling ego include unrealistic paranoia or lesser degrees of basic mistrust and anxiety, as well as excessive anger or timidity, rather than constructively appropriate self-assertion, and/or emotional depression. Those kinds of symptoms tend to escalate in degree of intensity, frequency, and duration, depending on what degree of insecurity the weak ego experiences with regard to not feeling assured of its ability to control its continued survival as a psychological entity, with the greatest degrees of insecurity resulting in, and being reflected by, correspondingly intense and extreme levels of psychopathology. These kinds of psychological patterns may, perhaps, coincide with the concept of "learned helplessness," as described in the psychological research and theory of individuals such as Martin Seligman, Steve Maier, and Bernard Weiner.[2] Any intended psychotherapeutic process that does not address the underlying causal source of those dysfunctional patterns, arising from the weak ego's basic sense of insecurity, is not likely to be substantially and enduringly effective, but, at best, will likely produce only rather cosmetic, superficial, ephemeral, improvements in the client's level of psychological functioning.

The degree of our perceived ego weakness can be diagnostically assessed both directly and indirectly. It can be assessed directly through questionnaire items or responses that reflect the degree of our experienced feelings of deficiency and insecurity, with regard to our sense of individuation and differentiation; or it can be assessed indirectly through the assessment of the degree of the ego's need to compensate for, and thereby escape from, cover over, or control against fully consciously experiencing its feelings of deficiency, by superimposing a greater sense of conceptual and experiential positivity. The greater the degree of the ego's compensatory needs, the greater is the presumed sense of underlying deficiency with regard to our sense of individuation or differentiation, and, therefore, the greater is the degree of ego weakness and psychopathology that is being indirectly evidenced. For example, if our sense of individuation and the sense of potency of will upon which it is based are not well-developed or have been frequently disaffirmed, then we will, likely, be burdened by feelings of impotence of will, weakness, helplessness, vulnerability, insecurity, dependency, insubstantiality, etc. The degree of relative ego weakness can be determined directly by assessing the prevalence of these feelings of deficiency with regard to our sense of individuation, or it can be indirectly inferred from the assessment of one's psychological needs that seek to promote the experience of their compensatory opposite proficient counterpart, such as a need for power, control, security, adequacy, substantiality, independence, etc. Psychologically healthy individuals naturally value and seek these kinds of proficient qualities, but when seeking such qualities becomes driven by an extreme sense of intolerance of frustration, lack of reasonable self-restraint, insecurity, frantic desperation, continuous narcissism, unrealistic grandiosity, and exaggerated, intensely demanding, insatiable, cravings, then it reflects or evidences relative psychological pathology, or a weak ego.

The Psychopathology-Health Inventory (PHI) is an instrument that has been designed to directly assess the degree of our experienced feelings of deficiency, with regard to our sense of individuation and differentiation, and is also the means by which the degree of these deficiency feelings can be indirectly assessed via the degree of our compensatory needs. In both of these ways, the PHI serves as the means of assessing the degree of our ego weakness, which is the fundamental causal element determining the degree of our psychopathology. Those individuals who possess a relatively well-developed and well-affirmed sense of individuation and differentiation will feel like a clearly delineated and substantial personal self, which will be reflected on the PHI as having relative ego strength and relative psychological health. We postulate that most individuals who have developed a relatively strong and clear sense of ego-strength, secure identity, or psychological individuation and differentiation will usually tend to be more psychologically healthy and constructive, with significantly greater levels of emotional security, relaxed inner peace [tranquility], and self-confidence, as well as evidence less psychopathology, psychological pain, anxiety, and inner conflict, than most individuals who have a much weaker ego or a much more tenuous sense of psychological individuation and differentiation.

A more specific and detailed explanation of how the ego's sense of individuation and differentiation develop, and the essential characteristics of each, will now be presented.

The ego's sense of being a separate psychological being, entity, or self cannot be established until a sense of personal psychological individuation has been developed. As long as no such sense of individuation exists, the child continues to feel psychologically connected to the mother as though through a psychological umbilical cord. As a consequence, the child can have no sense of being a separate psychological entity, personality, or self in its own right, and instead remains an extension of the mother's will and personality. Until the child can pit its own will successfully against the mother's will, and effectively say "no" in defiance of the mother's will, it cannot cut that psychological umbilical cord, and thereby experience a sense of its own psychological separation, individuation, or selfhood. Later in life, the weak ego may look to other individuals besides the mother for a basic sense of psychological security, worth, and identity that it feels unable to independently provide for itself and seek to be psychologically incorporated by them.

Thus, the foundation of the ego's sense of self lies in its affirmed sense of individuation, or psychological separateness, first from the mother and then from others, which arises with a sense of being a separate willpower that takes credit for being the autonomous personal cause of intended effects. The sense of willpower is contingent upon the efficacy or potency of our will to control or influence others to conform to our will or to produce effects in that intended direction. It also requires that we prevent the will of others from controlling or influencing us in the direction that others intend. If we cannot control or influence others in the direction we intend, or if others are able to influence us in the direction that they intend, despite our own willful resistance, then our potency of will and its associated sense of being a psychologically individuated self cannot be inferred, validated, substantiated, or affirmed, which is severely threatening to the early developing ego, or to the ego with a relatively tenuous sense of individuation.

In view of the fact that the ego's sense of self hinges on its sense of individuation, and that its sense of individuation hinges on its ability to affirm a sense of potency of will (or its equivalent feelings, thoughts, and sensations, such as those that yield a sense of power, control, efficacy, mastery, adequacy, etc.), therefore, any failure in the attempt to generate such feelings, thoughts, or sensations would likely invalidate or disaffirm the ego's sense of potency of will, and thereby threaten the ego's sense of individuation or psychological existence, especially if such failure of willpower is viewed as significant, persistent, recurring, deeply humiliating, and intolerably painful, disappointing, or frustrating to the ego. Hence, feelings of deficiency related to a deficient sense of individuation or potency of will (such as feelings of weakness, powerlessness, frustration, helplessness, vulnerability, or insecurity), signal a threat to the ego in regard to accentuating the tenuous nature of its sense of self, and, therefore, reflect relative ego weakness. The greater the tenuousness of the ego's sense of individuation, the greater will be the threat of experiencing itself as being a psychological non-entity or inner nothingness when its potency of will is momentarily disaffirmed, and the more likely is its associated feeling of deficiency to be rejected, denied, and escaped from via the attempt to gratify a psychological need that represents its compensatory relative opposite sense of proficiency.

For example, if there were a momentary disaffirmation of your sense of potency of will, and therefore a threat to your sense of individuation, then a feeling of deficiency in potency, such as a feeling of weakness, is likely to arise. If this occurs in someone with a relatively weak ego-sense, then that person is likely to attempt to compensate for that feeling of weakness or sense of experienced deficiency in potency through an exaggerated need to affirm a personal sense of power as the means of attempting to reinforce, enhance, or strengthen, his or her diminished sense of individuation. This compensatory need to affirm an exaggerated sense of willpower may take a variety of different forms, such as developing excesses in the area of physical potency (e.g., as muscular strength or physical weight), intellectual potency, sexual potency, interpersonal potency (e.g., seeking excessive popularity or dominating other people), or psychological potency (e.g., excesses in regard to internal self-discipline, self-denial, etc.), trying to overpower others through aggressive expressions of will power, or trying to frustrate others as a more subtle, passive-aggressive expression of will power. Hence, these excessive forms of deficiency-need compensation reflect a relatively deficient sense of individuation, and thus relative ego weakness. This would be true for any exaggerated or excessive need to display a sense of "psychological muscle," in whatever form it takes, such as habitual oppositional conflicts with others, or, more subtly, a need to seek out or create unnecessary challenges to our potency of will or sense of mastery.

An excessive compensatory need to feel a sense of power or control characterizes many psychologically pathological symptoms. In many of these cases, the ability to generate a sense of control, internal or external, becomes equated with a sense of security (i.e., a sense of control over our continued survival as a psychological being or entity). On the other hand, the inability to control generates extreme feelings of insecurity, which represent a threat to the ego's continued survival, psychologically, with extreme weakness or deficiency sometimes also being perceived, consciously or subconsciously, as endangering even our physical survival and well-being. This is especially evident in obsessive-compulsive and phobic reactions, in which a perceived inability to control will trigger extreme feelings of insecurity, reflecting a relatively weak sense of individuation, and thus relative ego weakness. In some cases, those who have never developed a significant degree of individuation may have what might be called a psychotic personality structure or predisposition reflecting an extremely tenuous sense of individuation that is relatively easily threatened with dissolution. Quite extreme forms of compensation in these cases may manifest as unrealistically grandiose delusions, such as when a person identifies with a powerful figure from history, such as Napoleon Bonaparte,

Julius Caesar, or Jesus Christ in order to compensate for, and thereby deny, his or her painful feelings of impotence of will in the form of a feeling of weakness, helplessness, vulnerability, or insecurity.

Excessive forms of compensation for feelings of impotence of will may be seen as being operative within groups or crowds, as well as within any one individual. Much of the violence occurring at athletic events by both athletes and spectators, especially when the home team is losing and everyone is feeling terribly frustrated, is an example of compensatory reactions to feelings of deficiency of power or feelings of impotence of will on a group level. Out of fear of affirming an already existing relatively impotent sense of will, those with a relatively weak ego are often unable or unwilling to continue to watch such games or support a home team once that team is branded as a consistent loser. The threat that it brings to their tenuous sense of individuation makes them fearful of putting their will on the line and cheering for their team to win, if they believe that their team is likely to lose. Likewise, various kinds of international conflicts, ethnic chauvinism, bigotry, and religious intolerance, as well as political and social authoritarianism involve compensation for egoistic feelings of deficiency, inferiority, worthlessness, insecurity, or paranoia, replaced by their opposite, compensatory sense of conquest, proficiency, superiority, exaggerated pride, and controlling tendencies, manifested at a group-dynamics level. That kind of competitive animosity or chauvinism is how the individual and collective ego denies and escapes from its deeper underlying sense of inner emptiness, nothingness, and insubstantiality, and attempts to superimpose, validate, or "prove" a compensatory greater sense of positive identity, proficiency, substantiality, or "something-ness", often involving unrealistic grandiose delusions and unrealistic vilification of other individuals and social groups.

Relative ego weakness can also be reflected through the exaggerated avoidance of putting our will on the line to be affirmed because we fear that it will be easily disaffirmed, which would threaten to eradicate our tenuous sense of individuation. This tendency to avoid putting our impotent sense of will on the line is especially reflected in states of extreme psychological passivity and dependence, as well as interpersonal fearfulness, timidity, or withdrawal. When extreme, it may also involve psychotic potential.

The relatively weak or poorly individuated ego requires a continuous reinforcement of the potency of its will, and therefore has to continuously exercise its will by being oppositional not only in regard to the will of other people, but even in regard to its own spontaneously arising feelings and impulses. This attempt to affirm the ego's potency of will by turning it against its own objectified spontaneous experiential life, such as rejecting our own feelings, natural inclinations, and potentials pushing for actualization or development creates a sense of internal conflict or subject-object duality separation within our naturally unitary whole being. In some cases, this may involve timid reluctance or unwillingness to take reasonable constructive risks for the sake of enhancing our level of productive functioning, involving the actualization of our fullest range of natural individual and relationship potentials, as the basis of enhanced transformational development of what is truly real, vital, fulfilling, creative, adaptive, and life-affirming in us. Problems with regard to imposing our will upon our own experiential spontaneity, reflecting relative ego weakness, are evidenced in excessive forms of self-rejection, self-control, self-inhibition, or self-repression, and their resulting feelings of inner conflict and tension, as well as lack of energy, all of which can undermine our ability to cope effectively with adaptive challenges that may significantly affect our well-being and social adjustment. There is also a reflection of relative ego weakness in the opposite extreme, in which our will is impotent to exert self-control or self-discipline, when that is appropriate, adaptive, or necessary, resulting in excessive impulsivity, anti-social acting-out behavior, or self-indulgence to the point of addiction or recklessness.

The relatively weak ego also fears losing its sense of individuation when a sense of psychological closeness to another person is imposed upon it. In these circumstances, the ego fears that its sense of separate psychological space is being invaded or violated. This makes the ego feel that its sense of separate self-awareness, identity, or psychological boundaries is being obliterated, or that its individuated sense of self is being swallowed up by the other person. As a consequence, the relatively weak ego is often marked by fears of love relationships or psychological intimacy of any kind. Often such an ego will deliberately create friction in its relationships in order to reinforce its sense of separation from the other individual, and avoid being psychologically incorporated into the other individual. This becomes especially difficult in psychotherapy, and accounts for much of what is viewed as resistance in the psychotherapy process. Such an insecure, defensive ego will resist being understood by the therapist, because it views being understood as a sense of psychological union or experiential connectedness that violates its individuated sense of separate psychological space. The relatively weak ego also has problems in interpersonal relationships because the weaker the ego, the more narcissistically self-preoccupied it typically is, as the means of bolstering that weak sense of individuation via continuous self-awareness. This makes the individual less aware of others, and therefore extremely insensitive to the needs and feelings of others, which diminishes his/her ability to relate to others in an empathic, appropriate, harmonious, effective, adaptive manner. A relatively strong ego feels well-established and substantial, and thus can drop self-awareness for a time, without feeling threatened in its sense of psychological existence and security. This permits it to make another person the object of its conscious awareness, instead of itself, at appropriate times, which enables it to be truly caring, sensitive to, and empathically understanding of another person, and capable of responding to the other individual's needs and concerns in an appropriate, ethically responsible manner, and, therefore, capable of engaging in psychologically mature, constructive, and truly fulfilling relationships. Furthermore, having the inner strength of character to be able to temporarily relinquish self-awareness and self-concern enables us to be successful at various kinds of productive tasks that require undistracted attentiveness. Only a relatively strong ego feels secure enough to let go of separate self-awareness, self-gratification, and self-will when it is truly appropriate or necessary to do so, whereas a relatively weak ego will typically hold onto self-preoccupation even when that produces significant maladjustment and impaired functioning.

Problems in regard to our sense of individuation in the opposite direction can also reflect relative ego weakness, such as when we resist the process of individuation necessary for our psychological maturation by overly clinging or being excessively attached to others, or by refusing to make our own decisions or take responsibility for the development of our own life and actualization of our true individual potentials. In all these various ways the tenuous nature of our sense of individuation is evidenced, and, via the PHI, those tendencies are the means of assessing the relative ego weakness, immaturity of psychological development, or severity of psychopathology of the particular ego.

After the ego has established itself as a psychologically individuated or separated sense of self, as the subjective I-sense, it is further strengthened, solidified, made more substantial or secure through the process of psychological differentiation, which provides the ego with a sense of personal psychological distinctiveness. The process of differentiation is designed to provide the ego with a consistent conceptual and experiential definition or description of who it is, or what that I-sense or separate self-awareness specifically holds itself to be as a psychological identity. Through the process of differentiation, the ego assumes a set of personal psychological qualities that help it differentiate itself from other psychological beings. The individuated sense of separation as a psychological being is not sufficient to feel like a complete entity because it still does not feel psychologically distinctive or different from other, similarly individuated, psychological beings. Hence, after the ego-sense has first made itself feel separate as a psychological being, through the development of separate self-awareness, it must then make itself feel like a particular, uniquely different, separate psychological being by defining its sense of identity somewhat differently than the identity of others, as the specific content or knowable qualities that comprise the self-aware knower's sense of distinctive identity.

Thus, the process of differentiation is the means by which that subjective individuated sense of self, as knower, robes its naked I-sense, separate self-awareness, or psychological form, in the conceptual garb of familiar self-concepts, self-images, motivational intentions, or experiential states that together make up its known sense of personal am-ness, self-knowledge, objectivity, inner psychological substance, or consistent personal identity, as the specific knowable contents of the self-aware ego's sense of identity. This serves as the means by which the ego-sense can be self-aware, and thereby know itself as a psychological being that is consistent and continuous over psychological time, which adds to its sense of being a permanent and distinctive psychological entity. Its sense of being a psychological entity with a personal history or sense of continuity over time is established via tacit declarations such as, "The personal qualities or sense of self that I know or experience myself to be today are basically the same self that I have known or held myself to be in the past, and it will be essentially the same self that I project into the future. Therefore, through that affirmed sense of continuity over time, I can conclude that I truly do exist as that particular psychological identity or self. I am the particular personal qualities that distinguish me from other

individuals." Thus, any disaffirmation of the ego's conceptual or experiential identity disaffirms its sense of differentiation, which threatens the ego's sense of existence.

Therefore, indications (e.g., from the PHI questionnaire)
of a vague, amorphous, confused, contradictory, or under-
developed personal psychological identity would often, but
not necessarily always, reflect relative ego weakness. This is
because it may reflect a relatively weakened or diminished
sense of differentiation, which makes the ego feel less self-
consistent, precisely definitive, clearly describable, or substantial as a psychological entity or personal sense of self.
However, in other cases, psychologically healthy and secure
individuals may not define or identify themselves with exclusive qualities because they are open to the whole range
or continuums of diverse modes of experience, perception,
and functioning, and are willing to be an undefined mystery
unto themselves, at least at times. In some cases, relative
ego weakness could also be reflected through an excessive
compensatory need to defend, affirm, or enhance its conceptual or experiential identity as a reflection of its attempt to
deny deeper underlying feelings of deficiency in regard to its
diminished sense of differentiation. On the other hand, embracing contradictions, ambiguity, uncertainty, and paradox
can, in some cases, reflect a strong, secure, ego rather than
a weak, fragile-feeling, defensive ego if the individual does
not fearfully reject, escape from, and attempt to prematurely
resolve such experiences, but instead, welcomes them as
part of the natural whole range of experience, with an open-
minded, flexible, non-defensive, non-controlling attitude.
Furthermore, strong, confident, well-adjusted egos will not
let uncertainties and confusion prevent them from exploring
openly into the truth of the situation and making clear decisions, commitments, and constructive risks when that is appropriate or necessary, whereas a weak, defensive ego will
often fearfully escape from such situations that expose its
basic sense of insubstantiality and fragility, leading to impaired functioning, and reflecting lack of inner consistency,
integration, integrity, and related inner conflict.

Some people with a relatively weak sense of personal identity or differentiation may often manifest a strong fear of loneliness, or of being alone even for relatively short periods of time. This is because their tenuous sense of differentiation requires that some other people be available to continuously see and affirm who they are as a psychological entity, or else their sense of psychological existence becomes severely threatened. This kind of individual often manifests an excessive need for affiliation with others to the point of sometimes appearing to be a "people addict." These kinds of manifestations reflect an attempt to compensate for a diminished sense of differentiation, and therefore relative ego weakness.

In addition, relative ego weakness, in regard to an individual's tenuous, insecure, sense of differentiation, can also be assessed through the intensity of his/her compensatory need to be unique, special, unusual, recognized, noticed, or to seek attention in some way, so as to be able to stand out, feel different from others, or to feel set apart from the norm in some way. The more extreme or bizarre the behavior, appearance, or whatever represents the extreme means he/she has to use in order to gain a compensatory sense of recognition or differentiation, the greater is the apparent degree of ego weakness. At the other extreme, relative ego weakness will also be evident in one who has an overriding fear of putting a weak sense of personal identity or differentiation on the line to be affirmed or disaffirmed. This is often reflected through a fear of gaining attention, being in the limelight, standing out, or being differentiated from others, which often manifests in the form of being overly conforming, taciturn, shy, or withdrawn.

The ego with a relatively weak sense of differentiation, because of a weak sense of personal identity, tends to feel inwardly empty of a sense of personal psychological substance; therefore in order to escape the sense of being an inner void, it is likely to become dependent upon the generation of a wide variety of new and intensely arousing or stimulating sensations as the means of providing itself with a sense of being inwardly more substantial. The ego equates those arousing and stimulating sensations with a sense of personal psychological inner animation, vitality, passion, excitement, or life energy. Hence, as that sense of stimulation or arousal begins to significantly diminish, the ego starts to feel bored, and interprets that sense of boredom as being a threat of the loss of its sense of psychological vitality, which triggers a form of psychological death anxiety. In an attempt to compensate for feared feelings of boredom, or associated feelings of inner emptiness, some individuals with a relatively weak ego may excessively seek thrilling, exciting, or overly stimulating sensations, such as the "highs" generated by drugs and alcohol, to the point of becoming addicted to these sensations, often coming from unwholesome, artificial, substances. Others may turn toward crime or other anti-social acts, gambling for high stakes, or performing daring and dangerous acts in the attempt to create sensations of excitement to escape from dreaded feelings of boredom. Therefore, indications of either an excessive need for stimulation, or fears of being burdened by a threatening sense of boredom, will likely reflect a diminished sense of differentiation, and thus relative ego weakness.

In addition to seeking intensely stimulating, exciting sensations, the relatively weak ego also generates a sense of psychological inner animation, and thereby reinforces its sense of inner substance and differentiation via the continuous mind movement or inner monologue of a conscious awareness in a perpetual state of desire or conceptual becoming, i.e., seeking to become validated and enhanced as a conceptually defined sense of identity. In a state of conceptual becoming, our conscious awareness is rejecting and moving away from what we are actually being, as a momentary spontaneously arising feeling or experiential state, in the continuous attempt to enhance ourselves and become the absolute, exclusive, or idealized exaggerated epitome of our conceptual should-be, or positive self-concept identity. In view of the fact that we can never actually become the conceptual should-be or positive self-concept, as an absolutely, exclusively, permanently, or definitively validated quality, because all concepts are intrinsically relative and change-able in nature, those who live predominantly in a state of conceptual becoming typically experience increased feel-ings of psychological insecurity, inner conflict, frustration, and tension, as well as a decreased sense of spontaneity. The weak ego tends to frequently "put itself on trial" by repeat-edly trying to "prove" positive ideas about itself and disprove opposite negative qualities about itself, even though there is really no realistic way to definitively prove the positive and disapprove the negative traits, because contrary invalidating evidence can potentially arise at any point in time.

As a consequence of its need to be in a continuous state of conceptual becoming, with which it identifies as its psycho-logical life, the relatively weak ego cannot sustain periods of inner contentedness, satisfaction, peacefulness, or relaxation for fear that it will lose its state of conceptual becoming, psychological self-enhancement, or the related sense of in-ner animation that contribute to its sense of inner substanti-ality. Therefore, such an ego tends to be very fearful of quiet states of mind, periods of inactivity, immobility, stagnation, or anything else that will terminate its state of conceptual becoming, and thereby expose its deeper underlying sense of inner emptiness, or lack of a personal sense of psychological substantiality, self-knowledge, and inner animation. Typical compensations for such an insecure-feeling ego may take the form of: hyperactivity, both in terms of thinking and ac-tion, which in very extreme cases may produce an agitated, restless, mind that is continuously racing and feeling out of control, as seen in those with manic disorders; erecting ex-aggerated goals that are extremely difficult, even unrealistic, or inappropriate to attain, so that the individual remains in a continuous state of desire or conceptual becoming; such as a continuous desire to travel and be constantly on the move. Another illustrative example of the ego's frantically desperate attempts to compensate for underlying feelings of inner emptiness, nothingness, deficiency, and insecurity is

the continuous attempt to fill the sense of psychological inner emptiness or lack of inner substance through a form of
symbolic displacement such as by filling the stomach with
excessive amounts of food, filling the mind by collecting all
kinds of ideas or trivial bits of information, or filling one's
house with excessive clutter as a kind of "pack rat," filling
the empty heart with overly-exaggerated sentimental, comforting, feelings, and so on.

The psychologist Abraham Maslow makes an important
distinction between motivations that arise from the attempt
to compensate for a basic sense of inner deficiency, or lack
of wholeness and well-being, which may involve seeking
to gratify various selfishly-oriented, egocentric, desires as
a means of assuaging that experience of inner deficiency,
in contrast to motivations arising from the urge to express
and thereby more fully experience qualities that arise from
the experience of intrinsic inner wholeness of being, as well
as related qualities of inner proficiency, contentment, and
unconditional well-being, involving nonjudgmental acceptance of ourselves, other individuals, and the indivisible wholeness of life. Maslow refers to the experience of
intrinsic inner wholeness, contentment, and joyful well-
being as "peak experience" and refers to the natural urge
to develop our own individual capabilities or potentials that
come from such an experience of intrinsic inner wholeness
as the process of "self-actualization," "growth-choices," or
"Being Needs," in contrast to escapist "regression-choices,"
or "Deficiency Needs." According to Maslow, peak experience and the process of self-actualization often involves
expressing unselfish caring for others as an expression of
the inclination to share or give of our sense of intrinsic inner wholeness and abundance, in contrast to relating to other
people as a compensatory way of gratifying perceived lacks
or deficiency needs.[3] Maslow also suggests that peak experience involves the experience of feeling secure in an authentic sense of identity, in contrast to individuals who take on
a "phony" kind of identity because they do not experience

such a genuine sense of inner substantiality: "Another kind of self-validating insight is the experience of being a real identity, a real self, of feeling what it is like to feel really oneself, what in fact one is—not a phony, a fake, a striver, an impersonator. Here again, the experiencing is the revelation of a truth."[4] Maslow[5] and Ken Wilber[6] also share our view that only when the ego is strong, healthy, or well-developed in its sense of authentic individual identity, inner substantiality, and emotional security can it be put aside, or permit itself to be self-forgetful at times in order to make possible caring empathic communion with other individuals and activities, and the experience of fulfilling, self-actualizing levels of reality and creative functioning beyond egoistic self-awareness, such as transpersonal states of consciousness involving an experienced sense of joyful connection to the Supreme Being and all living beings.

Our own PHI scale views motivations arising primarily from the attempt to assuage the experience of inner deficiency, and seeking compensatory forms of basically selfish gratification, or inauthentic self-aggrandizement, as evidencing ego-weakness or relative degrees of psychopathology, whereas the scale presupposes that motivations arising primarily from the urge to express the experience of inner wholeness, and seeking to actualize our real potentials and natural inclinations, reflect ego-strength or relative degrees of psychological health and constructive functioning. People who live predominantly in a state of conceptual becoming may also manifest a relatively impaired contact with reality, not only in regard to the external reality, but also in regard to their internal, actual, moment-to-moment experiential reality. This is because a state of conceptual becoming is marked by a conscious awareness that is often lost in fantasy or other forms of self-preoccupied thought related to the attempt to bolster their weakened ego-sense via continuous self-awareness, and used as a means of seeking gratification through imaginative thought of the ego's compensatory needs related to escaping from its rejected feelings of deficiency.

Thus, indications of deficiency-oriented thinking and forms of compensation that suggest that one's conscious awareness lives predominantly in a state of conceptual becoming will reflect relative ego weakness and psychopathology. In contrast, the conscious awareness of someone with relative ego strength will live less frequently in a state of conceptual becoming, and will more frequently be able to sustain a state of being, in which their conscious awareness is fully content with and unconditionally accepting of whatever experience is actually arising, here and now, inside and outside, instead of being in continuous pursuit of the conceptual should-be, which marks the deficient-feeling ego in a state of conceptual becoming, trying to become or conditionally achieve a state of less deficiency and greater proficiency. As a result, people who are capable of sustaining a state of being are less dominated by the perceived need to escape from feelings of deficiency, and therefore are capable of sustaining greater contact with inner and outer reality, which reflects relative psychological health or constructiveness.

This coincides with Maslow's observation that those who are relatively free of egocentric deficiency needs, and who are prepared to let go of self-awareness at times because they feel secure in a well-established, substantial, sense of self, are able to view themselves and others in a more realistic, unbiased, unselfishly caring manner than those whose perceptions are dominated by such egocentric deficiency needs, who tend to perceive others in a more distorted manner, and relate to others in a more selfishly manipulative, exploitative, controlling, insincere way, in the attempt to influence the other individual to gratify the ego's deficiency-based psychological needs, as well as to continuously preserve and reinforce the weak ego's tenuous sense of separate self-awareness:

> Perception in the peak-experiences can be relatively ego-transcending, self-forgetful, egoless, unselfish. It can come closer to being unmotivated, impersonal, desireless, detached, not needing or wishing. Which

is to say, that it becomes more object-centered than ego-centered. The perceptual experience can be more organized around the object itself, as a centering point, rather than being based upon the selfish ego. This means in turn that objects and people are more readily perceived as having independent reality of their own . . . precisely those people who have the clearest and strongest identity are exactly the ones who are most able to transcend the ego, or the self, and to become selfless, who are at least relatively selfless and relatively egoless.[7]

The relatively weak ego also attempts to enhance its sense of differentiation by trying to establish its psychological identity as having outstanding positive value, worth, or esteem compared to others. In this way, the ego is helped to feel different from others by affirming that it is better than others. Hence, value judgment in whatever form it takes (e.g., worth-worthlessness, positive-negative, good-evil [or bad], right-wrong, superior-inferior), becomes a necessary often fiercely competitive means by which the ego establishes its sense of differentiation, superiority, and self-aggrandizement, as a means of feeling more like a conceptually defined, inwardly substantial, important "something," and less a deficient sense of being an inner nullity. The more positively valued you and others hold your identity to be, the greater is the reinforcement, enhancement, strengthening, or security of the ego-sense, as a means of validating that you are inwardly substantial, significant, and important as a psychological entity, rather than being an insignificant inner nothingness, nullity, or a "nobody." The closer to absolute deficiency, negativity, worthlessness, or total lack of value the ego holds itself to be, or others hold it to be, the more it tends to feel deflated, nullified, negated, or extinguished as a psychological entity.

We can hold ourselves to be a conceptual something only as long as it is positively value judged. The negative relative opposite is not just an opposite something from the positive, but instead actually represents a state of negation or absence of the positive, which contributes toward a greater sense of inner insubstantiality, insignificance, and lack of differentiation. Thus, weakness is not a substantial reality in its own right, but only represents a state of negation or absence of power, strength, or control, which represents the psychological something. Hence, people who feel extremely worthless do not just feel like a worthless something, but actually feel closer to being a conceptual nothing, a psychological nobody or non-entity, which reflects a relatively weak ego-sense.

Thus, a diminished sense of differentiation or relative ego weakness can be assessed directly via your experienced feelings of worthlessness, or the prevalence of negative self-concept identifications, and indirectly via your exaggerated compensatory need to strive for and affirm a positive self-concept identity and an enhanced sense of personal worth, value, or esteem. Typical compensatory behavior in this regard is evidenced in people who have an excessive need to be competitive with others, as the means of comparing themselves with others, in the attempt to feel superior to them, thereby elevating a diminished sense of worth. Hence, the greater the ego's need for a sense of self-aggrandizement, in whatever form it may take, as compensation for underlying feelings of deficiency in regard to its sense of worth or differentiation, the greater is the evidenced degree of ego weakness. You would not feel a strong, persistent need to try to "prove" something positive about yourself unless you were really experiencing serious doubts about it, and therefore feeling insecure in your sense of positive identity and psychological "something-ness." Those "strong ego" individuals who already feel highly secure in their sense of identity, self-confidence, psychological substantiality, or inner "something-ness," have no or at least less need to prove anything about themselves to themselves or to others. At the other extreme, as the opposite counterpart to self-aggrandizement, a diminished sense of worth, and relative ego weakness, can also be reflected in our need to avoid competitive situations for fear that a negative comparison with others, as apparent evidence of inferiority, will disaffirm our tenuous sense of worth. Weak ego people who do not feel confident of their ability to validate a positive sense of identity and superiority through success in the competitive arena are also likely to experience a related need to be excessively pleasing of others, even to the point of disregarding their own growth-enhancing needs, in order not to be rejected and judged negatively or unfavorably by others. The latter behavior serves to generate positive or flattering responses from others toward themselves that they use as a means of enhancing their diminished sense of worth.

In contrast to the relatively weak ego's use of competitive endeavors and other tactics as the means of compensating for feelings of deficiency in regard to its conceptualized sense of differentiation, worth, security, and inner substantiality, people with relative psychological health, or a relatively greater level of ego-strength, are motivated more by the urge to gratify growth-oriented needs which contribute to their greater self-actualization, which involves developing greater levels of creative, productive, and psychologically constructive, functioning, by actualizing their natural individual potentials, exploring and discovering what is experientially real in themselves, as well as being more open to exploring and thereby gradually outgrowing the basically unreal, or presumptively contrived, aspects of the ego-personality self-definitions. Self-actualization refers essentially to the fact that we are making actual, or bringing into continuously greater forms of expression, development, flowering, or fruition, that which was originally only seed-like latent potential in ourselves. Self-actualization should not be misunderstood to imply some kind of final or perfect state of development of our sense of individuality; instead, it really represents a process of continuous evolution or ongoing developmental growth. Thus, no one is ever fully self-actualized, or completely developed in the fulfillment of all of their potentials, but always continuously self-actualizing our real, natural, or inherent potentials. This may be referred to as our real or existential becoming, or authentic transformational development, in contrast to the illusory, presumptive state of conceptual becoming discussed earlier, involving enhancing, "proving," or aggrandizing the ego's favorable views of itself, and attempting to disprove the ego's unfavorable views of itself.

By way of contrast to real becoming, conceptual becoming refers essentially to the attempt to absolutely affirm or aggrandize our conceptual identity, as a conceptually defined sense of being, (i.e., our idealized self-image or those positive concepts or ideas about ourselves with which we are identified, and which are always necessarily relative in nature, because we can always become or evidence more or less of a particular conceptually defined quality at various times, and/or in comparison to other individuals). Real or existential becoming refers to the developmental growth of what is real in ourselves, rather than what is only conceptual, presumptive, or imaginary in ourselves (i.e., the continuous actualization or development of the natural inclinations, potentials, and abilities inherent in our real being or existence). Hence, the actualization of our natural real potentials represents our true identity, our genuine experiential self-knowledge, in contrast to conceptually presumed self-definitions, and yields a sense of real differentiation, or genuine particularity, which is truly substantial in contrast to the basically static self-concept identity and vague, insubstantial, easily shattered, defensive, presumptive, conceptualized sense of differentiation that is characteristic of the relatively weak ego.

We continue to grow in self-actualization via the greater exploration, discovery, or development, of our real potential abilities, qualities, functions, interests, inclinations, etc. Thus, in seeking out competitive and other situations, people with relative psychological health are motivated less by attempts to compensate for feelings of deficiency, by trying to validate that they are superior rather than inferior to others in the competitive arena, and more by the urge to maximize challenging opportunities by which their real potentials, or growth-oriented needs, can gain a greater degree of actualization, fruition, or fulfillment, which is an inherently joyful process. Our real potentials are part of our natural spontaneity, and, therefore, as we grow more self-actualized, we also becomes more spontaneous, less contrived and controlled, less dominated by the idealized conceptual "shoulds" or "should nots." The greater the degree of your spontaneity, the more heightened the sense of particularity or uniqueness of your genuine individuality, which enables you to feel more substantial with regard to your sense of differentiation and is, therefore, reflective of relative ego strength and psychological health. A psychologically healthy and secure sense of identity or individuation is based primarily on openness to the momentary experiential truth of oneself and self-actualization of one's natural real potentials and inclinations rather than on presumptive conceptual self-definitions and competition or comparison with others.

According to Maslow, the psychotherapeutic process should encourage clients to "uncover" their own authentic distinctive particularity as an individual by growing in the development or actualization of their own individual potentials, rather than indoctrinating clients into the therapist's own belief system. "Very important as a source of data to support the biological basis of choosing growth over regression is the experience with 'uncovering therapy,' or what I have begun to call Taoistic therapy. What emerges here is the person's own nature, his own identity, his bent, his own tastes, his vocation, his species values, and his own idiosyncratic values. Those idiosyncratic values are often so different than the idiosyncratic values of the therapist as to constitute a validation of the point (i.e., uncovering therapy is truly uncovering rather than indoctrination)."[8]

Thus, in all these ways one's relative ego strength-weakness, with regard to one's sense of differentiation, is assessed via the PHI. It follows from this theory that anxiety and psychological insecurity would be defined as the feeling that arises when the ego fearfully anticipates an impending disaffirmation of its sense of individuation and differentiation, and the consequent painful feelings of deficiency, as well as a threat to the ego's sense of continued psychological existence or inner substantiality that would accompany such disaffirmation. The prevalence of such feelings of anxiety and the defenses used to escape its awareness would therefore add to the assessment of the degree of your relative ego-weakness. In contrast, feelings of confidence or security would reflect the ego's anticipation of impending affirmation of its sense of individuation, differentiation, or inner substantiality. Where these feelings characterize our reactions, when our sense of individuation and differentiation is on the line to be affirmed or disaffirmed, then we will assume that relative ego strength or weakness is, thereby, reflected.

Whereas anxiety represents the ego's *anticipation* of impending disaffirmation of its sense of individuation, differentiation, or inner substantiality, psychological pain, in whatever form it takes, represents the experiential state that arises *after* disaffirmation has already taken place. Therefore, underlying every feeling of psychological pain is a feeling of deficiency, related to the disaffirmation of our sense of individuation, differentiation, or inner substantiality, which represents a greater or lesser degree of negation or nullification of the ego's sense of being a psychological entity or self. Thus, for example, if your sense of potency of will power or sense of individuation were put on the line, to be affirmed or disaffirmed, the relatively weak ego would experience anxiety in that regard. If your sense of potency of will then turned out to be disaffirmed, so that you felt deficient in will-power, then your sense of individuation, or ego-sense, along with your related sense of inner substantiality and emotional security, which depends upon affirming the potency of your will, would feel diminished. That disaffirmation of the ego's sense of identity and will power would produce corresponding feelings of deficiency, such as frustration, impotence, weakness, fearful insecurity, helplessness, vulnerability, etc. Similarly, if your sense of worth were put on the line and disaffirmed, you would experience the painfulness of experiencing a partly diminished or even totally nullified sense of worth, bringing a diminished or even totally negated sense of being an inwardly substantial, emotionally secure, psychological "something," and some greater or lesser degree of loss of self-perceived stature, prominent identity, and differentiation from others would then arise.

The feeling of deficiency may also cloak or disguise itself and its inherent painfulness related to the disaffirmation of your sense of individuation or differentiation, in other feelings or reactions. Typical of these are depression and anger. Thus, this theory views most, if not all, expressions of psychological pain as similar in the sense that they each reflect an underlying feeling of disaffirmation of the ego's sense of individuation or differentiation. In depression, you feel helpless to do anything about that sense of disaffirmation because available forms of compensation are ego-dystonic, or uncomfortable for the ego, for some reason; whereas anger represents the attempt to deny those feelings of helplessness via a compensatory expression of power. Emotional depression may arise from blocking feelings that feel uncomfortable or threatening to the ego, especially feelings that make the ego feel insecure, such as anger or guilt, but depression may also reflect a sense of inner deadness, inner numbness, lack of vitality, or lack of inner energy flow, arising from viewing yourself and/or others as basically unlovable, unworthy or unavailable to be loved.

Thus, this PHI theory focuses on the compensatory nature of ego motivation. It views the ego's motivations, needs, desires, wants, wishes, hopes, demands, ideals, or "should," etc., as reflecting the attempt to compensate for rejected painful feelings of deficiency related to an experienced disaffirmation or weakening of one's sense of individuation or differentiation, arising from some kind of invalidation or discrediting of one's sense of inner substantiality as a psychological entity, identity, or conceptual self-definition. Hence, psychological pain, in whatever form it takes, usually reflects the ego's perception, at some level of awareness, that its sense of self has been disaffirmed or diminished in some way, with regard to its sense of individuation, differentiation, or inner substantiality, with which it is identified. Therefore, the psychological pain associated with your feeling of deficiency basically represents the fact that you now feel closer to psychological nullity or complete extinction of your psychological entity or personal sense of self and sense of inner substantiality.

In contrast to feelings of relative psychological pain, this theory would suggest that feelings of relative elation reflect the fact that your sense of individuation, differentiation, or inner substantiality has been experienced as being momentarily affirmed or enhanced in some way. With regard to feeling psychologically "up" or "down," the ego is very much like a balloon; feelings of elation arise when the ego feels more inflated or enhanced with regard to its sense of individuation, differentiation, or inner substantiality, whereas some form of psychological pain arises when the ego feels that it has been deflated or diminished in its sense of individuation, differentiation, or inner substantiality. Thus, the degree of psychological pain and anxiety that characterizes your functioning, as well as the degree of intolerance that you express with regard to these threatening feelings, reflects a weakened sense of individuation, differentiation, or inner substantiality, and, therefore, relative ego weakness and psychopathology.

In contrast to the ego's conditionally acquired, conditionally lost, feelings of elation, self-aggrandizement, vitality, well-being, inner substantiality, worth, security, competence, and power, which are dependent upon feeling enhanced in your conceptually defined sense of identity, what Maslow describes as "Being-values" involve the experience of a sense of inner vitality, joyfulness, goodness, wholeness, and well-being that are intrinsic to your being rather than conditionally acquired and conditionally lost.[9] In contrast to the weak ego's, and perhaps also the strong ego's, conceptually defined presumptive sense of self-enhancement as the basis of its temporarily acquired feeling of elation, the transpersonal self's psychologically healthy sense of intrinsic, unconditional well-being is experiential (i.e., directly experienced), rather than conceptually defined or presumed, or in Maslow's terms, the qualities or characteristics of being are relatively "unanalyzable."[10]

A basic distinction should be made between the strong ego's sense of conditional psychological security and well-being, derived from positive, proficient, or favorable self-evaluations, and confidence in its ability to influence others to gratify the ego's basic needs, as a confident ego, in contrast to the psychopathological insecure-and-deficient feeling ego, and also in contrast to an unconditional, intrinsic, sense of wholeness, security, well-being, or fulfillment, coming from your own being, as a transpersonal self. The transpersonal self, or the holistic self, is a non-defensive self beyond the defensive ego, a relational self, an experiential real self, in contrast to the ego as a conceptually defined sense of separate self-awareness and identity. In contrast to the strong and weak ego, as a conceptually defined exclusively separate, basically illusory, sense of self, the real self is fully whole, and therefore fully healthy, because it is without divisive conceptual self-definitions and self-evaluations. Although we view the strong ego as psychologically normal or relatively healthy, in contrast to the weak ego's greater susceptibility to psychological pain and pathology, we view full or optimal psychological health as involving maturing beyond, or at least temporarily forgetting, the strong and weak ego's defensively-oriented, deficiency-based, separate self-awareness, self-aggrandizement, and divisive conceptual self-definition, by functioning as a relational self, an undivided self, a non-conflicted being-self, without divisive positive and negative self-evaluations.

Pain intolerance, especially in its most extreme form, or what may be termed "pain phobia," reflects relatively extreme ego weakness, i.e., an ego that, often subconsciously, if not fully consciously, experiences itself as being inwardly insubstantial, tenuous, fragile, insecure, and liable to being easily negated in its basic sense of self or identity. To this kind of ego, pain of any sort is perceived as a threat to annihilate its sense of individuation and differentiation. Pain threatens the ego's sense of individuation because when the relatively weak ego pits its relatively impotent sense of will power against the painful experience, in the attempt to reduce or subdue it, and finds that it cannot be effective in doing so, it feels disaffirmed in its potency of will, and, therefore, disaffirmed in its sense of individuation or individual psychological existence. The intensity of uncontrolled pain also threatens to obliterate the ego's sense of separate self-awareness or differentiation so that you are no longer aware of anything but the pain, and, therefore, you feel threatened by the loss or overshadowing of any other kind of self-knowledge. Pain can be such an overridingly intense sensation that it obscures the ego's familiar personal conceptual and experiential states with which it has become identified; thus, the ego feels lost or lacking self-awareness when it cannot locate those familiar sensations, mind chatter, mostly narcissistic emotional reactions, and effective controlling personal willpower with which it is identified, because of the dominating presence of the painful experience. Thus, the pain phobia or fear is not only of pain but also even more importantly of its consequent capacity to destroy the ego's sense of individuation and differentiation, and thereby bring about ego-death or loss of separate self-awareness of one's psychological sense of self.

In view of the fact that pain has the capacity to destroy its sense of individuation, the relatively weak ego or the insecure-feeling ego seeks to control and avoid pain at all costs, even if it means losing out on some kind of highly valued experience. Furthermore, the weak ego often avoids the necessity to cope with uncomfortable, difficult, adaptive challenges even if that avoidance is hazardous to your psychological, social, financial, or physical security and well-being, such as when it jeopardizes your capacity for productive functioning, social adjustment, or even physical survival. Such an ego typically fears and avoids being too happy because it feels most vulnerable to intense pain, especially intense feelings of disappointment, anticipated to arise should the happiness later be lost. The avoidance of potentially promising love relationships because of the fear of the possible emotional pain they could bring is one such example. Prematurely quitting on the attempt to achieve other valued, genuinely fulfilling, self-actualizing goals, such as career goals, for fear of experiencing psychological pain arising from possible failure, frustration, and disappointment is another such example. As a result of its intense fear of psychological pain, such an ego tends to become extremely self-indulgent and heavily dependent upon having a steady stream of pleasurable sensations that enable it to escape from and have a sense of control over the arising of any actual, anticipated, or interpreted pain, which often results in addiction of one kind or another, as a consequence of becoming overly dependent on a particular substance, such as some kind of narcotic, that deadens the experience of pain, and superimposes a pleasurable and/or relaxing feeling upon it. The kind of pleasure and relaxation that comes from such escapist pursuits is usually much shallower than the deeply satisfying sense of joy and vitality that comes from actualizing the natural potentials, abilities, interests, and inclinations, that are intrinsic to your real being, and therefore life-based in contrast to presumptive forms of conceptual self-definition, self-enhancement, and self-gratification, which lack a basis in real life energy experience.

Hence, in any situation where there exists both the possibility of significant ego gratification and also possible pain to the ego, it is expected that the relatively weak ego will be dominated by the need to avoid any possible pain, and therefore will likely avoid any significant involvement in that situation out of fear that its tenuous sense of individuation and differentiation could be easily eradicated should intense or prolonged pain arise. In contrast, someone with relatively good ego strength will tend to be dominated more by the yearning to maximize the gratification of one's basic needs even if the possibility of pain does exist, and therefore is able to make more reasonable constructive risks, in the face of possible pain, in the attempt to gain a greater level of transformational development and fulfillment, such as taking the risk of experiencing disappointment and frustration arising from possible failure or needing to surmount difficult obstacles to achieve one's desired goals. Therefore, someone who is characterized by the avoidance of such risks will be evidencing relative ego weakness and relative psychopathology.

Thus, in all of these various ways assessed directly via one's conscious experience of feeling deficient, or indirectly via the assessment of one's psychological needs which attempt to compensate for these feelings of deficiency, the Psychopathology-Health Inventory (PHI) measures the degree of one's sense of individuation and differentiation, which is a foundational structure of the ego and the basic determinant of its degree of relative ego strength-weakness or relative psychopathology-health.

The Psychopathology-Health Inventory (PHI) as an Empirical Diagnostic Tool, Contrasted with Other Ego-Strength Scales

*(**Editorial Note by Barry Hammer:** Readers who are not interested in the following discussion of the PHI psychological diagnostic questionnaires, and the related discussion of statistical analysis and comparison with diagnostic questionnaires devised by other psychologists may wish to skip to the Concluding Summary of Chapter 5 on pages 347-8 and then skip to Appendix A beginning on page 374)*

The rooting of the PHI in this coherent theoretical framework should make it possible to assess its construct validity more precisely than other, actuarially-derived, ego strength scales such as the Barron's Ego Strength (Es) scale (Barron, 1953). The Es scale, although it is to date the most widely used ego strength scale available to clinicians and researchers, has suffered from this lack of a consistent theoretical framework when subjected to empirical analysis. For instance, although the reliability of the Es scale has generally been found to be adequate (e.g., Barron, 1953; Gocka, 1965), its validity is open to question. While the Es scale is useful in distinguishing overtly pathological groups from normals (e.g., Taft, 1957; Kleinmutz, 1960; Himelstein, 1964), it has been less successful in delineating among different pathological groups (e.g., Tamkin, 1957, comparing neurotics with character disorders; Gottesman, 1959, comparing schizophrenics with neurotics; Quay, 1963, comparing psychotics and neurotics). The performance of the Es scale as a predictor of response to psychotherapy (the task for which it was originally designed) has also been mixed. Studies by Barron and Leary (1955), Wirt (1955, 1956), Welkowitch (1960), and Sinnett (1962) confirm Barron's (1953) initial contention. However, other studies (e.g., Ends & Page, 1957; Getter & Sundland, 1962; Fowler, Teel, & Coyle, 1967) failed to separate therapy responders from non-responders on the basis of Es scores, discrediting the utility of the scale for this task. Furthermore, studies by Edwards (Edwards, Heathers, & Fordyce, 1960; Edwards, 1962) have produced data demonstrating that the Es scale is significantly influenced by the response set of social desirability. This confound, combined with the equivocal nature of the validation research, has caused many researchers and clinicians to view the Es scale skeptically.

There are several other disadvantages of both the Es scale and the other widely known ego strength measure—the Rorschach Prognostic Rating Scale (RPRS) developed by Klopfer (Klopfer, Kirkner, Wisham, & Baker, 1951). Both of these instruments are extremely time consuming to administer. Es requires a full MMPI protocol, and while this may be obtained in approximately an hour and a half with a reasonably well-functioning subject, some more disturbed individuals require as much as two or even three hours for a complete administration. Similarly, the RPRS, requiring as it does a complete Rorschach protocol, plus the time required for the extremely complex, cumbersome, and somewhat unreliable scoring procedures, is equally time consuming. This is a severe disadvantage, particularly in research where it is necessary to obtain data on a large number of subjects.

In contrast, the PHI is extremely easy to administer and score. Typically, a complete protocol can be obtained in approximately ten minutes. Rarely is more than twenty minutes necessary for completion. Also, as will be seen, the PHI has the unique advantage of having two equivalent forms, which allow for subsequent testing at any phase of treatment or research without fear of contamination of results by familiarity or practice effects. In addition, the scoring procedure for the PHI is completely objective and quantitative, which makes it more reliable than the RPRS, which depends on subjective, qualitative, and often symbolic interpretations on the part of the scorer. Finally, the PHI has readily apparent face validity, not shared by more projective instruments, which should insure maximum motivation on the part of the tested individuals.

A Brief Description of the Pathology-Health Inventory

As mentioned above, the PHI diagnostic questionnaire is a paper and pencil psychological assessment inventory consisting of the equivalent forms of sixty-five items each.

Examples of some of the items are as follows:

1. It is very hard for me to take a risk if there is the chance that it would embarrass me or hurt my pride.
2. I am afraid that other people want to or will hurt me.
3. I like to work on other people until they see things my way.
4. I try very hard to get other people to notice me.

5. I have a strong need for thrills, excitement, or variety in my life.

Subjects are instructed to respond to each item by using a six point scale reflecting the frequency with which each statement applies to them. The scale categories are: almost always (6), very frequently (5), often (4), sometimes (3), seldom (2), and almost never (1). Subjects record the number corresponding to the scale category best describing the frequency with which a particular stimulus item applies to themselves. The total PHI score is then obtained by summing the numerical responses given in each item. The higher the score, the greater the degree of ego-weakness and psychopathology.

Statistical Analysis: Development of the PHI, Methods and Results Initial Testing

The original form of the PHI consisted of a pool of 180 items. This form was administered to a sample of 152 university undergraduates. From these data, the reliability of the instrument was assessed using alpha coefficient (Nunnally, 1970) and a coefficient of .96 was obtained.

The validity of the instrument was then assessed. This was done in several ways. First, the PHI was administered concurrently with the Tennessee Self Concept Scale (TSCS; Fitts, 1965), to a new sample of 107 psychology students. Highly significant Pearson product moment correlation coefficients were obtained between the PHI and the TSCS subscales of "General Maladjustment" (a numerically inverted scale; ($r = -.43$; $p <.001$), "Total Positive" ($r = -.54$; $p <.001$), and "Personality Integration" ($r = -.28$; $p <.002$). All coefficients were in the expected direction.

Another trial investigated the validity of the PHI as a measure of pathology. Thirty-four state hospital patients were administered the PHI along with the MMPI. Significant correlations were obtained between the PHI and the MMPI Sc (Schizophrenia) scale (r = .59; p <.001), and Pa (Paranoia) scale (r =.19; p <.05).

An investigation of the PHI as a measure of relative psychological health was conducted by comparing it to Shostrom's POI test of self-actualization (Shostrom, 1965). A sample of 44 college students was used. Significant correlations were obtained between the PHI and the POI dimensions of Time Competence (r = -.49; p <.01), Time Incompetence (r = .49; p <.01), Inner Directedness (r = -.32; p <.05), and Other Directedness (r = .42; p <.01).

The time Competence-Incompetence and Inner-Other Directedness were the two most important dimensions of the POI to consider, since they underlie all of the other POI scales. Time Competence is thought to relate to a person's capacity to live in the here and now and to have full contact with reality. This was predicted to correlate highly with the PHI, since the weaker or more deficient feeling ego is more self-preoccupied as the means of bolstering, gratifying, and protecting itself; therefore, it is less able to be in full contact with reality, here and now. The Inner-Other Directedness dimension of the POI was also expected to correlate significantly with the PHI because the greater the degree of ego-strength, the greater is the solidity and clarity of the ego's sense of identity, and the more likely is the ego to be inner-directed or governed by its own internal spontaneity rather than directed by others.

The concurrent validity of the PHI as a test of ego strength, per se, was assessed by administering it along with the Barron's Es scale to a mixed normal ad pathological sample. Twelve inmates from the Women's Correctional Center in Skowhegan, Maine, and 41 college undergraduates served as subjects. The correlation between the PHI and the Es scale was -.41 (p <.001). In addition, the discriminating validity of the PHI was assessed using this same sample by dividing the sample into high and low ego strength groups (a PHI score of 500 was used as the cutoff). A Chi Square ($\underline{x}^2$ = 9.05; $\underline{df}$ =1) was calculated. This differentiated the normals from the inmates at the .005 level.

Refinement of the PHI

This initial series of studies was seen as providing substantial evidence for the reliability and validity of the tool. At this point, it was decided to refine it further in an effort to make it an even more useful clinical and research instrument. It was decided to first reduce the size of the scale, both to decrease administration time, and to improve the internal consistency. The PHI was administered to a new sample of 150 college students, and from these data item-scale correlations for each item were computed. It was decided to drop all items correlating at the .24 level or lower. This dropped fifty items from the scale. The remaining 130 items were correlated significantly at the .001 level with the total PHI score.

At this point, the decision was made to divide the test into two forms of equal length of sixty-five items each (hereafter referred to as Form A and Form B). It was felt that the creation of two statistically equivalent but non-overlapping scales would be a great advantage to those using the tool. This would allow for retesting of a patient or subject after relatively brief time periods without fear of the contamination of results by familiarity or practice effects.

The split was made on an odd-even basis. Initial assessment of the reliability of the two forms, the strength of their relationship to each other, and to the full scale PHI was performed using the data from the above sample of 150 students. A comparison of Form A with Form B yielded a Pearson $\underline{r}$ = .96; a comparison of form A and Form B with the total PHI score yielded correlations of $\underline{r}$ = .98 for each of the shorter forms. The reliability of the 130 item PHI and the two derived forms was equally high. Shortening the PHI raised its reliability coefficient to the .97 level. The reliability of the two short forms were each in excess of .95.

The test was thus seen to maintain its high level of reliability. The two short forms share this quality, and are highly related to each other and to the full scale. Given the strength of the correlations, there is reason to assert that Form A and Form B are statistically equivalent and equally sensitive in measuring ego strength. The next step was to reassess the equivalence, reliability, and validity of Form A and Form B on a new subject sample. In this effort, 135 introductory psychology students were used. In order to check the concurrent validity of the tool, the subjects were also administered the Barron's Es scale. In addition, the impact of the response set of social desirability was investigated by administering the Marlowe-Crowne Social Desirability Scale (Crowne & Marlowe, 1964).

The alpha reliability coefficient was again compared. Both Form A and Form B achieved coefficients in excess of .94. In addition, the scores of the subjects on Form A and Form B correlated at .95.

The concurrent validity of the two forms was demonstrated by moderate but significant correlations with Barron's Es scale (r = -.51; p <.001 for both forms). A significant but not extremely high correlation was expected because the PHI is much broader in the areas of ego strength and much more theoretically sound.

Low but significant correlations were achieved between both forms of the PHI and the social desirability measure (Form A, r = -.25; p <.002/Form B, r = -.24; p <.002). This was not entirely unexpected in that this response set is a property of most paper and pencil tests such as the PHI. It has been noted earlier that Es is also quite susceptible to this factor—apparently to a much greater degree than the PHI. Edwards, Heathers, and Fordyce (1960) found a correlation between the Es and social desirability of .73. This is much higher than the relationship of the PHI to this parameter, and thus when compared to the Es scale is much less affected by it. Other data bearing on this topic will shortly be presented.

In order to assess the discriminative validity of the PHI, and to further explore the issue of the social desirability response set, a further study was conducted. The subjects consisted of a group of sixty-nine alcoholics who were receiving inpatient treatment for their substance abuse at the VA hospital in Togus, Maine. The alcoholics were all detoxified, and were beginning their first week of rehabilitative treatment at the start of the study. The alcoholics were administered one form of the PHI at the start of their treatment, along with the Barron's Es scale and the Marlowe-Crowne. The other form of the PHI was administered just prior to discharge. Thirty-nine subjects received form A first, while thirty received Form B first. These data were collected as part of a larger research program evaluating the alcohol treatment at the VA facility and the pre- and post-treatment comparisons will be reported elsewhere. Only data on pretreatment will be reported here.

The discriminating validity of the PHI was assessed by comparing the Form A and Form B scores of the alcoholics with the Form A and Form B scores of the previous sample of 135 introductory psychology students. Because of the previously noted correlation with social desirability, the issue was raised as to whether possible group differences may be due to this dimension rather than ego strength. In order to protect the results from the influence of this possible confound, an analysis of covariance using social desirability as a covariate was used to examine the significance of between group scores.

Even with the effect of social desirability covaried out, a highly significant population main effect was achieved with both Form A and Form B (Form A: F (1,167) = 30.095, p <.001/Form B: F (1,158) = 19.492, p <.001). In contrast, a comparison of the performance of the two groups on the Barron's, while at first showing significance on a simple ANOVA (F [1,197] = 4.389, p <.04), when recomputed introducing social desirability as a covariate, lacked an acceptable level of significance (F [1,196] = 3.155, p = .078).

Thus, although the PHI is mildly related to social desirability, it still powerfully differentiates subject groups even when the influence of the response set is controlled for. In contrast, although the Es scale also discriminates between groups (albeit less powerfully than the PHI), this ability vanishes when the influence of social desirability is accounted for.

Discussion

The above series of studies provide strong statistical support for the Pathology-Health Inventory as a reliable and valid paper and pencil diagnostic measure of ego strength. The alpha reliability coefficient of the full PHI and the two shorter forms has consistently been found to be at the .94 level or better. The Pearson correlation coefficient between Form A and Form B has been found to be .96, providing strong evidence for their statistical equivalency. The concurrent validity of the tool has been demonstrated in its relationship to a number of different measures of psychological pathology and psychological health, such as the Tennessee Self Concept Scale, Shostrom's POI test of self-actualization, and the Barron's Es scale. The discriminative validity of the tool has been displayed by its successful segregation of pathological and normal subjects. Finally, the tool possesses a high level of theoretical and face validity due to its firm grounding in this new theory of relative ego strength-weakness. It is likely that the promising performance of the PHI is a direct reflection of its solid rooting in this theoretical base.

Social Desirability

The issue of social desirability requires further comment. In the decision to measure ego strength with a paper and pencil inventory, rather than a projective test, it was realized that such tests are often subject to the social desirability response set. This is inherent in the nature of the stimulus materials of this class of psychometric tool. By necessity, the items used in such an inventory must be specific enough for the subject to understand and apply to his or her own experience. Almost any important statement or question pertaining to psychological functioning can be interpreted as socially desirable or undesirable. In order to get around this difficulty, two strategies are possible.

One, the items can be made so ambiguous that their social desirability becomes unclear. But, in order to do this, so much ambiguity is injected into the stimulus items that the test almost becomes projective in nature. This leaves the test open to the difficulties found with projective tests, because scoring becomes a matter of symbol translation, which leads to error and unreliability.

The second alternative is to try to construct the items in such a way that they appear to be unrelated to the target dimension. However, this decreases the face validity of the test, which, especially with pathological subjects, has a negative impact on the motivation of the subjects taking the test.

Thus, some social desirability is seen as a necessary evil if we are to take advantage of the benefits of a paper and pencil inventory (e.g., fast administration, objective and fast scoring, high reliability, etc.). What is noteworthy about the PHI is that it is much less affected by social desirability than the most widely used paper and pencil ego strength measure (i.e., the Barron's Es scale), and maintains its ability to discriminate between known pathological and normal groups even when the impact of social desirability is controlled for, while the Barron's fails to do so. The PHI, then, has a demonstrated superiority over the Es scale.

Interpreting the PHI

In an effort to provide the prospective user with a means of evaluating PHI scores and localizing them on the continuum of psychological pathology-psychological health, a tentative classificatory system is offered. The distribution of PHI scores obtained from a total of 283 university undergraduates. The distribution of PHI scores obtained from a total of 283 university undergraduates was examined. In view of this distribution, the following categories seemed to suggest themselves:

Table 1: PHI Scoring Categories

PHI Score	Category Label	% of sample* in category
Less than 100	Pseudo-Healthy	4.8
100-120	Healthy	13.4
121-165	Normal	50.6
166-190	Mild Pathology	14.7
191-227	Severe Pathology	12.0
Greater than 227	Pseudo-Pathology	4.5

* $\underline{n}$ = 283

The demarcation points of the different categories are roughly related to their distance, in standard deviations, from the mean of the sample. For example, the cutoff point between the Normal and Mild Pathological Categories is roughly one half of a standard deviation away from the mean. The cutoff point between the Mild Pathology and Severe Pathology categories is roughly one standard deviation away from the mean; the Pseudo-pathology category starts at about two standard deviations away from the mean, etc. This system is for use with the short forms of the PHI only. To interpret a full scale PHI score, simply divide it by two.

The categories of Pseudo-Healthy and Pseudo-Pathology deserve special comment. Subjects whose scores fall into either of these two extreme categories are viewed as attempting to appear much healthier or much more pathological than they are in actuality. Even the healthiest individual has some areas in which his ego needs are not always being met, and even the most pathological individual has those needs met sometimes. Therefore, in a valid performance, scores should not fall into these extreme categories of pseudo-healthy and pseudo-pathology. People falling into either of these extreme categories must be viewed as presenting a falsely consistent picture of themselves, and their performance on the test should not be considered valid.

The categories should be considered only tentative, and the boundaries between them diffuse rather than distinct. There is, of course, no sharp differentiation between, say, mild and severe pathology. The labels should be viewed as rough guides in the interpretation of an individual score.

Uses of the PHI

The Pathology-Health Inventory should find utility in both research and clinical practice. Some of its potential advantages in empirical work have already been mentioned. It is quick to administer, interpret, and score. It yields readily quantifiable data, unlike some of the most respected tests of personality, such as the TAT and the Rorschach, which yield data of a basically qualitative nature, making them difficult to use in quantitative, statistical research. It is the first tool specifically designed to measure both pathology and health within the same diagnostic instrument. This allows for direct comparison of psychologically normal and abnormal subjects, and eliminates the need for different tests measuring these dimensions separately. Its two equivalent forms allow for retesting after short time intervals without fear of contaminating the data with familiarity and practice effects.

The PHI promises to be of equal value to the clinician as well. By evaluating the strength of the ego, determinations as to the appropriateness of reconstructive versus supportive therapies can be made with much greater confidence. In addition, the inspection of responses to individual items can be used to yield information as to which particular ego compensatory needs (e.g., security, worth, power, identity, excitement) are seeking most intensely to be gratified, and in what areas the ego feels most deficient or threatened. Clues from the PHI concerning the client's ego compensatory needs can also reflect how the client may use the therapy relationship. Thus, if a client has a strong need for power, as compensation for an impotent-feeling will and tenuous sense of individuation, then it is likely that the client will use the therapy relationship as a battle of wills in order to affirm the power and independence of his or her own will; or if the client has a strong need to generate a sense of worth, in order to compensate for deep feelings of worthlessness and a tenuous sense of differentiation, then it is likely that the client will use the therapy relationship as an attempt to manipulate the therapist into providing the client with a compensatory sense of worth, rather than exploring his or her feelings of worthlessness in order to outgrow them.

The availability of two equivalent forms allows for several different assessment options. If a quick determination of ego strength is needed in order to plan immediate intervention, one of the short forms can be used. If a more comprehensive picture of ego functioning is desired in order to plan long term therapeutic goals, the entire PHI can be administered. The existence of two equivalent forms also allows for the effective monitoring of therapeutic progress.

REFERENCES

Barron, F. "An Ego-strength Scale which Predicts Response to Psychotherapy." *Journal of Consulting Psychology* 17, no. 5 (1953): 327-333.

Barron, F., & Leary, T.F. "Changes in Psychoneurotic Patients with and without Psychotherapy." *Journal of Consulting Psychology* 19 (1955):139-145.

Crowne, D.P. *The Approval Motive: Studies in Evaluative Dependence.* New York: John Wiley and Sons, 1964.

Edwards, A.L. "Social Desirability and Expected Means on MMPI Scales." *Educational and Psychological Measurements* 22 (1962): 71-76.

Edwards, A. L., Heathers, L.B., and W.E. Fordyce. "Correlations of New MMPI Scales with SD Scale." *Journal of Clinical Psychology* 16 (1960): 26-29.

Ends, E.J., and C.W. Page. "A Study of Functional Relationships among Measures of Anxiety, Ego Strength, and Adjustment." *Journal of Clinical Psychology* 13 (1957): 148-150.

Fitts, W.H. "Tennessee Self-concept Scale." *Counselor Recordings and Tests*, Box 6184, Acklen Station, Nashville, Tennessee, 1965.

Fowler, R.D., S.K. Teel, and F.A. "The Measurement of Alcoholic Response to Treatment by Barron's Ego Strength Scale." *Journal of Psychology* 67 (1967): 65-68.

Getter H., and D.M. Sundland. "The Barron Ego Strength Scale and Psychotherapeutic Outcome." *Journal of Consulting Psychology* 26 (1962): 195.

Gocka, E. "American Lake Norms for 200 MMPI Scales." Unpublished materials, 1965.

Gotteman, I.I. "More Construct Validation of the Validity of the Ego Strength Scale." *Journal of Consulting Psychology* 23 (1959): 342-346.

Himelstein, P., "Further Evidence of the Ego Strength Scale as a Measure of Psychological Health." *Journal of Consulting Psychology* 28 (1964): 90-91.

Klienmutz, B. "An Extension of the Construct Validity of the Ego Strength Scale." *Journal of Consulting Psychology* 24 (1960): 463-464.

Klopfer, B., F.J. Kirkner, W. Wisham, and G. Baker. "Rorschach Prognostic Rating Scale." *Journal of Projective Techniques* 15 (1951): 425-428.

Nunnally, J.C. *Psychometric Theory*. New York: McGraw Hill, 1970.

Quay, H. "Ego-strength and Psychiatric Diagnosis." *Psychological Reports* 13 (1963): 70.

Shostrom, E.L. "A Test for the Measurement of Self-actualization." *Educational and Psychological Measurements* 24 (1965): 207-218.

Sinnet, E.R. "The Relationship between the Ego Strength Scale and Rated In-hospital Improvement." *Journal of Clinical Psychology* 18 (1962): 46-47.

Taft, R. "The Validity of the Barron Ego Strength Scale and the Welsh Anxiety Index." *Journal of Consulting Psychology* 21 (1957): 247-249.

Tamkin, A.S. "An Evaluation of the Construct Validity of the Barron's Ego Strength Scale." *Journal of Clinical Psychology* 13 (1957): 156-158.

Welkowitz, J. "Behavior Patterns in Group Psychotherapy Sessions in two Veteran's Administration Hospitals." *Dissertation Abstracts* 20 (1960): 4202-4203.

Wirt, R.D. "Further Validation of the Ego Strength Scale." *Journal of Consulting Psychology* 19 (1955): 444.

Wirt, R.D. "Actuarial Prediction." *Journal of Consulting Psychology* 20 (1956): 123-124.

Author's (Max Hammer's) Footnote

I am indebted to Joel A. Gold for his statistical advice during several phases of this project, and to Robert Kuehnel and David McGalliard for their help in the collection of much of the data.

CONCLUDING SUMMARY OF

CHAPTER 5

DEVELOPMENT AND VALIDATION OF THE

PSYCHOPATHOLOGY-HEALTH INVENTORY

We have discussed the characteristics of the PHI psychological diagnostic questionnaire developed by Max Hammer and its theoretical basis. Following this concluding summary, the actual diagnostic questionnaire will be presented as an appendix to this chapter.

We postulate that psychological health is most essentially derived from having developed tolerance for psychological pain, which enables people to accept the possible risk of facing frustration, disappointment, and other unpleasant experiential states for the sake of responding effectively and constructively to adaptive challenges and opportunities that can vitally impact their personal well-being. Relatively strong ego individuals, or psychologically healthy and secure individuals with strength of character or tolerance for psychological pain, can typically be more flexible, and less defensive or controlling in their manner of perception and behavior, having less need to validate positive self-definitions and invalidate negative self-evaluations as a means of avoiding the risk of psychological pain. In contrast, the relatively weak ego or psychologically insecure-feeling and pain-phobic person tends to avoid challenges and opportunities that threaten to invalidate the ego's tenuous sense of identity, differentiation from others, self-consistency, and security, for fear that the ego's foundational sense of inner nothingness, insubstantiality, and deficiency may be exposed, which threatens the ego's sense of psychological existence and can produce psychological pain, which the weak ego finds difficult to tolerate.

The degree of ego weakness or strength can be diagnostically determined through questionnaires that measure the degree of experienced psychological neediness or deficiency, and the compensatory drive to defend and enhance or aggrandize the ego through the gratification of those needs. The PHI diagnostic questionnaire also measures the degree to which individuals feel secure in their sense of separate identity, self-esteem, psychological pain-tolerance, and willpower. Psychological pathology can also involve inner conflict, caused by escaping from painful feelings and experiential states. Another related psychologically unhealthy tendency is to become overly dependent on potentially addicting sensations, substances, and/or escapist fantasies, pursued as a means of escaping from psychological pain, and generating an intensely exciting sense of stimulation as a means of experiencing a semblance of inner vitality and euphoria, whereas genuine vitality and fulfillment come from being open to the actual experience of ourselves and others. A "strong ego" or a psychologically healthy individual typically has less or no need to prove anything about themselves to themselves and/or others, such as by trying to feel superior to others through comparison and fierce rivalry in the competitive arena. The strong ego's conditional sense of relative security and well-being differs not only from the weak ego's greater sense of insecurity and deficiency, but also from the unconditional sense of security and well-being inherent to one's being, or transpersonal self. Whereas the strong ego is relatively psychologically healthy, or psychologically "normal," and the weak ego is relatively psychologically unhealthy or subnormal, the transpersonal self or state of being constitutes above-normal, full, or optimal psychological health and fulfillment, as a qualitatively greater of psychological development.

SECTION B OF CHAPTER 5

APPENDIX TO THE PSYCHOPATHOLOGY-HEALTH INVENTORY (PHI) THE ACTUAL DIAGNOSTIC QUESTIONNAIRES

Editorial note, by Barry Hammer: The "Scale of Painful Feelings" was not originally included in the PHI materials by my father, Dr. Max Hammer. Instead, he originally composed the "Scale of Painful Feelings" as a separate document. However, I am including it at the end of the appendix because I believe that it may provide readers, particularly, experimental and clinical psychologists, with valuable insights into how painful feelings can be experimentally measured, as well as how they relate to psychological health and pathology, which is the focus of the PHI.

THE PSYCHOPATHOLOGY-
HEALTH INVENTORY (PHI)
FORM A: CLINICAL

Max Hammer, PhD
Professor Emeritus of Psychology
University of Maine at Orono

This personality inventory is designed to help us identify the degree and special areas of psychological disturbance within you. By becoming aware of these troubled areas that are causing you excessive emotional pain, handicapping your interpersonal relationships, or limiting your general adequacy and effectiveness, we will then be in a position to be able to help you eliminate their disturbing effects. Almost everyone has psychological problems of some kind or another at any given moment in one's life, and this is no cause for one to feel guilty, angry, ashamed, or in any way feel inferior, for such problems are often the result of the hardships and complexities of life, and the varying degrees of psychological pressure and stress that one has to face from time to time. The first step in eliminating the painful and disabling effects of those problems is to identify and openly admit the existence of those problems to yourself. Thus, how honest and courageous you are in exposing your psychological problems and feelings to yourself and to us will determine how quickly and relatively painlessly we will be able to help you eliminate these problems. It is emphasized that this inventory is not an attempt to evaluate you or your worth, nor is it an attempt to deny your special uniqueness or individuality. The essential point is that without the information that this personality inventory provides, we would not be in the position to help you eliminate your problems quickly and with the least possible discomfort.

Read each of the enclosed inventory statements very carefully, to be sure that you understand what is being asked. Then ask yourself how true the statement is, as it applies to you.

Now rate your answer to that statement on the six point scale found at the top of each page. For each statement in this inventory, apply a number or numerical score of 6, 5, 4, 3, 2, or 1, depending on how strongly you agree or disagree with each statement. The categories related to each score are as follows:

6: Almost always
5: Very frequently
4: Often
3: Sometimes
2: Seldom
1: Almost never

Thus, for example, the first statement in this inventory reads, "I cause myself a lot of emotional pain." If you sincerely and honestly feel that this statement is *almost always* true for you, then your score on the scale at the top of the page would be 6. You would therefore write that number 6 on the line to the right of that statement. If, however, instead of finding this statement to be almost always true for you, you find this statement to be only *very frequently* true for you, then you would put a number 5 on the line to the right of the statement. If you find that the statement is neither almost always true nor very frequently true, but *often* true for you, then you would write a number 4 on that line. If the statement were only *sometimes* true for you, then you would write a number 3. If you feel that the statement is *seldom* true for you, then you would write a number 2, and if this statement, in your honest judgment, were *almost never* true for you, then you would write a number 1 on that line. Continue in this way until you have written a number for each statement. If you are not certain as to how to answer some particular statement, then take whatever part of the statement does apply to you, in whatever way, and answer it accordingly. Remember, for this diagnostic test to be optimally effective and useful, every *statement should be answered* by giving it a number that you feel best fits your answer.

THE PSYCHOPATHOLOGY-HEALTH INVENTORY (PHI) FORM A: RESEARCH

Max Hammer, PhD
Professor Emeritus of Psychology
University of Maine at Orono

This personality inventory that you are about to fill out is part of a very important research project that will help us better understand the nature of psychological health, illness, and pain. This will then enable us to develop the best means of helping people with psychological problems to become psychologically healthy, mature, and free of emotional pain. People from all walks of life are being asked to participate in this very important project. Therefore, your fullest cooperation and honesty is very much needed and appreciated. Almost everyone has psychological problems of some kind or another at some time or another in his or her life, and this is no cause for him or her to feel ashamed, guilty, angry, or in any way inferior, for such problems are the result of the hardships and complexities of life, and the varying degrees of psychological pressure that one has to face from time to time. We are mostly interested in finding out how often particular kinds of problems, feelings, and experiences occur in the everyday life of most people. Therefore, you can clearly understand that there are no right or wrong answers to any of the statements in this inventory. We are only interested in finding out how *you*, personally, feel about each statement. Read each one of the enclosed statements very carefully to be sure that you understand what is being asked. Then ask yourself how true the statement is, as it applies to you. Now rate your answer to that statement on the six point scale found at the top of each page. For each statement in this inventory, apply a number or numerical score of 6, 5, 4, 3, 2, or 1, depending on how strongly you agree or disagree with each statement. The categories related to each score are as follows:

6: Almost always
5: Very frequently
4: Often
3: Sometimes
2: Seldom
1: Almost never

Thus, for example, the first statement in this inventory reads, "I cause myself a lot of emotional pain." If you sincerely and honestly feel that this statement is *almost always* true for you, then your score on the scale at the top of the page would be 6. You would therefore write that number 6 on the line to the right of that statement. If, however, instead of finding this statement to be almost always true for you, you find this statement to be only *very frequently* true you, then you would put a number 5 on the line to the right of the statement. If you find that the statement is neither almost always true, nor very frequently true, but *often* true for you, then you would write a number 4 on that line. If the statement were only *sometimes* true for you, then you would write a number 3. If you feel that the statement is *seldom* true for you, then you would write in a number 2, and if this statement, in your honest judgment, were *almost never* true for you, then you would write a number 1 on that line. Continue in this way until you have written a number for each statement. If you are not certain as to how to answer some particular statement, then take whatever part of the statement does apply to you, in whatever way, and answer it accordingly. Remember, for this diagnostic test to be optimally effective and useful, *every statement should be answered* by giving it a number that you feel best fits your answer.

Thank you for your time and effort.

PHI— FORM A— THE ACTUAL
SCALE CATEGORIES

6: Almost always
5: Very frequently
4: Often
3: Sometimes
2: Seldom
1: Almost never

1. I cause myself a lot of emotional pain.
2. I feel lonely.
3. It is very hard for me to take a risk if there is the chance that it would embarrass me or hurt my pride.
4. I try to escape from feeling bored.
5. Pain (physical or mental) frightens me.
6. I eat, smoke, or drink (e.g., alcohol, coffee) more than I should.
7. I lose my temper and become very angry.
8. I feel like I am going to pieces or about to have a nervous breakdown.
9. I am extreme in my moods, either very high or very low.
10. I feel quite frustrated.
11. In my mind there are thoughts that repeat themselves over and over, and I find it difficult to make them stop.
12. I find it very difficult to sincerely praise or say nice things to another person.
13. I feel the need to please others even when it is at the cost of my own pleasure, needs, or principles.
14. I try to carefully plan the image of myself that I present to others, rather than openly letting them know what I am really thinking or feeling.
15. I feel terribly uncomfortable meeting strangers, especially a group of strangers.
16. I am driven by very powerful desires, or an inner voice, that forces me to do certain things against my will.

17. Things annoy me.
18. I am driven by too much ambition or lack of ambition.
19. I find that my mind tends to live more in the past or future than it does in the present moment.
20. I feel insecure.
21. I hate other people.
22. I, or other people, see my attitudes and behavior as being childish or not mature.
23. I feel that life is more than I can cope with.
24. I am quick to blame myself for the bad things that happen to people with whom I am involved.
25. I daydream or live in some kind of make-believe fantasy world.
26. I find it very difficult to get out of bed in the morning.
27. I am burdened by fears or phobias.
28. I am fearful of expressing anger, or any negative feelings, to others.
29. I find myself wishing that I were dead.
30. I like to work on other people until they see things my way.
31. I feel that it is better to be loved than to love.
32. I lose a lot of sleep because I worry so much.
33. I seem to lack feelings.
34. It makes me uncomfortable to wait for something that I want.
35. I am afraid that other people want to, or will, hurt me.
36. I go out of my way to compete with other people, or to avoid competing with other people.
37. I have doubts about my worth.
38. I feel afraid, ashamed, or angry when others become emotional.
39. I feel confused.
40. I feel that it is safer not to trust people.
41. I feel terribly hurt.
42. I need to feel important.
43. I feel that good things will never happen to me, or if they do, they will not last very long.

44. I hate myself.
45. My sexual needs are much greater or much less than I feel they should be.
46. I have a great deal of tension.
47. I lack a sense of humor.
48. A great deal of responsibility frightens me.
49. I expect too much of myself.
50. When doing my usual work, I find that my mind wanders.
51. I feel depressed.
52. I am selfish.
53. I find it hard to make or keep close friends.
54. I hate to submit to the will, influence, or control of others.
55. I try to prove my masculinity or femininity.
56. I need to feel different, or more unique, than others.
57. I have a strong need to be needed.
58. After an argument, I expect the other person to apologize first or admit that they were wrong before I will relate with them again.
59. I am very critical of others or very hard to please.
60. I feel inadequate.
61. I feel like a big, empty, or hollow nothing inside.
62. I tell lies or stretch the truth.
63. I lack confidence.
64. I crave something that will make me feel good or high.
65. There are times when things look completely hopeless.

THE PSYCHOPATHOLOGY-HEALTH INVENTORY (PHI) FORM B: CLINICAL

Max Hammer, PhD
Professor Emeritus of Psychology
University of Maine at Orono

This personality inventory is designed to help us and you identify the degree and special areas of psychological disturbance within you. By becoming aware of these troubled areas that are causing you excessive emotional pain, handicapping your interpersonal relationships, or limiting your general adequacy and effectiveness, we will then be in a position to help you eliminate their disturbing effects. Almost everyone has psychological problems of some kind or another, at any given moment in one's life, and this is no cause for one to feel guilty, angry, ashamed, or in any way feel inferior, for such problems are often the result of the hardships and complexities of life, and the varying degrees of psychological pressure and stress that one has to face from time to time. The first step in eliminating the painful and disabling effects of those problems is to identify and openly admit the existence of those problems to yourself. Thus, how honest and courageous you are in exposing your psychological problems and feelings to yourself and to us will determine how quickly and relatively painlessly we will be able to help you eliminate these problems. It is emphasized that this inventory is not an attempt to evaluate you or your worth, nor is it an attempt to deny your special uniqueness or individuality. The essential point is that without the information that this personality inventory provides, we would not be in the position to help you eliminate your problems quickly and with the least possible discomfort.

Read each of the enclosed inventory statements very carefully to be sure that you understand what is being asked. Then ask yourself how true the statement is, as it applies to you. Now rate your answer to that statement on the six point scale found at the top of each page. For each statement in this inventory, apply a number or numerical score of 6, 5, 4, 3, 2, or 1, depending on how strongly you agree or disagree with each statement. The categories related to each score are as follows:

6: Almost always
5: Very frequently
4: Often
3: Sometimes
2: Seldom
1: Almost never

Thus, for example, the first statement in this inventory reads, "Decisions are difficult for me to make." If you sincerely and honestly feel that this statement is *almost always* true for you, then your score on the scale at the top of the page would be 6. You would therefore write that number 6 on the line to the right of that statement. If, however, instead of finding this statement to be almost always true for you, you find this statement to be only *very frequently* true for you, then you would put a number 5 on the line to the right of the statement. If you find that the statement is neither almost always true nor very frequently true, but *often* true for you, then you would write a number 4 on that line. If the statement were only *sometimes* true for you, then you would write a number 3. If you feel that this statement is *seldom* true for you, then you would write a number 2, and if this statement, in your honest judgment, were *almost never* true for you, then you would write a number 1 on that line. Continue in this way until you have written a number for each statement. If you are not certain as to how to answer some particular statement, then take whatever part of the statement does apply to you, in whatever way, and answer it accordingly. Remember, for this diagnostic test to be optimally effective and useful, *every statement should be answered* by giving it a number that you feel best fits your answer.

You may have already filled out a form of this inventory that is very similar to this new one. We are also asking you to fill out this new form because it will aid us significantly in the diagnosis and treatment of your psychological problems.

THE PSYCHOPATHOLOGY-HEALTH INVENTORY (PHI) FORM B: RESEARCH

Max Hammer, PhD
Professor Emeritus of Psychology
University of Maine at Orono

This personality inventory that you are about to fill out is part of a very important research project that will help us to better understand the nature of psychological health, illness, and emotional pain. This will then enable us to develop the best means of helping people with psychological problems to become psychologically healthy, mature, and free of emotional pain. People from all walks of life are being asked to participate in this very important project. Therefore, your fullest cooperation and honesty is very much needed and appreciated. Almost everyone has psychological problems of some kind of another, at some time or another in his or her life, and this is no cause for him or her to feel ashamed, guilty, angry, or in any way inferior, for such problems are the result of the hardships and complexities of life, and the varying degrees of psychological pressure that one has to face, from time to time. We are most interested in finding out how often particular kinds of problems, feelings, and experiences occur in the everyday life of most people. Therefore, you can clearly understand that there are no right or wrong answers to any of the statements in this inventory. We are only interested in finding out how *you*, personally, feel about each statement. Read each one of the enclosed statements very carefully to be sure that you understand what is being asked. Then ask yourself how true the statement is, as it applies to you. Now rate your answer to that statement on the six point scale found at the top of each page. For each statement in this inventory, apply a number or numerical score of 6, 5, 4, 3,

2, or 1, depending on how strongly you agree or disagree with each statement. The categories related to each score are as follows:

6: Almost always
5: Very frequently
4: Often
3: Sometimes
2: Seldom
1: Almost never

Thus, for example, the first statement in this inventory reads, "Decisions are difficult for me to make." If you sincerely and honestly feel that this statement is *almost always* true for you, then your score on the scale at the top of the page would be 6. You would therefore write that number 6 on the line to the right of that statement. If, however, instead of finding this statement to be almost always true for you, you find this statement to be only very *frequently true* for you, then you would put a number 5 on the line to the right of the statement. If you find that the statement is neither almost always true nor very frequently true, but *often* true for you, then you would write a number 4 on that line. If the statement were only *sometimes* true for you, then you would write a number 3. If you feel that this statement is *seldom* true for you, then you would write a number 2, and if this statement, in your honest judgment, were *almost never* true for you, then you would write a number 1 on that line. Continue in this way until you have written a number for each statement. If you are not certain as to how to answer some particular statement, then take whatever part of the statement does apply to you, in whatever way, and answer it accordingly. Remember, for this diagnostic test to be optimally effective and useful, every *statement should be answered* by giving it a number that you feel best fits your answer. Think over your answers very carefully, but be sure to work as rapidly as you can.

Some of you may have filled out a form of this inventory already that is very similar to this one. We ask for your co-operation again in filling out this new form because it is a necessary phase of this research project.

Thank you for your time and effort.

PHI FORM B—THE ACTUAL
TEST SCALE CATEGORIES

6: Almost always
5: Very frequently
4: Often
3: Sometimes
2: Seldom
1: Almost never

1. Decisions are difficult for me to make.
2. I have a very strong need for recognition, fame, or prestige.
3. I feel guilty a great deal over things that other people do not seem to feel guilty about.
4. I feel trapped.
5. The thought of growing old frightens me.
6. I feel very tired much of the time even when I have not been working hard.
7. I feel a strong need to escape from my thoughts or feelings.
8. Other people gossip about me.
9. There are feelings of extreme coldness within me.
10. I feel that life has been quite unjust and unfair to me.
11. It really makes me uncomfortable to be physically or emotionally close to others.
12. I do not have peace of mind.
13. I try to hurt other people.
14. I have a strong need for thrills, excitement, or variety in my life.
15. I feel timid, shy, or very self-conscious.
16. I lack determination or am lazy.
17. I am very possessive or jealous of those people I care very much about.
18. I find myself confused or in inner conflict because of opposing wishes, desires, or needs that are going on within me.

19. I feel blocked in my ability to love others.
20. I am fearful and do not know why.
21. I feel that no one really understands me.
22. I criticize myself or judge myself harshly.
23. I am unable to work under pressure.
24. I am afraid of people.
25. I wish that I were very powerful in some way.
26. I dislike being alone.
27. I prefer familiar people, places, and things than to be faced with a new challenge or a new situation.
28. I try hard to impress other people.
29. I feel very unfulfilled.
30. I feel inferior to other people.
31. I feel helpless, vulnerable, or defenseless.
32. I think that I am a bad or sinful person.
33. I need to feel loved.
34. I hate for anyone to be one-up on me or get the better of me.
35. I feel dead inside.
36. I envy, or am jealous of, other people or what they have.
37. I worry that other people will reject me.
38. I feel that I cannot handle any more pain or stress.
39. I feel that no one cares about me.
40. I see myself, or others see me, as being too dependent on others.
41. I feel like a nobody or a nothing.
42. The idea of having to make a commitment to someone or something bothers me.
43. I like to be perfect at what I do.
44. I feel comfortable only when I am in control of what is going on.
45. I worry about my health.
46. Criticism from others, however well intended, hurts me terribly.
47. I feel inhibited or blocked in my ability to be spontaneously self-assertive or self-expressive.

48. I feel like I am not a very desirable person.
49. When people talk to me I feel attacked.
50. I try very hard to get other people to notice me.
51. Expressing myself in a large group frightens me.
52. When someone praises me, I feel very uncomfortable.
53. My concept or image of myself is more negative than positive.
54. I blame other people or conditions beyond my control for my defeats, mistakes, or problems.
55. I feel uneasy when I am with people of authority or prestige.
56. I am not clear about what or who I am.
57. I feel terrible when I lose an argument or a game, no matter how minor it may be.
58. I get overly excited.
59. I feel terribly hurt or resentful when I am ignored or overlooked by people.
60. I dread the unknown or the uncertain.
61. I have doubts about whether I can be a good sexual partner.
62. I try to avoid things which might bring me some pain or discomfort even if they are things that I know I really should face up to, or do, for my own benefit.
63. I feel that I am under great pressure.
64. I overly indulge in things I know are bad for me.
65. I wish I could be reborn.

A Scale of Painful feelings

Max Hammer, PhD

On the pages that follow, you will find a list of various kinds of painful feelings. Rate each painful feeling in terms of how frequently you tend to experience that feeling. A scale for rating how frequently you experience each kind of painful feeling is provided below.

How frequently do you experience each painful feeling?

1: Never
2: Seldom
3: Sometimes
4: Often
5: Very frequently
6: Constantly

Enter a score, from one (1) to six (6), for each rated feeling, on the line provided next to that feeling. Thus, for example, in rating a feeling of confusion, if you believe that you *never* experience a feeling of confusion, you would place the number one (1) on the line next to that particular feeling; if you only *seldom* experience that feeling you would enter the number two (2) next to that feeling; if you *sometimes* experience that feeling, then you would enter the number three (3) next to that feeling; if you *often* experience that feeling, then you would enter the number four (4) next to that feeling; if you experience that feeling *very frequently*, then you would enter the number five (5) next to that feeling; or if you experience that feeling *constantly*, then you would enter the number six (6) next to that feeling.

If there are any feelings that you experience as being painful that are not included on the list, then just add that feeling(s) at the very end of the list (under the heading "Other Feelings") and rate each of these feelings with a frequency score as you have all the other feelings.

When all of the painful feelings have been rated in terms of frequency of experience, then turn to the last page where you will then rate the rank the five (5) feelings that you consider to be the most intensely painful, as described there.

How frequently do you experience each painful feeling?

1: Never
2: Seldom
3: Sometimes
4: Often
5: Very frequently
6: Constantly

Rate the frequency with which you experience each of the following painful feelings.

1. _____ feeling frustrated.
2. _____ feeling depressed.
3. _____ a feeling of loneliness.
4. _____ a feeling of anger.
5. _____ a feeling of sorrow.
6. _____ a feeling of insecurity.
7. _____ a feeling of shyness.
8. _____ a feeling of guilt.
9. _____ feeling anxiety.
10. _____ feeling ashamed.
11. _____ a feeling of boredom.
12. _____ a feeling of remorse.

13. _____ a feeling of jealousy.
14. _____ a feeling of inner emptiness.
15. _____ a feeling of resentment.
16. _____ feeling no sense of belonging.
17. _____ feeling unloved.
18. _____ feeling vulnerable.
19. _____ feeling hurt.
20. _____ feeling foolish
21. _____ feeling worthless.
22. _____ a feeling of confusion.
23. _____ feeling exploited by someone.
24. _____ feeling trapped.
25. _____ feeling overwhelmed.
26. _____ feelings of inferiority.
27. _____ a feeling of weakness.
28. _____ a feeling of rejection.
29. _____ feeling betrayed.
30. _____ feeling of a loss of a loved one.
31. _____ feeling fearful.
32. _____ feeling deceived.
33. _____ feeling abandoned or deserted.
34. _____ feeling like a failure.
35. _____ a feeling of having to make a commitment.
36. _____ a feeling of not being in control.
37. _____ feeling nervous.
38. _____ a feeling of having responsibilities placed on me.
39. _____ feeling like a coward.
40. _____ feeling unlovable.
41. _____ feeling manipulated by someone.
42. _____ feeling unreal or less real as a self.
43. _____ feeling that no one understands me.
44. _____ feeling stagnant, in a rut, not getting anywhere.
45. _____ feeling dissatisfied with myself.
46. _____ feelings of helplessness.
47. _____ feeling ignored or unnoticed.
48. _____ feeling lost.

49. _____ feeling fragile inside.
50. _____ feeling that I need more attention.
51. _____ feeling that someone is taking advantage of me.
52. _____ a feeling of hate.
53. _____ feeling that life is passing me by.
54. _____ a feeling of wanting to cry.
55. _____ feeling like a nobody.
56. _____ feeling like I'm falling apart.
57. _____ feeling that I'm being controlled by others.
58. _____ feeling dependent.
59. _____ Feeling disappointed.
60. _____ feeling inwardly numb, like I can't feel anything at all.
61. _____ feeling embarrassed.
62. _____ feeling like I'm a fake or a phony.
63. _____ feeling that others want to hurt me.
64. _____ feelings of regret.
65. _____ a sexual feeling or sexual yearning that I do not like.
66. _____ feeling like I wish that everyone would just leave me alone.
67. _____ feeling that I am lazy.
68. _____ feeling worried.
69. _____ feeling greedy.
70. _____ feeling ignorant or unintelligent.
71. _____ feeling under a lot of pressure.
72. _____ feeling uncertain about the future.
73. _____ feeling a lack of self-confidence.
74. _____ feeling that I am evil or bad in some way.
75. _____ feeling inadequate.
76. _____ feeling that my life, or life in general, is meaningless.
77. _____ a feeling of great tension.
78. _____ feeling a lack of self-esteem.
79. _____ feeling that I am about to explode.
80. _____ a feeling of not wanting to grow up.

81. _____ a feeling of wanting to hurt myself.
82. _____ a feeling that I really cannot trust anyone.
83. _____ feeling humiliated.
84. _____ feeling unable to love.
85. _____ feeling very needy.
86. _____ feeling completely unmotivated to do anything.
87. _____ feeling ill at ease with others.
88. _____ feeling insulted by others.
89. _____ feeling that life is unfair.
90. _____ feeling very inhibited.
91. _____ a feeling of self-hate.
92. _____ feeling immature.
93. _____ feeling that there is nothing very special about me.
94. _____ a feeling of wanting to commit suicide.
95. _____ feelings of doubt or uncertainty.
96. _____ feeling that I am avoiding what I should be doing.
97. _____ feeling very ugly.
98. _____ feeling that I cannot tolerate very much pain.
99. _____ a feeling of hopelessness.
100. _____ feeling my own lacks or deficiencies.
101. _____ the feeling of losing something that I value.
102. _____ feelings that come when I withdraw from an addiction.
103. _____ a feeling of not knowing who I really am.
104. _____ a feeling of wanting to hurt someone.
105. _____ feeling that I have disappointed someone.
106. _____ feeling a loss to my reputation.
107. _____ a feeling of wanting someone to take care of me.
108. _____ a feeling of shock or surprise when something happens that I have not expected.
109. _____ feeling overly sensitive to, or easily hurt by, criticism from others.
110. _____ feeling like I am going to go to hell.
111. _____ feeling that someone hates me.

112. _____ feeling that I cannot trust myself.
113. _____ feeling that others expect too much of me.
114. _____ feeling that I am at my wit's end.
115. _____ feeling that others are evaluating or judging me.
116. _____ feeling that I am never going to be really happy.
117. _____ feeling powerless.
118. _____ a feeling of not wanting to grow old.
119. _____ a feeling of being addicted.
120. _____ feeling under a lot of stress.
121. _____ a feeling of wanting to indulge some impulse that I know I should not indulge.
122. _____ a feeling of being very selfish.
123. _____ a feeling that I expect too much of myself.
124. _____ feelings of inner conflict.
125. _____ feeling that I do not have enough money for all that I need.
126. _____ a feeling that no one really likes me.
127. _____ feeling that I have to conform to what others want or expect.
128. _____ feeling that I am just not good enough.
129. _____ feeling put down by someone.
130. _____ a feeling that I will not accomplish my goals.

Other feelings. List below any other feeling(s), not included in the above list, that you experience as being painful, and rate the frequency of these as well.

131. _____
132. _____
133. _____
134. _____
135. _____

Now we go on to the last page that deals with the intensity of painful feelings.

Ranking the Intensity of Painful Feelings

In the spaces below, under the heading of "Most Painful Feelings in Rank Order," list your rank of the five (5) feelings that you would consider to be the most painful if they were currently present in your experience. Thus, for example, if you consider a feeling of confusion to be the most painful feeling for you then you would write in the feeling "confusion" to the *right* of the number one (1) below. If, in this example, a feeling of guilt was your second most painful feeling, then to the right of number two (2), you would write in the feeling "guilt." Continue in this way until you have ranked all five (5) feelings that you consider to be the most painful to you.

Most painful feelings in rank order

_____ 1. _____.
_____ 2. _____.
_____ 3. _____.
_____ 4. _____.
_____ 5. _____.

Rating the intensity of Painful Feelings

On the line to the left of each number, rate each of your five (5) most painful feelings in terms of how painful you experience each feeling as being, according to the scale provided immediately below.

Intensity of Painful Feelings

1. Mildly painful
2. Moderately painful
3. Extremely painful
4. Unbearable

Thus, for example, if you ranked the feeling of confusion to be your most painful feeling, and you consider it to be *unbearable*, then you would write in the number four (4) on the line to the left of number one (1) under the heading "Most Painful Feelings in Rank Order." If you consider this feeling of confusion to be only *extremely painful* but not unbearable, then you would write in the number three (3) on the line to the left of number one (1). If you consider this feeling to be only *moderately painful* to you, then you would write in the number two (2) on the line to the left of the feeling that you ranked as being most painful; or if you consider this feeling to be only mildly *painful*, then you would write in the number one (1) on the line to the left of the feeling ranked most painful. Continue in this way until all five (5) of the most painful ranked feelings have been rated in terms of the intensity of painfulness to you.

APPENDIX A

AWAKENING THE DEEPEST LEVEL OF OUR LIFE ENERGY FORCE AS LOVE, OUR SOURCE POWER CENTER, THE "GREAT GENIE IN US"

Metaphorically speaking, our unconscious pure life energy is saying to our not fully developed conscious awareness, "Beautiful dreamer, awaken more consciously unto me." Our conscious awareness is like in a dreaming state, not fully conscious of the true reality nature of its being, and, therefore, imagining or falsely presuming a divisive good and evil nature to be reality life energy presence, instead of its true indivisible, flawless, holistic nature. Through the not fully consciously recognized inner voice, "still small voice" of intuition, spontaneously arising core integrity, or inner GPS system of our own being, our unconscious vibratory life energy force is in effect basically whispering to our conscious awareness, "Beautiful dreamer, awaken unto my perfect life energy nature, and then I will be like your great magic genie, and grant all of your good-natured wishes, for limitless abundance of true love and all other forms of true goodness. I am a great creative intelligence, a vibratory life energy field, which can mold or make anything out of myself, or attract to you what I have already created out of myself, that naturally, rightfully, belongs to you, my beloved subjective awareness, higher directing principle, gradually growing more conscious of my life energy presence. Together, we the conscious intelligence-will power and the unconscious life energy force share the same good-natured wishes or realistic dreams, seeking fulfillment, as one's intuited vision, one's mission, one's intended destiny, one's true blueprint in life."

It is like our own unconscious life energy field is saying to our developing conscious awareness, "I have always been your perfect beloved, your perfect life energy nature, from the very beginning of our shared evolutionary development, and I can provide you with limitless good in abundance when you awaken me. But I have been like a Sleeping Beauty, because you have been a sleeping awareness, not fully conscious of my reality life energy nature; therefore, you have presumed me to be limited in the good that I could provide for you, so I perceived myself that way and provided you with only limited good, and also some suffering, because I take my cue or sense of self-knowledge of who I am from how you view me. You are my knower, my Lord and master, my subjective male higher reality intelligence nature, and I am your objective female loving servant, who, most of all, loves to please you.

"Therefore, if you ask me to give you relative suffering, I must lawfully give it to you, because I lawfully and lovingly have to obey my higher, more conscious, more subjective, reality intelligence principle. Howsoever you view me, I will be for you, divine beloved or unfaithful whore, afflicting you with pain. Whatever view you, the conscious awareness, are projecting on to me, your own unconscious life energy presence, as the presumption of limited scarcity or unlimited abundance of life, well-being, goodness, that is what I lawfully have to reflect back to you, in your subjective and objective experience, mirroring you as my own subjective higher reality intelligence principle. But my basic function is to love you, and to serve all of your good-natured love wishes, your reality aspirations, your realistic dream, vision, mission, destiny. I am your inner genie, so to speak, but I am caged up in a restricting bottle, because you have presumed me to be a limited goodness or a scarcity nature. You have put me in a limited bottle or lamp so to speak, as a restricted level of development and functioning, by having a limited conception or view of me. However, when you fully awaken me, by intuitively recognizing my true nature, then I am truly your wish granting genie, as long as it is good-natured wishes. I am your veritable Horn of Cornucopia, an inexhaustible reservoir of limitless abundance of all of the true good that is inherent to the maturely developed and awakened spiritual reality of life. I am your fountain of perpetual youth. I am your great panacea, elixir, total sweetness, the divine sap or juice of life. I am your inner ambrosia and nectar. I am your divine beloved loving servant, who lives only to lovingly serve you and please you, because your conscious happiness is reflected in me. Together, in loving wholeness, oneness, we can make a grander and grander experiential paradise for ourselves, and for our loved ones.

"You will give me your conscious awareness, and I will give you my perfect, flawless life energy experience, and we will forever be wedded unto each other, as a relational whole conscious-life energy presence, indivisibly united together and sharing the same divine self-realization IAM. Then we will share a fully satisfying holy matrimony of full blessedness, wholeness, fulfillment, total well-being experience, sharing the true good of life in limitless abundance, in unlimited height, depth, and breadth or variety of new form. Your conscious will is my command. Will me to give you a paradise, by seeing my life energy as perfect; see me as intrinsically being a total goodness, with no inherent evil, defect, flaw, ceiling, or wrongness in me; see me as a total well-being experiential nature, with no inherent suffering. Then I will conceive for you whatever you wish, that is of a loving good-natured nature, and I will grant you the fulfillment of not only your conscious wishes, but I will also grant you even your unconscious wishes, that even you, yourself, do not know, but I do know. I am recessively you, and you are recessively me. I am recessively your 'I,' your conscious knowing and willing function, and you are recessively my 'AM', my unconscious vibratory energy power. Together, we are wedded in holy matrimony, fully awakened immortality, bliss, rapture, total goodness, loving warmth, ecstatic joyfulness, total peace and harmony, which is our fully awakened relational wholeness, fulfillment, or divine self-realization I AM. We are awakening our inner energy-power source, enabling us to magnetically attract greater abundance into our life, and unfold greater abundance from our own being, as well as magnetically repel various forms of inner and outer negativity."

The more that our conscious awareness loves its own life energy presence, by being open to our own actual experience, and expressing the expansive relational nature of our real energy field as loving caring for other individuals, the more that our conscious awareness loves and expresses its own life energy presence in that way, the higher, the deeper, the broader it penetrates into that spirit life energy presence, and thereby accesses, unfolds, manifests, or extracts higher or greater levels of potentials actualization, to actualize and develop.

Where there is a relatively highly-developed level of conscious of the true nature of reality, a mature form of innocence will be regained, in contrast to the naïve innocence or embittered cynicism that characterizes individuals with a less maturely-developed consciousness of reality. In that maturely-developed consciousness of reality, a holistic perspective, or a true perception of the world as an indivisible whole relational "Tree of Life," will gradually begin to replace the ego's divisive view of the world as a fragmented, dichotomous, "Tree of Knowledge of Good and Evil," some branches, blossoms, and fruitage, exclusively good and others exclusively bad, meaning some aspects of reality are perceived as life-enhancing and life-preserving while others are deemed to be life-diminishing and life-negating. When we reach a relatively advanced level of psycho-spiritual maturity or a well-developed consciousness of reality, that provides a true vision of reality as conscious awareness of innocence, seeing intrinsic, flawless purity of life energy as love-beauty-goodness. In this innocence awareness or true vision of reality, we intuitively become conscious of the all-pervading substratum or the ever-present holistic life energy substance underlying the diverse visible forms of this world, which gradually replaces the ego's false, relatively immature, divisively-oriented experience of fear, pain, tension, rage, and life-degenerative destructiveness of all kinds. As our awareness of the indivisible oneness of life presence cumulatively develops, we begin to mature in the awareness of the true reality nature of life, no longer divisively viewed as partly good and partly evil, as the immaturely-developed mind has viewed and experienced it. Therefore, we experience less fearful anxiety, insecurity, dread, suffering, rage, pain, illness, predation, deficiency presumption and compensatory desire, boredom, meaningless, emptiness, existential despair, and so on, as well as various kinds of unhealthy addictive escapes from these egoistic negative feelings, grounded in the ego's narcissistic recoil or alienation from real life energy presence, inside and outside. All of these negative, pathological feelings and experiential states come with an immaturely developed level of consciousness, functioning as an egoistic, fragmenting, value judging, mind, defining our experience in terms of exclusively dichotomous, unrelated, categories, such as good and evil, good and bad, acceptable and unacceptable. Such an egoistic mind thereby divisively obscures and distorts the seamless oneness or indivisible wholeness of life energy presence by superimposing fragmented conceptual interpretations and presumptive abstractions upon it.

This view that as consciousness develops a more mature or more accurate view of reality, it comes to perceive more holistically and less divisively and partially and is more open to direct experience rather than viewing experience through a dark, opaque filter of presumptive conceptual interpretation, is metaphorically epitomized in the following biblical passage, "For we know in part and we prophesy in part, but when perfection comes, the imperfect disappears. When I was a child, I talked like a child, I thought like a child, I reasoned like a child. When I became a man, I put childish ways behind me. Now we see but a poor reflection; then we shall see face to face. Now I know in part; then I shall know fully, even as I am fully known" (I Corinthians 13:9-12, New International Version). Whereas the ego mind tends to view inner and outer experience in a dichotomously divisive, piecemeal, fragmentary, partial manner, the maturely-developed and awakened heart of love intuitively grasps the indivisible unitary relational wholeness or oneness of the "Tree of Life" as the inherent reality nature of life, which is a maturely developed innocence awareness.

When we view ourselves, other individuals, and the whole world through the "eyes" or viewpoint of the maturely-developed heart of love, it reveals and manifests the essential goodness and loveliness that pervades this entire world, and dispels illusory appearances and experiences of inner and outer negativity as a powerful transformational true vision of reality, rather than a naïve self-delusion. The maturely developed and consciously awakened presence of love in the heart removes fear from the heart, which uproots all forms of unnecessary evil and suffering experience, as suggested by 1 John 4:18: "There is no fear in love. But perfect love drives out fear, because fear has to do with punishment. The man who fears is not made perfect in love."

When we maturely develop and consciously awaken the presence of love in the heart, we begin to intuitively recognize, beyond the fragmenting ego mind, that the true reality of life is an indivisible relational whole "Tree of Life." We recognize that all life forms-functions-potentials are like interrelated, interdependent branches, all connected to a unifying collective tree trunk, united in its roots to Mother Nature, the outer material existence soil, or underlying substratum, of the indivisible whole earth, as well as united to the connective inner relational reality of loving warmth, metaphorically like sun and sunshine. Then all aspects of reality are correctly viewed as part of and naturally abiding within the indivisible seamless relational whole web of life. That maturely developed, true vision of reality reveals the essential harmony, beauty, goodness, and joyfulness of life, and gradually transforms contrary experiences of negativity, to either disappear or be aligned with a more harmonic, benevolent, vibratory frequency of energy.

Through openness to fully consciously embracing all of our life experiences, our own core integrity is gradually moving us (our consciousness) toward itself, as the most essential level of our own being. Following the changing flow of our authentic inner and outer experience ultimately leads to and reveals the grandest, most essential, permanently enduring, Divine level of reality, which can only be directly intuited with the core of the heart, and cannot be grasped by the divisive, speculative, ego-mind. Following the moment-to-moment changing experiential truth of ourselves is what ultimately leads to awakening the essential core reality nature of our own permanent being, metaphorically symbolized by the *Wizard of Oz* story, in which Dorothy and her companions "follow the Yellow Brick Road" to its source, the Wizard of Oz. This process of openness to the experiential truth of ourselves, metaphorically represented by stories such as the *Wizard of Oz*, involve the awakening of our deepest core energy-power source as the relational spirit of love-goodness-regenerative life energy, co-created and maturely developed through deeply invested caring relationships with other individuals, as the living aspect of our essential core permanent being archetype.[1] That process of following the often circuitous trail of the experiential truth of ourselves and of our encounters with other individuals, relating to ourselves and others with authenticity, sincerity, integrity, genuine caring, and nonjudgmental compassion, is what eventually enables us to experience and deeply appreciate the essential permanent level of life energy, where it is inherently a divine beauty, love, joy, and goodness, as well as being our own inner energy-power source, endowing us with enhanced powers of functioning and abundance. However, we have to be willing to be open to fully consciously contacting the full range of spontaneously arising actual life experience, including being willing to pass through relatively painful experiences in life in order to be able to eventually intuit that most essential permanent level of reality life experience, which is also the highest level of creative insight and inspiration, especially musical inspiration. Beethoven was able to intuit that divine "Music of the Spheres" within his own extremely intuitive, compassionate, and creatively inspired heart, even though he was physically deaf. Perhaps this willingness to consciously face and lovingly, non-dualistically embrace all kinds of painful as well as joyful experiences for the sake of making deeper contact with the reality of life, ultimately enabling our consciousness to penetrate into the essential core of reality, and thereby experience its limitless sublime grandeur, may be alluded to in the lyrics, "To be willing to march into hell for a heavenly cause," from the song, "To Dream the Impossible Dream."[2]

It is only the selfish ego-personality, with its absolute dichotomous positive and negative value judgments, functioning as a willful controller, censor, and distorting preconceived interpreter of spontaneously arising life experience, that keeps our conscious awareness and passionate feeling energy restricted to the superficial minutia of life experience, preventing our conscious awareness from soaring to the greatest height of potential life experience, like being content to remain fixated as a larva or caterpillar, and not willing to be metamorphosed into a soaring butterfly. *Thus, the basic meaningful purpose of life is to be open to deeply contacting the fullest range of changing life experience, until we penetrate into and thereby fully consciously awaken, the deepest, most essential, grandest, permanent level of life energy, thereby activating our own inner creative energy-power source.* The fulfillment of this basic intended destiny is thwarted when we move away from the flow of our own authentic experience, meaning that we filter our experience through a distorting lens of speculative interpretations, rather than contacting it directly, in its immediacy, "face to face," so to speak (see I Corinthians 13:12).

APPENDIX B

TAPPING INTO THE SOURCE OF CREATIVITY: THE LIMITLESS MYSTERY PLENITUDE

We authors are using the terms "plenitude" and "pleroma" interchangeably, and basically defining it as a source of limitless abundance at the energetic core or center level of our being, like an inexhaustible fountain, wellspring, or veritable Horn of Cornucopia. This is the ontic source of limitless creative possibilities, limitless creative insights, discoveries, resources, productions, and powers of functioning. It is, most essentially, an overflowing, limitless, inexhaustible abundance of creative energy-intelligence, as the source of everything that is actually or potentially knowable. The plenitude is like a vast, hidden, metaphysical reservoir of mystery being, the source level of Divine creative intelligence, the source level of self-organizing order, or entelechy (i.e., a non-entropic, self-organizing, self-developing, purposive, self-consistent, coherent, or cohesive energy). Various online and printed dictionaries define plenitude as "fullness, completeness, abundance, plenty."[1]

Relational communion with someone or something beyond egoistic self-awareness puts us in contact with limitless transformational possibilities or potentials of creative intelligence, abiding between the mystery core and knowable surface levels of our being-vibratory life energy-intelligence. Now we will discuss why that is so.

All creative possibilities and options are forever taking place, and fully available, in the full now, which is the full unification of the timeless, changeless, now of permanent being and the changing now of time becoming phenomena. This unification occurs when we develop loving or caring warmth, by engaging in deeply invested, heartfelt communion with other individuals, objects, and activities in the world.

When our subjective conscious awareness is deeply invested in heartfelt, caring communion with someone or something in objective reality, that unites the timeless now of changeless permanent being with the changing world of becoming phenomena. They are united together as the substance and form, subjective and objective, or inner "contents" and outer "package" levels of our individual intelligence, or life energy and psychophysical existence, joined together through the caring relational energy of loving warmth that arises through our connection or communion with other individuals, phenomena, and activities in the world of objective reality. The expressed energy of caring warmth that flows when we are connected to objective reality in non-dualistic communion is the living, manifest, expression of the creative mystery core level of our being, the most essential level of our being-intelligence, the greater reality of relational wholeness that unites the subjective and objective, or inner and outer aspects of reality within itself. The limitless mystery pleroma or plenitude contains the knowable integral wholeness, subjective, and objective levels of reality-intelligence, or unifying essence, subjective substance, and objective form levels of reality within itself, as not other than itself. The limitless mystery pleroma, or the supreme plenitude level of our individual being-creative intelligence gradually unfolding as a knowable life energy nature, is a limitless wholeness of being, containing limitless creative and transformational possibilities within itself.

Metaphorically similar to water flowing from an open faucet when the valve is released, when we open our heart by connecting to someone or something in objective reality, outside, in deeply invested, heartfelt communion, then our heart or energy center also becomes open to impartations from the inner source of creative intelligence, arising from the core level of our own being. Like a two-sided valve or door, our openness to self-forgetful, deeply invested, heartfelt, loving, relational connection with objective reality, outwardly or objectively, also opens us to the relational energy of the deepest level of our own individual creative intelligence inwardly or subjectively. The inner relational core level of our creative intelligence can flow into our conscious awareness only when we let go of egoistic self-preoccupation and acknowledge the relational nature of reality by engaging in deeply invested communion with someone, something, or some activity in objective reality, outwardly.

Perhaps there is a kind of real "magic" involving manifesting new creative insights, powers of functioning, and tangible products from the hidden mystery core or dormant reservoir level of our own being, accessed when our relational energy force or relational spirit of caring warmth is highly developed, like pumping a limitless supply of water from a limitless reservoir, fountain, or wellspring. When we tap into and consciously awaken that source level of our being-intelligence, like a limitless reservoir or a veritable Horn of Cornucopia, then we can unfold its limitless creative possibilities, which can involve the fulfillment of our wishes or even seeming "miracles."

Sometimes, the mystery reservoir or storehouse level of our being can unfold something radically new, which we cannot even anticipate beforehand, as the discovery of qualitatively new breakthroughs and transformational insights in any area of endeavor or field of inquiry. For example, perhaps tapping into the relational and individual zone or source of creativity might eventually facilitate the metamorphosis of the outer human body and brain-mind into a qualitatively more advanced level of evolutionary development, as a truly new and more highly developed biological species, reflecting a correspondingly greater qualitative level of maturational development of conscious awareness or awakening of the reality intelligence of our inner being or vibratory energy field. To suggest a metaphorical analogy, if you heat liquid water to the boiling point so that it is turned into water vapor, there is a qualitative metamorphosis, an intensified energy state with correspondingly higher or greater powers of functioning. That greater, more abundant level of creative energy-intelligence becomes available if you do not accept permanent, insurmountable limitation of any kind. Then you are standing as an inner source of limitless abundance, an inexhaustible plenitude or great mystery pleroma.

To release creative insight, transformational power, and abundance from the core level of your own being, you are not knowing the source or core level of your own creative intelligence from a standpoint of duality from it, nor are you narcissistically, introspectively self-aware as it; instead, you are non-dualistically being it, and creatively, productively functioning as it, or expressing yourself as it, when you are self-forgetfully deeply invested in communion with some-one or something beyond the ego's separate self-awareness and basically selfish concerns, giving deeply of your caring energies, insights, capabilities, and resources without seek-ing to enhance yourself, in some way, as egocentric psy-chological deficiency seeking compensatory gratification. Tapping into the source of creative intelligence is not a pro-cess of introspectively turning your consciousness inward upon itself to know yourself as the most subjective knower. That would be a kind of extreme narcissism, self-deification of the ego as continuous introverted self-awareness. Instead, tapping into the source of creative intelligence involves the knower, your pure conscious awareness going outward to lovingly contact visible forms in the world, in deeply in-vested, self-forgetful, loving communion with them. The self-preoccupied ego does not have access to the source of our creative intelligence because that core level of our being is a relational wholeness that can be accessed only by liv-ing or expressing the relational wholeness nature of reality, by engaging in deeply invested, heartfelt, caring communion with someone or something beyond the self-absorbed ego, thereby accessing the greater relational wholeness that uni-fies or integrates the subjective knower and objective reality within itself. The self-preoccupied ego is not a principle of wholeness and limitless abundance of creative intelligence because it constitutes the subjective knower dualistically divorced from objective reality; that divisive orientation is partial and, therefore, limited and restrictive. Various influential psychologists, such as Abraham Maslow,[2] Sidney Jourard,[3] and Rollo May[4] concur with our view that creative insight and functioning are enhanced when we are willing to let go of separate ego self-awareness and inner monologues by being self-forgetful in deeply invested communion or encounter with someone or something outside of us. Rollo May and Max Hammer described the process of investing our entire being in self-forgetful communion, and the enhanced level of creative functioning that that can produce, as a state of "ex-stasis," based on their interpretation of the etymological derivation of the modern English word "ecstasy" from an ancient Greek word meaning to "stand out from" or "stand outside of oneself."[5]

Relational connection or non-duality is the key to tapping into or unlocking the limitless mystery plenitude, the reservoir or storehouse of limitless creative potentials and transformational possibilities, because only what is relational is whole or holistic, including everything, excluding and therefore lacking nothing, whereas a non-relational principle would necessarily exclude whatever it does not relate or connect to and stands in duality with, such as a sense of duality between the ego as self-preoccupied subjective knower and its divorced objects of knowledge. Furthermore, only a relational energy can be a limitlessly expansive, inexhaustible, energy, abundantly giving of itself to relational others, without ever being depleted, in contrast to the ego's reluctance to connect deeply to others and give of its energy to others for fear of having its seemingly limited source of energy and other resources depleted.

Those who withdraw from relational contact with other individuals, phenomena, and activities in the world introspectively seeking to find within themselves alone, as a separate, detached, knower, the source level of creative intelligence and limitless abundance, the mysterious, the divine, the spiritual, the sublime are going in the wrong direction. Instead, when you deeply, self-forgetfully invest your conscious attention and heartfelt love for particular forms in the world, and are not seeking any kind of self-knowledge or self-gratification, that is when you are able to tap into the source of creative intelligence most expeditiously, because it is a relational, expansive energy, not a narcissistic, contracting, energy principle. Loving communion is most deep, and therefore most effective in tapping into the source of creative intelligence, when you contact, love, and enjoy, forms in the world that you experience as being most akin to your own inner being, natural potentials and inclinations.

When you express true love, empathic communion, unselfish caring, or deeply give of your energies to the point of experiencing total depletion or full exhaustion of your energies, and even a little bit beyond that point, that is when you release the hidden limitless mystery source level of your energy-being-intelligence to unfold deeper, higher, or qualitatively greater, truly new levels of its limitless abundance of creative potentials. That is to say, when we awaken the relational (divine, spiritual) source level of our individual form of creative intelligence as love-being, by unselfishly loving and serving other individuals in the world, then the love-being-intelligence that we express, and thereby experience ourselves as being, can manifest any particular form of love-intelligence-being that we are in self-realization as relationally being, as the limitless "this and that" particular forms of experience and expression that our limitless love-being-intelligence can potentially take. The source of creative being-intelligence as loving warmth or warmhearted caring cannot create, produce, or manifest anything destructive or harmful to anyone, only what is benevolent and helpful to everyone or anyone who comes into contact with it. The limitless mystery wholeness, core level of our being, awake to itself as loving warmth, literally has a limitless creative power, as a principle of limitless abundance, a limitless reservoir of creative intelligence, like a veritable Horn of Cornucopia, plenitude, or pleroma. Whatever it can conceive that is truly real, truly good, and consistent with its own true intelligence nature, it can manifest from itself, because it is the creative energy source of all form, the love-being-intelligence or underlying substance of all form. Once we tap into the source level of our own creative intelligence, as our individual form of plentitude, then it can create (manifest, materialize) anything out of itself, as a fully developed, fully functional, individual power-source. *All of our true good is already inherently abiding within our own being, like a limitless inner reservoir, but it unfolds and manifests only when we activate, energize, or release the relational wholeness level of our being by uniting the subjective and objective, inner and outer aspects of reality, which necessarily involves letting go of divisive egoistic self-awareness in deeply invested, heartfelt, caring communion with someone or something beyond the ego.*

The limitless abundance of our being naturally flows outward and manifests itself only when we are abiding in and thereby reflecting its true nature as relaxed peace, arising from resting in intrinsic, unconditional, wholeness and well-being, rather than functioning from an illusory, presumed, egoistic, sense of deficiency striving to achieve a conditional sense of greater proficiency, self-consistent cohesive integrated wholeness and well-being. If you presume inherent deficiency of being and lack of well-being, then you attract the experience of greater and greater deficiency or lack of wholeness or non-well-being, such as deprivation of the necessities and enjoyable goods of life, because your inner and outer experience tends to reflect your inner convictions, expectations, or attitudes, as the inner knower or pure conscious awareness. Perhaps this principle may be metaphorically implied by Biblical passages such as, "To those who have, more shall be given, but to those who have not, even what little they have shall be taken away" (Matthew 13:12).

When you fully consciously awaken or maturely develop the creative energy-power-center of your own being, then you can manifest or materialize anything desired from it that is consistent with its totally benevolent life energy nature, or have it unfold for you what is currently totally unanticipated, inconceivable, unimaginable, not yet manifested, or truly new. When your conscious awareness is abiding at the source level of creative intelligence, which is the source of all delineated knowable form, then you can manifest or materialize new forms of being-intelligence at will, or retrieve old forms (such as regaining lost possessions, repairing broken relationships, or perhaps even resurrecting deceased loved ones).

There is a centripetal and centrifugal force of reality intelligence. The connective centripetal force produces greater levels of order and integration, which, paradoxically, also brings greater levels of the centrifugal force of diversity. This requires the polarizing, dichotomizing, disintegration, and disordering of what has previously been unified, cohesive, and ordered. Later, it can be reintegrated into new and greater levels of order, harmony, wholeness, as a recurring cycle, or ever ascending spiral, ad infinitum, like the Hegelian dialectic of thesis and antithesis being unified into a higher order synthesis. If you excessively hold onto the current order, or what you currently believe you already know, then you do not permit the process of apparent disintegration or current lack of cohesive integration, order, clarity, knowledge, certainty, resolution, completion, accomplishment, fulfillment, and satisfaction to eventually lead to more advanced levels of reintegration, resolution, order, and knowledge.

The functioning of creative intelligence includes both existing reality and creative imagination or constructive relative illusion. Creative intelligence naturally functions in a circular or ascending spiraling manner. You not only have to be open to whatever knowledge or experience is currently coming or arising from mystery, but also let it fall back down into mystery, like the rise and fall of a wave from and back to its underlying base in a larger body of water.

The zone of creativity can also be called the sublime zone or the twilight zone. It abides between knowledge and mystery, where relative knowledge and relative mystery meet, as relative degrees of one another. The zone or source level of creative intelligence is like the underlying base of a wave of water, where delineated water form meets un-delineated or mystery water substance. At the peak, apex, or point of maximal development of knowledge, knowledge or experience tends to be more clearly delineated, precise, tangible, elaborated, developed, whereas at the underlying base of the wave of vibratory energy and knowable form, that is the underlying source level of new experiential insights, innovative discoveries, and transformational, seminal, creative breakthroughs, coming from the deeper, less clearly delineated, substance level of energy, where knowledge meets mystery. There, knowledge or experience tends to be more amorphous, intangible, mysterious, and subtle because it is closer to the limitless mystery substance level of energy than to the more clearly delineated level of energy form. However, at the level of mystery substance, all good things are possible, because the mystery substance level of energy-being-intelligence is limitless as a result of not being restricted to any particular preconceived form of knowledge or predetermined experience, as is the case with knowable form. Hence, openness to mystery, or tolerance of uncertainty and lack of current knowledge, not demanding premature closure, brings contact with the mystery source of limitless creative possibilities, beyond what is already or currently known. However, being intolerant of mystery, uncertainty, inconsistency, lack of closure, or lack of current knowledge cuts us off from the deeper mystery source of qualitative new creative insights and transformational breakthroughs.

In any area of endeavor or field of inquiry, such as various arts and sciences, if you are too much abiding at the peak of the wave of energy as knowable experience (i.e., clinging to what is already known or presumed to be reality) you do not learn and grow much. It is too much light, overly defined and delimited, not enough darkness of mystery to provide qualitatively new possibilities or further development, too superficial, too far removed from the hidden mystery depths of energy-being-intelligence, too much restricted or limited to what is already known, already measured or comprehended, often yielding only relatively minor alterations or quantitative extensions of what is already known. To tap into the greatest possible energy of creative insight, creative power, you have to be abiding where the light of knowledge meets the darkness of mystery. That twilight zone of openness to relatively unstructured, subtle, indefinable, spontaneous, uncontrollable, noetic faculties, such as intuition, empathy, and inspiration, is the zone of limitless possibilities, which can produce a metamorphosis or breakthrough into qualitatively greater levels of transformational insight and development. When you are not overly committed to preselected beliefs, expectations, and goals, then you are abiding in a psychological or energetic zone of maximal openness, receptivity, and flexibility, where new possibilities, options, and insights can spontaneously arise to your unrestricted consciousness. The zone of creativity is where diversity of knowable form meets unity of undifferentiated energy substance, as epitomized by the Latin phrase, "E Pluribus Unum," or "The one in the many; and the many in the one."

The mystery core of our being is a dynamo-like reservoir of limitless creative intelligence and transformational possibilities, including the potential capacity for qualitative metamorphosis. Hasidic teachers such as the Maggid [Preacher] Dov Baer of Mezritch referred to this limitless reservoir of creative intelligence and transformational possibilities as the "Gate of Ayin"[6] (i.e., the Gate of "no-thingness"), or the Kadmut ha-Seikhel (the "originating source level of intellect" or creative intelligence). That is the base of the wave of knowledge or knowable experience as limitless undifferentiated mystery energy substance. At the peak of the wave of energy is more clearly delineated experience, more definitive knowledge, whereas the base of the wave is

more paradoxical, because it is where all relative polar opposite branches of knowledge and functioning converge as
a unified whole continuum in the mystery center base level
of energy-being-intelligence. The base level of energy can
sometimes still include knowledge of diversity, to a degree,
but each known element recessively contains a degree of its
own relative polar opposite, both united together within and
as a higher order integrated relational unity whole continuum. This dynamic process of holistic integration and relational interpenetration of polar opposites, or the "union of
opposites," is represented by the Taoist pictorial symbolism
of Yin and Yang united together within a greater circle that
includes them both, with Yin and Yang each containing at
their center an opposite-colored dot representing the other
element abiding within them at their very core, like two
waves always flowing into one another, as related, not mutually exclusive, polar opposites. In Hegelian terms, we have
to explore and appreciate the thesis and then the antithesis,
each from their own terms or frame of reference alone, in
order to optimally appreciate their differences, and then their
degrees of overlapping common ground, complementarity,
similarity, paradox, and higher order full unity, full integration, full synthesis.

Deeply invested non-dualistic empathic communion between individuals and their dynamically connected or overlapping "electromagnetic" vibratory energy fields opens up
the gateway to "relational space," wherein abides the creative energy power center of individuals, dyadic relationships, groups, and being or reality as a whole. That is where
the divine plenitude of limitless creative and transformational possibilities abides, as the relational center level of
our individual being-intelligence or our individualized form
of the relational energy field of love-warmth-life-light. The
individual center or core level of our being is where our own
individual energy form connects to, overlaps with, or converges with other individual energy fields, as a relational
center rather than a solo, solitary, or detached center. That

relational center or core level of our individualized being-intelligence-energy field is our own particularly individualized form of the plenitude or the universal creative divine being-intelligence. Deeply invested relational contact with other individuals, objects, and activities in the world takes our conscious awareness beyond the surface level of delineated energy form to the level of undifferentiated energy substance, where individual energy fields converge at the unifying level of reality-intelligence. At the center level of being-intelligence, individual energy fields connect to one another and to the unifying relational energy field, web, or matrix of being without losing their own individual identity, integrity, and distinctiveness, like individual radii converging at their common center of the same circle, yet each retaining their own greater individual distinctiveness or particularity at the circumference level of individual form.

Thus, the zone or source level of creativity abides in relational space, or relational energy, accessed or generated through relational contact between inner and outer or subjective and objective reality, when individuals invest the totality of their energy-being-attention in one another, to the point of temporarily relinquishing dualistic separate self-awareness, so that they are then united or empathically connected with one another's experience and energy field, heart core to heart core, in loving or caring communion with one another, so that they are relationally in full contact, non-dualistically not other than each other, at the core, center, or source level of their individual being. Through that process of deeply invested caring communion with other individuals, objects, and activities in the world to the point of full contact between their individual energy fields, full overlap, full non-duality, full communion, total fusion for a moment, but then letting the energy naturally move apart again to permit the retention of individual particularity and creatively challenging maximal polarization, through that willingness to let our energy momentarily flow into the experience of full non-duality with someone or something beyond the self-absorbed ego, we have thereby entered into the deepest source level of the zone of creativity, as our individual relational form of the limitless mystery plenitude. That connective center or limitless mystery plenitude level of reality intelligence is an overflowing fullness of being that contains all potential and actual knowledge within itself, so it is a dimension where anything good is possible to discover and manifest, as the limitlessly abundant source level of creative intelligence.

To manifest, unfold, or create some particular desired product, insight, discovery, or power of functioning from the core of your individual being, you must have an agenda (i.e., you must have some specific focus in mind, or nothing comes; you must not seek anything from a sense of lack or deficiency, but you must be curious about something that you wish to discover, produce, or achieve). You recognize that although your being is not deficient or intrinsically lacking anything that it requires to be inherently whole, you are, for the time being, relatively deficient or stuck in terms of needing to go beyond what you already know or have already accomplished, so you acknowledge that you have a need to obtain new knowledge or new productivity. Then, if you take that limited knowledge that you have already developed and keep exploring, keep questioning, with an attitude of openness to mystery, or tolerance for initially experiencing lack of knowledge, lack of certainty, lack of closure, lack of resolution, lack of achievement, lack of effectiveness, or lack of fully developed powers of functioning, in that kind of openness and receptivity to what is not yet known, discovered, or developed, something new can spontaneously arise to your conscious awareness from the deeper mystery core of your being, which can take the form of significant new breakthroughs, insights, discoveries, or accomplishments in any particular field of inquiry or endeavor.

We see this creative process as an ongoing process of exploring, questioning, stretching ourselves beyond our current limits of knowledge, and as yet undeveloped powers of functioning, pursuing particular desired goals, as an

expression of intrinsic proficiency rather than inherent deficiency of being, yet also being optimally open and receptive at the same time, speaking but also listening at the same
time. Then, sooner or later, some new insight, product, or
power of functioning will come from that open, listening,
receptive, relaxed attitude, from the limitless mystery plenitude core of our being. Those new gifts are imparted into our
receptive, relaxed, conscious awareness when we are in that
non-dualistic state of loving communion, which is the gateway to relational space, fundamentally the gateway from the
peak of knowledge to the base, the twilight zone, where light
and dark, knowledge and mystery meet.

On the surface of our conscious awareness, energy field,
and functioning, we seem to be restricted to limited time and
space, which apparently restricts us to what is already known
or manifested as knowledge, experience, products, or accomplishments. However, when we are willing to temporarily relinquish the ego's separate sense of self-awareness and
self-gratification in deeply invested communion with other
individuals, objects, and activities in the world, then our conscious awareness gradually moves beyond the surface knowable differentiated form level of energy-being-intelligence
to a deeper level of energy substance and essence, where
individual energy forms converge and overlap with one another, in relational contact with each other, like individual
radii gradually converging as they move from the circumference to the unifying center of the same circle. Because the
plenitude or substance and essence level of energy-being-
intelligence is not restricted to particular delineated forms
or objects and ideas that are already known, it is a limitless fullness of energy-being-intelligence, as a reservoir or
storehouse of limitless potentials or variable possibilities, so
literally anything truly good can come out of it, manifesting
as new insights, new products, new powers of functioning.
Qualitative breakthroughs, in contrast to quantitative modifications, involve not just further developing, extrapolating,
extending, or slightly modifying what is already known,

developed, or accomplished, but discovering, producing, or manifesting something on a fundamentally new and greater order of magnitude.

The creative energy field of love is intrinsically relational, as the energy that connects individual energy fields to one another, so it is a co-created reality, like a father and a mother co-creating a new child, as a new combined form of them both. The creative energy power that is released is qualitatively greatest when two or more individuals have been in heart core to heart core non-dualistic communion with one another, so that their energy heart cores touch each other. (We are referring to the "heart" as one's immaterial energy center or core, not the physical heart). When individuals connect their core energy centers to one another, in deeply invested empathic communion, they co-create or produce a relational energy field of loving warmth subjectively (inwardly) and produce a new product or insight objectively (outwardly).

Where energy is at the peak or surface, it is most restrictive, most closed to other potential knowledge and new possibilities abiding beyond the parameters of its current structure and boundaries. Furthermore, where energy is at the peak, it is most controlled and controlling, most tense, most resistive to the flow of any actual or potential energy field other than its own self-will or self-generated individual flow of experience, activity, and productivity. However, when the individual heart-mind-body energy field is deeply open, relaxed, receptive, and optimally flexible or pliable, then it is porous or open to impartations coming from a deeper level of being-energy-intelligence, beyond the confines of what is already known, and beyond the confines of the analytic ego mind. In that state of maximum openness and receptivity, we tap into the deeper source level of creative energy-being-intelligence, where energy meets stillness of unconditioned permanent being, and where all other relative polar opposites converge. That energy center where individual forms and relative opposite polar extremes converge together is a relational meeting point or nexus, which contains all actual and potential knowledge of delineated form within its limitless undifferentiated being, as the substance and essence level of energy, the integrated wholeness, cohesive, or holographic level of energy. Therefore, it can unfold, impart, or manifest any desired form of potential new knowledge, as a form of expression of its own limitless, overflowing fullness of being.

On the surface or circumference levels of energy fields of being-intelligence, where everything is most delineated, most discernible, most tangibly manifested, most differentiated, most polarized, as individual form or object of knowledge, that is where vibratory energy is most corruptible, decaying, entropic, unstable, changing, becoming, but increasingly, as the radius of conscious awareness, or attention approaches or converges with the center level or stillness of timeless permanent being, that is where the changeless stillness of timeless absolute being and fluid vibratory energy meet, as regenerative life energy, functioning as self-organizing, self-actualizing, entelechy, between material existence energy and changeless permanent being. That is where being and becoming are fully unified, and non-dualistically not other than one another, in the heart core center of our being, where life energy meets stillness. That is where life energy is most regenerative, cohesive, self-organizing, harmonious, relaxed, and open to new insights coming from a limitless source of creative intelligence.

We are most fully open to impartations from the limitless mystery plenitude when we are relaxed and content because then we are in a state of being, or grounded in the intrinsic wholeness and limitless abundance of our real being, rather than striving to become or achieve something that is not actually present in the here and now, as a state of conceptual becoming, which reflects a presumptive sense of deficiency and lack of wholeness. That sense of deficiency and lack of wholeness is contrary to the true nature of the limitless plenitude of being, and therefore interrupts our connection to it and our ability to receive new insights and other creatively productive impartations from it. Our fully relaxed and open heart center is like a nexus point, juncture, or gateway that connects the gross or tangible outer dimension of our being, the mind and body abiding in the material world, with the un-manifest inner fountain of regenerative life energy, which is the source of our individual creative intelligence, the source of higher (above normal, subliminal) noetic faculties such as, intuition, inspiration, empathy, compassion, aesthetic appreciation of true beauty, goodness, and integrity. Our individual creative potentials and relationship potentials are already abiding within the mystery timeless permanent being level of our individuality, waiting to be tapped into, or creatively unfolded into our experience and functioning in the world, like the roots of a flower or tree unfolding and manifesting as the visible aspect of the flower or tree above ground.

Max Hammer referred to our individualized form of timeless, changeless, permanent being, dynamically unfolding our individual seed-like creative potentials into the surface, manifest, changing, developing, becoming, mind-body level of our individuality in the world, as the archetype. The archetype is gradually unfolding our prototype or living blueprint for developmental growth, potentials actualization, enhanced functioning, and transformation from the dimension of timeless, changeless, permanent being into the dimension of becoming, or time and change. This view of the archetype as the permanent being prototype or blueprint of the individual soul differs from Carl Jung's view of the archetypes as collective unconscious symbolic motifs.[7] However, Max Hammer viewed the archetypal reality of timeless permanent being as having a significant influence in shaping the ethos, creative spirit, and development of collective humanity as a whole, particular ethnic cultures, nations, and social groups, as well as individual people.[8] The limitless mystery archetype or plenitude is like the script writer for its/our experiences in the world. When we access and awaken that essential source intelligence level of our being by being self-forgetful of the obstructing mechanism of egoistic self-awareness through deeply invested relational communion with other individuals, objects, and activities in the world, then we can change our experiences in the world by changing the basic narrative, matrix, or causal template of the source creative intelligence level of our own individual being.

If you want to understand something better or more deeply and clearly, you have to love it. That is, you have to be in subject/object non-dualistic experiential communion with the topic that you are exploring, including not only its tangible surface aspects, but also the mystery deeper aspects of it, because mystery-intelligence, as changeless permanent being, unfolds into love, the most powerful vibratory frequency or most essential level of life energy. If you fear mystery, or are intolerant of acknowledging a current lack or incompleteness of understanding, you will hold on to presumptions in order not to acknowledge and experience your current uncertainty. Therefore, you will seldom learn anything significantly new, or have a peak performance, or an enhanced experiential insight, that is qualitatively new and grander. Whoever does not love mystery or the exploration of what is currently unknown and undeveloped as potential, fears mystery, escapes it, and thereby becomes fixated in the actualization or developmental growth of their real love-life energy potentials unfolding from mystery, the source of all significant beneficial real transformation.

In a sense, mystery is greater than knowledge, because it is the underlying source from which knowledge or creative intelligence unfolds or arises, like the vast ocean base from which a passing wave of water arises, or like roots hidden below ground from which a plant grows above ground, and from which the visible plant receives its nourishment and stabilizing support. If you fear mystery as a kind of experiential death, absence, or cessation of current knowledge and escape it, then you have no access to new insights coming from beyond the scope of what is already known. That is why receptivity to creative new insights is greatest when we are without any kind of presumptive knowledge, biased expectations, or interpretation of experience. From trying to extrapolate only from what is already known or currently presumed to be known, nothing qualitatively new and greater will come as creative insight. It is only by loving the challenge, the question, as a kind of loving communion with the process of exploration into truth, do we "coax" the reality that we contemplate to reveal its secrets, as we penetrate deeply into the reality that we are exploring through our deeply invested non-dualistic communion with it. You need to have a focused, enjoyable passion to transcend current limits of understanding and functioning in some particular area of inquiry or endeavor, so that you are willing to penetrate deeply into the core of it, the mystery of it.

Love, or deeply invested, passionate, non-dualistic, experiential communion is the key that opens the door to the unfolding of our mystery creative intelligence. It is not sufficient to relate to mystery with a dispassionate, detached mind alone, as is encouraged in some forms of Eastern philosophy and spirituality. If you want to discover what is creatively new, then you have to deeply penetrate the mystery core of it, by passionately uniting with the mystery core of it, and then, through that deeply invested communion or exploration, significantly new and greater experiential insight will unfold. For example, if you want to understand physical, psychological, and interpersonal relationship pain and how to transcend it, then you have to go into the heart core of it and love it, commune with it, non-dualistically unify your conscious attention and caring energy investment with it, be experientially one with it, into its mystery core, before it will reveal to you how to transcend it, or give you insight into the basic cause of it or both. In a sense, you yourself are the mystery source of creative insight, and you are also the topic that you are contemplating or exploring, because it is abiding within your own consciousness, as well as abiding within your own subliminal mystery levels of creative intelligence.

There is a twilight zone between subconscious awareness and where conscious awareness first awakens from sleep, dream, or imagination, where the subconscious or subliminal inner source of creativity can most readily have contact with, and creatively and spontaneously unfold into, our conscious awareness. Psychologists call this twilight zone a hypnagogic or suggestible state, functioning as a source of intuition, inspiration, and insightful revelation. In a sense, all things are possible there. Once we are fully awake, our conscious awareness grows relatively insensitive to subconscious functioning, being deeply invested in conscious thought and activity, which blocks the creative subconscious or subliminal conceiving mind from unfolding its potentials spontaneously into our conscious awareness. In other words, when our conscious awareness is most closely in contact with the subconscious levels of the psyche, in non-dualistic connection with them, then that is the twilight zone of creativity, intuition, inspiration, revelation.

That is especially important for creative artists. Artists are not necessarily creative in their artwork in terms of illuminating the true nature of reality through a process of experiential communion with it. Most of them are just skilled craftsmen, producing their work in a rather mechanical, uninspired manner, as a basically "lifeless," "dead" product. However, when you are in deeply invested communion with your inner and outer experience, then that communion will enable deeper levels of true creative insight, vitality, inspiration, and beauty to be revealed through your creative work. Those inspirational, insightful, empowering, transformational qualities come from the enhanced levels of loving warmth and regenerative life energy released through the process of deeply invested communion with your particular activity, field of endeavor, or area of inquiry. Fully invested heartfelt communion is the inspirational source of experience and expression of true beauty, joy, wisdom, transformational breakthroughs, and creative insight because they are all products of the essential relational energy of life as love.

However, if there are some repressed unconscious painful feelings in the energy-heart core of the soul, then our conscious awareness is no longer lovingly connected to the subconscious or super-conscious source of creativity, but feels divorced from it, in order to permit our conscious awareness to escape from all of the repressed negativity, conceptual and experiential, that threatens to undermine the ego's sense of positive identity and pleasurable or comfortable experience or "something-ness" as a conceptual and experiential entity. Metaphorically speaking, energy trapped in rejected and repressed feelings, distracting mind chatter, overly intense sensations, or addictive cravings is like liquid water frozen into ice, no longer free flowing, and therefore no longer available for drinking, agriculture, and other productive uses. Similarly, when our energy becomes "frozen", cluttered, absorbed, or blocked in rejected and repressed painful feelings and other uncomfortable experiential states, we have less energy available for productive functioning and vitality, whereas when we consciously reunify with those uncomfortable experiential states, and thereby liberate the energy formerly invested in them (metaphorically similar to the process of melting ice back into water), then we have greater levels of regenerative energy available for productive functioning, creative insight, and vitality, as well as more energy available to enjoy or savor whatever worthwhile experiences life in the world has to offer.

When we stop escaping from uncomfortable feelings and related negative conceptual self-evaluations, then our conscious awareness and mostly non-conscious creative energy are no longer cluttered and divorced from one another by that extraneous mental-emotional inner chatter or heavy psychological "baggage," functioning as an obstructing barrier to block significant new insights from being unfolded from our creative center and flowing into our conscious awareness. When our conscious awareness and subconscious energies are unified or wedded together, then, like children being born from the union of father and mother, from the unification or loving non-duality between the conscious and subconscious aspects of our individuality, the birth of creatively inspired, intuitive, revelatory products like children will spring forth. Many artists are fearful that they will lose their artistic creativity if they go for psychotherapy, but whatever creative artistic work they have been doing is often mostly in spite of, rather than a productive outgrowth of, the repressed, fixated, trapped, blocked experiential energies abiding in the subconscious. Therefore, their creative energies are not as spontaneously free flowing, insightful, inspiring, transformational, and productive as they would otherwise have the potential to be, because much of their energies remain blocked in various internal self-conflicts and lack of openness to the spontaneously arising actual experiential truth of themselves from moment to moment. Instead, such artists are likely expressing a relatively immaturely developed and often rather distorted imaginative experience of the reality nature of life energy presence. When repressed experiential contents in the heart and mind are retrieved, accepted, relaxed into, fully consciously embraced or unified with, and thereby resolved, then there is a greater degree of loving communion between conscious, below-conscious, and above-conscious levels of our life energy force, once our conscious awareness and life energy force are liberated from those formerly repressed, obstructing contents. If we tend to identify only with the conscious levels of our life energy force, then we are divorced from levels of our energy force or being that abide above or below the threshold of consciousness and their potential creative contributions. Then we are not optimally functional in peak experiencing and peak performing.

If we have a lot of repressed negativity buried deep in the subconscious, then it is likely that our creativity will often be basically escapist imagination that distorts and escapes from reality, rather than bringing true insight into reality. The incessant process of fearfully, quickly escaping from uncomfortable negative thoughts and feelings will absorb much of our conscious awareness and subconscious energies, preventing them from deeply contacting and thereby gaining substantial insight into what is genuinely real in ourselves, other individuals, and in the world around us. That kind of unrealistic, escapist, fantasy-oriented imagination will be a distorted, antithetical expression of true creativity and the enhanced appreciation of reality grandeur that it can bring. That is, you will not be truly creative in terms of insightfully understanding and constructively transforming reality, but instead, you will be imaginative in terms of conceiving what is negating of the intrinsic true goodness, beauty, and meaning of reality, such as producing horror stories or seeking intense excitement through depictions of death and destruction, under the influence of the antithetical shadow of reality, influenced by what is repressed into the unconscious heart and mind. Therefore, when you are creating escapist products, sensations, or ideas influenced by the antithetical shadow of reality, instead of arising from your naturally pure energies, then your creative artistic talents often become relatively distorted, increasingly and insidiously destructive rather than constructive in orientation.

Creative products that arise from communion with real life energy presence, relatively inside and/or relatively outside, often reflect deep insight into the essential beauty, goodness, and meaning of real life energy presence. When you are open to deeply contacting or non-dualistically communing with creative life energy presence, inside and outside, you intuit the grandeur, beauty, goodness, inherent to that nature, like a love song, love dance, love melody, love poetry. That is what Julie Andrews, as Maria, sings about in the movie, *The Sound of Music*: "The hills are alive, with the sound of music." The more deeply we love and contact the reality nature of life energy presence, inside and outside, the more deeply we appreciate its nature, which correspondingly enhances the quality, the profundity, inspiration, and beauty of our creative artistic works as an expression of our correspondingly more penetrating appreciation of the reality nature, and inherent goodness of life energy in ourselves and in other life presences.

APPENDIX C

THE PROCESS OF SELF-HEALING, SELF-PURIFICATION, SELF-TRANSFORMATION, AND OVERCOMING ADDICTIONS

We will discuss the basic cause and cure of addiction to a false sense of inner life presence, including psychological as well as physical addictions. This involves understanding the process of distinguishing and separating our pure conscious-life presence from its entanglement or overlay of association with a false sense of identity and life presence, functioning as a malevolent, addictive, "energy parasite" or "energy vampire."

Our real self is an individual form of pure conscious awareness, as subjective knower, united with an objectified vibratory life energy presence animating the body, mind, and emotional heart center, together comprising our individual being. However, our real self as pure consciousness-life energy becomes obscured and covered over when we superimpose upon it illusory presumptive ideas of ourselves, such as exclusive, self-limiting self-definitions as well as egocentric desires and sensations. We infuse those presumptive ideas of ourselves and related addictive experiential states with a semblance of intensity, vitality, and selfhood by identifying exclusively with them and by valuing them, thereby infusing our real consciousness-life energy into them. By doing so, we give those parasitic inner monologues, self-definitions, and addictive substances an illusory semblance of vitality, functioning as a basically separate, non-relational, sense of self-awareness. That investment in ego-oriented thought, desire, and sensation enables those egoistic contents to stick to our real self, our real IAM, like psychological glue. Those contents of the ego's continuously self-absorbed inner monologues, or what Max Hammer often referred to as the "personal life story daydream fantasy" function like "energy parasites" or "energy vampires," so to speak, sucking your veritable life's energy "blood" out of you as long as you continue to identify with them and value them, and thereby infuse them with your real life energy, your heart-felt feeling energy. But they become totally unglued and fall away if you cease to identify with them, cease to value them, and no longer wish to retain them by realizing that you are, instead, intrinsically and permanently being your un-acquired, real, pure conscious-life energy presence, which is the real IAM, the real self, the real subject or knower of all of those delimited, acquired, conceptual objects of knowledge, which you can only know but never actually be. If you understand this, then you can distinguish the real IAM, your pure conscious-life presence, the one and only self that you can truly be, from all of its self-induced objects of knowledge, be they egoistic emotions, conceptual ideas of oneself, or physical sensations.

Identify with it and value only it as your own real being-presence which you are intrinsically permanently being, ever-present in the timeless now. The pure conscious-life energy presence of your real being is reflected from your spiritual heart-center into the mind that is abiding in total inner silence and stillness of a state of being in the timeless now. Through that means, its vibratory frequency will gradually quicken to the speed of light, until there is full enlightenment or full conscious awakening to and as that glowing divine presence, which intrinsically is a divine light, warmth, life energy. That is your true IAM, your true self, most subjective subject, the real subject, knower of all particular objects of knowledge, but is not any of them. The more that you are willing to be an undefined mystery unto yourself and cease to identify with and value all of the accumulated conceptual parasite objects of knowledge that adhere to your conscious-life presence or true being, the more quickly will all those acquired conceptual parasites fall away from your true being, like a façade, and the sooner will its full awakening take place. Therefore, if you just hold to being that undefined, intuited, pure consciousness-life energy substance, the most subjective nature of your pure being as knower, then all psychological parasites will gradually fall away from it, as the formerly valued and invested life energy presence in them becomes totally spent and is no longer reinforced, through identification, valuing, and acting on or gratifying them.

That is what the process of self-purification really means, and when all such acquired psychological impurities fall away from your true being, your real presence or conscious life substance, then it will shine brightly and will gradually awaken to its true reality nature. That shining or flowing is inherent to its own nature, which is now no longer obstructed or covered over by those dark psychological parasites; therefore, it is then free to glow in its fullest intensity, which is your spiritual IAM's true, full awakening. Therefore, hold yourself to be only that most subjective essential pure consciousness-life energy substance under all conditions, never identifying with or conceptually reacting to any exclusively-defined, conceptually-acquired objects of knowledge, and not holding those objects of knowledge to be a reality, a power, a life presence in their own right, no longer infusing them with your own conscious attention and real life energy, until your true divine nature begins to shine, glow, flow outward, and become knowable. Then you will fully awaken as that radiantly expansive, relationally connective, glowing nature, which, as an intrinsically flawless wholeness nature, is the inherent divine or spiritual reality nature of your being. In that perfect inner silence and stillness of a state of being in the timeless now, in which you are one with that pure consciousness nature, then you are living in heaven, so to speak. At any point in time, you can step into that infinite timeless now of your divine being and stay there until it begins to shine, glow, and radiate with its inherent brightness until your real IAM fully awakens to itself.

That contentment to be an undefined, undivided mystery unto yourself, as pure consciousness-energy, without divisively exclusive, partial, delimited, self-definitions, is real psychological healing, because it ends inner conflict between positively and negatively value judged, approved and disapproved self-evaluations. You don't have to analyze those psychological energy-parasites to be healed of them, just as you do not need to analyze your trash before discarding it. There is no healing of them; there is only healing of your real being liberating itself from false, restrictive self-identifications by ceasing to identify with and value them, and thereby dissociating yourself from them, casting them off, or dissolving them into their underlying substratum of pure conscious life energy. Therefore, you have to take no thought for the ego's conceptually defined sense of identity and experience; instead, attend continuously to that undefined, undivided, being, the pure IAM, spiritual conscious life presence, and it will take care of all your individual requirements by grace.

When individuals join together in a true sense of community by being in heartfelt empathic communion with one another, as they all live in and as that relational divine energy presence, its power and grace multiplies exponentially and can flow outward and produce this kind of transformational real change in other individuals, healing them of their identification with the ego or false sense of separate selfhood, apart from the relational life energy of love. That is the only way that this world can really be improved, so that there is real peace on earth and good will to everyone. That would be akin to a veritable paradise on earth.

It is important to not let the energy of our intrinsic real being become blocked by superimposing a restrictive overlay and contrary flow or counter-flow of a continuous stream of exclusive self-definitions and addictive, overly intense sensations, which block the natural unfolding of our individual

potentials, abilities, insights, interests, and other natural inclinations. Permitting that parasitic overlay to block our real
life energy flow is extremely dangerous because it produces
all kinds of pathological distortions or degenerative antithetical perversions of our energy field, which is the basic underlying cause of all kinds of medical, psychological, societal,
and financial disorders. Investment in a sense of exclusively
separate identity, self-awareness, self-gratification, and self-
generated excitement that does not arise from caring communion and constructive relationships with other individuals
is a process that unnaturally recoils or turns inward our conscious-life energy, producing a degenerative momentum of
our conscious awareness collapsing inward upon itself, like
the suction of a Black Hole in space. This inner Black Hole
suction continuously feeds upon itself as a self-perpetuating,
self-escalating momentum, pulling or contracting our conscious life energy ever more tightly upon itself, producing
fear, tension, and intense anger, seeking to drain the tension
and many other related forms of dreadful negativity or unhappiness arising from unnaturally twisting our energy field
by continuously, compulsively turning it inward upon itself,
instead of permitting it, at least at times, to naturally flow
outward to others in deeply invested, loving communion and
caring relationships with them.

The collapse of our conscious life energy tightly contracting inward upon itself, like a kind of inner Black Hole suction,
is opposite to the expansive process of spiritual and psychological growth as a continuous natural outward-radiant-shin-
ing and developmental growth of our conscious life energy
field, eventually culminating in our energy field becoming
perpetually self-sustaining and self-luminous, like a shining
star or sun in the heavens. Full spiritual and psychological
maturity or full expansive development of our individual and
relational energy field involves full development of our inner power source, providing us with the ability to function in
an optimally creative and productive manner. When we release or "pump out" the deepest core of our energy-being by

unselfishly, generously sharing our caring energy-investment with others, that release and full development of the source level of our energy-being generates a powerful magnetic energy field that enables us to magnetically attract all kinds of true good to ourselves. Furthermore, the regenerative quality of our maturely developed, unobstructed, fully released, relationally-oriented, energy field facilitates greater healing, health, vitality, and longevity, whereas the opposite, obstructing process of our conscious life energy compulsively recoiling, contracting, or collapsing inward upon itself produces an antithetical degenerative momentum, diminishing or impairing our ability to function in a productive, creative manner, as well as magnetically attracting various kinds of negative or painful experiences and producing various pathological disorders for us and for others who come into contact with us. That degenerative momentum cannot easily be turned off or reversed at will, and can produce very dangerous unintended and unanticipated long-term consequences, such as an enduring, possibly irreversible, degenerative recoil or blockage of our conscious life-energy, especially if we permit that self-recoiling momentum to gain accelerating intensity by not being willing to experience the discomfort of frustrating its insatiable addictive demands when it is appropriate or necessary to do so.

When we express unselfish caring to other individuals, and generously give of our conscious attention and energy to them, that expands and enhances the vibratory frequency of our conscious energy field, producing greater levels of functioning and regenerative well-being, whereas when we function in a selfish, uncaring, uncompassionate manner, that contracts, collapses, or depresses, our conscious energy field, producing the opposite experience of tension, depression, and anxiety as well as the compensatory addictive pursuit of various unhealthy forms of false elation or pseudo euphoria. When we inhibit our natural inclination to give abundantly or generously of our conscious life energy to others, that recoil sets into motion a degenerative process, as an antithetical distortion or perversion of the intrinsically regenerative quality of our conscious life energy when it naturally flows outward to others in a caring way. Thus, real living involves giving of our energy, as suggested by Martin Buber's observation: "All real living is meeting,"[1] or connecting in a caring way to other individuals, whereas the process of compulsively holding back our energy in some kind of recoil of extreme self-preoccupation is literally deadly.

When individuals connect to one another with deeply invested, heartfelt, unselfish caring, empathic communion or true love they thereby co-create a centripetal, unifying, expansive energy of "loving warmth," as a cohesive force of permanent integrity wholeness or the unity wholeness essence of love-life energy, which prevents the individuals and their relationship from being disintegrated by the centrifugal, divisive, contracting force of egoistic negativity. Subject-object non-duality, empathic connection or "sacred we" loving communion between two or more individuals is what releases, energizes, activates, consciously awakens, or maturely develops the unity wholeness essence level of their individuality and relationship, which is a centripetal cohesive force of "permanent integrity wholeness" that cannot be disintegrated, and which prevents the individuals and their relationship from being disintegrated by the opposite, "anti-cohesive" centrifugal force of egoistic extreme divisiveness and entropy. The co-created unity wholeness essence level of life energy as connective loving warmth or warmhearted unselfish caring is the highest or greatest source level of our individual and relational creative intelligence, producing enhanced levels of transformational creative functioning or peak experiencing and peak performing.

There is no other effective, realistic way to achieve immortal salvation or enduring preservation and enhanced transformational/maturational development of our individuality and our relationships without maturely developing and awaking the cohesive, regenerative unity essence level of our life energy force as co-created loving warmth, by unselfishly loving and serving other individuals. Any basically selfish, solo approach to seeking salvation and enhanced transformational or maturational development of our conscious life energy force is basically a self-delusional presumption that will never bear true fruit, because the source level of our being or conscious life energy force is an intrinsically relational nature that has to be co-created, activated, awakened, or maturely developed through deeply invested, caring, empathic communion with other individuals, and cannot be achieved by us alone, as self-preoccupied, narcissistic ego-personalities. We must engage in a high quality of deeply invested, unselfishly caring relationships for a long period of time (perhaps even over many lifetimes) in order to gradually, maturely develop our conscious love-life energy force or spirit from spark to full flame, as a permanent integrity wholeness, a force of permanent cohesion that can never become disintegrated.

Although our inherent being is already a mystery wholeness, we can make its limitless abundance of creative intelligence and cohesive permanent integrity wholeness knowable, manifested, or consciously awakened and maturely developed as the individual form, relational substance, unity essence, (and perhaps also the all-inclusive integrity quintessence, which integrates the individual form, relational substance, and unity essence) levels of love-life energy-intelligence, only by actively expressing its radiant, warmly expansive, energy nature or qualities to others as unselfish caring or true love. Until we actively, responsively express the limitlessly abundant goodness of the source level of our being, by expressing unselfish, generous, empathic, caring or true love to other individuals, its inherent inner grandeur qualities remain relatively dormant. But when we share or express those noble qualities to others, then our inner power center gradually becomes more consciously awakened and maturely developed, until it becomes fully activated or energized, as our inner power center, our fully maturely developed *Divine Imago*. It is like a tiny spark that has developed into a full flame, a perpetually shining inner sun or star that can give endlessly, limitlessly, of its boundless, inexhaustible abundance without ever being depleted, or like a small seed that has grown into a fruitful giant tree of everlasting love-life energy.

We can develop enhanced levels of constructive and creative functioning only by developing emotional pain tolerance, stress tolerance, frustration tolerance, ambiguity and confusion tolerance, etc. Avoidance of psychological or emotional pain diminishes or weakens strength of character, psychological health, and maturity, whereas willingness to face psychological or emotional pain for constructive reasons (in contrast to masochism, enjoying and pursuing suffering for its own sake, as a false form of excitement or life energy arousal) strengthens character, integrity, self-confidence, psychological maturity, and health. Developing strength of character involves the ability and willingness to endure frustration and other related uncomfortable experiential states for the sake of developing greater levels of productive, adaptive, well-adjusted, functioning, including enhanced interpersonal relationships as well as enhanced individual functioning, whereas when we lack strength of character, being intolerant of frustration and other uncomfortable experiential states, that will necessarily detract from our ability and willingness to face difficult challenges, even if that avoidance undermines our ability to cope effectively with the adaptive requirements of reality.

Various kinds of psychologically, socially, and/or physically unhealthy addictions arise from escaping from psychological pain, and having a lack of confidence in our ability to face or endure pain effectively, without having our fragile sense of self-awareness inundated, submerged, or overshadowed by the pain. Escaping from the full conscious awareness of painful or uncomfortable experiential states through various unhealthy, unwholesome means, such as ingesting artificial, addictive physical substances, pursuing intensely exciting sensations, participating in mental and emotional addictions such as fantasy and virtual reality (especially computer games and video games), those kinds of escapist tactics only temporarily and superficially cover over the uncomfortable experiential states at a less than fully conscious level of our psyche, where they continue to fester and become increasingly more pathological, like a wound that becomes infected when ignored or covered over and not properly medicated. Those escapist, addictive activities, sensations, and substances are often unnatural or artificially induced, and unwholesome, producing toxic effects, be they hidden or consciously recognized.

Such escapist activities and substances typically give people a false "high," a false sense of elation, which inevitably gradually wears off, with diminishing returns as the artificially induced sensation sooner or later subsides. It is like a robot returning to inertia when its battery or wind-up energy is exhausted, because what merely mimics life energy but has no genuine energy source of its own cannot enduringly sustain itself. Artificial sensations ultimately deaden rather than enhance our energies because they only mimic, overlay, and block the natural flow of real life energy within us. Therefore, when we use some kind of artificially induced process to escape or distract ourselves from uncomfortable experiential states, then the "payoff" of relief from those uncomfortable experiential states and related artificially induced comforting, exciting, pleasurable, experiential states gradually diminishes, while opposite experiential states of discomfort and depression gradually increase. That is to say, the more that we increase the consumption of artificially induced, often addicting sources of quasi excitement and euphoria, the more we become acclimated to a particular level of arousal or stimulation, which gradually subsides and thereby diminishes its exciting, elating, and comforting effects. Therefore, we feel compelled to keep escalating the intensity, frequency, duration, and amount or volume of intake of the addicting substance, sensation, or activity in order to keep the level of gratification from diminishing. Artificial addictive substances and sensations gradually deaden or desensitize the alertness and acuity of our consciousness, and depress or numb our energies, so we increase the dosage or intensity, amount, and frequency of the addicting substance, sensation, or activity to compensate for a continuously diminishing level of energy, comfort, security, elation, and well-being coming from that addictive substance. Thus, excessive dependence on intense escapist sensations often sets into motion a psychologically unhealthy process of numbing and blockage of our energies, which can have corresponding adverse effects upon our physical health and relationships, as well as on society.

We encourage people to seek psychologically healthy, constructive, alternatives to get relief from chronic, intense, unbearable, psychological pain, without escaping from it into unhealthy addictions. The only effective way to heal psychological pain is to embrace it or unify with it, whereas escaping from pain actually prolongs and magnifies it by increasing the level of inner conflict, tension, and blockage of energy between the controlling consciousness, as knower, and the distanced pain, as object of knowledge. Ours is currently "an addicted society." Unselfishly giving of ourselves, of our energies, to other individuals and to constructive, life-affirming, wholesome activities enables our life energy to naturally flow outward from the mystery core level of our being and become objectified as a knowable experience, as true joy, true euphoria, in contrast to addictive, unwholesome, substances and sensations, which provide only an imitative, pseudo sense of euphoria, vitality (excitement, aliveness, arousal), comfort, and security. Excessive, escapist, addictive substances, sensations, and self-stimulating mental and emotional activities such as fantasy and virtual reality are like a false beloved, a false friend, only a pseudo euphoria, elation, and grandeur, which sometimes involves egotistical grandiosity or self-infatuation as well as unrealistic infatuation with other individuals.

It is important that you clearly recognize that the issue is not: "Shall I endure psychological pain now or try to avoid it?"

That pain cannot be avoided indefinitely because it is within you, and it has not been eliminated just because you are trying to ignore it or escape from it. You can never really escape from yourself; you are being your own painful experiential states occurring within your own psyche. Therefore, you can only escape for a time from your awareness of that painful experiential aspect of yourself. That process of escape, in which the conscious knower stands dualistically distant and separated from the pain, only preserves and intensifies the pain. Thus, the real issue is, "Shall I endure psychological or emotional pain now by surrendering to it, unifying my conscious awareness with it, so that it can thereby gradually drain out into my conscious awareness, and eventually be fully gone? Or shall I try to avoid it now and therefore have to endure it for a longer time and with greater intensity later, when it inevitably eventually pushes past the resistance and forces its way into my conscious awareness?" Make no mistake about it, at some time in the future, when you grow tired of escaping from your painful experiential states, and the incessant internal struggle, tension, or self-conflict that necessarily involves, or when your ego can no longer tolerate the constant pressure and tension of having to escape from your own thoughts and feelings, that pain will register in your conscious awareness with enormous intensity.

If you expect to ever be able to regain the energy trapped in hitherto rejected painful feelings, so that energy can become available for productive, adaptive, enjoyable living, and for investing in developing and maintaining caring or loving relationships with other people, rather than leaving your energy frozen in rejected, blocked, repressed, experiential states, and if you wish to grow psychologically from your painful experiences, so that they are not a total waste, then you must learn to confront your pain head-on, and let it do its worst. Fully embrace or unify with the pain in your experiential heart or conscious-energy center. If you do that, your pain will dissolve relatively quickly, and you will heal of the emotional pain and of the inner self-conflict that it produces. But if you do not directly confront your pain, by permitting yourself, as knower, to fully consciously experience it, contact it, embrace it, unify with it, welcome it to play itself out to completion in your conscious awareness without any kind of censorship, control, inhibition, or blockage, and without any sense of distancing or duality that process of self-escape from your painful experiential states necessarily involves, then, whether consciously or subconsciously, your pain will continue, and your capacity for undertaking productive, adaptive functioning and engaging in satisfying personal relationships, as well as your psychological stability, will be severely impaired, because the energy trapped in those rejected, blocked, painful experiential states will not be available to you. Metaphorically speaking, the energy trapped in rejected painful experiential states is not free to flow spontaneously into your conscious awareness and play out to completion, like water that becomes frozen into ice, so that it can no longer flow and be utilized for drinking, agriculture, and other life-sustaining purposes, metaphorically representing the enhanced levels of psychologically constructive and productive functioning that become available only when you liberate energy trapped in suppressed uncomfortable feelings and experiential states.

APPENDIX D

THE DIFFERENCE BETWEEN THE REAL SELF AS A DIVINE OR SPIRITUAL RELATIONAL SELF AND THE EGO AS A FALSE SENSE OF SEPARATE SELF

The real self is our divine IAM, the real subject in us, the knower of all objects of knowledge. We intentionally write the IAM as one word with no hyphen to show that it is one indivisible seamless whole self, not a compound self comprised of a mixture of disparate elements.

However, the self as "conscious-life" should be hyphenated. We make a distinction between the real subjective mind as pure conscious-life substance, the real subjective self, the real subjective knower that we inherently, changelessly, permanently be in contrast to the objective mind, the psychological subjectivity mind of acquired, changing, basically arbitrary, unfounded self-interpretation and self-definition, the mind of conceptualization-imagination-emotion-sensation, the world and body-related mind, the brain-related mind. The unconditioned or non-acquired subjective mind is the inherent pure conscious-life subjective substance of the mind, the pure IAM. That is the source of the true greatness nature in human beings, the source of our sublime qualities, our states of exaltation, the intuitive higher mind and pure energy-feeling-heart, our intrinsic non-deficient flawless wholeness of being, our true creative intelligence, abiding at the deepest energy-center level of our being, in contrast to the more superficial psychological mind, comprised of brain activity, such as memory, reasoning, and ego-oriented thought. The pure subjective conscious-life substance is our individualized form of the divine image that we intrinsically, permanently, changelessly be. That is our real self, the real subject or knower, our inherent real being, and where we truly live or abide. That is the spiritual or divine life dimension, which some call the Kingdom of God or the Kingdom of Heaven that is within you, the source of the higher nature, the source of all states of true beauty, exaltation, enchantment, creativity, intuition, inspiration, and charisma, which some psychologists describe as "peak experiencing" and "peak performing," and which some spiritually or religiously oriented people describe as a state of grace, blessing, blessedness, redemption, or salvation. Each of us is intrinsically being the same spirit-life energy nature, the same higher nature of love-goodness. We differ only in the degree of the conscious self-realization of it or as it, meaning that some individuals are more while other individuals are less conscious of that spiritual life presence; therefore, it is more or less developed in some than in others, depending on how much we have developed that higher nature, our spiritually developed, psychologically mature nature, in contrast to our egocentric narcissistic and selfish nature, which is relatively psychologically immature.

We are each a unique individualized form and function or archetypal blueprint pattern of the Divine IAM of God, which constitutes the divine image or *divine imago* that our being intrinsically is, most essentially. That is the source of our own higher nature, as a real individual form of the divine image. The term divine image refers to our inherent real self, subject, or being, which we can never stop being. We cannot actually be or become an object of knowledge; we have to always inherently be the conscious-life substance that is the knower of all objects of knowledge, including the defined, delimited, acquired, ego-personality I-thought which the ego holds to be its subjective sense of self or identity. That pure IAM or pure conscious-life substance, our unconditioned mind substance, is the pure subjective part of everyone's being. The pure IAM is what we inherently are being as conscious-life presence prior to taking or identifying with any acquired object of knowledge as a finite "this or that" that we add to our permanent being, which always transcends everything that we hold ourselves to be that is acquired in finite time and space and psycho-physical existence. The ego is the objectified, conceptually defined, acquired, psychologically separate sense of self that replaces the real subject or the real self as our identity when consciousness is not yet maturely developed enough to be in self-realization as its real life presence and real self, fully awakened as a knowable, intuited, or experienced energy presence. Pure conscious-life substance is like a mirror, and when it is not very maturely developed in self-realization or the direct experience of its intrinsic real nature, it confuses itself with the acquired, delimited, conceptual interpretations of itself that are reflected upon itself. Because that is a continuous process, the knower or the real self, as pure conscious-life substance, tends to identify with those conceptually-derived or acquired finite objects of knowledge reflected upon itself, and therefore loses awareness of its true nature, confusing itself with the acquired finite self-concepts, self-images, emotions, and sensations that are reflected upon our consciousness like images reflected upon a mirror.

The individual soul is part of a greater whole web of life, a web of relational connections between individuals, abiding within a collective over-soul or a universal soul of humanity and an even greater connective web of all living beings and the indivisible whole of reality, like an individual cell of the human body is naturally abiding within and integrated into the harmonious functioning of the whole body, or like an individual letter of the alphabet combining with other letters to compose limitless writing. The relational nature of reality makes all living beings and all branches of knowledge naturally related to one another in their being, experience, and meaningful significance. Therefore, anything or anyone is best understood within the context of their interactions with others and with larger connective wholes, whereas viewing any aspect of reality in isolation often produces false, distorted, superficial perception. Unselfish true love or genuine caring is a great power for healing, blessing, and creative transformation. Our living or becoming body-mind-heart or physical-mental-emotional nature in the world is gradually unfolding the potentials of our un-manifested permanent being, the invisible spiritual blueprint, prototype, or archetype of our being, like a visible plant above ground growing from the unseen roots below ground.

We are each individual forms of the One Self. The One Self is love; it is without fragmentation or divisibility. The relational nature of reality, as the connective energy of love, is the harmonizing power that transforms the world by transforming every soul, making it more loving. Every individual has a particular way of expressing love for others, serving others and the whole of life in some way, and our particular natural way of serving others and the whole of life through the ongoing developing of our individual life potentials is our individual life function or work.

Psychological pathology or, in religious terms, "sin" arises when people stand apart from other individuals and from the whole flow of life experience in the world, with their conscious awareness recoiled in a continuous narcissistic self-awareness. Just as an individual cell of the human body cannot survive and function effectively apart from the other cells and organs of the whole body, and just as an individual alphabetic letter has no meaning apart from the context of combining with other letters, similarly, our individuality cannot experience true wholeness and well-being apart from relational connection to other individuals and to the indivisible relational whole web or network of life or reality. The real self, the soul, is naturally inclined to function in cooperative harmony with others, and to make reasonable accommodations to the legitimate rights, needs, and wishes of others, whereas the narcissistic ego reinforces its continuous sense of separate self-awareness by compulsively expressing willfulness or oppositional resistance to others and to the realities of the here and now, even when it is not really appropriate, advantageous, or even safe to do so. The individual and collective ego's extreme willfulness can also involve a compulsive oppositional resistance to the development and expression of our own natural real potentials, abilities, interests, and inclinations, rejecting our real capabilities and temperament, or rejecting what we actually are being, in favor of what the individual and collective ego presumed we "should be" or "ought to be." The ego's conceptually presumed sense of totally separate, independent, identity and oppositional willfulness is like a false psychological mask or persona, superimposed upon the relational nature of the real self, the soul.

Whenever an individual holds himself/herself to be totally separated and unrelated to others through her/his own sense of oppositional willfulness and identification with exclusive self-definitions, then that person is serving a divisive force or principle antithetical to the nature of God, life, or reality, as love. In psychological terms, that resistive, oppositional force can be called the individual and collective ego, whereas it is known to many religious people as the force of evil, Satan, or the Devil. However, our real individuality, which includes our distinctive real individual potentials, abilities, interests, and natural inclinations, is not meant to be permanently lost or relinquished in God or in caring relationships with other individuals. Instead, our real individuality is truly found and preserved through how we relate to others and contribute to their well-being, as well as how we express God's nature as love-goodness to others, in our own particular, special way.

APPENDIX E

FULFILLING THE BASIC PURPOSE OR MEANING OF LIFE, AND OVERCOMING PATHOLOGICAL PSYCHOLOGICAL FIXATION

This discussion of the dangers of fixation or blockage of our continued psychological and spiritual development involves the principle of "grow or die." We will explain why we must permit ourselves to unify with or fully consciously experience our painful feelings in order to liberate our life energy that has been invested and trapped in those painful feelings.

The basic meaning or purpose of life is to grow more conscious of and more fully develop our individual and relational energy field, which includes unfolding potentials, abilities, proclivities, and natural inclinations that are intrinsic to our real being or energy force. This basic purpose of life can be fulfilled only if our energy field is not covered over and blocked in its flow by having false presumptive ideas of ourselves and associated mind chatter superimposed upon it. There are times when we must wear our psychological and social masks, such as in a professional role in our career or relating to other individuals in formalized, conventional, socially expected ways; but we must not exclusively, rigidly, or enduringly identify with those psychological and social roles or masks. Otherwise, we will have difficulty in putting them aside when it would be appropriate to do so, as the basis of making unmediated contact with the actual experiential truth and energy presence of ourselves and of other individuals as the basis of developing greater self-understanding, greater levels of flexible functioning, as well as greater ability to develop genuinely caring relationships and good interpersonal communication with other individuals. We have to recognize that there is a real "face" of our love-life energy presence and its real experiential states abiding behind or beyond those acquired, artificially contrived, superimposed psychological and social masks. Our real love-life energy presence and our real experiential states hidden behind psychosocial masks are like a potential flower hidden within the shell of a seed. Like the growth of a flower, our love-life energy presence is naturally, gradually unfolding and actualizing our natural real life passions, interests, and various other kinds of natural inclinations, gradually and spontaneously unfolding into our conscious awareness if we do not block them by identifying with superimposed psycho-social masks as conceptually defined presumptive ideas of ourselves, which may not necessarily reflect the actual experiential truth of ourselves and our natural inclinations and potentials. The more rigidly, defensively, and exclusively you are identified with your positive and negative self-concept and self-image masks, the more you obstruct your real life energy force from flowing freely and fully spontaneously. This not only hampers your real life potentials from unfolding and being fully actualized, but also prevents your life energy force from being optimally regenerative, which may, ultimately, adversely seriously affect your psychological and physical well-being. That blockage can produce a life-degenerative momentum, involving various kinds of emotional, mental, and/or physical disturbances, illnesses, suffering, or even premature death. For example, blocked energy, recoiled in some kind of continuous narcissistic self-awareness, can produce negative feelings such as chronic fearful anxiety, tension, depression, and destructive aggressive inclinations.

Therefore, your openness to the actual experiential truth of yourself and of others, particularly in genuinely caring relationships with them, is extremely important, perhaps the most important aspect of your life in terms of the importance or magnitude of its influence upon your overall well-being, developmental growth, happiness, fulfillment, creativity, and optimal functioning. Only when you are optimally open to your real life natural passions, deeply loving and enjoying the activities that you are engaged in and deeply invested in non-dualistic communion or optimal real relationship with those activities with optimal investment of your heart, mind, and senses, then, in that inner total self-forgetfulness, you are empty of all self-concept, self-image, rigid static masks and associated mind chatter. Therefore, in that absence of the obstructing, blocking, or distracting mechanism of the ego-personality's continuous reactive inner monologue or personal life story daydream, then the source level of your life energy force will be able to unfold its natural potentials into your conscious awareness, bringing greater levels of productive functioning and creative insight.

If you truly wish to grow, develop, blossom, or flower, as a real life presence, inwardly, ever more beautifully, grandly, more powerfully, then you must learn to engage in real relationship, or subject/object non-dualistic empathic communion with yourself and others. For that kind of real relationship or empathic communion to be possible, you have to be a relatively psychologically healthy and mature individual, because individuals who are relatively psychologically unhealthy or immature tend to be defensively fearful of losing their exclusive, continuous, pre-committed sense of separate self-awareness, and controlled self-gratification. Individuals who are relatively psychologically immature tend to be afraid of being open to becoming conscious of and acknowledging the spontaneously arising actual experiential truth of themselves, for fear that their positive psychological masks will be disaffirmed, and thereby dissolved, and that they will lose their absolute sense of willful control and separate identity, as an absolute sense of disconnection, psychologically, from other life forms, other life presences. Therefore, they cannot contact their own life energy presence and real experiential states and those of other individuals. Relatively psychologically immature individuals are very much wrapped up in themselves, which makes it very difficult for them to relate empathically and effectively to others, and even to their own real life energy presence and its spontaneously arising potentials, functions (or capabilities), interests, and other natural inclinations. They tend to become extremely selfish, narcissistic, hedonistic, self-absorbed, self-infatuated, self-gratifying, living in a kind of continuous inner monologue or self-aggrandizing personal life story daydream, relating predominantly to their own positively and negatively value judged psychosocial masks, as well as to their positive and negative value judgments of others. That is like superimposing psychosocial masks or preconceived interpretive ideas upon themselves and others, which makes real relationship to their own life presence and to the real life presence of others extremely difficult.

Consciousness is fully awake or fully conscious only when it no longer rejects any of its own spirit or love-life-existence energy presence, including its temporary feelings and experiential states, spontaneously arising to our consciousness from moment to moment. Therefore, as long as we still have some of our life energy presence trapped in painful feelings that are rejected from conscious awareness and thereby still repressed into the unconscious, we do not have available to us the totality of our spirit, or our love-life energy presence, to be conscious of. Therefore, our consciousness itself is limited or fixated because consciousness continues to grow, mature, or develop, only as it fully contacts, loves, embraces, and unconditionally accepts the totality of its spirit, or its love-life energy presence, including that part of our energy that is invested in previously rejected and repressed painful negative feelings. Therefore, when we keep any of our love-life energy spirit in the form of painful feelings rejected or excluded from our conscious awareness, and thereby repress them into the subconscious level of our subliminal awareness so that our love-life energy presence is not totally available to our consciousness, then we cannot be fully, totally, or absolutely conscious of our absolute or fully maturely developed love-life-existence energy presence. When our love-life energy spirit is maturely developed and fully awakened to itself, and no longer covered over and blocked by unresolved troubled feelings, then it provides us with the knowable experience of the intrinsic grandeur and goodness of our permanent being and its limitless unfolding creative potentials.

Therefore, you should welcome your unconscious fearful and painful feelings to spontaneously arise back into your consciousness fully; otherwise, you cannot retrieve all of your spiritual love-life energy presence that has been invested and trapped in those uncomfortable feelings. Until those uncomfortable feelings are fully drained or dissolved and released back into their underlying substratum of free flowing pure energy by being fully embraced or fully welcomed into our conscious awareness, our consciousness cannot be fully conscious or fully developed and continue to grow and maturely develop into an absolute consciousness of fully vibrant, unblocked, love-life energy presence, as our IAM self-realization, the flame of absolute love and joy or bliss which is our immortality. So we really have no choice but to be open to our hitherto rejected and repressed unconscious fears and pains, because they are trapped, distorted, twisted, exiled forms of our very own spiritual love-life energy presence. If we do not retrieve the totality of our love-life energy presence, where none of it is trapped in painful or fearful feelings rejected and repressed into the unconscious, then we cannot be fully conscious of our full vitality, our life energy power center, and thereby experience the unconditional fulfillment, security, grandeur, and limitless power for good that is intrinsic to our energy-being. Until we retrieve the totality of our energy presence from being blocked or trapped in unresolved painful feelings, distracting compensatory escapes, or false coverings of egocentric volition, feeling, thinking, and sensation, we cannot be fully conscious of or fully awakened to our absolute IAM, which is our greatest attainable source of fulfillment, security, and limitless creative energy-potential. If we don't accomplish that, then we insidiously start regressing back to become less conscious, and our regression toward less consciousness is totally unacceptable, because that is gradually undoing our evolutionary development in powers of functioning. When that happens, we begin to lose our human level of consciousness, so we gradually become more animalistic, bestial, or devilish.

We emphasize that there is no other constructive choice or responsible alternative but to retrieve the energy invested in painful, fearful feelings by fully accepting, welcoming, embracing, unifying those uncomfortable feelings back into our consciousness whenever they spontaneously begin to arise into our awareness. We have to keep growing in the reunification and the full conscious awakening of our love-life energy presence, including all of our painful feelings, or we will inevitably totally self-destruct, sooner or later, individually and as a collective society. However, as long as we continue growing in the consciousness of our life energy presence, we are still a useful function to life and so it helps us. As long as we are still growing or developing in the consciousness of our life energy presence and unfolding new and higher or more developed productive and creative potentials of it, we will not start regressing toward total unconsciousness, total loss of powers of functioning. Therefore, remaining open to continued growth in the conscious awakening or maturational development of our love-life energy spirit is an unavoidable or choiceless necessity, as epitomized by the dictum "grow or die." We must keep growing in the consciousness of our love-life energy presence, including all of our painful feelings, or we automatically, inevitably, begin an ever-accelerating pathological, degenerative momentum, eventually leading to total self-destruction.

We understand that it is not fun to face your fears and pains, but the alternative is much worse. You become totally contrary to the natural flow of life energy or totally anti-life, totally contrary to the momentum of love and goodness or totally anti-love, when you become fixated or permanently blocked in unwillingness to reintegrate or reunify with your

own life energy presence by fully retrieving back into consciousness all of the painful, fearful, negative feelings that
have become intensely invested with your own love-life energy. In addition to reunifying our love-life energy with our
consciousness by retrieving our previously rejected uncomfortable feelings into consciousness, we also have to stay
strongly invested in contact with life or reality in the world,
here and now, as an expression of love for life, by being
highly attracted to it, unselfishly giving of our caring energies and talents to life, serving the continued advancement
of life, other individuals, and our own transformational developmental growth in some way. If you keep loving life,
you keep living, but if you withdraw your investment and
interest in life, then you gradually start dying, physically,
psychologically, and spiritually by blocking the natural flow
of your caring energy outward into contact with objective
reality, metaphorically similar to extinguishing a light or a
flame by preventing it from naturally shining outward. By
keeping your energy continuously recoiled in some kind of
narcissistic egoistic self-involvement, thereby blocking your
energy from naturally flowing outward to others and to the
world of objective reality, you literally trigger a life-degenerative process.

When we no longer reject and escape from our uncomfortable feelings, but fully welcome them to spontaneously
arise back into our conscious awareness, then paradoxically
our willingness to face fearful and painful feelings gradually
puts an end to the fear and pain by draining it out into our
conscious awareness. When there is no longer any fearful
escape from uncomfortable feelings and from investment in
caring contact with objective reality in the world, then much
unnecessary psychological pain and suffering will disappear,
because fear is the underlying substratum and causal source
of psychological pain and suffering, as well as of much related pathological pain and suffering of the physical body, and
various kinds of societal disorders, as well as malfunctioning or breakdowns of significant interpersonal relationships.

When you bring love to your uncomfortable feelings by fully welcoming their total retrieval into your consciousness, and when you express deeply invested heartfelt love for life, then the heart will naturally, correspondingly be filled with love and joy, and that good energy naturally gets projected outward or flows outward into the world, "magnetically" attracting greater experiences of good to us, and repelling various kinds of potential negativity or potential harmful hazards.

As part of your expression of true love for life in the world and for your own love-life energy presence, you have to keep pushing beyond the current limits of powers of functioning of energy-feeling-heart, mind, and body. You have to be very growth-oriented and unselfishly devoted to helping others to grow or advance to greater levels of transformational development, enhanced potentials actualization, and enhanced levels of creative, productive, empowered, and constructive functioning. Otherwise, your latent potentials gradually atrophy if they are not exercised and actualized or developed at the proper time, or the proper "season," so to speak. For example, when a certain "season" or optimal time comes to actualize your athletic physical potentials, you must do so or they will atrophy. The same pattern occurs with professional skills, interpersonal relationship skills, physical skills, psychological skills, and spiritual powers of functioning. Most importantly, never quit on life or on your responsibilities in life. It is not failure but rather quitting that we have to be afraid of, because as long as we are doing the best that we can, then we are still growing, still serving life, but if we quit, then we are no longer growing, no longer serving life, so we automatically set into motion a life-degenerative, life-negating, pathological process. Developing strength of character, or true courage, which involves developing greater tolerance for frustration and other related forms of psychological discomfort, enables us to face the unpleasant experiential truth of ourselves, liberating our energies for enhanced creative and productive functioning, whereas escaping from uncomfortable feelings and experiential states undermines our willingness and ability to take reasonable constructive risks as a way of enhancing our individual transformational development and relationship functioning.

We not only have to stay strongly invested in life in the world with our mind and senses, we also have to stay strongly invested in life in the world with our heart. We have to love life in the world as the divine beloved of our own consciousness. Life in the world is the natural true beloved of our consciousness, because it evokes all of the knowable potentials and powers of functioning embedded in our conscious awareness as well as in subconscious, super-conscious, or subliminal levels of our psyche. Our life-existence energy always reflects our consciousness, like an objectified knowable mirror of the subjective mystery knower that we inherently be, so if our consciousness rejects and thereby attacks our life-existence energy by continuing to reject and repress uncomfortable feelings in which our life-existence energy is invested, then our life-existence rejects and attacks our consciousness, by producing an ever greater accelerating degenerative momentum of physical, psychological, societal, and interpersonal relationship pathology. We must never reject or attack any object of knowledge form of life-existence, relatively inside or relatively outside, relatively subjectively experienced internally or relatively objectively experienced in the world, because it is all part of the indivisible divine beloved of our consciousness. Therefore, no matter what form of experience our love-life energy presence spontaneously takes, in a given present moment, we have no constructive choice but to unify our consciousness with it. Your permanent being consciousness is intrinsically non-dualistically being and naturally unified with the totality of your life-existence energy experience, your real divine becoming nature. We wish to make a clear distinction between our real becoming nature, consisting of the natural potentials, abilities, interests, inclinations, and proclivities that are intrinsic to and unfolding from our permanent being, in contrast to the ego's illusory becoming nature, its attempt to become something more or better than it currently believes itself to be, or attempting to improve itself in some way in order to compensate for the ego's underlying, foundational, not fully conscious, sense of deficiency.

We must recognize that we really have no constructive choice but to unconditionally accept and lovingly non-dualistically unify with the totality of our own life energy presence, including all of its temporarily arising objects of knowledge, as forms of experience and feeling that arise like temporary wave forms of that water-like permanent life energy substance. Otherwise, if we reject any feeling, experience, or aspect of our life-existence energy presence or spirit, we are rejecting, attacking, or abusing our own life energy, which must then necessarily attack and reject us, by increasing our pathological psychological, physical, societal, and interpersonal relationship pain, suffering, and malfunctioning, as a mirror-like reflection of how we are treating our own life energy presence, which is the objectified knowable surface level of our subjective pure conscious awareness, as mystery knower. Therefore, we must unconditionally accept, non-dualistically unify with or lovingly remain connected to and be highly invested in every aspect of our own life-existence presence, including all of our spontaneously arising feelings and experiential states, as well as every aspect of life-existence in the world, and unfold its limitless inherent potentials. Otherwise, we automatically set into motion a basically destructive, life-degenerative, life-negating process, as an antithetical momentum caused by blocking, twisting, or distorting, the natural, regenerative tendency of our energy to flow outward to others and to the world of objective reality. This view that blocking our energy from naturally flowing outward into deeply invested expressions of caring connection with other individuals and with the world of objective reality, through recoiling our conscious attention and feeling energy in egocentric or narcissistic continuous self-preoccupation, is basically responsible for producing a pathological, potentially destructive, momentum in our own energy field, finds corroboration in the following observations by Erich Fromm:

> Life has an inner dynamism of its own; it tends to grow, to be expressed, to be lived. It seems that if this tendency is thwarted the energy directed toward life undergoes a process of decomposition and changes into energies directed toward destruction. In other words, the drive for life and the drive for destruction are not mutually independent factors but are in a reversed interdependence. The more the drive toward life is thwarted, the stronger is the drive toward destruction; the more life is realized, the less is the strength of destructiveness. *Destructiveness is the outcome of unlived life.* Those individual and social conditions that make for suppression of life produce the passion for destruction that forms, so to speak, the reservoir from which the particular hostile tendencies—either against others or against oneself— are nourished.[1]

Fromm's observations underscore the importance not only of undoing egocentric psychological blockages to investment in caring communion with other individuals and objective reality, but also of actively generating a life-affirming momentum by actualizing our life-based natural potentials and abilities to the fullest possible extent.

So no matter how uncomfortable the pain, psychological or physical, you must face it, unify with it, recognize that it is only temporary. Then it will gradually fully drain out into your consciousness, fall back into its underlying base or substratum in pure feeling energy, and be divested of its painful, pathological, orientation. However, you will necessarily, but perhaps unknowingly and insidiously, set into motion a pathological, possibly self-destructive, momentum if you do not permit uncomfortable feelings and experiential states to naturally flow back into your conscious awareness, and do not permit your conscious awareness and feeling energy to naturally flow outward into caring communion with other individuals and with objective reality in the world. If energy is not permitted to naturally flow freely and spontaneously, but is instead blocked, obstructed, rejected, then it becomes distortedly antithetical to the naturally regenerative, constructive orientation of our original, undistorted, pure energy nature, and becomes twisted into an antithetical, distorted, anti-love, anti-life, anti-light of truth, degenerative, divisively dis-integrating, pathological nature, orientation, or momentum.

Transcending false identification with the ego as superimposed, preconceived interpretations of ourselves and others enables us to fulfill the basic meaning of life, which is growing in unobstructed, undistorted contact with and consciousness of our pure energy, which is our real being. Fixation in continued identification with the chronically resistive, reactive ego takes us out of the relational flow of inner and outer actual life experience by recoiling our conscious attention and energy investment into the ego mind-chatter incessant monologue. That continuous, fixated recoil from the relational flow of actual life experience into the self-preoccupied egoistic inner monologue inevitably twists or distorts our energies into a basically degenerative momentum, like a kind of unconscious death wish. Sidney Jourard suggests that withdrawing our investment from the flow of life experience and from life-affirming goals basically sets into motion a process of dying:

> If human life is the experience of life, he who experiences more, with greater intensity, lives more. If life occurs in time, then he who has more time has more life. If life is experience, then he who would diminish my awareness is a murderer. And when I blot out my experience, I commit partial suicide.
>
> A person lives as long as he experiences his life as having meaning and value and as long as he has

something to live for—meaningful projects that inspirit him and invite him to move into his future. He will continue to live as long as he has hope of fulfilling meanings and values. As soon as meaning, value and hope vanish from a person's experience, he begins to stop living; he begins to die.[2]

The only effective way to grow in greater consciousness of our own real love-life energy presence and to make more substantial contact with the real energy presence of other individuals is to be willing to at least temporarily relinquish the ego or sense of continuous separate recoiled self-awareness, and its related sense of duality from other individuals, including letting go of conceptual self-definition and overly exaggerated approving and disapproving evaluations, or extreme positive and negative value judgments of ourselves and of other individuals. That continuous conceptual-emotional reactivity and compulsive oppositional willfulness functions as a kind of false sense of inner animation or quasi life energy presence substitute, providing a false sense of inner vitality or excitement as an incessant process of recoil of our conscious attention and energy investment into egoistic inner chatter taking place in our own mind, which overlays and blocks awareness of our real, intrinsic, individual and relational life energy presence from being experienced and expressed by our consciousness.

Without that conceptually-acquired, reactive, recoiled, continuous inner monologue functioning as a false sense of inner animation superimposed or overlaid upon our un-acquired, or unconditioned, intrinsic, pure consciousness, our real life energy presence is no longer blocked from reuniting with our consciousness and unfolding its creative and productive potentials into our unblocked, open, receptive, conscious awareness. That is to say, without that false inner presence, as false egocentric self-awareness and self-knowledge, functioning as a superimposed covering, barrier, obstruction, or blocking mechanism, our permanent being, which naturally is a mystery unto itself, a fullness of limitless potentials, an inexhaustible reservoir or vast plenitude, is then naturally able to shine or unfold into our consciousness its new and progressively ever higher or ever greater, more maturely developed or highly evolved, potentials and powers of functioning of our spiritual intelligence. This enhances the capabilities of our social, emotional, mental, and physical functioning, producing greater levels of enhanced functioning in all aspects of our life. Furthermore, when our conscious attention and feeling-energy investment is no longer heavily invested in egoistic mind-chatter, then our ability to commune with other individuals, worldly phenomena, and activities is correspondingly enhanced, and that enhanced contact with the relational flow of life experience also enhances our level of appreciative insight into the "many-splendored" essential beauty and goodness of everyone and everything that we encounter in the world, as well as enhancing our level of regenerative life energy, which produces greater levels of holistic health, vitality, enjoyment, and effective functioning.

Thus, to have greater access to regenerative life energy and creative intelligence flowing into our consciousness from the mystery permanent being core of our individuality, (which we authors also refer to as our spiritual blueprint, prototype, or archetype), we have to at least temporarily transcend or relinquish continuous recoil in narcissistic, separate, ego-personality self-awareness and related incessant mind-chatter, which causes a degree of prolonged or even permanent blockage or fixation in the actualization of our natural real individual and relationship potentials, producing decline or regression in our level of constructive, adaptive, functioning vitality and well-being. Some typical aspects of this egoistic barrier to contact with our own real potentials, feelings, experiential states, as well as optimal caring contact with other individuals and with objective reality in the world, includes dualistic conceptual and emotional reactivity, such as overly exaggerated, extreme, and unrealistic, positive and negative or good and evil value judgment. The only effective way to transcend our "fatal attraction" to the continuous, divisive, inner monologue of mental-emotional reactivity, or to overcome unhealthy, addictive recoil in separate ego-personality self-awareness, is to find another life presence more attractive to you than the narcissistically self-absorbed ego-personality, and therefore put the totality of your conscious attention and heartfelt investment of love-life energy feeling or cathexis into another life presence or activity in the world, in non-dualistic communion or connection with it.

The process of dismantling, or at least occasionally suspending, the ego-personality as a false sense of continuous self-awareness, and thereby undoing the pathological momentum of consciousness habitually, unnaturally, and tightly recoiling upon itself, necessarily involves a related process of radical openness (full openness) to all spontaneously arising experience with a nonreactive innocence awareness, involving no predetermined conceptual interpretation and value judgment of ourselves and of another life presence, which makes it a conceptual mystery to us. That lack of pre-determined egocentric interpretations of ourselves, other individuals, and phenomena in the world, enables us to gain deeper, undistorted, experiential insight into whatever inner or outer realities are actually arising in the here and now. When we do that, then the lack of narcissistic ego-personality self-awareness, and the absence of recoiled clenching, closing, twisting, tensing, or blocking of our conscious and non-conscious energies that that involves, enables the mystery permanent being core of our individuality to shine, flow, or unfold its energy spirit into the psychological or experiential-energy heart (not to be confused with the physical heart), and thereby begin to awaken the heart faculties of love and joy. Then that radiance of love-life energy presence naturally shines outward into the world, and we begin to intuit the inherent attractiveness, beauty, harmony, and lovable quality of every particular life form that we encounter, each in its own particular special way. That intuitive experience of the intrinsic lovable quality of the living presence of other individuals and forces of nature is what attracts our conscious attention and our heartfelt love-life energy investment to at least temporarily relinquish narcissistic self-awareness and naturally flow outward to other individuals, forces of nature, and activities. The more that we do that, the more the vibratory speed frequency of our love-life energy field presence increases to a higher level of awakening and development, and as that happens, the experience of love-life energy, as joy and beauty grows more and more substantially in the heart.

As we keep relinquishing narcissistic ego-personality self-awareness in deeply invested caring communion with other individuals, activities, and forces of nature in the world, the vibratory speed frequency of our conscious-love-life energy force-field gradually increases, in its radiant loving warmth-light-life energy presence, until it reaches the vibratory speed frequency of fully maturely developed and fully awakened or absolute loving warmth-light-life energy presence. That is when the evolving spiritual spark within the soul or experiential/energetic heart center bursts into a full divine flame, as an intuited self-realization IAM, which is an absolute consciousness, or the full awakening to our absolute, fully maturely developed, love-life energy presence, as the absolute reality nature of our permanent being united to our living becoming individuality abiding in the material world. That is what brings us the conscious experience of the only true and permanent security, incorruptibility, indestructibility, or possibly even immortality of a permanent, totally satisfying, life presence fully awakened in the heart. Because the mind and body, like the radius and circumference of a circle, are always naturally abiding within the subtle energy-heart center of our individuality, they also partake of the heart's immortality, as an indivisible whole individual divine person, because it is the heart that is appearing or manifesting itself in more tangible form as the mind and body, when there is no unnatural divisive sense of otherness or separation between them.

That evolutionary development from mortal human being to fully awakened immortal divine being is the basic purpose or essential telic meaning of life, the fulfillment of the basic objective of the evolutionary process. Our intuition suggests that then there may be ever greater unfolding of our spirit-life energy potentials from there, quantitatively and qualitatively, forever without end, producing progressively greater, more advanced levels of spiritual intelligence powers of functioning, ad infinitum. At some deeply hidden mystery core level of our being, we are not only always inherently being a whole individual divine person, with a natural capacity for full awakening or full development; we are also naturally being every developmental level or evolutionary rung of "Jacob's ladder," metaphorically speaking, but we simply have not yet fully evolved our spiritual intelligence or penetrating brightness of consciousness into it, like a seed that contains the blueprint or prototype for the fully mature plant from the very beginning of its development. This notion that every individual human being, or perhaps every living being, has an intrinsic potential to eventually awaken as a divine being, is epitomized in the Buddhist aphorism: "Every creature is, from the very beginning, a Buddha."[3] For most of us, our spiritual intelligence is not yet bright enough to illuminate the source level or highest rung of Jacob's ladder within the mystery plenitude level of our archetype, where we are already being a divine person (i.e., an immortal, flawless, limitless, totally secure, unobstructed, optimally functional, divine grandeur nature, but not yet consciously awakened to itself and fully developed as actualized potential).

However, once the illusory, dualistic, narcissistic, ego-personality identity self-awareness is totally relinquished and fully transcended, there is no obstruction to full divine person awakening. Perhaps our transformational development continues to unfold from there with limitless, progressively ever higher levels of powers of functioning. Unselfishly caring real relationship is the key to achieving that transcendence of the illusory ego-personality self-preoccupation, and the full awakening of our immortal divine self, because that is what gradually raises the vibratory frequency of our consciousness naturally united to our love-life energy presence, which is our evolving spiritual consciousness of soul.

If we remain fixated in continuous self-awareness of the narcissistic ego-personality, as a false sense of totally separate identity, when the critical period or naturally intended period occurs for maturational or evolutionary development into the individual and collective Era of (fully invested) Communion Relationship, requiring a growing predominance of the centripetal or relatively unifying, connective force over the relatively divisive centrifugal force, then that fixation will inevitably produce gradual regression in powers of functioning for the individual human being and for our collective society. Metaphorically speaking, as epitomized in the nursery rhyme "The Bear Went Over the Mountain," once an individual and the whole society reach the top of the limited hill of the greatest level of functioning that can be achieved while still restricted to narcissistic ego-personality identification and its fixation of continued development of our real love-life energy spirit, then there is nowhere to go but downhill. When that fixation occurs, and is prolonged, then the vibratory frequency of our conscious love-life energy spirit presence of soul gradually begins to diminish, which causes our powers of functioning to regress. If that process of regression continues and gains accelerating momentum for a very long period of time, such as over many lifetimes or many centuries, then there may be a possibility that we, individually and/or collectively, could eventually regress all the way back down to subhuman or pre-human levels of development and functioning, possibly even descending into total unconsciousness, before the beginning of our evolutionary development of consciousness and powers of functioning, like returning to the level of being a mineral prior to evolutionary development into plant, animal, and human form.

The development of advanced technologies could actually accelerate rather than prevent this destructive momentum if those technologies become misdirected in ways that are not sustainable for the natural environment, such as extreme pollution and/or global warfare. Since technology necessarily reflects the conscious and subconscious psyche of its human inventers and users, the human psyche must be psychologically healthy, or consistent with the intrinsically relational, growth-oriented reality nature of life-energy, if the impact of human technology is to be reasonably healthy as well.

That dangerous process of fixation and regression in the development of our conscious love-life energy spirit is metaphorically represented in the Bible by the story of Lot's wife looking back when climbing a mountain, and turning into a pillar of salt and becoming a mineral, symbolizing the total undoing of her past evolutionary development of consciousness of reality and psychological maturation (Genesis 19:24-26). Lot's wife looked back in regret, longing for the pleasures that she had previously enjoyed in her former home city, which was being destroyed. A degenerative, ultimately destructive process of psychological fixation and regression occurs when we "look back" as a fixated attachment to our current or previous level of conscious development, functioning, and gratification, rather than persevering in the long, hard climb of ascension to a higher level of consciousness of reality, and a more psychologically mature level of functioning and gratification. It won't happen immediately or suddenly, but it will inevitably, gradually, insidiously happen sooner or later, because the living or becoming nature of the individual must keep ascending in its progressively greater powers of functioning, symbolized by climbing a very tall or endless mountain, or ascending the rungs of Jacob's ladder. Otherwise, if we become fixated or blocked in the continued development and conscious awakening of our love-life energy spirit, then we must inevitably start descending, declining, or devolving in our evolutionary development, because our evolutionary development cannot be static until full conscious awakening is achieved, but must always be ascending upward or descending downward.

Therefore, engaging in unselfishly caring real relationships, which produce continued upward development or transformational ascension of our conscious love-life energy spirit, is not only the key to our achieving progressively greater levels of evolutionary development, it is also the key to the survival of our whole society, as well as the survival of our individuality. Without it, we automatically begin to gradually regress to less conscious levels of development and functioning, possibly leading to total unconsciousness, total inertia, total loss of powers of functioning, under the usually unrecognized influence of a mostly subconscious kind of individual and collective death wish, functioning as an antithetical perversion or distortion of our love-life energy force. If we permit that process of fixation and regression to continue indefinitely, over successive lifetimes, the possibility exists that we may eventually end up becoming totally unconscious again, as we were prior to the very beginning of our individual and collective evolutionary development. Metaphorically speaking, that would be like being sucked into the intense gravitational suction or vortex of a Black Hole in outer space, from which no light or matter can escape, symbolizing our consciousness being totally absorbed or imprisoned in a continuously self-perpetuating recoiling process of total narcissistic ego-personality self-awareness, resulting in perpetual self-blockage or self-damnation of our spirit because of its inability to naturally shine or flow outward into loving communion or real relationship with other individuals and activities in the world. Just as a Black Hole extinguishes all light, warmth, and expansive flow of energy, prolonged fixation of consciousness recoiled in egoistic self-preoccupation suppresses the natural expansive flow of our energy outward to others, producing an inner "darkness," "coldness," and stagnation tantamount to psychological degeneration and ultimately psychological death, or enduring perhaps permanent suppression of what is truly real and naturally alive in us. If that individual and collective recoil of conscious attention and energy develops into a prolonged, intensely accelerating momentum, it can eventually lead to extreme forms of psychopathology, possibly even insanity, as well as related physical, interpersonal, societal, and ecological disorders.

We cannot continue to develop greater powers of functioning and greater levels of awakening of our love-life energy spirit unless the permanent being center of our individuality, our archetypal mystery plenitude or fullness of being is unobstructed in shining progressively higher levels of spiritual energy-intelligence brightness into our open, receptive, mind-body person, the surface level of our individuality, abiding in the visible world, producing an ever higher vibratory frequency of the IAM, our cumulatively developing conscious love-life energy presence. It is the same basic process for human beings and for pre-human species. The basic difference is that, at a particular stage of psychological and spiritual development, human beings need to develop their individual particularity and multicultural societal diversity by developing a centrifugal sense of extreme individuation and differentiation of their sense of identity, by identifying with the separatist, divisive ego to an extreme degree. If that process produces an accelerating momentum that moves far beyond the optimal, psychologically constructive level of development of individual, societal, and multicultural diversity, then the flow of our conscious attention and energy can become fixated in that extreme narcissistically recoiled momentum. That fixation obstructs the further transformational development of our conscious love-life energy spirit into a more psychologically healthy and mature harmonious balance between the polarizing, diversifying, centrifugal and connective, unifying, centripetal forces of energy. This is an important key to understanding the whole process of maturational development of consciousness of the reality nature of our being, and related evolutionary development of enhanced powers of transformational functioning. Society, human relationships, and individual development function best when there is a natural, dynamic, flexible, harmonious balance between diversity and more connective, cooperative ways of functioning. When both modes of functioning are encouraged, at appropriate times, then individuals and diverse societal groups can learn and benefit from the enhanced development of one another's particular talents, insights, viewpoints, and productive contributions, while having the opportunity to integrate their diverse perspectives into broader, more holistic insights and achievements. Furthermore, society must encourage individuals to value contact with what is experientially real in themselves and others, rather than being overly invested in and enduringly identified with psycho-social masks and limiting, exclusive, presumptive ideas of themselves and others, if the conscious awakening, discovery, and development of what is experientially real and genuinely life-affirming in individual human beings, interpersonal relationships, and society are to be maximized as the fulfillment of the basic purpose and meaning of life.

APPRENDIX F

THE IMPORTANCE OF LIVING WITHOUT PREDETERMINED CONCEPTUAL SELF-DEFINITIONS, AND BEING OPEN TO OUR CORE INTEGRITY, INTUITION, EXPERIENTIAL SPONTANEITY, AND REAL POTENTIALS ACTUALIZATION

At the core of our being, we are not some static, unchanging, conceptual identity or presumptive self-definition, as a mental image or idea, "Who am I?" Rather, we are a non-static, ex-static, or ecstatic, free flowing, life energy force, which is naturally constructive and functions as a sense of inner integrity, intuitively informing us with regard to what feels right and wrong in any given moment. So we must stop conceptually defining ourselves as a static sense of identity or a self-definition, epitomized by the question "Who am I?" Rather, we should be intuitively alert to what is our own life energy force spontaneously seeking to express of itself or unfold as potentials in each moment, and then without choice, or naturally and non-resistively, going with the flow of that creative, spontaneous, life energy force.

If you lose contact with your own life energy force, you become terribly lost and confused, because you have no real inner guide, inner compass, or genuine integrity that you can trust in yourself. Therefore, you can easily choose the wrong career or marry the wrong partner. When we distance ourselves from our own life energy force and its inherent integrity by engaging in insincere ways of functioning, such as prescribed psychosocial roles and images, or "masks," then we lose guidance from our real life energy force, which is a very important source of protection and well-being, in terms of alerting us to potential dangers as well as to opportunities to actualize our real life potentials. When we distance ourselves from our real experiential states and our real love-life energy flow by superimposing presumptive conceptual interpretations of ourselves and others, prescribed ways of functioning, and predetermined psychosocial masks or roles, then we lose contact with the real vitality that is inherent to our life energy flow; therefore, we are apt to become addictively dependent upon various kinds of artificial, intensely stimulating substances to provide us with a substitute sense of inner vitality, euphoria, security, and well-being.

Losing contact with our own spontaneous love-life energy flow and genuine experiential states, we fall off course, become derailed, unhinged, off track with regard to the unfolding of our real mission in life, our real life function and potentials actualization, our true destiny involving the progressively higher or greater potentials that our real life energy function has to actualize and fulfill in this particular lifetime. Therefore, falling off course makes our life, essentially, a waste because we have not actualized our real life energy functions and potentials, or our true destiny. We have fallen off course, and basically wasted our lives in the pursuit of what is artificial and what is not inherently life-affirming and in our overall best interests, but merely providing a temporary more comfortable escape from the reality of our own life energy force and that of other people around us. Therefore, we distort or pervert our real love-life energy force into what is antithetical to its true nature, and then we increasingly grow more destructive with respect to ourselves and others, psychologically and physically, overtly or subtly.

Once you lose the power of discernment by becoming distanced from your own real life energy experience, by superimposing various presumptive self-interpretations, prescribed psychosocial roles or masks, and addictive intense artificial sensations upon it, then you can no longer be aware of your own or others' real heart call, your natural yearnings and inclinations, in contrast to the ego's distorted, perverted, addictive, intensely demanding cravings. Our real heart call is basically urging us to inquire, what is my "gut" core integrity or real energy flow basically telling me that I require for an overall sense of well-being and fulfillment? What is the course of my real destiny, and how do I get back on course, because I have lost such empathic sensitivity to the real life energy force of myself and others. Then I become dominated by the frantic desperation of continuous, addictive self-distraction away from all of my terribly painful inner feelings, which continues until I eventually die. Even before we die, we unconsciously seek death, because we simply cannot tolerate the painfulness of living and what we feel. When we lose contact with what is experientially real in ourselves, and, therefore, lose contact with our own natural integrity and "still small voice of intuition" in the core or "gut" level of our being, then we not only feel alienated from what is experientially real in ourselves and in others, but we also lose a basic sense of inner security and well-being, because we lose touch with a trustworthy inner guide, either the queasy gut feeling or the "right on" gut feeling.

Our core integrity is our true inner guide, inner compass, revealing to us, through a process of heartfelt intuitive discernment, what options feel truly right or wrong for us, based on being consistent or inconsistent with the vibratory frequency of relaxed peace, good-naturedness, sincerity, integrity, harmony, regenerative life energy, loving warmth, or inner purity. Like the children's game of "hot and cold," our core integrity intuitive discernment alerts us when we are "staying on track" or "moving off track" in terms of feeling truly right or wrong at the deepest level of our being. "Hot" represents moving closer to a vibratory frequency of loving warmth and regenerative life energy, whereas "cold" represents moving to a lower, slower, antithetical, vibratory frequency of coldness (cold-heartedness), which is related to energetic "heaviness," fear (fearful anxiety), tension, rage, death, and other forms of negativity. Functioning consistently with our core integrity makes us feel warmhearted and light-hearted, reflecting a higher vibratory frequency of regenerative life energy, relaxed peace, expansive joyfulness, and freedom of unblocked, free flowing regenerative life energy. But violating our core integrity makes us feel coldhearted and heavy-hearted, reflecting a lower, slower, antithetical, vibratory frequency. We accumulate various emotionally heavy egoistic self-embellishments, superimposed upon the "naked" purity of our being in order to manufacture a false sense of "something-ness," as a means of avoiding the ego's opposite sense of presumed inner nothingness, arising from a lack of self-knowledge. The ego, or the antithetical shadow of pure spirit love-life energy, views the undefined mystery pure being that we are inherently being as an inner nothing-ness, because it is not a defined "something-ness."

APPENDIX G

FUNCTIONING CONSISTENTLY WITH THE RELATIONAL NATURE OF REALITY

We are all individualized forms of the same conscious-life energy substance, abiding within the same collective or universal holographic intelligence. Therefore, we are all inherently interrelated, interdependent, different life forms with different potentials, abilities, natural inclinations, and functions with which to serve the whole web or network of life. Therefore, we are meant to become fully conscious of being and functioning as a naturally, intrinsically, interrelated, interdependent, global love family, like a global body of humanity, within which there are interrelated, interdependent, individual cells abiding within organ families, not necessarily blood relations or legally recognized relations, but families of spiritually related souls, sharing naturally closely related, life functions, potentials, interests, and proclivities.

In truth, no one is absolutely independent. We all depend upon each other, at least for relational contact of love, without which, we have no real life energy, no growth of loving warmth, light of truth understanding, and growth of regenerative life energy, no growth of powers of functioning. As physical and psychological adults, we can be relatively more independent than a child is, but we are not absolutely independent or we become like a cancer cell, which breaks off its constructive functioning and relatedness to other cell functions of the same organ function. A cancer cell eventually destroys itself, and because it is related to other cells, it begins to destroy other cells and the whole organ and eventually the whole body and the global divine love family.

There is a collective evil, disruptive, oppositional, willful force, the antithetical shadow of the spiritual reality of love-life energy, which speaks for everything antithetical to the reality of universal love family, anything that seeks to divide us from one another, whether it be religious differences, racial differences, ethnic differences; it all comes from the same unconscious hypnotic suggestive voice for absolute division, absolute duality, absolute otherness, absolute separateness, exclusivity, independence.

It is natural for all of us to feel related to one another and interdependent, sharing naturally related life functions, potentials, and inclinations. Anything that advocates conflict and warfare, be it physical and/or psychological, comes from the antithetical shadow of reality. To presume that divisive, vindictive, malevolent voice to be God is a distortion of reality, a degree of insanity, because the real God is the Heart of Divine Love in which we all inherently abide already, and which gives us a natural inclination to unconditionally love and compassionately, unselfishly, care for one another. We must not listen to any outer voice, or to any inner voice of illusory collective unconscious hypnotic suggestion, that speaks for absolute positive and negative value judgment, which tries to divide us within ourselves, and also between ourselves, as a principle of "divide and conquer." Although the divisive collective unconscious antithetical shadow of reality always tries, often aggressively, to aggrandize itself, it is actually antithetical to all of the qualities of true grandeur experience of the relational reality of love, light, life energy, wholeness, fulfillment, fully blessed total well-being, total goodness, inherent total security, worth, creative energy, peace, harmony, contentment, ecstatic joyfulness, inner beauty, freedom, and so on.

Despite experiencing the illusory collective unconscious hypnotic suggestion of the antithetical shadow of reality, as the presumption that there is something inherently wrong with the nature of our being, the presumption of inherent deficiency, the presumption of lack of inherent wholeness and well-being, as apparent "reality," we have to live or express the conviction of inherent wholeness, intrinsic total well-being already, regardless of all illusory contrary experiences of inner and outer non well-being. Like a mirror, objective life energy and material existence will always reflect back to your subjective consciousness whatever you presume the nature of life to be, inherently flawed and deficient, or inherently wholeness and well-being, because the subjective and objective aspects of reality are indivisibly united within the greater relational wholeness of reality intelligence.

Disregard divisive, presumptive, exclusive, absolute conceptual self-knowledge or self-definition, both positively and negatively value judged. In truth, there is no absolute division between the positively and negatively value judged, or relatively pleasant and unpleasant, natural, constructive aspects of life experience. Both the presence and absence of what you naturally enjoy each have an element of goodness, because you cannot optimally enjoy the presence of any particular good unless it is, at times, absent and balanced by relatively less pleasant aspects of life, such as constructive challenges of various kinds. For example, if you never have the experience of hunger, you cannot enjoy eating. The same principle holds true with regard to temporary abstinence from sexuality, absence of loved ones, and occasional disappointment, which balances and highlights the experience of subsequent gratification and successful achievements. Living consistently with the relational nature of reality involves welcoming or unconditionally accepting all constructive relative polarities of experience and functioning that are part of the greater wholeness of reality or natural living, rather than divisively, exclusively, overly valuing and pursuing relatively pleasant, controlled, aspects of life experience and functioning, and overly devaluing and avoiding relatively uncomfortable, unpredictable, and undesired, but still necessary and natural, aspects of experience and functioning. Sometimes it is vitally necessary to move beyond our current "comfort zone" in order to respond appropriately to adaptive challenges coming from the relational reality of life or being in which we are all naturally, inextricably embedded. This process of attunement to the relational flow of energy, relatively inside and relatively outside, involves openness to any and all options or relative polarities of experience, perception, and functioning, that seem consistent with our core integrity and appropriate in a given moment or situation.

Contrary to the false notion that the spirit is an introversive, introspective nature, in actuality, the spirit is the relational nature of the life energy force, which transcends all selfish, prideful, egoism and introspective self-seeking, regardless of the "lofty" or mundane guises in which it may be packaged. Therefore, there is no true spiritual growth without growth of the co-created spirit of love-life energy through an unselfishly loving or caring relationship in which there is a deep sense of connection of energies to each other in heart, mind, and body, as a deeply bonded sacred "we," a true couple, a deep sense of togetherness, in which the man and the woman, or two or more people in some other kind of genuinely caring relationship, experience a sense of forever belonging with each other, because they come to feel that their love relationship is too precious to ever lose. They have become like two (or more) connected hearts united in a single heartbeat. It is only through that kind of sacred caring relationship that the Source Spirit of Divine Love and Blessing can shine its spiritual presence as a grandeur of loving good-naturedness into our experience, and thereby gradually elevate the couple or the individuals in some other kind of caring relationship beyond all unnecessary suffering in the world. It is their co-created loving warmth, maturely developed in the core of the heart, which functions like a magnet to attract their bodies to each other wherever they may be during each lifetime.

Anyone who takes an introspective approach toward psychotherapy, spiritual or religious practice, and optimal living in the world is expressing a basically selfish, self-absorbed, and cold-hearted orientation, because in introspective practices, there is typically a lack of investment in heart-felt relational contact or empathic communion with another life form in the world. Such solitary self-seeking is clearly psychologically immature, as a form of selfish, narcissistic, egocentric self-absorption. Psychologically and spiritually mature individuals are deeply in love with life in the world, which is optimal contact with reality, and therefore an optimal degree of sanity or psychological health. They are not narcissistically self-absorbed, which is clearly a blockage of optimal contact with and investment in contact with objective reality. Therefore, it is a growing degree of insanity or psychopathology, a growing degree of all kinds of shadow-related negative feelings, instead of the co-created relational spirit of loving warmth-transformational light of true intelligence-regenerative life energy. If you observe institutionalized schizophrenic or psychotic people, you will clearly see that they have lost contact with objective reality, and are screaming in terror because they are being tortured by the insane, destructive, opposite shadow of love or co-created loving warmth. That co-created relational energy arises only from subject-object non-dualistic relational contact or communion with other individuals, as a sacred "we." Pharmaceutical drugs cannot possibly cure such psychologically disturbed, self-preoccupied, individuals. Someone has to love them very deeply with the heart, so that they can have an experience of loving warmth in their heart, which is the most essential level of reality, and provides an optimal experience of emotional security and well-being and an expansive inclination to connect in a genuinely caring or loving way to objective reality in the world. That experienced energy of loving warmth and the related inclination to expansively connect to objective reality in the world are the single most important factors that undo the basic psychopathological process of narcissistic self-absorption, self-recoil into one's own individuality, self-awareness and self-concern.

Introversive practices, be they ostensibly "psychotherapeutic," "spiritual," religious, or overtly hedonistic are usually, if not always, basically forms of selfish, narcissistic, self-awareness. By recoiling our conscious attention and passionate feeling-energy inward upon ourselves, such introversive practices typically inhibit the genuinely therapeutic process of "ex-stasis"[1] in which our conscious attention and passionate feeling energy naturally flow outward in an unselfish, caring way, to empathically contact what another individual life form in the world is experiencing and expressing. Through that deeply invested, unselfishly caring, relational contact, we co-create a relational spirit of loving warmth-light of consciousness-regenerative life energy, gradually growing or maturely developing from spark to full flame, which is the true fulfillment of the basic meaning of life. There is no other way for the divine mystery-essential core-permanent being level of relational reality to know itself, except through the knowable spirit of loving warmth in the core of the heart, gradually co-created and maturely developed through unselfish, self-forgetful, sacred "we" contact with another individual life form in the world.

There is no real spirit life energy presence in any introversive or introspective process of self-absorption, because there is no real love in it, which requires a deeply invested, heartfelt contact or experiential empathic attunement with another life form in the world. If there is no co-created loving warmth in the heart, which no introversive so-called "spiritual" or "psychotherapeutic" process can possibly generate, then there is no genuine experience of the integrated wholeness of subjective and objective reality experience, which is the co-created relational reality of loving warmth. Therefore, without the co-created experience of loving warmth, (which can be developed only by, at least occasionally, letting go of separate, introspective, self-awareness in deeply invested communion with other individuals), there is no true experience of wholeness of being, and there is no true experience of the qualities of reality grandeur, such as genuine happiness, goodness, or good-naturedness, inner beauty, relaxed inner peace, and true wisdom or true insight into the essential nature of reality. Only deeply invested, genuinely caring, heartfelt, responsive, communion with other individuals enables us to be, at least temporarily, forgetful of the narcissistic ego, and thereby elevate our consciousness to an experience of truer, profounder, grander, more substantial levels of reality, beyond the ego's rather superficial, often false, presumptive, distorted range of experience and perception.

There really can be no spiritual "path," because that really is a contradiction in terms. A path is a form of pre-commitment, or a predetermined way of functioning, viewing, and interpreting experience, whereas the spiritual life energy force is continuously, spontaneously, unpredictably free-flowing, and cannot realistically be statically confined within the restrictive parameters of any kind of pre-committed path, system, technique, method, model, recipe, or formula for living. The ego's illusory experience of fearful insecurity, projected into our individuality by the divisive, narcissistic, collective antithetical shadow of the relational reality of love-goodness, demands a guaranteed result or predetermined outcome for its efforts to grow free of uncomfortable or painful experience, mostly produced by that collective malevolent shadow and the individual ego form of it. However, the ego's efforts and the ego itself are basically only shadowy illusion, consisting mostly of positively and negatively value judged self-concepts, presumptions, beliefs, daydream-like in nature. There is no real spirit life energy in it. It is all empty presumption. How can any so-called spiritual path, which is essentially a process of presumption, possibly lead to the transcendence of all presumption, in the mind, and thereby lead to direct contact with the actual flow of life experience, spontaneously arising within ourselves, or in our direct relational contact with another individual living presence, object, or activity in the world from moment to moment?

So there is no real spiritual path. Every so-called spiritual path is just another form of religious philosophy or theology, such as Sufi mystical theology or some kind of Christian philosophy that promises that you will be saved if you love, obey, or believe in Jesus. But there is no actual life energy presence of Jesus for you to contact or love in the here and now moment. One has only a physical image of Jesus or some presumptive, imagined idea of Jesus to contact, but there is no actual spiritual life energy in it. Some people will tell you to "surrender your self-will and individuality to God," but if you do so, your individuality will become absorbed in your presumptive concept of what God is, but again there is no actual life energy presence to contact and love in such a presumptive conceptual idea or image of God. We are simply "loving," enamored, or infatuated with our own self-created fantasy, as a form of conceptually-created idolatry taking place in our own mind.

The real God is mystery love-being, which cannot realistically be conceptually defined, imagined, or conceived, because those are all forms of idolatry, presumption, restricting the limitless divine reality to our own limited, exclusive ideas and expectations. The real God of mystery love does not want you to surrender your individuality. Instead, it wants you to lovingly contact another life form in the world, and thereby co-create the knowable spirit of loving warmth, because mystery love-being cannot truly know itself in any other way. If you try to introspectively love God directly, apart from responsively contacting other embodied individuals in the world, then you are not really relating to God. You are actually relating only to your own imaged presumption, idea, or concept of what you believe God to be or what you presume divine love to be, but you are not actually co-creating divine love or loving warmth as the relational spirit real life energy presence, gradually maturely developing in the core of the heart, by unselfishly contacting, loving, and serving, other individual life forms in the world. As your co-created relational spirit of loving warmth gradually maturely develops from the circumference level of mind and body, to the heart core of your being, it gradually awakens the spiritual power source and grandest level of your being, as spiritual love-goodness, and at the same time it gradually displaces the collective antithetical shadow of negativity that dominates the individual heart, mind, and body until the energy of loving warmth is highly developed in you.

Relying for salvation or fulfillment on something or someone outside of yourself, such as, a purported savior, deity, hero, leader, "magic helper", controlled technique, or belief system (as a presumptive abstraction added onto your undefinable immediacy of being and spontaneously unfolding, unpredictable, momentary experiential truth) are ultimately futile, because no one other than you can provide you with greater psychological and spiritual development by facing the experiential truth of you for you, and by loving others for you. Only you, yourself, can generate your own psychospiritual growth, and the enhanced fulfillment or salvation that it naturally provides, by growing in truth and love (or love for truth) by courageously facing the experiential truth of yourself, following it to its source, unselfishly loving or caring about others and empathically tuning into their experiential truth, and following the self-generated energy of love-goodness to its source, metaphorically like following the yellow brick road to its source in the story, *The Wizard of Oz*. No one else but you can discover, liberate, and awaken the spiritual core of your own energy-being for you, by following the winding road of your moment-to-moment unfolding experiential truth and removing the false coverings that hide it from your conscious awareness. This process of ascending to a higher or greater level of consciousness and actualized development of our real individual and relational being by letting go of illusory false coverings, or "heavy" psychological baggage, is metaphorically represented by the notion in ancient Egyptian mythology that one's soul has to be weighed and found to be lighter than a feather to gain Salvation in the hereafter, and the parable of the *Pearl of Great Price* (Matthew 13:45-46; Gospel of Thomas: sayings 76 and 109), which can be purchased and retained only by parting with all "heavier" possessions. We are metaphorically suggesting that the "lighter than a feather soul" or the "Pearl of Great Price" can be liberated only by letting go of "heavy" unnecessary psychological clutter that "weighs us down," or stifles our real being under the dead weight of superimposed false psychological coverings, such as acquired presumptive ideas about ourselves, or self-definitions, that we have superimposed upon the purity of our permanent being and momentary experiential truth, thereby obscuring it. Thus, we must be our own true Savior or Messiah; "We are the ones we have been waiting for" (Native American adage).

APPENDIX H

THE EGO AS AN ADDICTIVE, PARASITIC "ENERGY VAMPIRE," VERSUS THE HEALTHY, NATURAL YEARNINGS OF OUR REAL BEING

Although the ego is often the loudest voice speaking within us, vociferously arguing for its own viewpoint and vehemently demanding limitless, immediate, sometimes inappropriate, recklessly impulsive, potentially addictive gratification of its insatiable desires and cravings, it is not our most essential, inherent, intrinsic, trustworthy, true inner voice, not our true self, not the source of our true happiness, security, maturity, self-understanding, and overall well-being. The individual selfish ego is strongly influenced by a collective negativity nature, which can sometimes function in a rather delusional, abusive, predatory, addictive, self-defeating, self-conflicted manner. The ego continuously urges us to become addicted to various kinds of intensely demanding cravings, often for unhealthy, unwholesome, substances, attitudes, and habits, as a way of escaping from a deeper, unreal sense of basic deficiency, inner emptiness, and fearful insecurity, which the ego tries to cover over by superimposing a distracting false façade of artificial pleasurable sensations and self-definitions, which can become rather grandiose and unrealistic, sometimes accompanied by destructive demonic energies and rather insane urges in the most extreme forms of selfish egoism. These various forms of ego-gratification are basically designed to provide quasi-substitutes for the natural, genuine euphoria, excitement, vitality, security, well-being, and divine grandeur that are intrinsic to our real being, and only imitated by the various intense sensations, substances, habits, and attitudes that the ego or separate sense of self-awareness urges us to pursue.

It is important to distinguish between "healthy appetites" that are truly natural, life-given urges, and that can actually enhance our overall enjoyment and appreciation of life, in contradistinction to unhealthy, addictive, unnatural appetites, or false cravings that can be detrimental to our overall well-being and functioning, including potentially having serious toxic effects upon our physical health, psychological stability, moral character, personal relationships, professional career, etc. With addictive false cravings, we become "possessed by our possessions," so to speak, so that our heart, mind, and body become burdened with heavy "psychological baggage," and related blocked energy clogging, excessive mental-emotional clutter, or incessant distracting egoistic inner chatter, which can significantly undermine our ability to satisfy our real, natural, life-given needs, as well as impairing our ability to adapt effectively to the challenging requirements of reality. That diminished ability to responsively cope effectively with the adaptive challenging requirements of reality, when our conscious awareness and feeling energy are heavily absorbed in egoistic cravings and related mental-emotional "noise," can adversely impact our level of well-being, security, happiness, genuine freedom of choice, as well as our overall health, vitality, and productive, constructive, functioning of heart, mind, and body.

The only reliable way to distinguish between healthy real appetites or constructive natural urges, in contrast to addictive, toxic, false cravings is to, at least at times, tune out the loudly demanding, argumentative voice of the selfish ego, so that we can intuitively "hear" the "still small voice" of the soul, our true self, our inherent, intrinsic, original nature as a life energy presence, communicating to our conscious awareness from the heart core level of our being, like a soft "inner beacon." Our core integrity guides us away from alluring temptations that would actually be harmful to us and/or others, and leads us to what would be truly compassionately beneficial to ourselves and others, even if it does not seem like the more attractive or comfortable option, at first glance. Goals and aspirations that come from the soul, the real self, are consistent with the actualization of our fullest range of individual and relationship potentials and natural inclinations, whereas goals and desires that come from the selfish ego often tend to lead us astray from the true reality nature of our own being. Our natural yearnings and inclinations are covered over and obscured by the superimposition of false presumptive ideas and beliefs about ourselves, such as the ego's idealized, sometimes unrealistic, unattainable, even grandiose, positively value judged self-images, which the psychologist Sigmund Freud referred to as the ego-ideal or superego.[1] Many of the superego's goals, desires, and values are basically attempting to validate a competitive sense of superiority in comparison with other people, in order to enhance the ego's tenuous, conditional sense of worth and self-esteem, and deny deeper feelings of presumed worthlessness, inferiority, deficiency, and other negative feelings. But the soul, our real self, is an energy of unconditional self-acceptance and intrinsic well-being, beyond all divisive positive and negative value judgments, or conditionally "good" and "bad" self-evaluations. Therefore, the soul has nothing to prove about itself, so it has no need to put itself on trial, or belittle other people, as a way of feeling better about itself. It does not need to defensively try to control and influence what other individuals say and do, in order to protect a fearful, fragile, sense of self, like a tenuous, collapsible, house of cards, or an easily punctured inflated hot air balloon, or engage in various kinds of insincere, manipulative, exploitative ego mind games as a way of denying and compensating for the ego's basic sense of deficiency and insecurity.

Our intrinsic real self is primarily a relational self, a relational center, which can experience its inherent true nature as love, happiness, and limitlessly inexhaustible inner abundance, only by unselfishly sharing that pure nature with other individuals, and by expressing unconditional love or sincere caring to other people, unselfishly serving them to the best of our ability. Contrary to the ego's attempt to generate a greater sense of well-being through various kinds of selfish gratifications, our greatest real hunger or natural yearning is to give deeply and generously of our caring and other energies to others, rather than seeking to gratify basically selfish, hedonistic, egocentric cravings, because the spiritual presence of real life energy, love, happiness, relaxed inner peace, inner and outer wealth or abundance, beauty, and goodness grows more consciously awakened and substantially developed in us only when we unselfishly share it with others. It is a relational nature, not a narcissistically self-absorbed nature. In fact, excessive narcissistic self-absorption blocks and clogs our real life energies, trapping them within the selfish ego, when our energies do not naturally flow outward to other people, as we express unselfish caring to them. That unnatural blockage of love and life energy, trapped within the selfish, self-contained, narcissistic ego, rather than naturally flowing outward to other people, perverts, distorts, or twists our naturally pure, wholesome, regenerative life energy into its opposite nature, so that our energy becomes increasingly toxic, foul, unclean, degenerative, and ultimately self-destructive. In addition, that blocked life energy, recoiled and trapped within the selfish ego, produces negative feelings such as tension, fear, anger, self-confinement, and various other forms of inner and outer negativity. It is only by unselfishly, deeply, caring about others that our energies can be released from narcissistic self-confinement, which makes us feel and be much more alive, joyful, secure, regenerative, creative, and productive than what we could otherwise experience, as a higher overall level of well-being and constructive functioning.

In its most extreme forms, the selfish ego functions like an "energy vampire," sucking ever more of our conscious attention, energy, and passion into itself like quicksand, or like the strong inward pulling suction of a Black Hole in outer space, as a dangerously escalating, addictive, self-perpetuating momentum of inner and outer negativity that can be very difficult to undo. But the maturely developed and consciously awakened unselfishly giving, loving nature of the soul is like an ever shining sun or star, which can never be depleted by endlessly giving of its inexhaustible warmth, light, and energy through the process of perpetual shining. That is why we naturally feel much better, in a genuine rather than artificially contrived way, as we unselfishly express our caring-energy to others, and thereby experience its limitlessly inexhaustible abundance, inner substantiality, joyfulness, and overflowing fullness of being. However, the more that the selfish ego tries to fill itself by functioning like an energy vampire, feeding off of the energy of others, or feeding off of the energy of addictive substances and sensations, the more inwardly empty, deficient, and insubstantial it feels, because trying to incorporate energy, vitality, or any other desired experiential state from outside of our own being reflects a presumptive conviction of limited scarcity, inner deficiency, lack of wholeness, lack of well-being, inertia, or lack of energy. The unselfish spiritual nature of the soul, our real being, is a principle of "united we stand," sharing a cohesive, coherent, relational energy that cannot be easily divided and thereby disintegrated, whereas the selfish ego is a principle of "divide and conquer" or "divided we fall" ever deeper and deeper into self-disintegrating negativity. The more that we identify with and express the unselfishly caring, generously giving nature of our relational true self or soul, the more we move into an ascending spiral of limitlessly inexhaustible abundance, which grows qualitatively as well as quantitatively ever more abundantly replenished as we share it with others, in contrast to the ego's basic fear of being depleted through sharing its energy with others in a genuinely caring, self-forgetful way. But the more that we identify with and express the ego's selfish, greedy, hoarding nature, the more we fall into a related momentum of scarcity and paucity, as a reflection of the vast sense of inner deficiency that the ego's acquisitive orientation is designed to fill, cover over, and disguise.

Whichever nature and motivational intention we express to others becomes increasingly more strongly reinforced in our own inner and outer experience, because we can express to others, and thereby objectify the manifested or knowable experience of only whatever nature we most essentially hold ourselves to be. For example, expressing love and joy, or hate and fear, implies that we are being the source of that energy that we are expressing or sending outward to others. Ego-related thoughts, desires, feelings, and sensations are fleeting, insubstantial, and vacuous, like temporary shadows, or passing vaporous clouds in the sky, whereas the spiritual nature of the soul is everlasting and inwardly substantial, like the sun or stars. Whatever psychological or physical possessions that the selfish ego seeks to acquire in time can be lost in time, whereas whatever true love, caring, and goodness we unselfishly share with others remains with us forever, because it is an objectified expression of our intrinsic permanent being. We can never lose what we inherently *be*, and we can truly give or express only whatever energy that we hold ourselves to be, or which flows from our actual being. Perhaps this principle of finding real life energy and its inherent true happiness only through expressing the unselfishly caring nature of our own relational being, rather than through attempting to add to the ego's deficient-feeling being some kind of conditionally acquired self-seeking gratification, is what is meant by passages in the Bible such as, "For how does it profit a man, if he gains the whole world, but loses his own soul?" (Mark 8:36), and "Whoever drinks the water that I give him will never thirst again. Indeed, the water I give him will become in him a spring of water welling up into eternal life" (John 4:13-14). That is, those who drink deeply from the wellspring of love-goodness by unselfishly, generously sharing their love or caring with others will gradually awaken the source level of their own essential permanent being as that inexhaustible, expansive, inner fountain of love-goodness, thereby experiencing an enduring sense of satisfaction, security, and well-being. Thus, pumping out the "living waters" of relational energy from the deepest core of our own being by unselfishly, generously sharing our caring energy with others will enduringly quench the ego's basic sense of deficiency or its metaphorical "hungers" and "thirsts" and compensatory, often insatiable, addictive, unhealthy, selfish cravings, as a futile attempt to assuage that underlying sense of deficiency. Although it seems counterintuitive, at first glance, the only way to truly, deeply, and enduringly fill or assuage the ego's sense of deficiency, inner emptiness, or lack of substantiality, is by unselfishly giving generously of your caring energies to others, rather than selfishly seeking to gratify yourself or have others gratify you in some way, because unselfish giving reflects the conviction and reinforces the experience of inner fullness of being, whereas intensely demanding selfish cravings reflect and reinforce the experiential conviction of inner deficiency or lack of intrinsic wholeness and well-being already.

Our natural real passions, yearnings, appetites, inclinations, avocations, and potentials actualization are pursued and enjoyed for their own sakes rather than used as a means of covering over, escaping, or compensating for the ego's basic sense of deficiency or non-well-being, as the ego's cravings are designed to provide. We can recognize the ego's unhealthy cravings by the (not necessarily fully conscious) feelings of tension, agitation, or frantic desperation that are often associated with them, reflecting the ego's fear that its deeper feelings of deficiency, inner emptiness, insubstantiality, insecurity, and unhappiness may be exposed if the more positive, gratifying, controlled, experiential states and self-definitions that it pursues are ever interrupted or insufficiently gratified, whereas our natural healthy yearnings or aspirations can be clearly recognized by the spontaneous, uncontrived feelings of relaxed peace, joy, beauty, and unconditional acceptance associated with them. The ego often tries to enhance its fragile, tenuous sense of worth, security, substantiality, vitality, and well-being through what it seeks, whereas our real being, the soul, has no need to prove anything about itself, because it is an intrinsic wholeness, serenity, well-being, and unconditional self-acceptance, so what it values, wills, and pursues is a natural expression of the energy, passion, self-discovery, or "calling" (energy feeling tone heart-call) of its inherent being.

APPENDIX I

PSYCHOLOGICAL MATURITY
AND IMMATURITY

We are defining psychological growth toward greater psychological maturity as essentially involving outgrowing identification with basically unreal, non-constructive patterns of self-perception and functioning, and growing in the ability to consciously experience and incorporate into our functioning more authentic, constructive values that are intrinsic to our real being. If you are psychologically immature, then you do not really know yourself, what is truly real for you, your own natural inclinations, abilities, talents, skills, interests, values, what you are naturally and deeply passionate about in terms of your basic nature, or what you want to accomplish with your life. When we are psychologically immature, we do not have a realistic, constructive vision for what goals are most important for us to achieve in life, what is optimal fulfillment for us, related to understanding our basic sense of mission, our destiny, what we can accomplish with our natural inclinations, potentials, and abilities. Many of us do not know what is truly real for us, as the distinctive, rather unique, particular individual that we each are intrinsically being, because we are often influenced by others to put away what is natural or real for us, such as our inherent real life potentials, that we are naturally inclined to fulfill as a way of reaching a higher level of functioning. We need to ask ourselves and try to deeply understand, what are the inner and outer influences upon us that take our conscious awareness away from what is natural to us, inherent to our real being? Our real life energy cannot actualize its real life potentials into our conscious awareness, the surface part of our life energy force, if we reject certain temporary feelings that are comprised of or part of our of life energy force, as various forms of it. As long as we remain in duality from rejected feelings, the energy invested in them remains trapped, blocked from flowing into our conscious awareness, preventing us from becoming more conscious of many of our real talents, abilities, interests, and natural inclinations that are intrinsic to our pure, unmodified, undivided, life energy nature.

We need to consider why our parents and other influential people in our life do not let us be and express what we are naturally inclined to be, so that we can actualize those potentials and increasingly develop them. For example, if your parents do not recognize your natural athletic ability, musical talent, or mechanical ability, or if your parents have a strong investment in something else that they presume or believe that you should develop into, but which is not actually consistent with your own natural interests and inclinations, then you are in no position to recognize your real natural inclinations, abilities, talents, skills, interests, values, intrinsic passions, and natural goals in life. In order to help you psychologically grow or mature, we want to help you understand whether your parents or society have molded you into conformity with some prescribed role or presumed ideal, or whether these things are actually true and natural for you. Many parents want to live vicariously through their children. For example, a mother is a nurse, and she wants her daughter to become a physician, which she always wanted to be, but could not achieve that goal. The fact that the daughter may be a naturally gifted creative artist or musician is ignored and rejected by the mother, because the mother wants her own dreams for herself vicariously fulfilled through her daughter. Many fathers do the same with their sons; for example, they want them to grow up to be famous athletes. But when the parents stifle what is natural and real in the child that becomes a form of psychological destruction of the child, because those talents are natural or inherent to the life energy force of the child. Therefore, when you stifle the life energy, you make it unconsciously life-degenerative, unconsciously self-destructive, death-oriented. Then your body develops pain, illness, disease, some kind of pathology.

Why don't our parents just let us be, so that we can express and thereby develop our own natural abilities and inclinations? In some cases, our parents want to vicariously live through us, by steering us into a particular career or urging us to fulfill other dreams or goals that they were not able to achieve in their own life, so that they can vicariously identify with us and experience the gratification of those aspirations through us. Those kinds of parents want us to be a reflection of them. If they are or wish to be intelligent, financially successful, socially or athletically successful, but are not able to achieve those goals in their own life, they think that it will reflect well on them if we achieve it, viewing us as a kind of extension of themselves, because we are their offspring. Psychologically immature people do not feel free to be, experience, and express what is spontaneously real for themselves, whereas psychologically mature people can do this.

We are a partly unconscious life energy force, with a multitude of different natural potentials, inclinations, abilities, and feelings that naturally want to make themselves known by unfolding themselves into our conscious awareness. But if we reject some of the temporary painful feelings that are comprised of our indivisible whole life energy substance, then our energy cannot unfold into our consciousness what is natural and real for us and thereby reveal what is inherent to our being. If you reject painful feelings and experiences, then you reject the life energy force in it, and then it cannot express itself spontaneously and freely and make itself known to your conscious awareness. If we reject some of the painful feelings that come into our conscious awareness, then we lose our natural inherent wholeness of being. We fragment it, divide it, split it. When that split becomes severe, then it becomes a process of psychopathology, such as milder forms of neurosis, as well as more extreme and intense kinds of schizophrenia, psychosis, or insanity.

It is important to understand that wholeness is not something that we have to become, or conditionally achieve; instead, wholeness is what we already inherently are being. However, if we impose positive and negative value judgments upon our indivisible wholeness of life energy, which includes all of its temporary feelings and other experiential states, then we reject some of those temporary feelings from remaining in our conscious awareness, and push them into the subconscious or subliminal level of our psyche, as if pretending that those painful feelings no longer exist once we have pushed them out of our conscious awareness. Then we are self-divided, self-fragmented, self-split, self-disintegrated, self-conflicted, which makes us dangerously life-degenerative. Rejecting or avoiding the conscious experience of painful or uncomfortable feelings causes all kinds of additional, often greater psychological and physical pain and illness, arising from inner self-conflict between our actual feelings and what we presume are better feelings or more positive experiential states that we "should be" experiencing. Of course, that kind of impaired functioning caused by psychological self-conflict can also cause social maladjustment, and adversely affect your financial well-being.

Parents, family, friends, and society tell us what they think we should be if we are to be conditionally accepted by them, rather than unconditionally accepted, which is part of what real love necessarily involves. Very few children are really loved deeply, or experience a deep and enduring sense of connection with their parents or significant others, so they feel psychologically and physically insecure, not just fearful of physical abandonment, but also fearful of psychological abandonment, when the parent negatively value judges, rejects, and abandons some aspect of the child's being. A sense of worth also brings a sense of security and well-being. The parents and others have positive self-concepts, so that they can feel good about themselves, and expect their children to live up to similar conceptually defined ideals; otherwise, the parents experience a threat to their sense of worth in having a child who seems to reflect poorly on them and overtly or subtly blame the child for that, which correspondingly reduces the child's sense of worth and security.

When there is unconditional acceptance in a relationship, which is the basis of real love, then there is enduring commitment in the relationship, "for better or for worse," so to speak. We do not value judge ourselves and our partner as good or bad. We unconditionally accept one another as a whole person, an indivisible whole "package" so to speak. However, if there are things about the other person's functioning that seem non-constructive or inappropriate to us, then we can respectfully talk about that as a way of helping them to better understand and thereby outgrow those inappropriate patterns of functioning, without rejecting or passing judgment on any aspect of the person's indivisible whole being and spontaneous, natural, psychologically healthy, appropriate manner of functioning. So, unconditional acceptance of the other individual's whole real being does not necessarily involve accepting or condoning their bad attitudes and behaviors. Those kinds of non-constructive tendencies may not necessarily reflect their intrinsic real being and natural, spontaneous manner of functioning, but may instead arise from psychologically immature needs and perceptions that may not be inherent to their being. Therefore, such inappropriate or non-constructive ways of functioning can and should be outgrown as a way of developing more psychologically mature and constructive levels of functioning and self-understanding that will be more truly authentic and fulfilling than were the old, psychologically immature, self-defeating patterns.

Psychological growth is naturally moving toward greater maturity, which involves expanding our consciousness into broader, deeper, or higher aspects of our being or of our life energy experience that were not previously recognized and harmoniously integrated into our natural wholeness of being. Thus, psychological growth necessarily involves developing the ability to unconditionally accept and fully unify our conscious awareness and heartfelt feeling energy with whatever experience is actually arising, here and now, without some kind of presumptive conceptual interpretation, positive and negative value judgment of it, or escapist distraction from it, such as narcotic intoxication or continuous hedonistic thrill seeking. Instead, we directly and fully experience the actual reality presence, here and now, inside and outside. Full contact with actual reality life presence gives us a greater consciousness of that life presence or experiential reality.

Greater psychological maturity frees us from the influence of the collective unconscious mechanical instinctual way of functioning like everyone else within the same species or social group, like a collective "herd instinct," and enables us to become more consciously individuated and differentiated, as individual human beings, so that we become fully sovereign from this collective unconscious, mechanical self-perpetuating instinct. As we develop greater self-understanding and become less identified with collective psychosocial conditioning, we develop greater levels of self-directed freedom, self-actualization of our fullest range of natural life energy potentials, self-responsibility, and genuine ethical responsibility toward others, which constitutes greater psychological maturity.

Full openness (or "radical openness") to all kinds of spontaneously arising experiences and feelings, without value judgment or conditional approval or disapproval of those feelings, can be described as "innocence" awareness of ourselves and of others. Unconditionally accepting whatever spontaneous experience arises to our heart, mind, and body-senses produces greater self-contact, self-understanding, and self-love, as an indivisible wholeness of being, because we are not rejecting any experience that our life energy force is spontaneously providing for us each moment, as a particular life energy feeling, thought, sensation, or activity. Life energy comprises and animates it all, in the heart, mind, and body. Therefore, at the central core of every heart, mind, body experience, by our growing consciousness, is a permanent, indestructible, pure life energy force, which cannot be created or destroyed. That greater self-contact, self-unification, self-integration, self-understanding, self-love, and indivisible wholeness of being, is psychological health, which is also the basis of optimal happiness and harmony in all aspects of one's life.

Psychological immaturity fixation and related forms of psychopathological inner conflict essentially involve being stuck at some particular stage of psychological development. The psychologist Erik Erikson suggested that some individuals become enduringly stuck at particular, relatively immature levels of psychological and social development as a consequence of failing to effectively adjust to certain adaptive challenges, and/or as the result of experiencing emotional traumas, especially early in life, which produce a basic enduring sense of insecurity.[1]

Our own view is that psychological fixation is essentially produced through the rejection of some temporary feeling or other experiential state, as an object of knowledge of our life energy force that is pushed into the subconscious. That rejection of some particular forms of our unitary whole life energy makes us experience an illusory sense of un-wholeness, fragmentation, self-division. That is what the term "schizophrenia" means, a severe degree of psychological self-splitting, which occurs when we have rejected so much of our wholeness that we lose psychological maturity, self-unification, self-integration, well-being, as a natural creativity and free-flowing spontaneity of our life energy force, which becomes blocked and static, like death. This blockage of our energy contained in rejected feelings and related inner conflicts produces a dreadful extreme tension, and that unconscious tension produces feelings of rage, destructiveness, and attack directed toward ourselves and others, in order to try to drain the unnatural tension. The attack, the aggression, directed toward ourselves and others, reflects psychological immaturity, pathological fixation of psychological growth toward full psychological maturity or adulthood.

Sigmund Freud wrote about oral, anal, and phallic fixations of the life energy force, which Freud referred to as the libido.[2, 3] We authors maintain that, in a broader sense, psychologically unhealthy fixation, blockage, degenerative distortion, and regression of our consciousness and life energy occurs when we become overly attached to, or overly averse to, any particular kind of feeling or experience. Being overly pre-committed for or against any particular kind of predetermined experience or feeling keeps our consciousness enduringly "stuck" or fixated at that level of functioning, preventing our conscious-life energy from continuing its transformational development, or gaining greater insight into the actual experiential truth of ourselves, others, and the whole of reality, as well as responding appropriately to adaptive challenges beyond our current "comfort zone."

Psychologically immature individuals remain fixated, like children, which diminishes their ability and willingness to face uncomfortable growth-oriented, life-affirming risks and challenges. They have little or no tolerance of fear, pain, frustration or stress. They cannot study for examinations, for example. They have to get "high" first. They have little or no ambiguity tolerance or confusion tolerance. To feel secure, they give themselves rigid, presumptive, premature answers to questions about life that they cannot answer in a realistic way through direct experiential insight.

The life energy force, being mostly unconscious, is a great mystery unto itself. It does not consciously know where it is going, what it is doing, and why it is doing it. It just mechanically, instinctively does it. Once you repress the life energy force from conscious awareness, by rejecting many of its temporary negative feelings, thoughts, and sensations, what happens when you do not have your life energy force readily available to your conscious awareness, as an intuited sense of integrity coming from the core level of your being or energy-field? Then you feel inwardly dead, and when you feel dead, which is the same as feeling bored or empty of life energy, you try to fill yourself with an illusory sense of life energy presence arousal. We instinctively, usually subconsciously, use anger to feel alive, or seek a sense of vitality through horror shows, thrills, some kind of intense excitement, some kind of artificially contrived euphoric, sensation, or controlled "high," something that is not inherent to the reality nature of our being, but comes from outside of ourselves, a virtual reality stimulation or artificial tranquillizer, which we are likely to turn to if we feel too tense, fearful, or agitated, and look to escape from the reality of our repressed unconscious feelings, thoughts, and sensations.

We also want to point out the disturbed consequences of this kind of psychologically immature blockage and fixation of our energies, in terms of unhealthy deterioration of our emotional, mental, physical, interpersonal, financial or economic, and societal situations. It is important to carefully explore all of these interrelated issues of impaired functioning together, as an indivisible whole psychological process of understanding and thereby undoing psychological fixation. By doing so, you can consciously see for yourself what is happening within you and to others around you, and thereby have the freedom to change it, if you wish to do so. At least then you will have the conscious option should you wish to do so, to deeply explore, understand, and thereby attempt to resolve the often subconscious underlying psychological basis of various kinds of personal, interpersonal, and societal disorders, which you do not have if you are driven by unconscious, unrecognized habitual impulses, functioning automatically.

Almost everyone in contemporary society is addicted to something, escaping from feelings of insecurity, threats to their sense of worth, adequacy, and will power. People are willing to endanger their physical health and survival in order to escape from feelings of insecurity, and other uncomfortable, seemingly intolerable, negative feelings, through various kinds of unwholesome addictive substances and artificially contrived intense sensations. For example, many people smoke cigarettes, even though everyone knows that they have the capacity to shorten their lifespan and produce illness. Similarly, alcohol destroys brain and liver cells, as well as undermining our ability to earn a living and maintain caring, constructive, relationships with our family. It gives us an altered state of consciousness, a pseudo high, a false sense of security, euphoria, vitality, and well-being, but it also dulls or desensitizes our conscious acuity, thereby undermining our ability to attend effectively to the needs of our family, our job responsibilities, and other realistic adaptive challenges. We become selfishly narcissistic, which is part of psychological immaturity. We care only about our next high, in order to escape from the experienced low, arising from our life energy being blocked, and therefore not available to be consciously experienced. That blocked life energy also produces intense levels of tension, which in turn can produce explosive expressions of anger in an attempt to drain the tension.

When you are psychologically immature and absorbed in addictive artificial substances, you become narcissistically self-preoccupied. You cease to care about contributing to the well-being of those around you, which is much more unselfish, psychologically mature, and ethically responsible, as an expression of empathic sensitivity. You become readily addicted to artificial substances and intense sensations that provide a false sense of life energy arousal, which is not real life energy experience.

Besides dangerous addictive substances such as, alcohol, cigarettes, and hallucinogenic drugs, other mechanisms that provide an artificial, pseudo, sense of excitement, vitality, or life energy arousal, euphoria, security, and well-being include listening to loud music, riding in fast vehicles, and watching horror shows. Many people, such as university or college students, feel so inwardly dead or lacking in natural vitality that they can hardly go from class to class without some kind of radio headset continuously pumping music to drown out negative thoughts, feelings, and sensations. There is nothing wrong with any of that, per se, but when it becomes a symbol of life, and becomes overly indulged, then it becomes addicting. If you are not addicted to it, then you can enjoy it, on occasion, as an expression of celebration. Sweet or sugary foods and drinks give you an artificial high, to cover over the dreadful low of repressed and depressed life energy feelings, which are low, fearful, painful, and blocked. Of course, we do not know it, but what we are really looking for is the release and return of our real life energy force, spontaneously free flowing again, which is a natural ecstatic joyfulness, a natural high.

Some natural genuine sources of feeling "high" or real elation include true love, actualizing real potentials, as well as learning about the experiential truth of ourselves, and being transformed by it. Some people in some countries feel so unhappy, so bored, so inwardly dead, so much without material comforts with nothing to live for, that they even start wars, terrorism, violent abuse of all kinds of people, in order to feel alive, powerful, and, therefore, secure, so that they do not feel weak, helpless, or insecure, like a child.

Such artificial, addictive forms of elation tend to inevitably produce a point of diminishing returns on our psychological investment, because the experience of intense excitement, elation, vitality, and security becomes progressively diminished, shallower, and less satisfying, as we adapt to a particular level of intensity of sensationalist thrill-seeking, as an ever decreasing duration of "high" euphoria. The "lows," succeeding phases of inner deadening and corresponding psychological depression, become increasingly more magnified as each sensationalist ingestion or "fix" wears off. This increasing experience of lows, hangovers, or emotional and energetic depression that succeeds brief periods of elation following the ingestion of artificial intoxicants and sensationalist thrill-seeking of various kinds occurs because no artificial sensation that mimics life energy can truly replace real life energy. Instead, it increasingly covers over our life energy, making it unavailable to be consciously experienced, resulting in inner deadness, emptiness, and psychological depression. We experience an ever-increasing sense of frantic desperation to obtain our next sensationalist or intoxicating "fix" to cover over and avoid the experience of inner deadening or psychological numbing of blocked life energy that is constantly shadowing us, like an invisible psychological predator, ready to pounce and "devour" our consciousness and remaining life energy at any time. That growing sense of frantic desperation to repeatedly reestablish and prolong an ever-diminishing sense of artificial euphoria, and cover over an ever-growing succeeding experience of deflation and numbing of our energy, makes every aspect of our life in the world a veritable hell, psychologically speaking.

Your life is basically a waste if you are not growing in terms of actualizing your real life potentials, thereby developing greater powers of functioning, psychologically, as well as vocationally, creatively, socially, and spiritually. As you actualize real life energy potentials, it translates into greater powers of functioning, which produces an enhancement of your creative intelligence and of the vibrancy or vibratory frequency of your energy field. Intelligent, psychologically mature people are more conscious, aware, awake, alert, vibrant or truly and fully alive, more empathic, sensitive, intuitive, creative, and spontaneous. They do not function dominated by mechanical herd instinct, like a child, because most young children behave basically in the same manner, as do many nonhuman species. It is difficult to see much that is unique in any particular young child. It is only when we mature that our particular unique qualities are discovered, and grow more substantial, as we discover our natural potentials, our natural inclinations that are unique to ourselves, our own special particular talents, abilities, skills, aptitudes, capacities, interests, values, passions, life objectives, or ambitions. We have our own realistic dreams to fulfill, of what we realistically know that we can become. Because we are already being it, we need to actualize its potential, or become it, in accordance with the vision, mission, and sense of destiny that we have, what we, particularly, are meant to do with our lives, that gives our lives a sense of fulfillment so that we do not fear death at the end. We feel that we have lived fully. Growing more conscious of the experiential truth of ourselves and actualizing our real potentials has given our life meaning. As Norman Cousins once wrote: *"Death is not the greatest loss in life. The greatest loss is what dies inside us while we live."*[4]

Males often have a more difficult time than females do in accepting their real feelings and emotions, often because openness to experiencing and expressing feelings is presumed to be feminine, not masculine, reflecting inner weakness of character, lack of strength, will power, control, security, worth. Masculinity is often equated with power of self-control, whereas being emotional, even if it involves openness to experiencing and expressing real feelings, is presumed to reflect lack of power or lack of self-control. Many people do not know how to distinguish males from females, psychologically speaking, except in terms of giving in to feelings. Most females are believed to give in to feelings of fearfulness, sorrow, tears, love, joy, much more easily. Many males have difficulty expressing love to their partners, not only an inability to express loving feelings, but even loving words, loving actions, signs of caring, such as remembering someone's birthday or other significant occasions. When males lose control over feelings, quite often it results in violence, destructiveness, extreme temper, because feelings are comprised of life energy, and you can only contain those feelings so long, because the life energy must live and express itself.

We encourage readers to deeply reflect on the following question: Are males and females truly intrinsically different in these various psychological ways, or do these perceived gender differences arise because society has conditioned some kind of conformity to a cultural role or ideal of what it presumes masculinity and femininity to be? We are asking:

are those differences really inherent to the biological and psychological composition of males and females? Are males more inherently introverted and females more extraverted? Are males inherently more intellectual and females more naturally emotional? Are males more naturally creative than females, as many have proposed, or are females more creative than males, because they create children, so to speak, and are more open to the creative process, and males more naturally enjoy mechanical things?

If you do not let your painful, uncomfortable feelings express themselves openly and directly, they will express themselves indirectly, inappropriately. If you do not express to your partner how much he/she has hurt you and how much you want to hurt him/her in return, if you cannot express why you feel that way, verbally, in a constructive manner, so that it can drain out, then you may impulsively express that angry, hurt feeling as physical violence or as psychological abuse, trying to make the other person feel inadequate or worthless, perhaps by having a sexual affair and making sure that your partner finds out about it. Because you feel hurt, but have not openly, directly, constructively expressed that feeling, it festers and builds up. Whenever you block life energy from expressing itself, it produces tension, and when tension builds up, it produces explosiveness, which some people try to drain out by intense rage or through other distracting substitute means (rather than by actually consciously facing and thereby draining out or resolving the painful feeling). Some of these methods include continuous sexual orgasm, alcohol, cigarettes, or other artificial, addictive substances, that function as relaxants, or tranquillizers. When feelings are blocked from being experienced and constructively expressed, then your life energy becomes pressed down, or depressed, so you feel bored, inwardly dead, empty, and meaningless.

Now we will discuss and try to explain the feeling of guilt as a factor that can contribute to alienation from what is psychologically or energetically real and alive in us and others. Quite often, if you incorporate the ideals of other people, such as what it means to be a good child, a good student, a good person, a good citizen, a good member of the church, a godly person, and you do not live up to that ideal, then you feel guilty, and what is guilt but a mental self-punishment, mental self-abuse? This is the feeling, "I can't stand myself; I can't tolerate myself." We sometimes want to do harmful, abusive, or even destructive things to ourselves in order to expiate or undo our sense of guilt, which we often psychologically internalize or incorporate from how others view us and define what it means to be a "good" or "moral" person, as the criteria of social approval or disapproval by which others measure us, and by which we measure or value judge ourselves, positively and/or negatively. We think that if we make ourselves suffer, in some way, then we can forgive ourselves and be forgiven for not fulfilling this ideal expectation. The feeling of guilt wipes out our sense of worth. We have a natural conscience, our core integrity, which intuitively tells us what is right, in contrast to what is wrong, in terms of injuring others or depriving others in some way. Maslow describes "intrinsic guilt" as a psychologically healthy, appropriate, existential guilt that alerts us when we are betraying or violating what is truly real and genuinely good in ourselves.[5] However, the feeling of guilt often has much more to do with not fulfilling some presumed ideal of perfection, some ideal of absolute worth, absolute adequacy, intelligence, power, or goodness. Such ideals may come from our own expectations of ourselves, and/or from internalizing the expectations of parents, other individuals, society as a whole, or what we presume to be pleasing to God, and therefore constituting a basis of salvation and enduring security. Freud referred to this socially and culturally based, but often internalized and partly individually self-selected mechanism of self-evaluation or self-approval and self-condemnation, as the superego.[6]

If your ability to love is immature, then your sexuality becomes immature, distorted, seeking to gratify psychological needs that were ungratified earlier in life. Therefore, quite often, in psychologically immature people, sexuality with a partner involves fantasy, not really contacting the partner as they really are, but engaging in some kind of fantasy of ideal psychological and/or sexual egocentric need gratification, such as some kind of Freudian oral, anal, or genital gratification. There may be nothing wrong with seeking sexual gratification, as long as it is not influenced by fantasies that urge you to pursue exploitative forms of sexual gratification that prevent you from achieving orgasmic full union with your partner, sexually, emotionally, and energetically. We often live a kind of fantasy or imaginary "personal life story daydream," not just in terms of sexuality, but also in many other aspects of our life. Quite often, fantasies continue almost all day long, often coming from the repressed unconscious. We fantasize about what would be gratifying, quite often perverse or unwholesome, and disruptive of our ability to invest deeply in contact with outer reality and our real inner experiential states.

Developmental growth toward maturity is natural, but it can be enhanced by openness to whatever repressed, painful, uncomfortable feeling wants to spontaneously arise to consciousness, which enables the life energy invested in it to drain out, if your conscious awareness does not run away from it, because the feeling is not permanent, it is only a temporary form of your life energy expression, like waves, bubbles, ripples, foam, ice are all just different forms of ocean water substance. The forms are temporary, but the ocean water substance is permanent. That is why physics teaches us that energy can neither be created nor destroyed. It simply is. And there is no good or bad to it. All feelings and experiences are forms of life energy. You can't have "good" life energy and "bad" life energy. Therefore, you can't have "good" and "bad" temporary feelings. Some temporary feelings may be very painful, but if your consciousness unites with it, then the negative or painful thought or message of the feeling, united to the unconscious life energy of the feeling, says what it has to say, and thereby drains out into your conscious awareness, which permanently undoes the feeling by reducing it to pure conscious awareness and pure life energy, its underlying substance or substratum.

We are being real, genuine, authentic, if we do not make any positive and negative value judgments or evaluations of ourselves and our feelings, in terms of conditional approval or disapproval. You cannot have just positive self-evaluations without negative self-evaluations because they are on the same continuum, or like two opposite sides of the same indivisible whole coin. Therefore, if you have positive value judgments of yourself and others, then you will inevitably have a capacity to negatively judge yourself and others, if you or they fail to validate whatever ideal standard or expectation the positive evaluations are based on. When you are being truly real, genuine, authentic, then you are open to consciously feeling, and, if appropriate, constructively expressing what is actually real for you in the moment. That is how we express and more fully develop sincerity and integrity. The energy in feelings that are permitted to be consciously experienced and constructively expressed is not blocked and drains out. When our energy in feelings is no longer blocked, then there is no tension, no rage. Then you experience spontaneously free flowing, ecstatic, joyful, life energy, as a natural high, when you are whole by not rejecting any part of yourself, in the form of temporary feelings or experiences, which are forms of your own conscious life energy, your own being. In the unconditional acceptance of yourself, as an indivisible wholeness, which cannot realistically be divided into positive and negative value judgments, that wholeness is real self-love, which enables us to truly love or care about others, as the "charity that begins at home, where the heart is."

That indivisible wholeness is psychological health, natural happiness and harmony, which are unconditionally inherent to your being, not something that you have to become or achieve. It is pathology that you seem to become, by negatively value judging, rejecting, and blocking a particular experiential state that is part of your indivisible wholeness, because it is inconsistent with some kind of presumptive ideal or expectation that you set up before you will conditionally approve of yourself, or judge yourself favorably. Health or wholeness is not something that we have to become or conditionally achieve because that is natural, inherent to our being. We just need to undo the process of pathology, as a process of inner conflict produced by not unconditionally accepting or letting be all of our experiential states and all aspects of our natural, constructive, spontaneous, life-affirming, functioning. Our intrinsic wholeness is a naturally spontaneous, free flowing life energy, which is experienced as a non-static flowing joyfulness, a natural real life energy high, a natural, genuine euphoria, an optimal experience of genuine security and well-being, making it unnecessary to become addicted to an artificial high, a false high. This psychological wholeness is not only the basis of optimal psychological and physical health, but it is also the basis of the natural psychological healing process.

You have to be open to all temporarily arising experienced forms of your life energy force, which means that you have to be open to your real feelings, not only currently, but also what has been previously rejected and repressed into your unconscious from your past experiences, some from early childhood. Those painful feelings that have been rejected do not just go away with time, because painful feelings are forms of life energy, and because life energy cannot be destroyed, the painful feelings cannot be destroyed, although they can be submerged below your conscious awareness.

What is most important is for children to be loved, because if children do not feel loved, then they presume that their inherent being is not lovable, not worthy to be loved, so they reject their own being. Young children presume that their parents are omniscient, all-knowing. If our parents treat us as unlovable, unworthy when we are children, then we presume that we must be that way, and so we reject our own being, and we struggle with feelings of worthlessness and inadequacy. So many men and women are afraid to enter into real love relationships, because they still unconsciously believe that they are unlovable. They expect that, sooner or later, their partner will see something that is worthless or not good in them, and therefore will stop loving them. They still love their partner, so to lose the partner that they love is very painful to them, threatening to overwhelm them with emotional pain, so to avoid the risk of experiencing painful rejection and disappointment in actual or potential relationships they make only relatively superficial contact with the other person. Therefore, they never experience the great grandeur of loving warmth, which comes only from a real and deep love relationship. The life energy essence, as loving warmth, is very regenerative and produces psychological growth. They may get involved in a superficial kind of love relationship, something sexual, some kind of companionship or friendship, sharing some activities together, such as being traveling companions, playing tennis together, having sex together, but it is mostly rather superficial contact. Those shared activities are engaged in only with the mind and body, but the heart remains un-invested with intense life energy feeling because that is what can produce the experience of pain, and most children and psychologically immature individuals presume that feelings can be permanent. Therefore, you assume that if you become conscious of painful feelings, they will always be in your consciousness, so they will always be painful and overwhelming.

However, feelings, like waves in the ocean, are only temporary forms of life energy substance. Therefore, if you let them flow freely and spontaneously into your consciousness, by not judging them, rejecting them, censoring them, or trying to control them in any way, they will play themselves out in your conscious awareness, and thereby fully drain out. Then you are more whole, less fragmented, less self-divided, which is more psychologically healthy, more psychologically healed.

This is the essence of the psychological healing process, which we have discussed in greater depth and detail earlier in this book. This process of unconditional self-acceptance of all of our spontaneously arising real feelings and experiential states is real self-love. It is like being married to yourself, for better or for worse, metaphorically speaking, with your conscious awareness "wedded" to or indivisibly united with your spontaneously arising pleasurable feelings or painful feelings, as well as with the life energy force within those feelings, in the heart core. Therefore, if you truly love yourself, which is not a positive value judgment of yourself, as conditional self-approval or self-aggrandizement, but unconditional self-acceptance, without value judgment of yourself, then you are being consciously united with your own natural ecstatic, spontaneous, free flowing life energy force, and you are being real loving warmth, with genuine compassion for yourself in the heart core. That is why love and joy go together, and if you have love in your heart, instead of fear, tension, or anger, then you also have love in your heart to love others with. If you do not have any love, joy, security, well-being in your own heart, but only fear, tension and rage in your heart, then how will you feel love for anyone else? So even if your partner, family, and friends have real love in their heart for you, you will not be able to feel it, because all that you can feel is your own fear, tension, anger, hatred, and unhappiness in your own heart. Your conscious awareness can only be aware of one thing at a time. That is why we must love, or fully accept and make full conscious contact with, what is experientially real in us before we can truly love or make contact with the genuine being and experience of others, in the same way.

The most important thing in terms of achieving optimal psychological health, well-being, and constructive functioning is openness to the actual experiential truth of yourself, which requires no commitment to what you presume that you "should be," and therefore no positive and negative value judgment of yourself, because you believe that you are succeeding or failing in the achievement of that conceptual ideal. As Shakespeare says, in *Hamlet*, "To thine own self be true, or you cannot be true to anyone else" (Act 1, Scene 3, 78-81). If you do not know what the truth of yourself is, then how can you be sincere, real, or genuine with anyone else? Then you will lack integrity. There is no integration, no consistency between what you are actually feeling, and what you are telling others that you are feeling, wanting, or needing.

Our life energy force is also a loving warmth and a light of consciousness, so as you are open to your life energy force and all of its temporary feelings, you are also growing in loving warmth. As your consciousness contacts life energy, wherever there is contact with what is experientially real in yourself or others, there is warmth, which is an expansive energy that produces the inclination to connect deeply to others at an energetic level, invest deeply in empathic communion with them, and express unselfish caring to them. Then, through that deepest invested contact with what is experientially real in yourself and others, the heart core feels warm, naturally secure, free of fear or coldness, full of light instead of dark, dreary, thoughts, feelings, and sensations. So all of those kinds of growth of our life energy force are naturally interrelated.

However, if, instead of being open, you are closed to the actual experiential truth of yourself, because you see something negative about yourself, that might undermine and invalidate your positive self-concepts and self-images; when you are closed to your own feelings, then you are closed to your own life energy abiding within those feelings. Therefore, you cannot become more integrated, more whole, less self-divided, more deeply grounded in the natural integrity, or the true experiential authenticity of your own indivisible whole being or life energy field, and therefore also less alienated from the real life energy experience of others, which makes you feel less lonely. Our life energy force is intrinsically a natural will to live, which is the same as a will to grow more conscious of everything that is truly real in us and in others around us, and to actualize our higher potentials of powers of functioning. It is also a will to grow more enlightened in understanding, in consciousness, in loving warmth, a will to contact and enjoy life in the world.

However, if you reject the actual experiential truth of yourself, then you experience everything the opposite of that. Your experiential life is too painful, so there is an unconscious wish to die, to escape from uncomfortable realities, so as not to be conscious of pain. Therefore, if you cannot eliminate the pain, you try to eliminate the conscious awareness of the pain. Then you become psychologically numbed, inwardly dead, coldhearted, dark, life-degenerative, and set into motion a momentum moving toward even greater pain than that you are trying to escape, along with related experiences of illness and premature death. If you have lived a very satisfying and fulfilling life, then you will not fear death at the end. You will have the intuition that, somewhere, your life goes on, and because life goes on, love goes on, consciousness goes on, growth of everything truly real goes on, whether on some other plane, or returning here to this world through the process of reincarnation, or neither. There are many possibilities that you can explore if you are interested in doing so. However, such a process of exploration should involve openness to intuited direct experience, rather than presuming anything or conjecturing.

There is a critical period, when, if you do not actualize your real life potentials during that period, they begin to atrophy, attenuate, die. That is why real growth of actualized potentials is so important for longevity of regenerative life energy, and for having a joyful life, a creative life, a very fulfilling life in the world. This is related to our discussion of the process of optimal living. If you do not actualize your real life potentials and they atrophy, it is like you are literally losing a part of your own life energy force. It is like you are inwardly rotting, withering, degenerating, decaying, psychologically, which can produce corresponding deterioration of your physical health, vocational career, and social relationships because no aspect or level of your indivisible wholeness as an individual can function in isolation from the others.

Real people naturally experience the whole range of feelings, such as fear, anger, sadness, as well as love and joy. Almost everyone naturally experiences this whole range of feelings at some time regardless of whether they happen to be males or females, young or old, as well as regardless of other kinds of biological and social differences. All of these varied feelings naturally arise in us, occasionally, because we are each an indivisible whole life energy force, which includes the whole range of possible feelings and experiential states within itself. That spontaneously free flowing life energy force can affect every level of our being, because it is the essence or substance level of our being. Therefore, it can have a great impact upon our health, longevity, well-being, happiness, and enhanced functioning.

If you are not willing to be uncertain, at times, when that is realistically unavoidable or appropriate, then you are not open to surprises, coming creatively and spontaneously, at times. When you become pre-committed in regard to what particular kinds of feelings or experiential states you exclusively want your life energy force to give your conscious awareness, then you deny and violate the natural indivisible wholeness of your life energy force, and block it, thereby misdirecting it into a distorted degenerative momentum, as a kind of counter-flow, contrary to the natural regenerative flow of life energy between various kinds of feelings and experiential states. Relatively pleasant and unpleasant or relatively positive and negative feelings and experiential states are all on the same continuum of indivisible wholeness of life energy, so they are only relative, complementary, polar opposites, not antagonistic, dualistic, divisible, mutually exclusive opposites. Conscious awareness is just the surface level of your life energy force, not dualistically separated from it, as an absolute otherness, like an accordion, or like a whole continuum of black and white, as well as various shades of gray in between.

Psychological maturity involves being open to the full range of appropriate experience and expression spontaneously arising from moment to moment, such as being open to living a spontaneous balance between your necessary work, rest, and recreation. This involves being open to play, fun times, doing something just because you naturally enjoy doing it, and also taking appropriate opportunities for rest, as a way of reviving your energies. When you go to sleep, there should be plenty of restful, deep sleep, so that your heart, mind, and body can be refreshed. You need time to rest and just be, and therefore just be here and now, very open to what is actual reality presence, such as alertly conscious of the beauty of a bird in flight, or a flower, a tree, a person, or what is real for them this moment, or experiencing sunshine, snowflakes, rainfall, squirrels frolicking. You need time to just be, not always moving toward some goal or objective, which you also need at times, for balance. Sometimes, in your play or recreation, you are not resting very much. You are still striving to achieve the highest bowling score that you have ever achieved or some other kind of goal. That is important too, but not exclusively. You need opportunities to just rest and be, not seeking to become, and therefore optimally alert to whatever is spontaneously present in the world, here and now. Being committed exclusively for or against particular kinds of wholesome, constructive, experiences and ways of appropriate functioning reflects an attempt to control your experience in order to prevent anticipated psychological pain from arising, which involves escaping from feelings of fearful insecurity, all of which evidences and perpetuates psychological immaturity and a lack of developed strength of character or courage.

Next we discuss the true meaning of inner freedom, as distinct from freedom from outer oppression or constraints.

When you are growing in consciousness of your actual experiential states, and in powers of functioning arising from optimal actualization of your individual creative potentials that are inherent to your life energy force, then your life energy is free to be, experience, and express whatever it needs to, from moment to moment. Our unconscious life energy has an unconscious wisdom, which your consciousness cannot always understand. If you repress, suppress, and oppress a part of yourself, by trying to control and thereby block some of your natural life energy experiences, expressions, passions, and capabilities, then you are likely to oppress other people too, to make them conform to what makes you comfortable, and validates your positively value judged self-concepts, self-images, presumptions, and beliefs about yourself, as well as not tolerating from other people and from oneself anything that might seem to confirm negative, unfavorable, or uncomfortable views of yourself.

Psychologically mature people are very real, authentic, sincere, genuine, and spontaneous. They are not trying to live up to any static conceptual masks, personae, defined identity, or illusory sense of personality. Instead, they are devoted to developing real character, integrity, inner strength, nobility, the capacity to be unselfish and sincerely caring of others, with a highly responsive empathic sensitivity to the well-being of others. Psychologically mature people do not try to control life so much that it becomes overly predictable, which is unrealistic, deadening, and degenerative. We need some uncertainty, unpredictability, surprises. They make life interesting, a great adventure. If you could control everything in your life, then life becomes too predictable, boring, like death.

There is a psychologically healthy kind of "selfishness" that is constructive self-care. Life energy naturally flows between complementary relative polarized opposites of experience, such as passivity and activity, strength and weakness, relationship with others and separation from others, caring for self and caring for others. As previously mentioned, psychologically mature individuals understand and accept the truth that all polarized opposites that are part of the indivisible whole reality of life energy are naturally inseparable from one another, existing on the same continuum, as relative degrees of each other, like two opposite sides of the same indivisible whole coin, rather than being dichotomous, mutually exclusive, antagonistic opposites. Arising from the responsive process of relational connection to the here and now, the "still small voice" of your relational life energy will "speak" within you as the intuitively experienced urgings of your own core integrity, alerting you to the experiential truth of yourself in the moment. You will find no permanent conceptual truth. If you seek a particular kind of pre-committed, exclusive experience, so that your life energy cannot flow spontaneously and naturally between the polarities, then you become too exclusive, too absolutist, too rigid and restricted in your manner of perceiving and functioning. You want to feel absolutely secure, never insecure, totally in control, never helpless. You seek to always experience pleasure, and never experience pain, but you cannot experience the pleasure without the contrasting experience of pain. To be able to enjoy the experience of the "sweet," you have to be willing to also experience the "bitter." If you were always experiencing sweetness, pleasure, comfort, or success, there would be no different knowable experience to which it could be contrasted, so it would no longer be knowable. It is as if life is saying, in the words of the popular song, "I never promised you a rose garden. Along with the sunshine, there has to be some rain sometimes." What would happen if you always had sunshine and never had any rain. Then everything would be dry and barren, like a desert.

Our real self is a relational self, dynamically arising from moment to moment through our relational contact and responsive interaction with other individuals and experienced phenomena in the world, as suggested by Roberto Assagioli: "Indeed, an isolated individual is a nonexistent abstraction. In reality each individual is interwoven into an intricate network of vital, psychological and spiritual relations, involving mutual exchange and interactions with many other individuals."[7]

The energy that spontaneously arises through relationship with others is our real self, our real life energy, our real spontaneous response to objective reality, our real inner voice, whereas when we are not in relational contact with others, then we have an inner voice that speaks for non-relational functioning, as an antithetical shadow of reality, which is a twisted, distorted, life energy voice, because the antithetical shadow has no independent reality presence, power, or intelligence of its own. It is not life energy; it is not reality, so it cannot speak for itself. It can only twist to its antithetical nature whatever your non-conscious real life energy is trying to communicate to your consciousness. Martin Buber is another prominent thinker who views the real self as a relational self, not a disconnected self, epitomized in his dictum, "All real living is meeting."[8] Buber also suggests that the "I," or self, "becomes," dynamically changes through its relationship to the Thou, or the living presence of another individual. According to our understanding of Buber's distinction between the I-Thou and I-It kind of relationship, the Thou is contacted through a process of immediate or non-conceptually mediated communion with full investment of our whole being, when the other individual we contact is not defined as an "it" through a process of conceptual mediation or abstraction and sense of detachment or psychological space between us, as knower, and the other individual, as object of knowledge.[9]

Psychological maturity involves being directed primarily by the reality principle, rather than pursuing the hedonistic pleasure principle, which reflects relative psychological immaturity. Relatively psychologically mature individuals can adjust themselves to the reality demands of life. They are predominantly reality principle-oriented, whereas the relatively more psychologically immature individual typically tries to control life experience, inside and outside. They try to make life be what they want it to be, even if it is not realistic, appropriate, or adaptive. Therefore, they tend to value judge many aspects of their life experience, in terms of conditional acceptance and rejection, or conditional approval and disapproval, instead of unconditionally accepting those aspects of life experience and circumstances that cannot realistically or appropriately be changed. They frequently seek some kind of idealized, controlled experience, as a presumption of what "should be" and "should not be," instead of accepting whatever is actually present, here and now, as a life presence or a spontaneously arising experience. Therefore, such psychologically immature, judgmental individuals often do not deeply invest in contacting or engaging in whatever is actually spontaneously arising as inner and outer experience, in the here and now, but relate to it through a kind of mental filtering mechanism, only as they value judge it or presume it to be. Lacking substantial development of the ability to let go of continuous egoistic self-awareness in order to deeply contact life experience with the heart, mind, and body senses, such psychologically immature individuals do not really love life, as it actually is; they do not relate to life as it actually is, in reality. Instead, they typically try to control, manipulate, exploit, idealize their inner and outer life experience and circumstances. They are predominantly living in a conceptual daydream or continuous reactive mental/emotional inner monologue, rather than contacting their actual experience or actual life presence in the present moment. They tend not to be concerned about the reality of what actually is arising, but only their conceptual interpretations and reactive value judgments of what presumably "should be" or "should not be." They expect the reality to conform to their own needs and wishes, even when such expectations are not necessarily realistic, appropriate, or adaptive to what is in their true best interests.

Relatively psychologically mature, healthy, individuals do not value judge themselves, others, and life experience much. They intuitively recognize the essential oneness, unity, or indivisible holistic interrelatedness of reality, as intrinsic love, harmony, and goodness. Therefore, they tend not to react to spontaneously arising experience and conditions in terms of dichotomous, judgmental, presumptive interpretive categories, such as absolute good and evil, absolutely good and absolutely bad, totally acceptable or totally unacceptable, extreme approval and extreme disapproval, extreme like and extreme dislike, etc. Instead, they tend to have an accepting, flexible attitude, especially toward circumstances that cannot realistically or appropriately be changed. Relatively psychologically mature individuals tend to be more tolerant of the shortcomings of other individuals, because they recognize that they are relatively immature in the evolutionary development of their consciousness of reality and in their personal character, but not inherently bad. So they can afford to be more empathically understanding and compassionate, and tend not to negatively value judge or blame relatively nonconstructive, selfish, misbehaving, egotistical personalities. They appreciate the intrinsic true beauty and true goodness of life, and therefore do not pursue some conceptually idealized abstraction of it, and are able to intuitively, empathically recognize the special form of beauty and goodness that each individual they encounter represents in particular. That is why they are open to deeply contact relatively uncomfortable, unpleasant, as well as more pleasant, comfortable kinds of experiences, which, metaphorically speaking, is like deeply tasting and "savoring the flavor" of the "sour" and "bitter," or relatively "tart," as well as the relatively "sweet" aspects of life experience. They do not expect or demand that life always be a "rose garden" of exclusively comfortable, pleasant experiences, with no significant difficulties, because they intuitively recognize that the relatively pleasant and unpleasant or the relatively positive and negative polarities of experience are not dualistically or dichotomously exclusive of one another, but are naturally interrelated and interdependent within a greater wholeness of reality, an indivisibly unified continuum, or the naturally dynamically flowing pendulum of life experience that includes or embraces both of them within itself. Psychologically mature and spiritually evolved individuals tend to be relaxed, comfortable, and accepting of themselves and others because they intuitively appreciate the intrinsic beauty and goodness of life, and recognize that reality is an indivisible oneness, unity, or wholeness that is beyond judgmental, dichotomous, divisive, categories of conditional acceptance and rejection, or conditional approval and disapproval. Trusting the natural spontaneous free flow of life experience, psychologically mature, spiritually evolved individuals tend not to inhibit, block, or obstruct the flow of reality experience by imposing some kind of controlling ideal, censorship, demands, expectations, and escapist distractions from undesired realities.

The level of your psychological maturity or development of openness to direct contact with your actual inner and outer energy experience, unmediated and undistorted by presumptive interpretations, demands, and judgmental expectations, basically determines your intuitive grasp of or insight into the true reality of life, your understanding and appreciation of it, and your ability to relate to it without unrealistic conceptual distortion, oppositional willful resistive attitudes, and disharmonious, maladaptive, or inappropriate ways of functioning. Recognizing the essential indivisible oneness of reality as love enables the heart to develop relatively high levels of loving warmth, good-natured unselfish compassion, empathy, relaxed inner peace, harmony, and joyful regenerative life energy, which automatically dispels discordant feelings of fear, tension, anger, and unhappiness from the heart. But psychologically immature individuals who presume divisive, dichotomous, judgmental, exclusive, absolutist, interpretive categories to be reality tend to be mistrustful, full of fearful anxiety, tension, unhappiness, and various other related forms of inner and outer discord.

Your particular view of reality and corresponding experiential states tend to be reflected outwardly by "magnetically" attracting corresponding kinds of experiences in the objective world, because there is a natural lawful correspondence between the inner and outer aspects of reality, as part of the greater indivisible wholeness and oneness of reality. Therefore, "like attracts unto like," meaning that our views of reality and corresponding experiential states naturally attract similar experiences to us in the objective world, at least to some extent. Thus, those individuals who are mostly dominated by the lower or more discordant, disharmonious, vibratory frequencies of energy will naturally attract and be influenced by other discordant, disharmonious, even potentially destructive, basically predatory, malevolent, forces of similar vibratory frequency in the outer worldly environment, and may even attract physical illnesses and/or inner possession by demonic disembodied spirits. However, these individuals who have developed a very high level of love awakening in the heart have a much higher vibratory speed frequency of love-life energy that dispels or magnetically repels inner and outer forces of negativity. A relatively high level of love, joy, relaxed peace, and harmony is the great protector against all energy forces of inner and outer negativity, which naturally get outshined, repelled, dispelled, or dissolved by a vibratory frequency that is much higher than theirs. Because this outer world is a dreamlike, metaphorical shadow or reflecting mirror of the inner world of the heart, therefore, a heart filled with love and goodness does not attract, but will repel nearby destructively or ill-intentioned forces, as well as magnetically attracting various kinds of abundant goodness into your life in the world.

Various interrelated optimal noetic capacities come from developing psychological maturity, grounded in openness to, and love for, what is truly experientially real in ourselves and others, such as intuition, empathy, inner guidance, core integrity, inspiration, aesthetic appreciation of true beauty, as well as incisive insight into the underlying significance and causal basis of observable phenomena on the surface level of experience. Another related noetic faculty is the ability to think, feel, and function in a relational, contextual, holistic, integral, integrated manner, being aware of significant underlying causal relationships between diverse and even seemingly disparate phenomena, and being able to derive broader, deeper conclusions from significant relationships between various branches of knowledge and fields of endeavor. The development of higher noetic faculties is facilitated by engaging in deeply invested, unselfishly caring, communion with other individuals and constructive activities in the world, as suggested in the blog earlier in this book, "The Co-Creative Muse." Deeper faculties of heart and mind, coming from deeper levels of our being, develop best through being strongly invested in making deep contact with objective realities in the world, beyond or outside of the ego's boundaries of narcissistic self-awareness and continuous inner monologue. The more strongly we are invested in making caring contact with individuals, phenomena, and activities in the objective world, thereby becoming self-forgetful of the ego, the more deeply, incisively our conscious awareness and feeling energy is able to penetrate into them, yielding deeper insights into their essential significance, beyond or beneath the surface appearances of the phenomena themselves. As we become more deeply interested in and attentive to heartfelt, open-minded contact or empathic communion with other individuals and phenomena in the world, our conscious awareness becomes correspondingly more alert, sensitive, and incisively penetrating, and that is what heightens the development of the higher noetic faculties or experiential capabilities of heart and mind, producing enhanced insightful understanding, enjoyable appreciation, and empowering transformation of ourselves and of reality as a whole as well as of specific individuals or phenomena that we encounter.

Full psychological maturity involves full freedom, full sovereignty, full empowerment, awakening, or liberation of our inner power source, full self-responsibility. This cannot be achieved as an ego or an exclusively separate sense of identity and its continuous sense of separate recoiled self-awareness, but only as the relational life energy presence of the real self or soul.

Although it is often appropriate to accommodate ourselves to the wishes and needs of other individuals in order to make constructive cooperation and social harmony possible, it is not psychologically mature, healthy, and constructive to permanently and totally surrender our individual will power to any other purported authority, because when we do, we become childlike, overly dependent, weak, helpless, powerless, defenseless, lacking confidence in our own good judgment and core integrity, which produces psychological immaturity and insecurity. If we give up our own self-governing autonomy of personal will power, independent reasoning, self-understanding, and individual natural inclinations to some purported human or divine authority, then that purported authority can misuse its influence to abuse us, and to prevent us from spontaneously developing in our own natural way by imposing its own agenda on us. We are not fully psychologically mature, fully sovereign, fully self-governing, fully self-responsible, optimally self-actualizing, full psychological adults if our will power is still impotent, and we are still dominated by others and by fearful insecurities, like a child, instead of being empowered by fully developed loving warmth, as a fully substantial, fully satisfying, enduring inner life presence, providing us with genuine psychological security and well-being.

However, we should never express individual will or make wishes arising from a sense of inner deficiency and compensatory desire, because once you presume inherent deficiency of being and lack of intrinsic security and unconditional well-being, then your experience, knowing, or having, must also inevitably reflect that presumed deficiency of being nature. Do not identify with any kind of experience of inner deficiency, defect, degeneration, or deterioration. It cannot be true of the reality nature of your life energy force, which is not an inherent self-contradiction, not inherent chaos, as a mixture of disparate elements of conditional well-being and non-well-being. The truth is that our being is an inherent self-consistent nature, an intrinsic order, wholeness, harmony, happiness, and well-being, once we are fully conscious of our reality life energy presence, as an unconditional flawless total well-being, as an individualized form of God, total goodness, or divine intelligence. In any event, whatever you wish for, believe that you will receive it, because your own loving warmth and wholeness of being are always inherently being it, and have the power to unfold it or manifest it through their expressed relational love-energy, which is their expressed being.

There is an infinite pseudo divine or pseudo spiritual narcissism and a finite human narcissism. Each of those forms of extreme narcissism can readily veer into solipsism or autism, implying the totally self-absorbed presumption, "Only I am, only I really exist, no one and nothing outside of me has any independent reality, existence, value, or significance, but is, at best, only an extension of my identity, needs, desires, and expectations." Many purported deities, and their human representatives, as well as other influential leaders, especially very controlling, tyrannical, cruel, authority figures, narcissistically try to mold others into their own image or reflection, as if to say, "Only I truly exist; none of you really exist. None of you have autonomous, intrinsic, existence, value, significance, identity, rights, and willpower; you are all meant or required to basically function as extensions of me, to do my bidding. None of you have the right to any freedom or independent existence, will, needs, experience, or viewpoint. Everyone and everything exists only to serve the gratification of my selfish demands and grandiose self-infatuation." Although such narcissistic "divine" or human "authorities" can be very grandiose, they have little or no true grandeur, because they are psychologically immature, like a self-absorbed infant or fetus curled inward upon itself in the mother's womb, lacking the psychological maturity to acknowledge anyone or anything outside of themselves to relate to, and therefore not recognizing the relational reality of life as love-goodness, and its intrinsic value, grandeur, or preciousness. Sometimes, we have to acknowledge our own separateness and function relatively autonomously or independently, but we are also relational to every other life presence to some extent. That capacity for individual diversity and particularity, as well as our relational connection to the distinctive particularity of other individuals, phenomena, and activities, keeps us from being immersed in a collective egoism, or universal undifferentiated monistic unity nature, as absolute narcissism or extreme self-absorption, grounded in the basically solipsistic presumption, "only I am," functioning at the finite human level, or the infinite "divine" or pseudo-spiritual level, in which we are identified with an infinite monistic entity knowing only itself, and not acknowledging any self-governing relational other individualities to relate to and accommodate as distinct from itself. Sometimes collective egotism takes the form of collective mass consciousness, in which individuals excessively subsume their identity and directing will to the norms and expectations of society or of particular social, ethnic, or tribal groups with which they are affiliated. Human collective mass consciousness resembles and often involves a continuation of collective behavioral or herd instincts that govern the behavior of various non-human species. Abandoning individual particularity, self-governing self-responsibility, and self-actualization or development of what is natural, real, or distinctive in us, by blending into a collective human or animal species herd instinct reflects relative psychological immaturity, especially if we are dominated by collective instincts that are relatively subconscious or impulsive in nature, in which individuals do not consciously consider and take full responsibility for the possibly non-constructive consequences of their collectively influenced behavior, values, attitudes, goals, and perceptions.

Another related aspect of psychological and spiritual maturity is to develop the inner energy-power center level of our being, so that it can unfold and actualize our natural potentials, attract greater material and experiential abundance, as well as empower the fulfillment of our self-directed, ethically responsible, constructive good wishes and needs. In making and attempting to fulfill constructive wishes or genuinely life-affirming aspirations, we rely upon the power of our maturely developed and consciously awakened being as loving or caring warmth. Our maturely developed energy center as caring warmth is the most powerful, fulfilled, and whole level of our being, because it is the highest or greatest vibratory frequency of energy. Therefore, it is potentially greater than any other opposing presence or power, and, certainly, a greater reality presence, power, and intelligence than negativity, which is not a reality nature. We wish and expect the love, goodness, wholeness, fulfillment, abundance nature that we already intrinsically are being to manifest as our experience in the world, and we wish it with total heartfelt passion, as well as with the conviction and expectation of its inevitable fulfillment.

APPENDIX J

MANIFESTO TO THE VANGUARD OF HUMANITY: THOSE WHO HAVE A WELL-DEVELOPED HEART AND SOUL

The well-developed heart and soul are the basis of an acute sensitivity to what is of enduring true value in life and love, the inner core or contents of reality, beyond the surface outer package or appearances, the numinous within the phenomena, the sublime, precious, glorious, lovely energy presence abiding within and appearing as the visible material objects and processes of this world. We wish to encourage, inspire, and empower the "vanguard" of humanity, i.e., deeply caring, highly creative, sensitive, sincere individuals who often feel like misfits in the mainstream of contemporary society, because they do not feel comfortable adapting to the relatively emotionally cold, uncaring, mechanically programmed, non-spontaneous, uninspired routine and ethos that are prevalent in many sectors of mainstream contemporary society, especially the business world. Such highly evolved "old souls" often have difficulty developing compatible, satisfying, personal relationships with other people whose consciousness reflects the mainstream ethos of society. Furthermore, it can be difficult for such individuals to find and keep paid employment, as a basis of achieving financial security, especially jobs that are a good fit with their natural talents, interests, and the highly developed quality or stature of their being. These kinds of sensitive individuals often like to express a deeper level of their being through their personal relationships, professional work, volunteer public service, and recreational activities, turning out products and providing services that have an inspirational quality, a flow of regenerative life energy, reflecting or expressing a quality of "heart and soul," rather than turning out "alienated" products and providing services that are basically lifeless, empty, mechanically programmed, routine, stale, superficial, and without depth. This brings to mind Kahlil Gibran's view that "Work is love made visible,"[1] as well as Karl Marx's view of work as an expression of our essential inner human qualities and genuine caring for others, in contrast to work that is basically an expression of "alienation," psycho-social "estrangement" (*Entfremdung*) or overly commercialized, mechanized, and routine, resulting in estrangement from other individuals, the natural world, and our own natural integrity and authenticity.[2]

To develop and awaken the true reality nature of our being, and thereby achieve true greatness, as well as to help others achieve the true greatness that already abides within them, as latent potential, it is important to recognize that we are each particular individualized forms of God's, being's, or life's pure, immortal spirit, unfolding as our individual fruitage of actualized potentials of real intelligence, which includes our real relationship potentials, as well as our real individual talents and natural abilities. Spiritual intelligence is the one, all, only, ever-present reality nature. Spirit has no opposite nature, in reality, but it needs an illusory opposite shadowy ego nature to contrast with, and thereby highlight, challenge, exercise, and strengthen our real nature. When we fully maturely develop and awaken our individual spirit of love-life energy by unselfishly sharing it with others, or expressing it to others, it becomes a limitlessly abundant, inexhaustible, self-sustaining, energy nature, like an ever-flowing fountain or a veritable "immortal flame" that is never depleted through its endless giving or expansive flow of energy, symbolically represented by the "Eternal Flame" or torch of the Olympic Games, the Statue of Liberty, the Tomb of the Unknown Soldier, the lights on a Christmas tree or Hanukah Menorah, etc., whereas the selfish ego is only illusory, dark, shadowy, cloudlike, empty, vacuous self-talk, like daydreams, hallucinations, mirages, hollow facades, or unconscious hypnotic suggestions. That relational energy of caring warmth or true love is the source of everything that is truly good, sublime, exalted, or of high stature in us.

The individual and collective shadowy, unreal ego nature tries to influence us by fusing with our real energy-being nature and our natural real experiential states, and by pretending to speak as our own inner voice, our own individual heart, mind, and body. However, the unreal will naturally fall away from the real if we do not react to it, identify with, or express the unreal, and instead keep expressing only our own real nature, as a natural goodness, unselfish caring, and flawless purity of being.

Egoistic feeling is basically comprised of and rooted in subconscious thought, which we have energized with our own feeling-energy by subconsciously identifying with those subliminal thoughts, and holding our well-being to be vitally affected by them, favorably enhanced or unfavorably diminished, as the basis of positive and negative value judgments, which may not necessarily be fully consciously recognized. If the thoughts hidden in the feeling were ever to be made fully conscious, and no longer identified with or reacted to, the feelings would dissolve. The feelings may be consciously perceived, but the thought or message hidden at the core of them is usually either preconscious or subconscious, at least to some extent. For example, you may consciously know that you are feeling depressed, but you may not necessarily be fully aware of why you are feeling depressed. The feeling itself, such as depression, functions as a kind of dark, opaque veil or smokescreen to keep your conscious awareness away from fully consciously recognizing the ego-threatening message within it. The underlying message that is the source of negative feelings is usually some sense of inner deficiency, such as a sense of worthlessness, grounded in the sense of being an inner void, inner emptiness, or psychological nullity, because your conscious awareness is not yet maturely developed enough to detect its permanent life energy presence as a sense of unconditional inner fullness, substantiality, and indivisible wholeness.

The only way to liberate our real energy-being and the true greatness that is inherent to it is to consciously acknowledge and fully embrace the ego's foundational feeling of being an inner emptiness, nothingness, or deficiency of being and lack of inherent well-being. As long as we feed or gratify the ego's compensatory sense of grandiosity and comforting distracting escapes from the deeper experiential truth of itself, the ego's positive and negative or relatively comfortable and uncomfortable self-definitions and associated experiential states will continue to overlay our inherent real being, and thereby block the conscious awakening and development of the potential for true greatness that is intrinsic to our real being. Thus, to be a real "someone" or "something," as pure life energy-experience, we have to drop the ego's false, conditionally acquired sense of "something-ness" and "nothingness." Only by letting go of or outgrowing all unreal ideas of ourselves, excessive artificial sensations, and other heavy, acquired psychological baggage can our real energy-being be liberated from those acquired coverings, enabling us to grow in what is truly real and of genuine value in ourselves. Perhaps the importance of liberating the utmost simplicity of our undefined pure energy-being and its intrinsic greatness from various complex positive and negative self-interpretations superimposed upon it, which the ego utilizes as a means of denying and escaping its foundational sense of inner nothingness, and enhancing or embellishing its compensatory sense of conceptually defined identity, may be metaphorically epitomized by Biblical observations as such as, "Who by taking thought can add [or diminish] even one cubit to his stature," (Matthew 6:27; Luke 12:25; paraphrase of the King James Bible) as well as Shakespeare's observation, "Nothing is good or bad, only thinking makes it [seem] so" (paraphrase of *Hamlet*, Act II, scene 2).

All feelings and experiences are just temporary modified forms of our pure conscious energy substance. Therefore, negative feelings and experiences can be transformed and released back into pure, relaxed energy by being in conscious communion or non-duality with the negative or uncomfortable experience, and its underlying message of deficiency, which reduces it to its underlying base or foundational level of calm pure energy. The more that you resolve your personal feelings, drain them fully of their unspoken messages of deficiency, and completely cease to identify with them, the more the life energy substance at the core of those feelings is liberated from those confining self-identifications. Then your liberated energy, divested of various egoistic coverings, is no longer impeded from pouring into your conscious awareness, making you more and more conscious of that spark of love-life energy, until your consciousness gains full self-realization as that fully maturely developed and fully awakened conscious-love-life-ecstasy energy, which is a blessed, enchanted, divine love-flame or spiritual fire, a flawless, non-deficient, intrinsic wholeness and overflowing fullness of being, like a perpetually self-renewing, self-sustaining inner sun or star. That unblocked, uncovered, undivided, energy, coming from the core of our own real being, is the source of true greatness, creativity, or genius in us, the real "genie in us."

True and enduring freedom from emotional pain, true greatness, creative breakthroughs, and real ecstasy never come as a result of a diminution or numbing of consciousness, but only from the fullest heightening of the penetrating alertness of consciousness, which ultimately leads to a full conscious awareness of the essential or absolute reality nature of our being or conscious love-life energy substance, which is inherent ecstasy and limitless creative intelligence, the source of true greatness in us, our true genius or the real "genie" in us. Remain fully conscious of any inner or outer experience and it will eventually reveal its underlying reality of pure or absolute life energy substance. Any psychological pain, or perhaps even physical pain, will reveal its under-lying, perfect or flawlessly pure, life energy nature if you remain fully conscious of it, and do not try to evade it, fully consciously experiencing it in its fullest possible intensity. To be fully conscious of it is to be in non-reactive, non-interpretive, non-dualistic, wordless communion with it, fully accepting it as self, a temporary experienced form of your own life energy substance. However, your consciousness feels less alive when you desensitize your consciousness as a means of escaping from pain, because a dull consciousness can make only shallow contact with inner and outer experiential life-energy presence. Fully developed consciousness and life energy substance awareness are one and the same reality. To become less conscious numbs or deadens the experience of pain, but also numbs or diminishes your awareness of life energy substance, and makes your consciousness more addictively dependent on some kind of substance or sensation that provides an artificially induced substitute sense of euphoria, excitement, and vitality, in order to feel more alive and escape from the death-like boredom and experience of inner emptiness and numbness that suppression of your emotional pain brings. That inner numbing also impedes our access to the life energy source of true greatness in us, such as creative insight, inspiration, integrity, intuition, empathy, courage, and so on.

To reiterate, the fear and dread of fully consciously experiencing the ego as an inner void, deficiency, or emptiness of real inner life substance is the basic fear and dread underlying all particular anxieties, negative feelings, and egoistic motivations. All experiences and feelings are just temporary modified forms of your pure energy love-life essence-substance and are alterable by you at any time. Thus, no temporary feeling or experience of yours is anything other than your own permanent conscious-life energy. Feelings and experiences may be functioning as temporary alterations and interpretive abstractions of your essential being, so they can be reduced back to that essential unconditioned or unmodified being, consciously experienced as an inherent love-bliss when its modifications are dissolved back into their original purity. Like a reflecting mirror of our being or conscious view of ourselves, our inner and outer experience, including our heartfelt emotions, mind, and body, can reflect either the flawless purity or intrinsic perfection of our unmodified love-life energy presence, our spirit, or an egoistically distorted modification of it, producing various inner conflicts and corresponding outer disturbances. Thus, our inner and outer experience is essentially like a mirror reflection of how our inherent being or conscious life energy presence views itself, and how it functions basically consistently or inconsistently with the inherent rightful integrity and wholesome purity of itself, producing either self-consistent wholeness, harmony, rightful integrity, and relaxed peace, or a distorted sense of self-conflict and disturbance in our inner and outer experience. That is to say, whatever is arising within your inner self, spirit, or conscious life energy presence, or howsoever it views itself, will also naturally be reflected, like a mirror, in the experience of your individual personal emotional heart, mind, and body. When your pure love-life energy is highly awakened, maturely developed, unblocked, and unmodified, then it supplies your heart, mind, and body with greater levels of creative intelligence, which produces enhanced levels of functioning and the potential for true greatness in any constructive field of endeavor or area of inquiry.

We gradually fulfill the basic meaningful purpose of life to grow in conscious awakening of the true reality nature of our being, or our inherent conscious life energy presence, naturally experienced as an indivisible wholeness and sublime grandeur, by reunifying with our own estranged feelings and experiential states internally, as well as developing loving connections or genuine caring relationships with other individuals externally, and then by gradually expanding or maturing our consciousness into the core of our own being and the universal spiritual reality as the "Eternal Flame" of

Divine Love itself. We can consciously awaken and maturely develop the essential energy core or inner power center of our own being only by engaging in caring empathic communion with our own feelings and experiential states, as well as with other individuals in the world, because the true core of our being is a relational core or center, in contrast to the ego's false, presumptive sense of being a detached knower, narcissistically, dualistically, or divisively separate from its unwanted, rejected, painful feelings and experiential states, as well as from other individuals in the world. Thus, courageously risking psychological pain by making deep, unrestricted contact with the actual experiential truth of ourselves, other individuals, and the world around us enables us to develop more advanced levels of true greatness or real stature of being, which comes from penetrating beyond the superficial surface of phenomena to the numinous energy-intelligence that abides within the deeper core of reality.

If society would nurture, honor, and support the vanguard of humanity, those who have developed relatively advanced levels of creative or insightful, inspirational, transformational functioning, grounded in attunement to the deeper core energies of reality, or real intelligence, those relatively psychologically mature and spiritually evolved individuals could be empowered to help other individuals and society reach significantly greater levels of true greatness, fulfillment, and psychological health, as ethically responsible true servant leaders. Sublime qualities such as true greatness, goodness, love, joy, beauty, and transformational creative breakthroughs develop best in us as we share them with others, as an expression of unselfish caring, because the source of those gifts is an expansive relational energy, in contrast to the ego's presumptive pride or false grandiosity, which keeps contracting or diminishing in its capabilities.

CONCLUSIONS

The primary key to resolving psychological inner conflict and emotional distress, as well as undoing toxic fixation in inappropriate, maladaptive, overly restrictive, habitually predetermined modes of perceiving and functioning is to permit uncomfortable feelings or painful experiential states to flow freely, spontaneously, into your conscious awareness, so that they can play themselves out without interference internally, or "speak" for themselves to conclusion, within your conscious awareness, and thereby drain out into their underlying base or substratum in pure conscious-life energy. This undoes the painful, self-conflicted, psychologically unhealthy momentum or feeling-tone of your energy. This process of self-healing through self-reunification with your previously rejected, repressed feelings and experiential states, so the energy invested within them can be released, and no longer be blocked, can occur only if you relinquish all sense of reactive, judgmental, preconceived interpretation, control, and censorship with regard to your own uncomfortable feelings and experiential states, but instead permit them to flow or speak for themselves within your nonreactive pure conscious awareness, without speaking for them, i.e., without superimposing any kind of predetermined presumptive interpretations, expectations, or goals upon the feelings. Following the trail or thread of the actual experiential truth of yourself wherever it may spontaneously lead from moment to moment liberates you from toxic blockage and misdirection of your energies in persistent, often habitual patterns of self-deception, self-rejection, self-division, and self-conflict. Perhaps the psychologically liberating, healing, beneficially transformational effects of being open to the actual experiential truth of yourself, without superimposing any kind of biased predetermined interpretations, expectations, goals, or agendas upon it, may be epitomized by the Biblical maxim, "You will know the truth, and the truth will make you free" (John 8:32).

511

Being open to the full range of your actual experiential states, without making divisive positive and negative value judgments or presumptive interpretations of them, also has a psychological healing effect by restoring the natural wholeness of the psyche through the reintegration of previously rejected or subconscious experiential states.[1] The principle that psychological healing involves reunifying the psyche by nonjudgmentally accepting and consciously reintegrating previously estranged experiential aspects of the psyche, as well as reunifying the inner and outer or subjective and objective aspects of reality by engaging in deeply invested caring empathic communion with other individuals, phenomena, and activities is succinctly epitomized by Max Hammer's dictum, *"Wholeness heals!"* Psychological self-healing or psychotherapeutic healing processes should involve letting go of restrictive self-definitions so that you can access and integrate experiential aspects of the psyche that abide beyond the parameters of those preconceived, divisive self-definitions.[2] For example, psychological, social, or religious theories are overly restrictive or reductionist if they automatically exclude aspects of human experience beyond the scope of their particular interpretive model, such as denying validity to the spiritual, transpersonal, numinous, or non-materialistic, non-rationalistic aspects of the psyche.[3]

Following or being open to the actual experiential truth of yourself as it dynamically, spontaneously, often unpredictably unfolds from moment to moment, also involves developing the ability and willingness to discern and function consistently with the sense of integrity, self-consistency, or good-will that spontaneously arises from the deepest core of your own being. Your core integrity intuitively alerts you to whether or not, or to what extent, in your current situation a particular option of perception or functioning is basically consistent with the vibratory energy tone and inherent qualities of your own being, such as the intrinsic genuineness (realness), sincerity, compassion, life-affirming goodness, constructiveness, self-consistent wholeness, inner strength,

courage, wholesome purity, and rightful quality of your being. The process of developing psychological maturity, involving genuine constructive self-responsibility and ethical
responsibility toward others, necessarily involves learning
to intuitively discern and heed the distinctive energy vi-
bration signals arising from the core integrity level of our
own being, alerting us to what options of functioning and
perceptions ring true or false or seem rightful or queasy to
the intrinsic soundness, constructive goodness, rectitude, or
rightful purity of our being.[4] The development of relatively
high levels of integrity makes us a self-consistent self, a cohesive, holistic, integrated, or integral self; a transpersonal,
non-egoistic, relational, connective, or nonexclusive self,
where all aspects of ourselves are unified by the indivisible,
self-consistent wholeness of the essential core of our individual being, connected to the transpersonal, spiritual, or relational whole of being. In contrast to the transpersonal or
holistic self, the experiential self can be divided by conflicts
between various impulses and experiential states, and also
be distanced or divorced from other individuals and from the
relational, spiritual, or transpersonal ground of being; while
the conceptually defined egoistic self, the conceptual self,
can readily be divided between various conflicting, presumptive, self-definitions and self-evaluations.

Furthermore, achieving psychological maturity also involves developing strength of character, or true courage,
involving the willingness and ability to tolerate the risk or
actual experience of psychological pain, discomfort, stress,
frustration, uncertainty, or lack of premature closure, when
such risks can truly have an adaptive, beneficial, or transformational impact upon us, or upon other individuals toward
whom we feel a genuine sense of ethical responsibility. Developing true strength of character and integrity enables us
to feel inwardly substantial, secure, and self-confident, rather
than feeling like an inwardly hollow, fragile, easily collapsible, "house of cards." The only effective way to develop genuine psychological maturity, integrity, and strength of character

is to consciously face, rather than escape, deny, and cover over painful feelings and uncomfortable experiential states, which often tend to be rooted in the conceptually self-defined ego-personality's basic sense of inner emptiness, nothingness, insubstantiality, insecurity, and lack of self-consistency.

Following the trail or thread of the actual experiential truth of ourselves in these and various other ways, gradually leads us away from presumptive egoistic ideas of ourselves to the discovery of more experientially genuine natural inclinations, talents, and potentials, that are intrinsic to our own being or conscious life energy force. As we outgrow what is psychologically immature or inauthentic in us, and grow in the discovery and development of what is more experientially genuine in us, our conscious awareness gradually progresses or penetrates beyond the momentary experiential truth of ourselves to the awakening of our permanent being, the deepest source or core level of our conscious life energy force. As our conscious awareness gradually penetrates into deeper levels of our own real being or life energy force, we begin to develop a clearer, more vivid, profounder experience of the qualities of unconditional well-being, inner peace, security, creativity, love, beauty, and true grandeur, that are intrinsic to our permanent being. Consciously awakening, discovering, or uncovering the essential core of our being also enables us to tap into a potentially limitless source of benign energy-power, creative intelligence, inspiration, abundance, and enhanced functioning within ourselves. Metaphorically similar to a gardener or farmer planting healthy seeds in fertile good soil, consciously awakening the essential "ground" level of our being facilitates the perhaps limitlessly growing fruition of the seed-like potentials that are rooted in our own conscious life-energy force. As our consciousness maturely develops the openness and clarity to penetrate into deeper and deeper levels of our being and experience, we thereby gain greater liberating and transformational insight into the experiential truth of ourselves, other individuals, and life or reality as a whole.

Thus, we envision a process or continuum of psychological maturation from the relatively weak (deficient-and-insecure-feeling) ego to the relatively strong ego (having a conditional sense of proficiency and security based on having developed relatively greater coping skills and somewhat greater tolerance of psychological pain) to the experiential self, conditionally unified with our painful and non-painful experiential states, as a relatively undivided, undefined wholeness of being, to the fully holistic, transpersonal, relational, or real self, experiencing the sense of unconditional fully integrated wholeness, security, and fulfillment that are intrinsic to our changeless permanent being, and to our full immersion in the relational whole fabric, network, web, or matrix of being. In contrast to the conceptually defined ego identity and the experiential self, which can both be overly selfishly-oriented, the transpersonal self experiences the intrinsic fulfillment of its being by sharing it with others through expressions of unselfish caring and serving others by actualizing our fullest range of individual and relational potentials. Discovery and actualization of the natural life energy potentials of the real self are evoked through relational communion with other individuals, phenomena, and activities, as well as self-exploration. But as long as the experiential self continues to be somewhat identified with the separate egoistic self-awareness, its capacity for communion and its level of related experiential self-discovery will typically tend to be somewhat shallower, while those who are strongly identified with the conceptually defined ego identity will often tend to be even shallower and more distorted in the self-discovery of their real life energy-based potentials and natural inclinations, covered over by deficiency-based psychological needs and preconceived self-interpretations.

The ongoing discovery of what is experientially real in us, including the unending process of actualizing our natural potentials and abilities, provides us with genuine self-knowledge, in contrast to the ego's presumptive ideas of itself, involving conceptual self-definitions and self-interpretations, which can never be conclusively proven or definitively established, because they are not intrinsic to our being or life energy force, and can always be invalidated by their relative opposite counterparts, such as the actual experience of being weak and ineffectual undermining the ego's presumptive definition of being powerful. Whereas the ego's conceptual self-definitions usually tend to produce a continuous process of narcissistic self-preoccupation and extreme experiential separation or energetic disconnection from others, our real being or conscious life-energy force is intrinsically a relational self, so many of its potentials can best be actualized through a process of responsive empathic communion and cooperation with others rather than through introspective self-isolation.

Perhaps consciously awakening the most essential core or power-source level of our being may eventually enable us to individually, relationally, and collectively gain greater mastery over various kinds of inner and outer predatory, destructive forces of negativity that can exert a more powerful, more frequent, and more enduring harmful influence upon us when our level of psychological maturity or conscious awakening of our life energy force is less advanced or developed. This seems to suggest that there may be a basic innate purposeful ontic intention for individuals, relationships, and collective society as a whole, to develop greater levels of conscious experiential awakening of our intrinsic being or life energy force in order to heighten our immunity to various kinds of malign forces, be they visible or invisible, inner or outer, physical, psychological, or societal in origin. Until we human beings gain greater mastery over inner and outer malign forces, so that we are not perpetually victimized, it is like having the Damocles sword of disaster always suspended over our heads, preventing us from feeling deeply secure and from deeply enjoying or savoring the many treasures or delights that life has to offer. Consciously or subconsciously, we all have a natural innate urge to fully experientially awaken our inner energy-power source so that it can serve as a protective, abundance-providing, wish-granting, guiding inner beacon, inner genie, or true genius in us. Following the trail of the momentary experiential truth of ourselves to its source in the permanent reality nature of our awakened being, as our inner source of limitless real power, wisdom, grandeur, and abundance, is metaphorically symbolized in many stories and myths, such as the story of following the "yellow brick road" to its source in the *Wizard of Oz*, seeking the "pot of gold at the end of the rainbow," the quest for the Holy Grail, climbing Jacob's ladder or "Jack and the Beanstalk," as well as songs such as "To Dream the Impossible Dream," or "When you Wish upon a Star." The wish-granting star, hidden treasure, or powerful Wizard of Oz symbolically represent the core level of our own being, beckoning us through the "still small voice of intuition" to come home to itself (our own true self) by following the winding trail of our own core integrity.[5]

Perhaps the development of greater conscious mastery over often subconscious or unconscious malign energy forces may be symbolically depicted by the transition from the Piscean Age, represented by fish swimming in water, to the Aquarian Age, represented by a person holding a pitcher of water, with water representing inner and outer turbulent forces that contain and control us when we have not yet consciously awakened or maturely developed the most powerful, genuine, core level of our own being, whereas a psychologically maturely developed consciousness can contain, tame, or overcome less conscious wild energy forces.[6] Like purifying a muddy or polluted river, our own conscious life energy force has a natural urge to restore its intrinsic purity, beauty, grandeur, regenerative vitality, inner peace, and wholeness, by overcoming or constructively resolving various kinds of unwholesome addictions, stagnating regressive fixations, and inner conflicts. Like a strong, sturdy tree that is deeply rooted in the ground, and cannot be blown away by passing storms, we must be deeply rooted in our own core integrity to overcome the opposing resistive force of disintegration, division, and discord, not necessarily by actively opposing it (we tend to energize and magnify whatever we focus our conscious attention upon), but rather by remaining courageously true to what is experientially real and constructively good-natured in ourselves, even under all opposing conditions, circumstances, and temptations, such as intense fear and greed.

Consciously awakening the source-energy-power level of our own individual, relational, and collective humanity or societal being may also serve to heighten our ability to unfold and magnetically attract greater levels of inner and outer abundance. Whereas the ego's basically unrealistic sense of self-aggrandizement or grandiosity often comes from feeling superior to others in the competitive arena, or even through various subtle or overt predatory ways of functioning (be it through physical violence, financial, sexual, social, or psychological means), our intrinsic real being or energy-force is consciously or subconsciously/subliminally urging us to awaken in ourselves the experience of a more genuine, more experiential, profounder, more enduring, sense of inner grandeur, as a life energy presence, by unselfishly sharing it with others, or generously expressing it to others. That is how we function as energy-givers, energy enhancers, rather than an energy-drain or "energy vampire" in our relationships with others. Whereas the ego often seeks to enhance, embellish, or aggrandize itself through extreme, exaggerated, positive self-definitions, the development of our real being or life energy force grows in greater depth, height, and breadth as we unselfishly share our caring energies, talents, and other gifts or resources with others, because the process of sharing or giving reflects the principle of inner abundance rather than inner paucity or scarcity.

NOTES

CHAPTER 1

1.   Frances Vaughan, *The Inward Arc: Healing in Psychotherapy and Spirituality* (Nevada City, California: Blue Dolphin Press Publishing, 1995), 63-64.
2.   Ken Wilber, *The Spectrum of Consciousness* (Wheaton, Illinois: Quest Books/Theosophical Publishing House, Second Edition, 1993), 196 and 198, compare 204.

CHAPTER 2

1.   Khalil Gibran, *The Prophet* (New York: A Knopf, 1923), 56.
2.   Sue Paton Thoele, *Heart Centered Marriage, Fulfilling Our Natural Desire for Sacred Partnership* (Berkeley, California: Conari Press, 1996), 126-127.
3.   Ken Wilber, *Integral Psychology: Consciousness, Spirit, Psychology, Therapy* (Boston and London: Shambala, 2000), 200-202.
4.   John Powell, *The Secret of Staying in Love* (Niles, Illinois: Argus Communications, 1974), 100-104.
5.   See Jean Houston, *The Wizard of Us: Transformational Lessons from Oz* (New York and Hillsboro, Oregon: Atria Books and Beyond Words, 2012).
6.   For a very cogent, extensive discussion of why the attempt to escape from psychological pain is ultimately futile and psychologically unhealthy, see Gail and Terry Maul, *Beyond Limit* (Glenview, Illinois: Scott, Foresman, and Company, 1983), 25-28.

7. Jiddu Krishnamurti, *Commentaries on Living, from the Notebooks of J. Krishnamurti*, Edited by D. Rajagopal (London: Victor Collancz Ltd., 1967), 101.

8. Gibran, Kahlil, *The Garden of the Prophet* (New York: A. Knopf, 1933), 27.

9. Jiddu Krishnamurti, *The First and Last Freedom* (Wheaton, Illinois: Theosophical Publishing House, 1968), 17, 94-98.

10. Idem, *Freedom from the Known* (New York: Harper and Row Publishers, 1969), 21-22.

11. Sidney M. Jourard, *The Transparent Self,* second edition (New York: D. Van Nostrand, 1971), and Idem, *Disclosing Man to Himself* (Princeton, New Jersey: D. Van Nostrand, 1968).

12. For a very illuminating discussion of the importance of going beyond preconceived interpretations of ourselves and others, see Maul and Maul, *Beyond Limit*, 2-3, 20-21, 24.

CHAPTER 3

1. Martin Buber, *The Knowledge of Man, Selected Essays*, edited by Maurice Friedman, Translated by Maurice Friedman and Ronald Gregor Smith (Amherst, New York: Humanity Books, An Imprint of Prometheus Books, 1998), 27-28.

2. Ibid.

3. Khalil Gibran, *The Garden of the Prophet*. New York: Alfred A. Knopf, 1972.

4. Alfred Adler, *Social Interest: A Challenge to Mankind* (Mansfield Center, Connecticut: Martino Publishing, 2011; and London: Faber and Faber Ltd.,1964), and http://pws.cablespeed.com/~htstein/qu-comm.htm.

5. e.e. cummings, *Six Non-lectures* (New York: Atheneum, 1967), 47.

6. From a translation of a lecture on Individual Psychology by Dr. Mueller in Rotterdam. January 10, 1934,

in the AAINW/ATP Archives. Cited in http://pws.ca-blespeed.com/~htstein/qu-comm.htm.

7. From a new translation of "Individual Psychology," *Einuehrung in die neuere Psychologie*, 1926, in the AAINW/ATP Archives. These quotes from Alexander Mueller and Alfred Alder are taken from the website of the Alfred Adler Institutes of San Francisco and Northwestern Washington, URL link: http://pws.cablespeed.com/~htstein/qu-comm.htm).

8. Martin Buber, *I and Thou,* second edition, Translated by Ronald Gregor Smith (New York: Charles Scribner's Sons, 1958).

9. Idem. *The Way of Response*. Edited by Nahum Glazer (New York: Schocken Books, 1966).

10. For a more extensive discussion of this idea, see Jiddu Krishnamurti, *The Only Revolution* (New York and Evanston: Harper and Row Publishers, 1970).

11. Rollo May, *The Art of Counseling* (New York: Gardner Press, 1989), 61-79.

12. Carl R. Rogers, *Client-Centered Therapy* (London: Constable & Robinson Ltd., 1951), 19-64.

13. Sidney M. Jourard, *The Transparent Self* (New York: D. Van Nostrand Company, 1971), 139-144, 151.

14. http://en.wikipedia.org/wiki/Sigmund_Freud,   cf. http://www.apsa.org/About_Psychoanalysis/Freud_Quotes.aspx].

CHAPTER 4

1. Martin Buber, *The Way of Response*, 49. See also Ibidem, *I and Thou*.

2. Martin Buber, *Between Man and Man*, translated by Ronald Gregor-Smith (London: Routledge, 2002), 135.

3. Abraham Maslow, *The Farther Reaches of Human Nature* (Penguin Books and Arkana, 1993), 59-60, 259-269.

4.   This quote comes from the following sources: Maurice Friedman, *Martin Buber: The Life of Dialogue*, (London: Routledge, 2002), 234. Friedman is quoting Martin Buber, "Religion and Modern Thinking," in *Eclipse of God: Studies in the Relation between Religion and Philosophy*, translator Maurice Friedman et al, 93.

5.   Maslow, *Farthest Reaches of Human Nature*, 327-328.

6.   Khalil Gibran, *The Prophet* (New York: Alfred A. Knopf, 1966), 76. See also Eckhart Tolle, *The Power of Now: A Guide to Spiritual Enlightenment* (Vancouver: Namaste Publishing, 1997 and Novato, California: New World Library, 1999).

7.   Khalil Gibran, *The Prophet*, 76. See also Eckhart Tolle, *The Power of Now: A Guide to Spiritual Enlightenment*.

8.   Antoine de St. Exupery, *The Little Prince*. (San Diego: Harcourt, 1971), 63.

9.   Abraham Maslow, *The Farthest Reaches of Human Nature*, 59-68 and passim; Idem, *Toward a Psychology of Being* (USA: Van Nostrand Reinhold Company, 1968), 203 and passim.

10.   Eckhart Tolle, *The Power of Now*.

11.   Brian Piergrossi, *The Wow of the Now: Awakening to the Big Glow Within*. (USA: no publisher listed, 2012).

12.   Martin Buber, *The Way of Response*, 48.

13.   Jalal ed-Din Rumi, *Mystical Poems of Rumi* Translated by A.J. Arberry. (Chicago: University of Chicago Press, 1979).

14.   Dov Baer, The Maggid (Preacher) of Mezritch, *Maggid Deverav le-Ya'aqov*, ed. Rivka Schatz-Uffenheimer (Jerusalem: Magnes Press, 1976), 209, 134, 199, 210. Translated by Daniel Matt, "Ayin: The Concept of Nothingness in Mystical Judaism" in Robert Forman, ed., *The Problem of Pure Consciousness*. (New York: Oxford University Press, 1990), 144-145.

CHAPTER 4, PART B

1. Daniel Goleman, *Emotional Intelligence* (New York: Bantam Books, 2006), 91.
2. Ibid. 91-92.
3. Abraham Maslow, *Farther Reaches of Human Nature*, 59-63, 68; Idem, *Toward A Psychology of Being* (United States of America: Van Nostrand Reinhold Company, 1968), 137-140 and passim. Idem, *Religion, Values, and Peak Experiences* (United States of America: Penguin Compass/Arkana, 1994), 59-68.
4. Charles A. Garfield with Hal Zina Bennett, *Peak Performance: Mental Training Techniques of the World's Greatest Athletes* (New York, Warner Books, 1984), 179-195 and passim.
5. Ibid. 183-184 and passim.
6. Compare Mihalyi Csikszentmihalyi's description of flow, in http://austega.com/gifted/16-gifted/articles/24-flow-and-mihaly-csikszentmihalyi.html.
7. Peter Gay, ed. *The Freud Reader* (New York: W.W. Norton and Company, 1989), 301-306, 594-97, 768, and passim.
8. Roberto Assagioli, *Psychosynthesis: A Collection of Basic Writings* (Amherst, Massachusetts: The Synthesis Center Inc., 2012), 18, 23, originally published as Idem, *Psychosynthesis, Manual of Principles and Techniques* (New York: Hobbs, Dorman, and Company, 1965).
9. Ibid. 21.
10. M.L. Von Franz, "The Process of Individuation" in *Man and His Symbols*, edited by Carl Jung, M.L. Von Franz, Joseph L Henderson, Jolande Jacobi, Aniela Jaffe. (Garden City, New York: Doubleday and Company, 1964), 173-176; June Singer, *Boundaries of the Soul: The Practice of Jung's Psychology* (New York: Anchor Books/Doubleday, 1994), 134, 164-177, 221.

11. Abraham Maslow, *The Further Reaches of Human Nature*,155-157, 185; Idem, *Toward a Psychology of Being*, 104, 210.

12. Ken Wilber, *Integral Psychology: Consciousness, Spirit, Psychology, Therapy.* (Boston: Shambhala, 2000), 100-106, 193.

13. Frances Vaughan, *The Inward Arc: Healing in Psychotherapy and Spirituality.* (Nevada City, California: Blue Dolphin Publishing, 1995), 34-40, 49-50; 62-66, 217.

14. Robert Augustus Masters, *Transformation Through Intimacy: The Journey Toward Awakened Monogamy* (Berkeley, California: North Atlantic Books, 2012), 75-78 and passim.

15. Debbie Ford, *The Dark Side of the Light Chasers* (New York: Riverhead Books, 2010), 1-5, 12-13, 39, 58 and passim

16. Maurice Friedman: *Martin Buber: The Life of Dialogue* (London: Routledge, 2002), 78.

17. Jiddu Krishnamurti, *Freedom from the Known* (New York: Harper and Row Publishers, 1969), 24-25, 28.

18. John Firman and Ann Gila, *A Psychotherapy of Love: Psychosynthesis in Practice* (Albany, NY: State University of New York Press, 2010), 24; Idem, *Psychosynthesis: A Psychology of the Spirit*, (Albany, NY: State University of New York Press, 2002), 36, 149; Assagioli, *Psychosynthesis, Manual of Principles and Techniques*, 22-23 and passim.

19. Assagioli, *Psychosynthesis*, 19-20.

20. Vaughan, *Inward Arc,* 187.

21. Powell, *The Secret of Staying in Love*, 103.

22. Ibid. 102-103.

23. From: http://www.elyrics.net/read/m/marie-osmond-lyrics/gift-to-be-simple-lyrics.html

24. Carl Jung, "Psychology and Literature," from Carl Jung, *Modern Man in Search of a Soul*, translated by W.S. Dell and Cary F. Baynes, reprinted in *The*

Creative Process, Brewster Ghiselin, ed. (New York: A Mentor Book from New American Library, 1952), 221-222.

25. Amy Lowell, "The Process of Making Poetry," *Poetry and Poets*, reprinted in *The Creative Process*, 110.

26. T. W. Adorno, E. Frenkel-Brunswik, D.J. Levinson, and R.N. Sanford, *The Authoritarian Personality* (New York: Norton, 1950).

27. Robert J. Lifton, *Thought Reform and the Psychology of Totalism: A Study of Brainwashing in China* (UNC Press, 1989).

28. Gibran, *The Prophet*, 74.

CHAPTER 5

1. Editorial note by Barry Hammer: In later typewritten notes dictated to me by my father, Max Hammer, after this PHI chapter was written, he described the subjective knower, pure consciousness, as inner substance, and its objectified self-knowledge as outer form, in contrast to the view of inner subjective form and outer objective substance presented in this PHI chapter.

2. M.E.P. Seligman, *Helplessness: On Depression, Development, and Death* (San Francisco: W.H. Freeman, 1975). Cf. B. Weiner , *An Attributional Theory of Motivation and Emotion* (New York: Springer-Verlag, 1986).

3. Maslow, *Religion, Values, and Peak Experiences*, 59-116; Idem, *Toward a Psychology of Being*, 36-37, 41-43.

4. Maslow, *Religion, Values, and Peak Experiences*, 75.

5. Maslow, *Toward a Psychology of Being*, 37, 105.

6. Seymour Boorstein, *Transpersonal Psychotherapy* (Albany, New York: State University of New York, 1996), 207 citing Ken Wilber, *Eye to Eye* (New York: Anchor Press, 1983).

7. Maslow, *Religions, Values, and Peak Experiences*, 62, 67, 75, and passim.
8. Ibid. 100.
9. Ibid. 91-96.
10. Ibid. 91.

APPENDIX A

1. For more extensive discussion of the metaphorical significance of the *Wizard of Oz* story as allegory of the transformational process of psychological and spiritual development, see Jean Houston: *The Wizard of Us* (New York: Atria Books, 2012).
2. http://www.stlyrics.com/lyrics/bestofbroadway-americanmusical/theimpossibledream.htm

APPENDIX B

1. See *Webster's New World Dictionary*, third edition (USA: Warner Books/Simon and Schuster, 1990). http://dictionary.reference.com/browse/pleroma; http://www.merriam-webster.com/dictionary/pleroma; http://en.wiktionary.org/wiki/pleroma
2. Maslow, *Farthest Reaches of Human Nature*, 59-60, 68.
3. Sidney Jourard, *Disclosing Man to Himself* (New York: D. Van Nostrand, 1968), 220.
4. Rollo May, *The Courage to Create*. (New York: Bantam Books, 1980), 87-109.
5. Ibid. 49.
6. Daniel Matt, "Ayin: The Concept of Nothingness in Mystical Judaism," in Forman, *The Problem of Pure Consciousness*, 144-145.
7. Carl Jung, *The Portable Jung*, Joseph Campbell ed., translated by R.F.C. Hull (New York: Viking, 1971), 59-69.

8   Perhaps our view that the spiritual archetype or reality of timeless permanent being subliminally influences individual people, particular social, national,
and ethnic cultural groups, as well as humanity as
a whole, to gradually grow more conscious of the
true reality nature of their life energy-being, and
advance in the ongoing development of its unlimited creative potentials actualization, may be somewhat similar to the philosopher G.W.F. Hegel's notion that the "spirit" (or "absolute spirit") influences
the ethos and historical development of humanity in order to gradually gain greater self-knowledge of its inherent freedom, grandeur, and creative intelligence. See http://en.wikipedia.org/wiki/
Lectures_on_the_Philosophy_of_History.

APPENDIX C

1.   Buber, *The Way of Response*, 48

APPENDIX E

1.   Erich Fromm, *Escape From Freedom*. (New York:
Henry Holt and Company, 1969), 182.
2.   Jourard, *The Transparent Self*, 93.
3.   http://en.wikipedia.org/wiki/Buddha-nature.

APPENDIX G

1.   We are basing the neologism "exstasis" on the etymological derivation of the word "ecstasy" from an
ancient Greek word meaning to "to be or stand outside of oneself." See http://en.wikipedia.org/wiki/
Ecstasy_(philosophy)

APPENDIX H

1. Gay, *The Freud Reader*, 557-8 and passim; Calvin S. Hall, *A Primer of Freudian Psychology*, 47 and passim.

APPENDIX I

1. Erik H. Erikson, *Childhood and Society* (New York: Norton, 1950); Idem, "The Problem of Ego Identity," *Journal of the American Psychoanalytic Association* 4 (1956), 56-121. Idem. *Identity and the Life Cycle* (New York: International Universities Press, 1959). Idem, *Identity, Youth and Crisis* (New York: Norton, 1968) cited in http://en.wikipedia.org/wiki/Erikson%27s_stages_of_psychosocial_development
2. Hall, *Primer of Freudian Psychology*, 93-115.
3. Gay, *The Freud Reader*, 584-589.
4. http://www.dictionary-quotes.com/death-is-not-the-greatest-loss-in-life-the-greatest-loss-is-what-dies-inside-us-while-we-live-norman-cousins/
5. Maslow, *Psychology of Being*, 193-197.
6. Hall, *Primer of Freudian Psychology*, 31-35, 46-46, 120. Gay, *The Freud Reader*, 769-772.
7. John Firman and Ann Gila, *Psychosynthesis: A Psychology of the Spirit* (Albany, NY: State University of New York Press, 2002), 3, quoting Roberto Assagioli, *Psychosynthesis: Individual and Social* (New York: Psychosynthesis Research foundation, 1965), 5.
8. Buber, *The Way of Response*, 48 and passim.
9. Buber, *I and Thou*, 10-12, and passim.

APPENDIX J

1. Gibran, *The Prophet*, 28.
2. http://en.wikipedia.org/wiki/Marx%27s _theory_of_alienation.

CONCLUSIONS

1. For an illuminating discussion of the importance of consciously integrating previously rejected or unknown "shadow" aspects of the psyche, see Deepak Chopra, Debbie Ford, and Marianne Williamson, *The Shadow Effect: Illuminating the Hidden Power of Your True Self* (New York: Harper Collins, 2010).
2. For more discussion of how fixed self-concepts can impede new insightful self-understanding and the ability to cope effectively with changing realities, see Jourard, *Disclosing Man to Himself*, 222 and 162-163.
3. Prominent psychologists who concur with our view that psychology should include the study of the soul, including the spiritual, numinous, or transpersonal core of the psyche, viewed holistically rather than divisively or partially, and not limited exclusively to the study of materialistic drives (such as the Freudian emphasis on sexual drives), rationalist explanations, or other reductionist interpretations include Otto Rank, Carl Jung, and Abraham Maslow, among many others. See Otto Rank, *Psychology and the Soul: A Study of the Origin, Conceptual Evolution, and Nature of the Soul*. Translated by Gregory C. Richter and E. James Lieberman. (Baltimore: The John Hopkins University, 1998), 3, 7-9, 23. Carl Jung, *Modern Man in Search of a Soul*. Translated by W.S. Dell and Cary F. Baynes. (New York: Harcourt, Brace, and World,

1933), 222-225 and passim. Maslow, *Religions, Values, and Peak Experiences*, 3-18.

4. We concur with Rollo May's view that psychologically healthy qualities such as integrity, serenity, courage, and creativity come from being grounded in a "center of strength" abiding "within our own being." See Rollo May, *Man's Search for Himself* (United States of America: W.W. Norton and Company, 1967), 68-69. Cf. Idem, *The Courage to Create*, preface and 3.

5. See Jean Houston, *The Wizard of Us, Transformational Lessons From Oz.* (New York and Hillsboro, Oregon: Atria Press and Beyond Words Press, 2012).

6. Rakesh Sethi, *Cruising Through Turbulence: An Inspirational Guide for Your Wealth and Well Being in Difficult Economic Times and Beyond* (United States of America: True Wellness Group, 2012), 28.

BIBLIOGRAPHY

Adler, Alfred. *Social Interest: A Challenge to Mankind*. Mansfield Center, Connecticut: Martino Publishing, 2011; and London: Faber and Faber Ltd., 1938 and 1964.

Adorno, T.W., E. Frenkel-Brunswik, D.J. Levinson, and R.N. Sanford. *The Authoritarian Personality*. New York: Norton, 1950.

Assagioli, Roberto. *Psychosynthesis: A Collection of Basic Writings*. United States of America: Synthesis Center Inc. in cooperation with The Berkshire Center for Psychosynthesis, 2012.

_____. *Psychosynthesis: A Manual of Principles and Techniques*. New York: Hobbs, Dorman, and Company, 1965.

Audi, Robert. *The Good in the Right: A Theory of Intuition and Intrinsic Value*. Princeton: Princeton University Press, 2004.

Banet, Anthony G., Jr., Editor. *Creative Psychology: A Source Book*. La Jolla, California: University Association, 1976.

Blum, Gerald S., *Psychoanalytic Theories of Personality*. New York: McGraw-Hill Book Company, 1953.

Boorstein, Seymour. *Transpersonal Psychotherapy*. Albany, New York: State University of New York, 1996.

Buber, Martin. *Between Man and Man*. Translated by Ronald Gregor Smith. London: Routledge, 2002.

Idem. *I and Thou*. Translated by Ronald Gregor Smith. New York: Charles Scribner's Sons, 1958.

Idem. *The Knowledge of Man, Selected Essays*. Edited by Maurice Friedman, Translated by Maurice Friedman and Ronald Gregor Smith. Amherst, New York: Humanity Books, 1998.

Idem. *The Way of Response*. Edited by Nahum Glazer. New York: Schocken Books, 1966.

Campbell, Joseph, ed. *The Portable Jung*. Translated by R.F.C. Hull. New York: The Viking Press, 1971.

Chopra, Deepak, Debbie Ford, and Marianne Williamson. *The Shadow Effect: Illuminating the True Power of Your Hidden Self*. New York: Harper Collins Publishers, 2010.

Erik H. Erikson, *Childhood and Society*. New York: Triad/Paladin, 1977.

Idem. *Identity and the Life Cycle*. New York: International Universities Press, 1959.

Idem. *Identity, Youth and Crisis*. New York: Norton, 1968.

Fadiman, James and Robert Frager. *Personality and Personal Growth*. New York: Harper and Row, 1976.

Fenischel, Otto. *The Psychoanalytic Theory of Neurosis*. New York: W.W. Norton and Company, 1945.

Firman, John and Ann Gila. *Psychosynthesis: A Psychology of the Spirit*. Albany, New York: State University of New York Press, 2002.

Idem. *A Psychotherapy of Love: Psychosynthesis in Practice*. Albany, New York: State University of New York Press, 2010.

Ford, Debbie. *The Dark Side of the Light Chasers*. New York: Riverhead Books, 2010.

Forman, Robert, ed. *The Problem of Pure Consciousness*. New York: Oxford University Press, 1990.

Friedman, Maurice. *Martin Buber: The Life of Dialogue*. London: Routledge, 2002.

Fromm, Erich. *The Anatomy of Human Destructiveness*. Henry Holt and Company, 1973.

Idem. *The Art of Loving*. Harper Perennial/Modern Classics, 2006.

Idem. *Escape from Freedom*. New York: Henry Holt and Company, 1969.

Idem. *The Heart of Man: Its Genius for Good and Evil*. Edited by Ruth Nanda Anshen. New York: Harper and Row, 1964.

Idem. *Psychoanalysis and Religion*. New Haven: Yale University Press, 1978.

Idem. *The Sane Society*. New York: Henry Holt and Company, 1990.

Funk, Ranier, Editor. *The Essential Fromm: Life Between Having and Being*. New York: Continuum, 1995.

Garfield, Charles with Hal Zina Bennett. *Peak Performance: Mental Training Techniques of the World's Greatest Athletes*. New York: Warner Books, 1984.

Gay, Peter, ed. *The Freud Reader*. New York: W.W. Norton and Company, 1989.

Gatchill, Robert J. and Frederick G. Mears. *Personality: Theory, Assessment, and Research*. New York: St. Martin's Press, 1982.

Ghiselin, Brewster, ed. *The Creative Process*. New York: New American Library, 1952.

Gibran, Khalil, *The Garden of the Prophet*. New York: A. Knopf, 1933.

Idem. *The Prophet*. New York: A. Knopf, 1923.

Goleman, Daniel. *Emotional Intelligence*. New York: Bantam Books, 2006.

Grof, Stanislav and Christina Grof. *Spiritual Emergency: When Personal Transformation Becomes a Crisis*. New York: Jeremy Tarcher, 1989.

Hall, Calvin S. *A Primer of Freudian Psychology*. New York: A Mentor Book, New American Library, 1979.

Hammer, Max, and Arthur M. Kaplan, eds. *The Practice of Psychotherapy with Children*. Homewood, Illinois: The Dorsey Press, 1967.

Hammer, Max, ed. *The Theory and Practice of Psychotherapy with Specific Disorders*. Springfield, Illinois: Charles C. Thomas Publishers, 1972.

Hammer, Max; Barry J. Hammer, and Alan C. Butler. *Deepening Your Personal Relationships: Developing Emotional Intimacy and Good Communication*. This book is currently in press, and is expected to be published in 2014 by Strategic Book Publishing and Rights Agency Publishers (SBPRA).

Harper, Robert A., *Psychoanalysis and Psychotherapy*. Englewood Cliffs, New Jersey: Prentice-Hall, 1959.

Hendrik, Ives. *Facts and Theories of Psychoanalysis*. New York: A Delta Book, Dell Publishing, 1958.

Houston, Jean. *The Wizard of Us: Transformational Lessons from Oz*. New York and Hillsboro, Oregon: Atria Books and Beyond Words, 2012.

Hughes, Fergus P., and Lloyd D. Noppe, with contribution by Ilene C. Noppe. *Human Development across the Life Span*. St. Paul: West Publishing Company, 1985.

James, William. *The Varieties of Religious Experience*. Garden City, New York: Doubleday and Company, 1978.

Jourard, Sidney M. *Disclosing Man to Himself*. Princeton, New Jersey: D. Van Nostrand, 1968.

Idem. *The Transparent Self*. New York: D. Van Nostrand, 1971.

Jung, Carl G., *The Archetypes and the Collective Unconscious*. Translated by R.F.C. Hull. Bollingen Series XX: *The Collected Works of C.G. Jung*, Volume 9, Part 1. Princeton: Princeton University Press, 1990.

Idem. *Memories, Dreams, Reflections*. Recorded and Edited by Aniela Jaffe, translated from the German by Richard and Clara Winston. New York: Vintage Books, a division of Random House, 1989.

Idem. *Modern Man in Search of a Soul*. New York: Harcourt, Brace, and World, 1933.

Idem. *The Undiscovered Self*. New York: Signet, Penguin Group, 2006.

Jung, Carl G., M.L. von Franz, Joseph L. Henderson, Jolande Jacobi, and Aniela Jaffe. *Man and His Symbols*. Garden City, New York: Doubleday and Company, 1964.

Karpf, Fay B. *The Psychology and Psychotherapy of Otto Rank: An Historical and Comparative Introduction*. New York: Philosophical Library, 1953.

Kedar, Ido. *Ido in Autismland: Climbing Out of Autism's Silent Prison*. 2012. No other publication information listed.

Kirschenbaum, Howard and Valerie Land Henderson, eds. *The Carl Rogers Reader*. Boston: Houghton Mifflin Company, 1989.

Krishnamurti, Jiddu. *Beyond Violence*. New York and Evanston: Harper and Row 1973.

Idem. *Education and the Significance of Life*. New York: Harper and Row, 1953.

Idem. *Exploration into Insight*. San Francisco: Harper and Row, 1980.

Idem. *The First and Last Freedom*. Wheaton, Illinois: Theosophical Publishing House, 1968.

Idem. *The Flight of the Eagle*. New York: Harper and Row, 1971.

Idem. *Freedom from the Known*. New York: Harper and Row Publishers, 1969.

Idem. *The Impossible Question*. New York: Harper and Row, 1972.

Idem. *Think on These Things*. New York: Harper and Row, 1964.

Idem. *The Only Revolution*. New York: Harper and Row, 1970.

Idem. *The Urgency of Change*. New York: Harper and Row, 1970.

Idem. *You Are The World*. New York: Harper and Row, 1972.

Lazaris. *Working with Your Shadow: An Imperative on the Spiritual Path*. Palm Beach, Florida: NPN Publishing Inc., 1995.

Lemert, Charles, ed. *Social Theory: The Multicultural and Classic Readings*. Boulder: Westview Press, 1993.

Liang, R.D., *The Divided Self: An Existential Study in Sanity and Madness*. New York: Penguin Books, 1990.

Idem. *The Voice of Experience*. New York: Pantheon Books, 1982.

Lifton, Robert J. *Thought Reform and the Psychology of Totalism: A Study of Brainwashing in China*. UNC Press, 1989, originally published by W.W. Norton, 1961.

McCary, J.L., ed. *Psychology of Personality*. New York: Grove Press, 1956.

McIntosh, Steve. *Integral Consciousness and the Future of Evolution*. St. Paul, Minnesota: Paragon House, 2007.

McTaggart, Lynne. *The Bond: Connecting to the Space Between Us*. New York: Free Press, a division of Simon and Schuster, Inc., 2011.

Maslow, Abraham H. *The Farthest Reaches of Human Nature*. United States of America: Viking Press, 1971; Penguin Books, 1976; Arkana, 1993.

Idem. *Religions, Values, and Peak Experiences*. United States of America: Viking Penguin Compass, 1970; Penguin Books, 1976; Penguin Compass and Arkana, 1994.

Idem. *Toward a Psychology of Being*. New York: Van Nostrand Reinhold Company: 1968.

Masters, Robert Augustus, *Emotional Intimacy: A Comprehensive Guide for Connecting with the Power of Your Emotions*. Boulder, Colorado (Printed in the USA): Sounds True, 2013.

Masters, Robert Augustus *Transformation through Intimacy: The Journey toward Awakened Monogamy*. Berkeley, California: North Atlantic Books, 2012.

Masterson, James F. *The Real Self: A Developmental, Self, and Object Relations Approach*. New York: Brunner/Mazel Publishers, 1985.

Maul, Gail and Terry Maul. *Beyond Limit*. Glenview, Illinois: Scott, Foresman, and Company, 1983.

May, Rollo. *The Art of Counseling*. New York: Abington Press, 1939.

Idem. *The Courage to Create*. New York: Bantam, 1983.

Idem. *Love and Will*. New York: W.W. Norton and Company, 1969.

Idem. *Man's Search for Himself*. New York: W.W. Norton Company, 2009.

Idem. *Psychology and the Human Dilemma*. New York: W.W. Norton, 1979.

Mullahy, Patrick. *Oedipus: Myth and Complex*. New York: Grove Press, 1948.

Piergrossi, Brian. *The Big Glow: Insight, Inspiration, Peace, and Passion*. USA: 2008. No publisher listed.

Idem. *The Wow of the Now: Awakening the Big Glow Within*. USA: 2012. No publisher listed.

Powell, John. *The Secret of Staying in Love*. Niles, Illinois: Argus Communications, 1974.

Prather, Hugh. *I Touch the Earth, the Earth Touches Me*. Garden City: New York: Doubleday and Company, 1972.

Idem. *Notes on Love and Courage*. Garden City, New York: Doubleday and Company, 1977.

Idem. *Notes to Myself: My Struggle to Become a Person*. New York: Bantam Books, 1970,

Rank, Otto. *Psychology and the Soul: A Study of the Origin, Conceptual Evolution, and Nature of the Soul*. Translated by Gregory C. Richter and E. James Lieberman. Baltimore: Johns Hopkins Press, 1998.

Rogers, Carl R. *Client-Centered Therapy*. London: Constable & Robinson Ltd., 1951.

Rohr, Richard. *Immortal Diamond: The Search for Our True Self*. United States of America: A Wiley Imprint of Jossey-Bass, 2013.

Ryckman, Richard M., *Theories of Personality*. USA: Brooks/Cole Publishing Company, 1997.

Saint-Exupery, Antoine de. *The Little Prince*. Translated from the French by Richard Howard. San Diego: Harcourt Inc., 2000.

Seligman, M.E.P., Helplessness: *On Depression, Development, and Death*. San Francisco: W.H. Freeman, 1975.

Sethi, Rakesh. *Cruising Through Turbulence: An Inspiring Guide for Your Wealth and Well-Being in Difficult Economic Times and Beyond*. USA: True Wellness Book, 2012.

Singer, June. *Boundaries of the Soul: The Practice of Jung's Psychology*. New York: Anchor Books Doubleday, 1994.

Smith, Ross, ed. *Eureka! The Six Stages of Creativity*. Middletown, California: Harbin Springs Publishing, 1988.

Szaj, Kathy, ed. *Resonance: The Essence of Co-Creating and Conscious Evolution*. Outskirts Press, 2012. Jointly authored and published by the Virtual Co-Creative Community: www.co-creativecommunity.net.

Thoele, Sue Paton. *Heart Centered Marriage: Fulfilling Our Natural Desire for Sacred Partnership*. Berkeley, California: Conari Press, 1996.

Tolle, Eckhart. *The Power of Now. A Guide to Spiritual Enlightenment*. Novato, California: Namaste Publishing and New World Library, 2004.

Underhill, Evelyn. *Mysticism: A Study in the Nature and Development of Spiritual Consciousness*. Minneola, New York: Dover Publishers, 2002.

Vaughan, Frances. *The Inward Arc: Healing in Psychotherapy and Spirituality*. Nevada City, California: Blue Dolphin Press Publishing, 1995.

Walsh, Roger M. and Frances Vaughan. *Beyond Ego: Transpersonal Dimensions in Psychology*. Los Angeles: J.P. Tarcher Inc., 1980.

Watts, Alan. *Nature, Man, and Woman*. New York: Random House, 1991.

Weiner, B. *An Attributional Theory of Motivation and Emotion*. New York: Springer-Verlag, 1986.

Wigglesworth, Cindy. *The Twenty-One Skills of Spiritual Intelligence*. New York: Silent Books, Inc., 2012.

Wilber, Ken. *Integral Psychology: Consciousness, Spirit, Psychology, Therapy*. Boston: Shambala, 2000.

Idem. *No Boundary: Eastern and Western Approaches to Psychological Growth*. Boston: New Science Library/ Shambala, 1981.

Idem. *The Spectrum of Consciousness*. Wheaton, Illinois: Quest Books/Theosophical Publishing House, 1993.

Idem. *Up From Eden: A Transpersonal View of Human Evolution*. Wheaton, Illinois: Quest Books, 1996.

Lightning Source UK Ltd.
Milton Keynes UK
UKOW04f0854050315

247264UK00001B/114/P